From PE DREAD to DELIGHT

Transforming Young People's Experiences in Physical Education

Lee Sullivan

Scholary

First published in 2025 by Scholary

The Dutch Barn, Bremhill Grove Farm, Chippenham, Wiltshire,
SN15 4LX, United Kingdom
Scholary is an imprint of Scholary Ltd

© 2025 Lee Sullivan

All rights reserved. No part of this book may be reprinted or reproduced or utilised in any form or by electronic, mechanical, or other means, now known or hereafter invented, including photocopying and recording, or in any information storage or retrieval system, without permission in writing from the publishers.

British Library Cataloguing in Publication Data.
A catalogue record for this book is available from the British Library.

ISBN: 978-1-0687095-7-9 (pbk)
ISBN: 978-1-0687095-8-6 (hbk)
ISBN: 978-1-0687095-9-3 (ebk)

Contents

Foreword   9

The End   13

Chapter 1: Direction   21
Lee Sullivan, Dr Margaret Whitehead, Professor Liz Durden-Myers, Matthew Trowbridge and James Mooney

Chapter 2: Realistic   53
Lee Sullivan, Professor Liz Durden-Myers, Phil Cocks, Anna Sheppard

Chapter 3: Experiences   75
Lee Sullivan, Paul Sammon, Kate Reynolds and Shaun Wilkinson

Chapter 4: Assessment   97
Lee Sullivan, Will Swaithes, Jon Campbell and Will Grove

Chapter 5: Disengaged   133
Lee Sullivan, Justen O'Connor, Grace Cardiff and Neil Moggan

Chapter 6: Delight   161
Lee Sullivan, Scott Kretchmar, Jordan Wintle and Rhys Meredith

Chapter 7: Excellence   185
Lee Sullivan, Emerick Kaitell, Katie Hart, Catherine Fitzpatrick and Vicki Gill

Chapter 8: Learning   209
Lee Sullivan, Professor Ash Casey, Ryan Parker and Nathan Walker

Chapter 9: Inclusion   237
Lee Sullivan, Shrehan Lynch, Simon Scarborough and Faith Newton

Chapter 10: Guides   **265**
Lee Sullivan, Professor Shane Pill and Ben Shields

Chapter 11: Holistic   **289**
Lee Sullivan, Vicky Randall, Kate Clough and Megan Lockett

Chapter 12: Training   **313**
Lee Sullivan, Ryan Ellis, Ben Holden and Sue Pye-Beraet

The Beginning   **333**

Afterword   **337**

List of Figures

Figure 1: The Elements of Engagement	35
Figure 2: Initial MOVE Notes	37
Figure 3: MOVE Intent	40
Figure 4: ABC (and D) of PE	59
Figure 5: Purpose of Assessment in Physical Education	99
Figure 6: Dylan William (2013) Quote	107
Figure 7: The Disconnected Curriculum	115
Figure 8: Student Log	116
Figure 9: Progress Tracker	117
Figure 10: Student Reflection	118
Figure 11: Reflection Assessment Practice	120
Figure 12: Physical Education Lesson Reflection	121

Figure 13: Methods used to collect student voice	139
Figure 14: ACCEPT Student Voice	141
Figure 15: Establish how the lesson went for the students	175
Figure 16: What were the barriers to students achieving full success?	176
Figure 17: Were they able to master the skills or want to improve?	176
Figure 18: What activities do the students want to do in a unit?	177
Figure 19: Student Ownership	178
Figure 20: Respectful Celebrations in PE	178
Figure 21: Core or GCSE PE?	189
Figure 22: Freire, teaching, and learning: Culture circles across contexts	197
Figure 23: Bronfenbrenner's Ecological Systems Theory	198
Figure 24: Primary Concept Curriculum, Lee Sullivan (2023). PE Scholar.	215
Figure 25: Newell's Constraint Model (1986)	230
Figure 26: Visualising Social Justice Terminology in PE	242
Figure 27: The Ally Continuum	256
Figure 28: Learning Episode	276
Figure 29: Kings Court First School PE Intent	328

List of Tables

Table 1: UK PE Aims	27
Table 2: Key Literature Findings of Meaningful PE	164
Table 3: Multi-Sports Day Carousel	200
Table 4: Pedagogical Approaches	220
Table 5: Outline of Key Areas of Social Injustice	245
Table 6: Form of Guidance with Teaching Styles	273

Acknowledgements

I would like to express my heartfelt gratitude to the following co-authors of this book: Dr. Liz Durden-Myers, Dr. Margaret Whitehead, Matthew Trowbridge, James Mooney, Phil Cocks, Anna Sheppard, Paul Samman, Kate Reynolds, Shaun Wilkinson, Will Swaithes, Jon Campbell, Will Grove, Justen O'Connor, Grace Cardiff, Neil Moggan, Scott Kretchmar, Jordan Wintle, Rhys Meredith, Emerick Kaitlell, Katie Hart, Catherine Fitzpatrick, Vicki Gill, Professor Ash Casey, Ryan Parker, Nathan Walker, Shrehan Lynch, Simon Scarborough, Faith Newton, Shane Pill, Ben Shields, Vicky Randall, Kate Clough, Megan Lockett, Ryan Ellis, Ben Holden, and Sue Pye-Baraet. Your insights, dedication, and contributions have been instrumental in shaping this work, and I am deeply thankful for your collaboration.

I extend my appreciation to my colleagues at Upton Court Grammar School and Desborough College, whose unwavering dedication to creating positive and meaningful experiences for every student in our care serves as a constant source of inspiration. I am particularly grateful to the teachers who generously gathered invaluable insights from their students' experiences: Aaminah Hussain, Kiera Wylie, Jon Campbell, and Simon Scarborough. A special note of thanks goes to Tracey Healey for her patience, thoughtful guidance, and invaluable feedback throughout this process. I am also deeply thankful to my friends at PE Scholar, whose unwavering support, inspiration, and commitment to PE continually go above and beyond for the benefit of everyone involved in the field.

I owe a profound debt of gratitude to Dr. Liz Durden-Myers for her unmatched expertise and solution-focused approach to Physical Education. This book is as much yours as it is mine.

Lastly, to my family—Kimberley, Amelia, Theo and Jaxson—thank you for your endless love, patience, and unwavering belief in me.

Foreword

Forewords often begin with a respected figure explaining why the book is important and encouraging readers to explore its pages. But in a book focused on transforming young people's experiences in physical education (PE), it feels only right to start with their voices. These real voices, often overlooked, are at the heart of the narrative this book seeks to address.

In this foreword, you'll hear from them—unfiltered, honest, and at times, uncomfortable. Their experiences demand our attention and must shape how we, as educators, leaders, and advocates, envision the future of PE. To move from PE dread to delight, these voices cannot simply be heard; they must drive real, meaningful change. Their experiences are what make this book so important.

Charlotte Sessions – Age 16

When I first joined the school in year seven, I was put with a male teacher who was slightly sexist. Being a girl dealing with a sexist PE teacher was incredibly frustrating. I remember feeling uncomfortable when this teacher would make comments that seem to favour the boys over the girls, often praising their efforts and skills while then downplaying ours. This felt like no matter how hard I tried my efforts were just overlooked and dismissed.

This kind of experience can really impact some children's confidence in sports. It makes it harder to enjoy PE when it feels like your teacher would rather you weren't there. I believe that your teacher should be a role model that encourages all students regardless of gender and pushes them to pursue their interests and abilities in sports. This made PE in school more like a chore than a beneficial subject in my education. I always dreaded the days I had PE on my timetable because it always involved lots of pressure to perform well in sports that I'm not good at. I remember feeling anxious when I had to change for PE.

The changing rooms also had a negative impact on the overall PE experience. I always felt uncomfortable and awkward. It felt like there was a lot of pressure to change quickly, especially with everyone around you. The lack of privacy was stressful, and I was often insecure with my looks. It always felt like I was being judged. The whole atmosphere in the changing rooms felt very unwelcoming, there can be bullying which always made it hard to relax. Instead of the changing rooms being a space to prepare for sports, it was a space where my insecurities were projected. This had a big impact on my confidence and motivation to participate in PE.

I think PE should be an environment where teachers should promote fun and fitness while helping improve their students' individualism as well as their team building skills rather than pushing them into a shell of worry. Teachers can do this by just listening to the students worries and making the environment safe, not putting extra stress on the students. It's just the simple things like checking up on them and making sure they still have a smile on their face when they come to PE.

Dareen Janah – Age 15

PE always felt like a chore instead of an enjoyable sport. Because PE felt like a chore, I just wanted to stand in the background during a game, doing nothing. It wasn't just me who felt like this; I would say a lot of girls did too, and many of them skipped PE lessons in the toilets because they couldn't be bothered to participate due to a lack of motivation. PE teachers would force them to do something or face consequences, which, personally, I thought was annoying. It made me hate anything sports-related because it always had that negative connotation. If I were a PE teacher, I would've asked the girls in my class what they wanted to do to get a collective response, whether it be a simple Just Dance lesson or a basketball one.

Mayah – Age 15

In Year 7 and 8, I never used to contribute to any activities in PE This was mostly because I never got used to the fact that I was the tallest out of everyone. This made me feel extremely uncomfortable, as I felt out of place and wasn't used to being the tallest around. In addition to being the tallest, I was also very quiet and never had the confidence to speak out loud or communicate with the people around me. It made me feel quite upset, as I knew that doing sports was what I loved. The fact that I couldn't even enjoy my PE lessons made me almost give up on building the confidence to engage in them. Growing up, I always dreamed of playing basketball. I would always play with family or friends, which made me think I was brave enough to carry that into secondary school. If I were a PE teacher, I would communicate with all students to ensure they feel comfortable enough to engage in the activities. If not, I would ask them for their opinions on what they wanted to do to make sure everyone feels included.

Immy – Age 12

Before the lessons began in primary school, getting changed for PE was horrible. The school was on a hill, and we had to go outside. We could not go inside as the hall was not big enough. It always seemed to be wet. There was so much grass, which I did not like.

We had to do some activities in houses. I didn't like it because we would always lose. We tried really hard but still lost. This made me feel sad. What is the point in trying if we always lost? It felt all about the winners. I took part in activities but often because they forced me to. If I said no, I would have lost playtime or been given a detention.

FOREWORD

I didn't like the PE teacher. There was something about him that made me feel like I couldn't talk to him about how I wasn't enjoying PE. If I said I did not want to do it, he would not care. None of the girls wanted to do it. Activities were more suited to the boys. At break time, they played football. I remember only one girls' football session. All the other sessions were with the boys, who were rough.

Changing in front of everyone made me feel embarrassed. The teacher timed us getting changed and gave merits for the first person ready. I didn't change slowly on purpose, but it just took me longer. It was horrible. Wearing thick socks used to really stress me out because I didn't like wearing them, but we had to because it was part of the PE kit.

On sports day, it was annoying when the parents watched because it felt daunting being in front of them all. I had to step in as captain and go first even though I didn't want to.

If I had been the PE teacher, I would have let us come to school in PE kit, like during Covid. Our school changed it back to normal and didn't explain why. It would have been better if we didn't have to change in front of everyone. I would have tried to make it more fun for everyone and would have listened to students and how they were feeling.

The End

The PE Past, Present and Future
In this book, I deliberately start with "The End" because it is essential to understand the destination to appreciate the journey fully. I would like you to consider how you might feel upon your retirement, having given years of your life to physical education and teaching. I would like you to consider the impact you will have made, what people would say about you, and the legacy you will leave behind.

Reflecting on the end of a career, no matter how long or short your contribution to PE may have been, offers a powerful perspective on the purpose and impact of our efforts within the subject. Starting with the end in mind allows us to identify what truly matters in our teaching practice. It prompts us to consider the legacy we want to leave behind and the kind of experiences we want our students to remember. This approach helps us focus on the broader picture, ensuring that our daily actions align with our ultimate objectives. "To begin with the end in mind means to start with a clear understanding of your destination. It means to know where you're going so that you better understand where you are now and so that the steps you take are always in the right direction," (Covey, 2004, Page 98).

I want to offer a glimpse into what your retirement celebration could resemble. Think of it as a "Christmas Carol" moment, where we're visited by ghosts of our past, present and future, showing us a version of PE that's within our grasp if we're willing to change our approach now. However, as a subject, if we continue as we are, the reflections upon our retirement might look somewhat different. David Kirk (2010) offers three possible futures for PE: radical reform, more of the same or the risk of PE becoming extinct.

So let's consider two retirement futures and ask yourself, what will your PE future look like if you continue as you are?

Your Retirement Future 1
As your journey as a PE teacher reaches its conclusion and your career in education draws to a close, you find yourself standing amidst the celebration of your retirement, reflecting on the profound transformation that has unfolded. The sports hall, once a space fraught with apprehension, now pulses with the vibrant energy of movement. It's been an extraordinary journey, one marked by both triumphs and trials, yet throughout it all, your unwavering commitment to your purpose has remained steadfast.

You sit and talk to your past students and reflect fondly on the lessons you once delivered. Lessons where movement and learning were not just encouraged, it was celebrated. Lessons which prioritised learning and movement competency, aiming for every student to build the skills and confidence to engage in physical activity. Despite movement competency being a priority, you should be proud that you were able to create a culture where failures and mistakes were welcome and embraced. Holistic development was always central to your delivery. In your lessons, and through PE, students have had the opportunity to immerse themselves in learning that could benefit other aspects of their lives too.

Central to your team's success has been the belief that everyone, regardless of background or ability, deserves to reap the benefits of movement. Your PE curriculum had been carefully crafted to reflect the needs and interests of your students, ensuring that every child felt included and valued. In the environment you created, students felt safe to express themselves, knowing that their voices were heard and respected.

Perhaps most importantly, your students developed a positive relationship with movement, understanding its significance in their lives beyond the confines of the lessons. They've come to value the learning of PE not just as a requirement but as an opportunity for personal growth and self-discovery.

As you bid farewell to this chapter of your career, you do so with a heart full of gratitude. You should be immensely proud of how far you've come. Some students have come from dread to delight and others have continued or strengthened their relationship with physical activity. Your students have embraced the joy of movement, and you have no doubt that they will carry this love with them for years to come.

Your Retirement Future 2

Reflecting honestly on your journey as PE teachers, would you acknowledge that there were shortcomings and missed opportunities along the way? Despite your best efforts, the atmosphere in your lessons often fell short of celebratory; instead, some of your students viewed PE with indifference or even disdain. In your pursuit of excellence, you inadvertently excluded those who might have engaged for other reasons…. perhaps those who needed you the most? The holistic development of the whole child often took a backseat to narrow performance metrics, leaving many students feeling unfulfilled and disconnected from the learning experience.

Despite your intentions, your curriculum failed to reflect the diverse needs and interests of your students, resulting in disengagement and apathy among the majority. In the PE environment, positive experiences and inclusivity were not always prioritised, leading to feelings of alienation and insecurity among certain students. As a result, rather than fostering a positive relationship with movement, many students viewed PE as a chore, lacking relevance and meaning in their lives. Your failure to address these fundamental issues meant that, for many students, the journey from dread to delight remained elusive, leaving them disillusioned and disheartened by their PE experiences. But this wasn't your fault, was it? It was the system; the government; parents; children themselves; the exams taking over the sports hall; the weather; the class sizes of thirty plus; etcetera. You did your best given the circumstances, didn't you? How aware were you of students dreading your lessons? Did you notice? Did you stop to wonder why?

I believe we have a genuine opportunity, whilst we are custodians of PE, to take children from dread to delight or from delight and continue to yet more delight . However, to do so, we need to really reflect on why some young people dread PE and consider what is in our control to move them to a place of delight.

Taking PE From Dread…

PE is at a pivotal moment. As I argued in my previous book, Is PE in Crisis?, the subject cannot remain rooted in outdated practices that focus solely on the physical, cater primarily to the already able, and leave many students feeling disengaged or even alienated. Instead, we have an opportunity to reimagine PE as something that genuinely supports every student, empowering them to discover and thrive in their own unique movement journey. This transformation is not just necessary—it's essential to ensure that PE becomes meaningful, inclusive, and a source of lifelong value for all. Together, we can redefine its purpose and impact for the better.

Dread can be defined as: to fear greatly; to be in extreme apprehension of something or to be reluctant to do, meet, or experience. Far too frequently, students approach PE with a sense of dread, often leaving without gaining anything positive from the experience, feeling disheartened or embarrassed, and ultimately disengaged from physical activity long after their school days. Just ask some adult friends, family or colleagues what their PE experiences were like at school. It's a concerning trend, especially considering that the majority of PE teachers aim to instil a lasting passion for movement in their students. However, despite our best intentions, our current practices seem to be pushing many away from embracing physical education. Why is that? What simple steps could you take to change it?

We must find ways to take any student that experiences feelings of alienation, exclusion or humiliation in PE to feelings of belonging, value and ownership. This is their story that we play a part in. We are not the final destination in PE, we are a very important part of the movement journey that our students are embarking on. Our actions can either propel their journey with momentum and meaning or derail it entirely.

To Delight…
As Scott Kretchmar said in his article "Ten More Reasons for Quality Physical Education" (2006), "one of the greatest things about physical activity and play is that they make our lives go better, not just longer. It is the quality of life, the joy of being alive" (page 6). Imagine a subject in which every student felt a feeling of long-lasting satisfaction and pleasantness, where they actively sought out opportunities to engage further and that genuinely supported the formation of active habits. THAT is delight in this subject. THAT is what I want to help make happen. Whilst not every student may start at dread, nor will every student find delight, it is imperative that we consider the totality of the PE experience for all students so that each one can discover their own unique joy in PE and physical activity. **If the heart of every student beats with movement potential, then PE should be the rhythm that brings it to life.**

An Aspiration, not a Destination
Delight in PE might not be attainable for all, but it is something we should all aspire to. Delight should not be considered as an end destination or an absolute. As Dr Justen O'Connor reminded me in conversation about this introduction, "we rarely work in a world of absolutes, rarely is a learning journey linear, and rarely does the world work in binary ways and whilst we can strive for delight, I very much doubt we are going to reach delight for all students in all activities, all of the time."

You can still create a supportive and productive learning environment even when a child doesn't bring their kit, feels insecure, lacks some competence, or may not be sleeping or eating well because of a tough home life. PE will not solve these problems or make everyone competent, but it has to accommodate these issues and provide an inclusive space for all students. Whilst I will write about a utopian version of PE, I am aware of the challenges we face. It is highly unlikely that you will have a classroom full of socially connected, fit, confident, and injury-free children. So, while I acknowledge that achieving delight for all will be a difficult and complex journey, this book will unapologetically aim for it, providing strategies to create positive experiences and relationships with PE, regardless of the challenges.

Who Should Read this Book?
In his book 'Winning' (1992), legendary coach Frank Dick (renowned for his pioneering work in athletics, insights into human performance and motivation) discussed the differences between who he calls mountain and valley people.

Valley people are drawn to the familiarity and security of the lowlands, where the terrain is predictable, and risks are minimal. They are comfortable with the status quo and resist change, preferring the safety of routine. Their primary concern is avoiding failure, and they often settle for mediocrity rather than striving for greatness. Valley people tend to make excuses for their shortcomings and blame external factors for their lack of success.

Conversely, mountain people embrace change as an opportunity for growth. Mountain people are not deterred by the possibility of failure; instead, they see it as a natural part of the journey towards success. They take calculated risks and are willing to push themselves beyond their comfort zones in pursuit of their goals. Mountain people are resilient in the face of adversity, viewing setbacks as valuable learning experiences that propel them forward.

This book is for mountain people or those open to becoming one. It is for PE teachers who recognise flaws in the current approach but refuse to wait for change to trickle down or engage in idle complaints about the state of PE. Instead, they take proactive steps to enact change within their own school. It is for PE teachers, that if the right tools were available, seek to navigate themselves out of the valley. This isn't about revolutionising the entire world; it's about reflecting and challenging how PE is taught and experienced within their own context. Are you a mountain person? Could you become one? If so, then I hope you read on.

How to Use this Book

My aim is that each chapter will draw you into the heart of a significant PE-related concern. I hope to navigate crucial content and research findings for educators to ponder in light of the issues presented. Furthermore, each chapter includes insights from experts in specific areas of PE and teachers with experience of applying evidence-informed approaches, providing practical solutions that bridge the gap between research and real-life PE in school practice. The chapters will highlight the 'dread' and offer considerations to shift to 'delight'.

Chapter Overview

D	Direction	to	**D**	Delight
R	Realistic		**E**	Excellence
E	Experiences		**L**	Learning
A	Assessment		**I**	Inclusion
D	Disengaged		**G**	Guides
			H	Holistic
			T	Training

Each chapter will follow a 4-part structure that will aim to provide you with **IDEAS**:

Part		Title	What will be covered
1	**I**	Insight	Insight into the issue/topic
2	**D**	Delve	Delve into related research
3	**E**	Expert(s)	Hear from experts on the topic
4	**A**	Apply	Hear from those addressing the issue in their school
	S	Summary	Considerations and reflections from chapter

This book is not intended as a step-by-step manual or even a how to guide. Rather, I hope it serves as a catalyst for critical reflection, encouraging readers to challenge thinking, explore current research, and inspire and innovate teaching practices.

I hope that certain aspects of this book will strike a chord with you. It's perfectly acceptable if there are areas where you disagree; diversity of opinion is valuable. Regardless, it aims to stimulate your thinking on the reasons behind your approach, the methods you employ, and the content you deliver in your practice. Only you know your context and what might work in it.

Through A Different Lens

We will delve into several crucial topics in PE, aiming to provide compelling arguments for approaches and instructions that enhance student experiences, meet various needs and support more of our students on their journey towards 'delight'.

Two focal points will be the research behind physical literacy and meaningful PE. We will further explore each concept (physical literacy in chapter 1 and meaningful PE in chapter 6) but, for now, it's vital to acknowledge the profound influence of viewing PE through different lenses. By applying these lenses and adopting new perspectives, educators can gain fresh insights, develop innovative strategies and make more informed decisions that prioritise more engaging and meaningful experiences for their students.

This book will focus on the issues we can control as teachers, and by applying the aforementioned lenses, improve our day-to-day practice. As PE teachers we often have to work within the confines of other structures such as wider school or national policies. That which is beyond our control should not deter us from continuing to advocate for meaningful change within our own spheres of influence. While we may not always have a direct hand in shaping policy, we can still strive to foster innovation, collaboration, and excellence in our own practice and in our own schools. By addressing students' needs, offering quality education, making research-based decisions, and promoting best practices, we can greatly impact their lives and the field of physical education.

We can only control the controllable. With that in mind, and while there are numerous contemporary issues in PE such as primary PE training, swimming provision, facilities and funding, this book acknowledges that it cannot cover them all. Instead, this book will concentrate on matters that can be directly addressed by those in the profession - not by governments or governing bodies, but by the frontline leaders of PE every day: us, the PE teachers.

Leaving a Legacy

In my first book, 'Is PE in Crisis?' I spoke about leaving a legacy, something I feel incredibly passionate about. We are all mere custodians of PE and we must ensure that we leave PE in a better place than we found it. When we do get to our retirement or leave the profession, what will our students say about the impact we had on them and how will we have left the subject to the next PE teachers that will follow in our footsteps?

I will not fix PE with this book and I will certainly not fix the world. I do however hope that I can support PE teachers to make informed decisions about their PE delivery that could positively impact thousands of students around the world. I sincerely hope that will be my legacy.

Welcome to From Dread to Delight, a journey into transforming young people's experiences in PE for practitioners seeking to foster a genuine love for PE, physical activity, and sport in every student.

References

Kirk, D. (2010). Physical Education Futures. Routledge; UK.

Kretchmar, S. (2006). Ten more reasons for quality physical education. Journal of Physical Education, Recreation and Dance. 77(9), 6–9. https://doi.org/10.1080/07303084.2006.10597932

Swaithes, W. (2022). Book Review: Meaningful Physical Education – an approach for Teaching and Learning (2021). Accessed 5 April 2024. Available at: https://www.pescholar.com/insight/book-review-meaningful-physical-education/

Stephen R. Covey (2004). The 7 Habits of Highly Effective People: Powerful Lessons in Personal Change. Simon and Schuster UK

Chapter 1: Direction

Lee Sullivan, Dr Margaret Whitehead, Professor Liz Durden-Myers, Matthew Trowbridge and James Mooney

Part 1.1 – Insight
Lee Sullivan

Direction, akin to a navigation compass, plays a pivotal role in navigating the complexities of PE practice and pedagogy, shaping the educational landscape for both educators and learners alike. In this chapter we will confront not only the need for direction but also the conspicuous absence thereof, which manifests as confusion, conflict, and stagnation within PE.

Reach for the Moon

In 1962, along the corridors of NASA's sprawling headquarters and amidst the hum of computers and the chatter of scientists, a humble janitor named Frank Wilson quietly went about his work. His days were spent sweeping floors, emptying trash cans, and ensuring the cleanliness of the facility, a job he had done diligently for years.

President John F. Kennedy visited NASA to tour the facilities and meet with the brilliant minds behind the nation's space program. As he made his way through the building, he stopped to chat with various employees, eager to learn about their roles in advancing the nation's space exploration efforts.

Amidst the sea of engineers and scientists, one figure stood out to him – Frank, the janitor. Frank's unwavering commitment to his work, despite its seemingly humble nature, caught Kennedy's attention. Kennedy approached Frank and asked him one simple question: "What do you do here?" With a sense of pride in his voice, Frank replied, "Mr. President, I'm helping to put a man on the moon."

President Kennedy was struck by the profound sense of purpose and dedication evident in the janitor's words. Here was a man whose role, though seemingly minor in the grand scheme of NASA's mission, embodied the spirit of ambition and unity driving the nation's efforts to conquer space. Frank's words reinforced the idea that everyone, no matter their job title, plays a crucial part in achieving a common goal. Frank knew that without him completing his role, others might be unable to fulfil theirs. He believed in the vision and the part he played in realising it. From that day on, Frank's simple yet profound answer became a symbol of the unity and purpose that drove NASA's mission to reach the moon.

This story serves as a reminder to all that success in any endeavour requires a clear vision and direction, with every individual contributing their unique talents and efforts to bring that vision to life. However, the absence of a unified direction and vision has led to discord within the PE community. Unlike NASA, where a clear purpose guides every individual, PE not only lacks a universally agreed-upon mission, but receives numerous mixed directions, resulting in inconsistencies in its delivery and implementation.

Power of 'Why'

As expressed by Ni Chróinin et al. (2019), 'the 'what' and 'how' of teaching are most powerful when they are led by a 'why'. Having the ability to articulate your 'why' is crucial for inspiring and guiding meaningful action and innovation in physical education. It serves as a compass, guiding decisions about curriculum, teaching methods, and interactions with students. A leader in PE who can clearly communicate their 'why' not only motivates and engages their team but also fosters a shared sense of purpose and direction. It can support a team to make better informed decisions, prioritise workload and reflect on practice. Most importantly, this clarity of purpose enables educators to align their efforts and resources towards common goals, ultimately driving positive outcomes for students and the broader community. Just as it did with Frank Wilson for NASA, your intent should unite and inspire all stakeholders, providing a clear direction and purpose for the teaching and learning experiences in your educational setting.

Stronger than the Struggle

Mark Twain once famously said 'the two most important days in your life are the day you are born and the day you find out why.' Teaching is undeniably challenging, particularly in the current climate marked by financial constraints, escalating behavioural issues, heavy workloads, and difficulties in recruiting and retaining staff. In the face of these obstacles, it's crucial for educators, including those in PE, to have a clear sense of purpose driving their efforts. This means that your 'why' – your reason for being an educator, a PE teacher, a leader – must be powerful enough to withstand the difficulties you face. It's this sense of purpose that propels you forward, even when the path seems daunting or the hurdles insurmountable. Your 'why' needs to be stronger than the struggle.

Unifying the 'Why'

I've had the fortunate opportunity to address large gatherings of physical educators at PE conferences. One of the presentations I deliver challenges teachers to reflect on why they teach PE and what they aspire to achieve through their teaching efforts.

Once teachers have had a go at articulating their 'why', I pose a simple question: "is your 'why' to create elite athletes or win trophies with extracurricular teams?" Notably, no one has ever stood up in response. However, when I inquire whether their primary goal is to foster a lifelong love of physical activity and/or cultivate competence and confidence in movement, nearly everyone rises to their feet, with only a few variations.

It seems, from my experience at least, that PE teachers are in it for the right reasons. However, these educators often find themselves navigating conflicting expectations from various stakeholders regarding the fundamental goals and objectives of PE, which ultimately impacts the 'what' and the 'how' of our delivery.

Eyes off the Prize

As much as PE leaders have their own vision for PE, so many are pressured and therefore understandably influenced by the groups that follow, even if that means contradicting their own why. Leaders end up pandering to the few rather than supporting the many:

- **Policy Makers:** Over the years various governments have used PE as a way of addressing issues within society. In England, PE has been delivered to create fit and efficient workers, for example. It shifted to building strength through German and Swedish gymnastics, and then again to improving fitness in preparation for war, specifically after the Boer War. Following World War II, PE was aimed at improving hygiene and developing team sports. The Government continues to pledge funds (though many argue not enough), via multiple policies, to encourage engagement in physical activity and promote the positive impact that regular exercise can have on the nation's physical, and now mental health. In other countries (Wales, New Zealand, Scotland, Australia, etc.) governments have introduced a more holistic PE National Curriculum that aims to nurture physical literacy and lifelong engagement.
- **Senior Leaders:** Senior leaders have the students' best interests at heart and face incredibly tough challenges themselves. PE leaders are often under pressure to conform to systems that are better suited to other subjects or aligned with the school's broader strategic aims. The demands placed on PE leaders to use school-specific language, improve GCSE outcomes and uptake, and assess students using harmful labels remain a source of frustration for many. It is crucial to recognise that senior leaders, unless they have been PE teachers themselves, may view PE through the lens of their own experiences as pupils. Without our guidance, they may not fully appreciate how PE has evolved or

the profound impact it can have.By clearly communicating the core purpose of PE—to contribute to every student's holistic learning and development—we can demonstrate how PE is essential to fostering skills, confidence, and well-being that extend far beyond the gym or sports field. Helping senior leaders understand this modern vision ensures they see PE as a vital component of the curriculum, one that supports the broader educational journey of every student.

- **Parents:** Pressure from parents might influence PE teachers to focus on extracurricular provision and the number of clubs or competitive teams that are offered. Therefore, curriculum design can be based on competitive sports that will support their performance outside of school time and run a plethora of clubs that might limit lesson planning and preparation time. Parents may also recall how PE was when they were at school and be unaware of the aims we now embrace.
- **Society:** I have fallen foul of thinking the aims of society and the media were the responsibility of PE. I thought it fell on PE to fix obesity, mental health issues, physical health decline and other global issues that needed fixing. The media and society pile pressure onto PE teachers to fix the ills in society, believing that PE is the sole answer to some very complex issues.

Eyes on the Prize: Students

Maybe the group that should be driving our intent are the group that have been ignored for far too long? The idea of a student-centred approach is one where teachers place the learner at the forefront of the educational process, focusing on their needs, interests, and abilities.

A student-centred approach allows teachers to tailor instruction to meet individual student needs, promote student engagement, motivation, inclusivity and ownership of learning. Student-centred methods can also support holistic development by addressing physical, social, emotional, and cognitive competencies.

In their 2016 article titled 'Seven Student-centred Principles for Smart Teaching in Physical Education,' Thomas Nathan Trendowski and Amelia Mays Woods illustrate the application of Susan Ambrose's (2010) 'seven researched-based principles for smart teaching' from classroom-based instruction to the context of PE:

1. **Prior Knowledge:** Acknowledging that students enter courses with existing knowledge, beliefs, and attitudes that can either facilitate or impede learning. Recognising and building upon prior knowledge is crucial for effective instruction.
2. **Organisation of Knowledge:** Understanding how students organise and connect new information based on past experiences and the role of knowledge in their lives. Helping students make meaningful connections between concepts enhances learning.

3. **Motivation:** Recognising the importance of students' motivation in regulating their approach to tasks. Providing personally relevant and enjoyable activities, setting attainable goals, and fostering a positive learning climate can enhance motivation.
4. **Development of Mastery Skills:** Emphasising the acquisition and integration of component skills to achieve mastery. Using curricular models and providing ample practice opportunities with appropriate challenges promote skill development.
5. **Goal-directed Practice:** Structuring practice sessions around specific goals, providing targeted feedback, and ensuring sufficient practice time. Setting SMART goals, offering feedback, and maintaining an appropriate motivational climate are essential for effective learning.
6. **Students as Social, Emotional, and Intellectual Learners:** Recognising students' social, emotional, and intellectual dimensions and their influence on learning. Creating a positive learning environment, promoting task-involved learning experiences, and addressing students' emotional needs enhance learning outcomes.
7. **Students as Self-directed Learners:** Encouraging students to monitor, regulate, and reflect on their learning processes. Teaching self-management skills, fostering self-regulated learning behaviours, and providing opportunities for student-led activities and reflections promote autonomy and responsibility in learning.

As we journey through this book, my aim is to underscore the profound alignment among various student-centred approaches such as physical literacy, model-based practices, meaningful PE, and concept-driven PE. Together, these principles have the potential to significantly enhance students' experiences in physical education. These seven principles offer a foundational framework for our exploration.

Part 1.2 – Delve
Lee Sullivan

Purpose Before Practice
For too long, it is the 'how' of PE that has driven the 'why'. The curriculum delivery has informed how much or little value is placed on the subject. Kirk (2010, 2012) contends that physical education's capacity to inspire, involve, and cultivate lifelong participation is often called into question, with apprehensions that, without significant reform, the subject faces the risk of extinction. Kirk argues that change within PE is inevitable. It is time for us as a profession to face the brutal truth: PE needs to change in order to survive. To do so, PE leaders need a clear understanding of what PE is and what it can achieve. Without clear guidance from policymakers or beyond, we are forced to come together in our own context in order to effectively communicate the vision and value of PE in our own schools. It's time to put purpose before practice.

Defining PE
When the Concept Curriculum (Sullivan, 2021) was published, it was met with a huge amount of positivity and was adapted around the world in the weeks and months that followed. It was also met by a few less than enthused observers too. Some argued that this approach 'just wasn't PE!'. This got me thinking, well what is PE?

If you were hoping for a clear and universally agreed definition for PE in this book, I am afraid you will be disappointed. It just doesn't exist. David Kirk (2010) recognises the difficulties in defining PE and highlights the numerous definitions in existence that are varied and agenda-led. Whilst no agreed definition of PE exists, many do refer to the physical domain, meeting the broader aims of education and imply health as an outcome.

Kirk presents the notion that PE goes beyond statements of 'beliefs, values and aspirations'. Kirk wrote that 'Physical education is defined by what is said, done and written in its name', (page 1). He presents this as the id^2. Essentially, Kirk suggests that the true essence of PE lies not only in the ideals and intentions expressed about it but also in the actual practices, actions, and representations associated with it.

Therefore, with no agreed definition, Kirk argues that the id^2 for PE has become that of sport-techniques. That is what many believe PE is, which might explain the resilience to the idea of anything other than that approach 'just isn't PE'.

If defining PE is problematic and offers little help to practising PE teachers, it is therefore up to us as PE leaders within our schools to consider the purpose of PE in our context. In this next section of the chapter, I will present research that might inform your own purpose for PE in your setting. Although presented as individual visions for PE, that is not the case in reality and there can be a combination of all/some or perhaps even none to make up your own beliefs to the purpose of PE in your school. My hope is to to challenge and inspire your thinking. Durden Myers (2018) articulates how professionals 'not having a clear answer to the value, role and purpose of physical education can be just as damaging as having an answer that undermines the subject. Physical education teachers, as educational professionals, are the custodians of the subject and they need to be able to champion and advocate the educational value of the subject in a clear and succinct way,' (p.193).

Purpose of PE: Leave it to Policy Makers?

The absence of a clear definition of PE presents a significant challenge, compounded by the varied messages regarding its purpose or objectives. Within the United Kingdom alone, the Departments for Education in Scotland, Wales, England, and Northern Ireland each provide distinct perspectives on the aims of PE:

Table 1: UK PE Aims

Country	Purpose of PE (as defined by respective Department for Education)
England	A high-quality physical education curriculum inspires all pupils to succeed and excel in competitive sport and other physically demanding activities. It should provide opportunities for pupils to become physically confident in a way which supports their health and fitness. Opportunities to compete in sport and other activities build character and help to embed values such as fairness and respect. (DfE, 2013)
Northern Ireland	Personal Health Aims; have an understanding of healthy; eating and the importance of exercise; develop positive attitudes towards an active and healthy lifestyle, relationships, personal growth and change; become aware of key issues which affect their physical, social and mental well-being and that of others; develop an awareness of their own personal safety (Council for the Curriculum, Examinations & Assessment, 2023).
Scotland	Physical education (PE) is a programme of activities that aims to provide children and young people with learning experiences that enable them to develop the knowledge, motivation and ability to lead a physically active life. (Education Scotland, 2023).
Wales (Health and Well-Being)	The Health and Well-being Area of Learning and Experience (Area) provides a holistic structure for understanding health and well-being. It is concerned with developing the capacity of learners to navigate life's opportunities and challenges. The fundamental components of this Area are physical health and development, mental health, and emotional and social well-being. (Wales Government, 2019).

The aims for physical education across the UK share several common themes. They all highlight the importance of promoting holistic development and well-being among children and young people. These aims focus on cultivating enjoyment and achievement through a variety of progressively challenging activities, fostering physical confidence, supporting overall health and fitness, and encouraging participation in competitive sports and other physically demanding activities. However, the curricula across the UK nations reflect different contexts and timelines. England's curriculum, being the oldest and largely pre-pandemic, arguably needs revision to remain relevant in today's world. Meanwhile, Northern Ireland and Scotland have more current frameworks, with Northern Ireland and Wales, in particular, addressing contemporary societal needs and challenges. These differences highlight the importance of adapting PE delivery to the unique needs and contexts of students, ensuring the subject remains meaningful and relevant. Ultimately, while physical education will always align with governmental priorities, it is the responsibility of educators to bring it to life, creating experiences that truly benefit children and young people beyond the confines of policy.

Purpose of PE: Sport?

One criticism that is often voiced towards policy makers is the inability to distinguish between PE, physical activity and sport. PE is not sport! However, frustratingly, PE is often referred to as sport. As we will explore later in this book, that does not mean that sport is a dirty word or cannot be used to deliver PE effectively, but they have varying aims and using one to drive policy in another is problematic.

The Association for Physical Education (AfPE) published their Health and Position Paper (2015) to provide their definitions and differences for physical activity, PE and school sport:

- Physical Activity is a broad term referring to all bodily movement that uses energy. It includes all forms of physical education, sports and dance activities. However, it is wider than this, as it also includes indoor and outdoor play, work-related activity, outdoor and adventurous activities, active travel (e.g. walking, cycling, rollerblading, scooting) and routine, habitual activities such as using the stairs, doing housework and gardening.
- Physical Education is the planned, progressive learning that takes place in school curriculum timetabled time and which is delivered to all pupils. This involves both 'learning to move' (i.e. becoming more physically competent) and 'moving to learn' (e.g. learning through movement, a range of skills and understandings beyond physical activity, such as cooperating with others). The context for the learning is physical activity, with children experiencing a broad range of activities, including sport and dance.
- School Sport is the structured learning that takes place beyond the curriculum (i.e. in the extended curriculum) within school settings; this is sometimes referred to as out-of-school-hours learning. Again, the context for the learning is physical activity. The 'school sport' programme has the potential to develop and broaden the foundation learning that takes place in physical education. It also forms a vital link with 'community sport and activity'.

Using sport to drive PE has long been a bone of contention for many in PE due to the perceived prioritisation of competitive outcomes, drive towards elite participation, lack of acknowledgement of other motivations to be physically active and of holistic physical development, to name but a few. However, it can't be denied that sport is a major part of PE.

The evidence of engaging in sport is clear indicating that it can lead to better mental health (higher self-esteem and life satisfaction), lower psychological ill-being (reduced levels of depression, anxiety, and stress), and improved social outcomes (improved self-control, pro-social behaviour, interpersonal communication, and fostering a sense of belonging) Eather, Wade, Pankowiak and Eime (2023). However specialising in specific sports can be detrimental to long-term engagement. As suggested by Chorley, Ribbeck, Szybinski and Brenner (2023), athletes who engaged in early sport specialisation often withdrew from their respective sports due to burnout.

If sport is to serve as the purpose for PE in any context, it must be diverse and ensure that students are exposed to a variety of sports and physical activities. Allowing them to explore their wider interests, develop a range of skills that have educational value will hopefully prevent the risk of burnout associated with early specialisation.

Despite criticisms, PE continues to focus on sports, often conflating it with health benefits. Government policies and cultural beliefs reinforce this, leading to the 'sportification' of PE, where competitive sports overshadow other physical activities. In their research paper, 'The Continuity of PE-as-Sport: Exploring Secondary School Students' Accounts of the Meaning and Purpose of Physical Education in England,' Matthew Berkshire, James Mason, and Jack Hardwicke (2024) argue that shifting away from a sport-centric curriculum toward a more holistic approach could benefit a broader range of students. Without this shift, PE risks serving only those who enjoy and excel in competitive sports, potentially alienating contemporary youth who favour informal lifestyle sports. Their study suggests that a critical examination of the role of sport in PE is necessary, emphasising the need for greater student voice and choice and calls for ongoing scrutiny of who benefits from the current PE structure. The research also advocates for efforts to redefine PE beyond traditional performance-oriented sports to help all children lead healthy, active lives.

Purpose of PE: More PE?

Mikael Quennerstedt (2018) said in a lecture presented at the AIESEP World Congress: "the only real sustainable aim for physical education is more physical education". Quennerstedt argues that the primary goal of physical education should be to provide more physical education opportunities, where diverse ways of experiencing the world through physical activity are not only possible but encouraged. Additionally, the presentation highlighted the significance of starting with the purpose of education before determining what and how to teach.

Quennerstedt emphasises the importance of viewing education as educative, where the goal is not just to impart knowledge but to foster personal growth and development. Secondly, he argues for a certain view of the child, one that recognises their individuality, capabilities, and potential for growth. Thirdly, Quennerstedt stresses the significance of teaching as an ongoing process of making informed decisions about why, what, and how to teach, guided by normative judgments about desirable outcomes.

Barnard Flory, Tischler, Sanders (2014), offer a similar purpose by suggesting that 'physical educators should do whatever is necessary to ensure that children "want" and "know" how to engage in physical activity when they leave the school building and continue through adulthood,' (Page 9).

The idea of PE informing positive physical activity habits was also discussed by James MacAllister (2013), as he defined a physically educated person as: 'those who have learned to arrange their lives in such a way that the habitual physical activities they freely engage in make a distinctive contribution to their wider flourishing.' In essence, if we are aiming to develop physically educated students, we must cultivate individuals who integrate physical activities seamlessly into their lives to support them achieving a comprehensive state of well-being and fulfilment that extends beyond physical health alone. However, beyond this structured view, it is crucial to emphasise the joy and love of movement that we, as educators, strive to instil in our students. Developing physically educated individuals isn't just about creating habits; it's about nurturing a genuine passion for being active—helping students discover activities they love and empowering them to embrace these as part of their identity. By fostering this deep appreciation, we aim to inspire students to seamlessly integrate physical activity into their lives, not as an obligation but as a source of happiness, vitality, and overall well-being.

Purpose of PE: The Physical Domain?

Few will argue that the bread and butter of PE is to develop movement competence and the ability for children to interact with their environment on a physical level. 'Movement is an integral part of life from the moment of conception until death, and a child's experience of movement will play a pivotal part in shaping his personality, his feelings, and his achievements. Learning is not just about reading, writing and maths. These are higher abilities that are built upon the integrity of the relationship between brain and body,' (Goddard Blyth, 2005, Page 5).

This foundational aspect of movement lays the groundwork for a lifetime of physical activity, how one interacts with their environment and their body. Movement competence encompasses fundamental motor skills, coordination, balance, agility, and other physical abilities essential for participation in various sports and physical activities.

Purpose of PE: Meaningful Experiences?

The idea of meaningful PE and the supporting research has encouragingly proven popular in recent times. In a major review of literature, Beni et al. (2017) found evidence of several provisional features of meaningful experiences. These features include: social interaction, fun, challenge, motor competence, personally relevant learning, and delight.

These elements align with other educational theories such as self-determination theory (Deci & Ryan, 2000) and provide a framework for designing and delivering PE that is engaging and impactful for students. By incorporating these features into PE programs, educators can strive to create experiences that resonate with students on a deeper level, fostering their motivation and lifelong engagement in physical activity. We will delve much deeper into this topic in chapter 6.

Purpose of PE: The Whole Child?

Arnold's conceptualisation of PE as education in, through, and about movement, outlined in 1979, has been a key driver for the Australian Council for Health, Physical Education and Recreation (ACHPER) curriculum direction and the Australian Curriculum and Assessment Authority (ACARA) guidelines for Health and Physical Education curriculum development. Shane Pill applied Arnold's framework to sport:
- education in sport, focusing on skill acquisition for efficient movement
- education about sport, understanding the structure and objectives of sports
- education through sport, encompassing social, cognitive, moral, and emotional learning through sport participation.

Whilst PE is not purely sport, we must acknowledge that sport makes up a large majority of the PE curriculum. PE has been delivering education in and about sport for years, and claiming to educate through sport. This holistic ideal and going beyond merely the physical domain is an important part of my own vision for PE and one that we will delve into greater detail later in this book. It is also important to note that whilst PE can be a means to achieve all other ends, it is also an end itself. The act of moving and being active is a valuable activity itself and one that must not be lost in any 'version' of physical education.

It is also suggested by Quennserstedt (2018) that physical education should encompass 'learning to move' and 'moving to learn'. Through a focus on developing body awareness and physical literacy. Body awareness is a holistic ability to understand where our bodies are in space and how our bodies move. The concept of physical literacy was first presented by Margaret Whitehead in her book "Physical Literacy: Throughout the Lifecourse," published in 1993. Whitehead defines physical literacy as 'the motivation, confidence, physical competence, knowledge and understanding to value and take responsibility for engaging in physical activity for life' (2019, page 12).

Purpose of PE: A Unifying Concept?

The concept of physical literacy encompasses four interconnected elements - affective, physical, cognitive, and behavioural - that evolve over a person's lifespan. While physical literacy is often associated with PE, its scope extends beyond the school years and can be nurtured at any age, profoundly impacting quality of life.

However, the field of physical literacy is not without controversy, with divergent definitions and applications leading to confusion among practitioners. Some interpretations focus solely on skill acquisition and physical competence, hindering the widespread adoption of a physical literacy-informed approach in education. Despite challenges, physical literacy has garnered significant global interest as a cherished concept with far-reaching implications. A recent Sport England physical literacy consensus statement (2023) set out to outline the collective understanding and agreement on the concept of physical literacy among key stakeholders in the sports and physical activity sector in England. The statement defines physical literacy as 'our relationship with movement and physical activity throughout life'. It underscores the importance of developing physical literacy across all age groups to enable individuals to lead active, healthy, and fulfilling lives. The statement also highlights the role of physical education, sport, and physical activity in fostering physical literacy and calls for collaborative efforts from various sectors to promote physical literacy across society.

Many advocate for integrating physical literacy into a school's culture akin to literacy and numeracy, as it correlates with sustained physical activity throughout life. Regardless of background or age, everyone has the potential to enhance their physical literacy and engage in lifelong physical activity, with motivation serving as a key driving force. This paradigm shift has prompted policymakers worldwide to reassess approaches to children's physical development and lifelong physical activity participation.

In the absence of a clear definition and differing opinions on the core objectives of PE, the concept of physical literacy emerges as a potential unifying force for the field. Picture a scenario where we collectively enhance students' competence and confidence, equip them with the knowledge and understanding regarding the significance and mechanics of physical activity and sport, fostering not only an appreciation for physical activity but also a lifelong motivation to engage. If this were the outcome of our efforts in PE, the impact would be truly profound.

Durden-Myers, Green, and Whitehead (2018) delineate seven fundamental principles for physical literacy-informed practice in physical education. These principles encompass:

1. **The Individual:** Placing the individual at the core of physical literacy and PE pedagogy.
2. **Promoting Motivation:** Creating autonomy-supportive, mastery-focused learning environments that inspire enthusiasm and encourage progress.

3. **Confidence:** Enhancing participants' confidence in their ability to succeed and make strides in physical activities, celebrating achievements and efforts to bolster self-esteem.
4. **Physical Competence:** Fostering the development of physical competence through meaningful engagement with various activity environments, allowing time for practice and refinement.
5. **Developing Knowledge and Understanding:** Integrating knowledge and understanding to enrich engagement in physical activities.
6. **Devolving Responsibility:** Encouraging students to take responsibility for their participation, fostering structure, values, and inner-discipline.
7. **Using Feedback/Charting Progress:** Employing positive, competence-based feedback to fuel intrinsic motivation, involving students in assessment tasks and criteria co-construction, self-assessment, and evidence presentation.

You have been presented with a clear case as to the need for a 'why', or intent behind your PE delivery. This will serve your driving force. I hope the research provided has given you some food for thought as to why PE exists in your school and the impact you can have on the students you teach through physical education. It's important to articulate this intent clearly to all stakeholders in a concise and memorable way, considering what you hope to achieve through your curriculum before you can focus on how you aim to achieve it.

Mid-chapter reflection

What new insights have I gained from this chapter so far?

How does this knowledge reinforce or challenge my current beliefs or practices?

Are there areas or concepts I still need to explore further?

Have I identified any gaps in my team's understanding or practice
that need addressing?

How can I share or apply this learning to positively influence others in my team or school?

Part 1.3 – Experts
Dr Margaret Whitehead and Professor Liz Durden-Myers

Physical Literacy
Building from Lee's compass analogy, PE has lots of complementary and competing forces manipulating the compass needle. Not having a robust understanding of your direction as a PE teacher or department can certainly amplify the risk of being pulled off course.

Having a clear vision of the purpose and ultimate goal of PE, or in other words the intent of your PE offer, will help to guide how you organise and structure the implementation of your curriculum and ultimately help to increase the impact you have working towards that goal.

There are multiple purposes or goals for PE out there, whether it be to deliver on the PE National Curriculum, develop sporting prowess, nurture physical development or the wider holistic development of the child, support health and wellbeing, promote active lifestyles, encourage character development, reduce obesity, improve academic attainment and so on. It is completely understandable to be lost in a sea of options not knowing how to set a clear course to a secure destination. This is where physical literacy could help provide some clarity in helping PE have a stronger and clearer direction and purpose.

What is Physical Literacy?
Physical literacy has increased in popularity and acceptance as the underpinning goal of physical education in recent years (Durden-Myers and Bartle, 2023). The concept was reconceptualised in the late 1990s and early 2000s by Dr Margaret Whitehead (Whitehead, 1993; 2001) and has since been developed to form a robust concept for use not only within education but across multiple sectors and throughout the life course (Whitehead, 2010; 2019).

Simply put, physical literacy aims to develop lifelong engagement in physical activity. While there are multiple definitions of physical literacy out there, the most widely accepted is the one offered by the International Physical Literacy Association which defines physical literacy as:

> "the motivation, confidence, physical competence and knowledge and understanding to value and take responsibility for engagement in physical activity for life" (IPLA, 2017)

In England, a recent development has also been facilitated by Sport England. In September 2023 after a period of consultation with a range of stakeholders Sport England launched their Physical Literacy Consensus statement which aimed to create a common definition and shared language for physical literacy across a range of sectors in England. The consensus statement defines physical literacy as:

CHAPTER 1: DIRECTION

"our relationship with movement and physical activity throughout life" (Sport England, 2023)

Whether you adopt the Sport England (2023) or IPLA (2017) definition the message remains clear that the purpose of physical literacy is to unite a range of sectors under a common framework to support lifelong engagement in physical activity. This mission has lots of synergies with the potential for PE to shape engagement in physical activity now and inform engagement later in life.

Why is Physical Literacy important?

Physical literacy highlights the importance of holistic development to promote active participation in physical activity. The different domains that are integral to engagement in physical activity are outlined as:

- **Move** (Physical Competence)
- **Connect** (Social / Value)
- **Think** (Knowledge and Understanding)
- **Feel** (Motivation and Confidence)

The table below outlines that when any of these areas are not secure there is likely to be a barrier to participation.

Figure 1: The Elements of Engagement

The elements of engagement

Move (Physical Competence)	Connect (Social / Value)	Think (Knowledge and Understanding)	Feel (Motivation and Confidence)	Behaviour
No	Yes	Yes	Yes	Frustrated
Yes	No	Yes	Yes	Disconnected
Yes	Yes	No	Yes	Confused
Yes	Yes	Yes	No	Disengaged
Yes	Yes	Yes	Yes	Engaged

Opportunities

Adapted from Durden-Myers (2020)

Our role as physical educators is to provide as many opportunities as possible to positively influence the elements of engagement. By focusing on the holistic development of physical activity in our lessons we are more likely to be able to unlock physical activity engagement now and throughout life.

What does Physical Literacy look like in practice?

Physical literacy informed practice would promote engagement in physical activity throughout life by creating a positive relationship with movement and physical activity. Key to achieving this aim would be a commitment to:

1. the holistic development of the individual (move, think, feel and connect)
2. the importance of a range of positive and meaningful experiences (scope, sequence and pedagogy)
3. ensuring that physical activity and movement experiences are personalised and inclusive (pupil-centred approach that also creates a sense of belonging).

Therefore, how you shape your PE intent, implementation and how you report on the impact of your PE offer needs to consider how each of these three points are achieved at each level. This is not an exhaustive list of how physical literacy can inform your practice, instead, this is the starting point from which you can begin to set your direction.

Summary

Physical literacy is increasingly being drawn upon in physical education as a unifying concept that provides clarity while also allowing for personalisation and contextualisation to meet the needs of your pupils, environment and school community. There has been criticism that physical literacy is just another initiative that will be 'here today' and possibly 'gone tomorrow', but from our experience and from how the concept is taking root all over the world, we believe that taking the time to develop your understanding of physical literacy and embedding it within your PE offer will be a secure investment for both you, your department and pupils.

CHAPTER 1: DIRECTION

Part 1.4 – Apply

Articulating Our Intent
Matthew Trowbridge

A Revelation

Some of our best ideas often come when we least expect them. I vividly recall in 2022, just as I was about to cut the grass on my front lawn, when I had a breakthrough that would transform how we structure, deliver, and assess Health & Wellbeing/Physical Education at our school. This moment of clarity became a revelation that shaped our approach moving forward. A proverb from Chaucer, circa 14th Century stated, "From little acorns grow mighty oaks". I ran into my house and immediately jotted down on an envelope what had come into my head. The following image laid the foundations of the work that has been carried out by our department, developed around the acronym MOVE.

Figure 2: Initial MOVE Notes

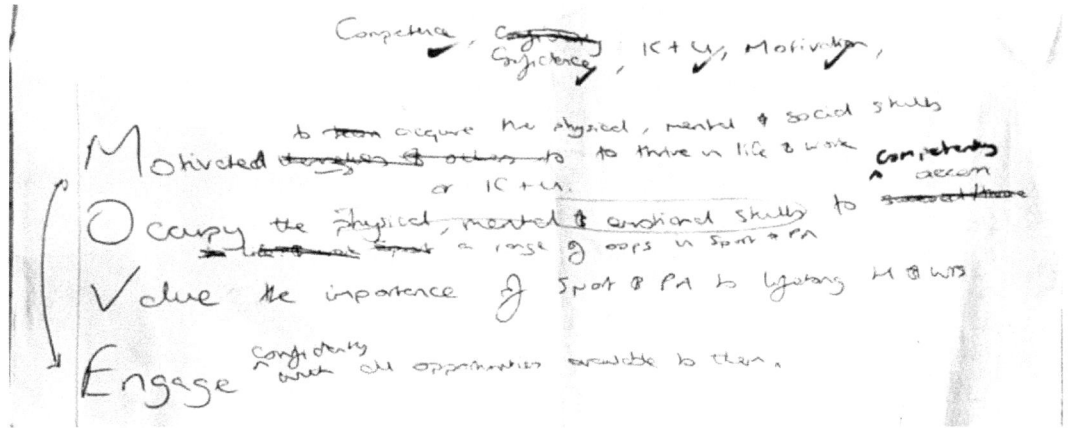

Realising Our Intent
I also recall a key question that I often reflect on from my interview for the post at Aberdare Community School (ACS) in 2020… "what will health & wellbeing look and feel like in the school, with you in the role of Director of Sport and wellbeing?" At the time, I was honest and replied, "I'm really unsure". In context, the New Curriculum for Wales (NCfW) was snowballing towards its launch in 2022, but there was still a lack of clarity of how this could be delivered in

each school. However, I highlighted my desire to gain a feel for the school, use the professional research I had undertaken so far in previous roles and utilise contacts from lead schools targeted for piloting change to shape the way we would deliver it at ACS. The truth is, when it came to my vision for PE, I was unsure of what I wanted it to be. In the early phase of my new post, I was navigating the typical demands of starting at a new school—while, as the astute reader will quickly recognise, facing the added complexities of doing so in 2020!

Whilst aiming to maximise opportunities to launch health & wellbeing (PE) lessons, I considered pupil and staff voice to reflect on the practices that had gone before me. It was clear to see that ACS was a hugely successful sporting school. Prior to COVID they had won both the football and rugby national cups at senior level.

Although staff voice called for this to return within the department, it was also noted that PE was missing opportunities to engage all with this competitive delivery at its forefront. There were many examples of where the department and staff had combatted this perception of competitive PE, with innovative ideas to branch out from the 'traditional' and wonderful examples of attempting to log learners' journeys, skills and progress in lessons. Although lovely practice, it felt a little tokenistic and would always cause debate in staff meetings as to the need and purpose of it. Something was missing and we needed to shift to align with the New Curriculum for Wales.

I asked each member of the team to reflect on their personal 'why'—why they chose to become a PE teacher and what impact they hoped to have on our students? This reflection was important because it gave us a chance to reconnect with our core motivations and evaluate whether we were currently meeting these goals in our practice. I collected all the team's 'whys' and used them as a foundation for building our shared intent. By aligning our new direction with the values and aspirations of the entire department, we ensured that everyone was invested in the journey ahead, and that our collective purpose was rooted in the very reasons we each became educators.

Articulating Our Intent

The vague nature of the proposals, delivery structure and setup of the new curriculum meant that in our school it was very much up to middle leaders to drive ideologies behind their Area of Learning Experience (AoLE) and what they would look like in ACS.

As we embarked on these changes and I began to rethink what PE should look like in our school, it became clear that a unified intent was essential before leading any significant transformation. We needed to take a step back as a team and carefully consider what we were hoping to achieve with our curriculum and, more importantly, why? Having a shared vision would provide clarity and direction, ensuring that every member of the department was working towards the same goals. This unified intent wasn't just about agreeing on a new framework—it was about establishing a foundation that would guide our future decisions, making sure that any changes were purposeful and aligned with our collective values. Only then could we effectively implement lasting, meaningful change.

At that point, we started to work in our own capacity and MOVE was developed on the envelope that summer. It appeared to address the direction in which the department had planned to move. The Rubik's cube was beginning to align. The centre colours at the core foundation with MOVE and the corner pieces were more freely revolving, or teaching intentions through a concept approach to break an enigma that has, for so long, caused us many headaches. The dormant enigma had now been broken. As a leader, I was excited to gain the valuable insight of the team in developing MOVE into a living, breathing curriculum.

I returned to school during INSET that September and presented this intent to our department. Following all the discussions, ideas, debates and direction…finally we had found something to build our foundations on. Presenting this real 'flow' moment to the department had won their hearts and minds and we established professional partnerships to develop each letter and thread of the acronym more profoundly. Previous departmental time had been spent working on collaborative Jamboards, deciding on two things:
- What are characteristics of a successful learner in PE?
- What are the qualities we would like to see in our learners to prepare them for an active and healthy lifestyle?

Suddenly, we had a structure to attribute them to. Everything was falling into place. The holistic approach we had earlier discussed could now be evident in everyday PE. Fundamentally we had tied in the Statements of "What Matters", the Progression Steps, the Four Purposes of the New Curriculum for Wales (Welsh Government, 2020), and our belief of what types of learners we should be fostering in Health & Wellbeing/PE. Skills beyond the physical would be able to flourish, combined with our intention and plan to approach teaching and learning from a concept delivery providing learners with visibly holistic PE.

Trust the Process

A crucial step in bringing this vision to life was developing a unified curriculum intent that the entire PE team could rally behind. This wasn't something that came from one person; it was a collaborative effort that required input and reflection from all members of the department. Each of us brought different experiences, ideas, and perspectives to the table, and together we were able to shape a curriculum that aligned with both our collective goals and the broader objectives of the New Curriculum for Wales.

This unified approach was essential, not only for clarity in delivering lessons but also for ensuring that every team member was fully invested in the process. By involving everyone, we created a shared sense of ownership and purpose, which has been instrumental in moving forward. As we refined and solidified our intent, it became clear that this alignment was key to fostering consistency across lessons, ensuring that all learners, regardless of their teacher, would experience a curriculum that was cohesive and intentionally designed to promote both physical and personal growth. Professionals were using departmental and directed INSET time with purpose and motivation (hallelujah!). A buddy system was developed to design the threads for each of the MOVE characteristics in twos, bringing our developments back to follow up meetings to share, peer-critique and refine. This carefully intertwined Progression Step language from the NCfW, the key themes from the Four Purposes of the NCfW, whilst embodying a "Know, Show, Grow" output that could be delivered and evidenced in physical education. Trusting the process allowed us to move from fragmented ideas to a holistic and purposeful curriculum that truly serves our students.

Figure 3: MOVE Intent

Impact

Our MOVE model has led to many reflective opportunities as a group of staff. We actively look for developments to enhance our delivery, utilising the *"Know, Show, Grow"* approach from the Concept Curriculum 2.0. This ties in directly with assessment opportunities for holistic success and reward in Health & Wellbeing/PE lessons.

CHAPTER 1: **DIRECTION**

It has also allowed me to personally reflect on the common difficulties we often encounter with the 'grey' areas of PE, where many learners still view it as 'Sport'…often reinforced by parental experiences of physical education. This resulted in me evaluating what PE actually is, offering an update and viewpoint on the traditional AfPE document showing how overlaps occur but the key differences between each (AfPE 2019). Highlighting how neither are mutually exclusive in our pursuit to deliver high quality physical education, but rather an opportunity to approach things from a range of angles in our delivery. (Trowbridge, 2023).

Conversations at parents' evenings are now based around the MOVE assessment model, whereby we have used descriptive terms in the *emerging, acquiring, developing, securing, mastering* qualifiers. Each phase aligns with the Progression Steps listed by the NCfW displaying how behaviours, skills and experiences can be measured in our lessons, without a tick box of physical skills/ability of pressured performances. Conversations of our intent commonly happen when engaging with stakeholders and parents, explaining our ambition to keep learners' learning, contributing and developing in Health & Wellbeing lessons 'beyond the physical'.

It is not a perfect working model. I don't think it ever will be. We still encounter hardcore resistance as we continue to alleviate barriers to learning and create learning that invokes an environment with far more psychological safety. However, we do now see learners aiming to engage in PE for varied, individual personal goals. We are always reassessing our delivery, encompassing physical literacy, choice and social values as learners progress through the school. As a result, we are piloting a new tracking tool which already feels a little less 'tokenistic' than the one mentioned earlier in this part of chapter. All of which, I feel, adds currency to what we are delivering in our Health & Wellbeing AoLE, capturing the requirements of the new curriculum purposes and statements of what matters. So much so, that our SLT has now adopted the *"Know, Show, Grow"* approach to pastoral teaching of behaviours like 'Respect' during tutor time. Our intent provides the clarity and direction needed to make key decisions about what is most important to us and has genuinely been a game-changer.

References

Association for Physical Education. (2019). Definitions of school sport, physical education, and physical activity. [Online] Available at: https://www.afpe.org.uk/news/624058/Definitions-of-Physical-Education-School-Sport--Physical-Activity.htm [Accessed on 9th Oct 2024].

Durden-Myers, E. J. (2020). Operationalising physical literacy within physical education teaching practice through professional development. PhD Thesis. Accessed Online: July 3rd 2024. Available at: https://uobrep.openrepository.com/handle/10547/624942

Durden-Myers, E. J. and Bartle, G. (2023). Physical literacy enriched physical education: a capabilities perspective. Children, 10(9), 1503. https://doi.org/10.3390/children10091503

International Physical Literacy Association (IPLA). (2017). Definition of Physical Literacy. Accessed online: 3rd of July 2024. Available at: https://www.physical-literacy.org.uk/

Sport England. (2023). Physical literacy consensus statement for England. Accessed Online: 3rd July 2024. Available at: https://www.sportengland.org/news-and-inspiration/physical-literacy-consensus-statement-england-published

Sullivan, L. (2021). Is PE in crisis? Leading meaningful change in physical education. Scholarly.

Trowbridge, M. (2023). "What are we doing in PE today?" PE Scholar [Guest Blog]. [Online] Available at: https://www.pescholar.com/insight/what-are-we-doing-in-pe-today-the-relationship-between-physical-education-physical-activity-and-sport/ [Accessed on 9th Oct 2024].

Welsh Government. (2020). Curriculum for Wales: Guidance. [Online] Available at: https://gov.wales/curriculum-for-wales [Accessed on 9th Oct 2024].

Whitehead, M. (1993). Physical literacy [Paper presentation]. International Association of Physical Education and Sport for Women and Girls Congress, Melbourne, Australia.

Whitehead, M. E. (2001). The Concept of Physical Literacy. European Journal of Physical Education, 6(2), 127–138. DOI: 10.1080/1740898010060205

Whitehead, M. E. (Ed.) (2010). Physical Literacy: Throughout the Lifecourse. London: Routledge.

Whitehead, M. E. (Ed.) (2019). Physical Literacy: Across the World. London: Routledge.

Physical Literacy Informed Curriculum Design
James Mooney

Sport is for anyone; PE is for everyone – our rationale for change
Sport's role within Physical Education is a hot topic, but a deliberate and thoughtful use of sport can create an impactful programme of study. Done well all students can reap the benefits of learning through carefully selected sports and physical activities, as opposed to blindly following a list of activities that have no meaning or value to the learning taking place. Although a list containing a broad variety of sports can meet the national curriculum, we know PE and sport offer so much more than this. We believe that all students are entitled to a PE offer that meets their needs and brings about a 'love for learning'. This meant that we had to look towards engaging all of our student body, not just those who already loved sport.

My role as the Multi Academy Trust Lead for PE, School Sport and Physical Activity was and continues to be to drive school improvement through the subject. This encompasses many facets, including the guardianship of our curriculum, our assessment of learning and the pedagogy used to enact the subject. This involves bringing together key experts from across the trust including Heads of PE, Primary PE Leads and expert practitioners to continually develop and review our curriculum.

When we first came together to shape a trust curriculum, we identified physical literacy as a key concept to underpin our curriculum. Physical Literacy promotes a holistic approach to PE where PE is bigger than just playing sport. It suggests that everyone will engage in activity for different reasons and will be able to access the benefits (in this case learning) across different domains. By using the different domains, we can better meet student needs and therefore build positive relationships with movement. If we get this right, all our young people will be confident in the skills, knowledge and understanding they have developed, leaving them motivated to be physically active for life.

Alignment is a Dirty Word - A Multi Academy Trust Approach
Alignment is a dirty word when talking about a centralised curriculum across a Multi Academy Trust. It often gets misunderstood that a trust will provide a top-down approach to curriculum, directing staff to what needs to be taught - often down to individual lesson plans. As a trust we don't do this. Our trust curriculum is built from the ground up, empowering the experts within the trust to continually shape what our young people need to know to develop value and meaning within our subject.

7 years ago, physical literacy was identified as an approach to curriculum design that was common across all of our schools. We believe it provides the foundations for us to build a

more holistic curriculum without removing the physical from physical education. Further to this, by using a physical literacy informed approach, we could identify what we believed were the most important aspects of a physical education curriculum, so it stays robust against contextual challenges faced by each individual academy in the trust. This meant that each school could design a programme of study to deliver the common key knowledge whilst meeting the demands of their context, the needs and interests of their young people and overcoming the barriers to differing available facilities.

We were fortunate that a year into this process, we connected with our Youth Sport Trust regional development manager who put us in contact with Will Swaithes who spent time with our Heads of PE unpicking our vision and affirming our beliefs. This helped us to confirm our vision, as we have learnt more about our practice. "Learning Through Movement" has now evolved into "Building positive physical activity experiences for life".

We talk a lot about lenses – Curriculum Design

We ask staff and students to view our curriculum knowledge through different lenses to develop understanding. This could be viewing it from a sport or activity perspective or a different role, for example as a coach rather than a performer, or finally viewing it through a conceptual lens like physical literacy. By layering the lenses, it allows all stakeholders to develop a clearer understanding of what PE is. By focusing on the outcomes of the PE National Curriculum through the Physical Literacy lens, we have identified the key knowledge that can be delivered through any physical activity. This knowledge will provide students with the opportunities to develop characteristics to be successful.

My Movement - Physical Competence (Physical):
An individual's ability to develop movement skills and techniques, tactics and strategies.
My Knowledge - Knowledge and Understanding (Cognitive):
An individual's ability to identify qualities that influence effective participation by following rules and regulations or improving their own and others' performance.
My Mentality - Motivation and Confidence (Affective):
An individual's ability to develop their confidence, empathy and resilience through sport, physical activity and play
My Behaviours - Engagement in Physical Activities for Life (Behaviours):
An individual connecting with others to work as a team through communication, taking on roles and leading others.

We call this central knowledge "the pillar" of our curriculum, which provides a stable platform for "the flame" that represents the contextual programme of study, where each academy can deliver activities and sports which reflect the needs of their young people and meet the needs of the national curriculum. It also meant we were not aligning activities which would be limited by prior experiences, expertise, funding, facility, and cultural beliefs.

Each lesson now has two learning intentions, where we are able to focus on what is important for the students to learn. One of these is always related to My Movement, focusing either on a skill, technique, tactic or strategy in order to build competence within the chosen activity or sport. We believe that every student has the capacity to improve their movement and develop confidence.

The second intention will come from one of the three other My Strands which targets the needs of the learners. This will target the anchor that young people have to physical activity to provide meaning or value in the activity. This will create an access point for positive experiences, across different domains such as the cognitive domain (My Knowledge), affective domain (My Mentality) or social domain (My Behaviours). This approach allows us to create learning experiences that meet the deeply personal relationship that individuals have with physical activity.

Demonstrating Progress

As the knowledge we have identified transcends each activity, we are able to revisit this knowledge and secure it before asking our young people to re-engage with increasing difficulty. We have done this through using different taxonomies to understand how application of knowledge can be progressive across each of the My Strands we are learning.

Early iterations just relied on students learning new knowledge to show progression, and this was our stumbling block. Having been very protective of our approach, we now reach out to different experts to quality assure our approach and offer feedback. Dr Nicholas O'leary at the University of Wolverhampton was generous enough to look at progression over time and directed us towards understanding that knowing and doing more can be how we interact with key knowledge, not just accumulating more of it. By asking our students to interact differently with knowledge over time allows us to inter-lever learning and add challenge or complexity without overloading content.

Students are now asked to "think like a... performer/captain/coach etc" when sharing declarative understanding, where each role will ask them to describe, explain, analyse and evaluate decisions. We now also ask students to perform with increasing challenge using command words such as replicate, demonstrate, combine and adapt to show procedural understanding.

This precise use of vocabulary is explicitly linked to the age-related descriptions we use for assessment guidance. This aligns with the early conceptual work within physical literacy, that the capacity to improve is always present and that improvement builds confidence. Further to this, we can show progression through the other access points - for those whose anchor to physical activity isn't performance-based -allowing these students to show improvement in other learning domains.

Assessment across the trust has three elements: the ongoing assessment over time, diagnostic and the collection of "Snapshot" data collection points using a formal assessment piece. The three elements will inform our holistic assessment of a student's ability. As our assessment criteria is based upon the common knowledge of our curriculum content, we have been able to ensure that performance is not a limiting factor for students, so all students can achieve progress in PE. This means that we can give feedback to students on their relationship to movement with something that is meaningful to them, providing them with next steps that are of value to their learning journey.

To quality assure our more recent curriculum iteration we engaged with Professor Liz Durden-Myers, Bath Spa University, PE Scholar and IPLA,. Her in-depth knowledge of physical literacy and teacher education offers great insight into what we do. Learning from positive experiences through PE Deep Dives across all phases and showcasing our work at the Youth Sport Trust national conference, , we needed to really look at how PL had informed our assessment strategy and the wording we used within our curriculum policies. By allowing Liz to challenge this, we have been able to refine policy to support leaders and classroom teachers to better articulate what we do and even more importantly, enact it for our young people.

Data Tells but Stories Sell

The impact of our curriculum can be seen in various ways across the trust and fundamentally comes down to how well we are achieving our intended outcomes. Although I'm pleased to say that as a trust we secured positive progress 8 and achieve great 9-4 outcomes, this only gives you a very small insight into the impact of our PE curriculum. There are far better ways to unpick its impact… let me tell you some stories.

"PE is my happy place… It's my happy place because it makes me feel like I belong here"
Arri, Year 4

Within PE, we are now better able to meet the needs of our young people. Using pupil voice, we hear how students now find value and meaning within PE. It's not an accident that this has occurred as we are able to build programmes of study that allow students to experience activities and sports which interest them in their unique context. Students have also shared that they have more opportunity to experience success and recognise that PE can be engaged with in various ways and for various reasons that are not solely high performance. Further to this, they have recognised that being successful in PE has allowed them to be successful in other subjects or areas of school life.

It's often a common misconception that a holistic approach to PE will decrease performance and that physical literacy just means supporting all to engage. However, it's more about meeting people at their level and supporting them to improve, and as we have become more skilled at delivery, we have been able to maintain high performance as well as increase the opportunity for all to engage with appropriate-level competition. Last year, we provided an additional 2,500 opportunities for students to engage in targeted intra-trust competition where there is currently no avenue for them to represent their school. Furthermore, we have continued to excel in various activities including athletics, cross country, basketball, football, cheer and golf where we continue to be successful on a regional and national level in the existing school-based competitions.

Being recognised as a strong trust is important to us and we recognise the importance of our civic responsibility, particularly when a young person's education experience is largely a postcode lottery. We embrace this civic duty by engaging and working in various networks, from sitting on a MAT trust advisory board, to fulfilling the role of Oak National PE Expert and supporting our active partnership to deliver professional development Our positive influence on the wider PE landscape has led us to be recognised by our peers as a best practice approach for a multi academy trust, winning the Youth Sport Trust Outstanding Practice Award in 2024. Previously one of our Primary PE Leads was recognised as the Primary Curriculum Leader of the Year 2023 (case studied by the Department for Education (DfE) and other national organisations).

Finally, although we don't do things for our regulatory body, Ofsted, we are now subject of choice for an inspection and we have received excellent feedback across all phases including our SCITT provision in 6 inspections over the last 18 months. This has often been a stumbling block for concept or holistic approaches to PE as documented by recent DfE publications, the Research Review in PE (2023) and Levelling the Playing field (2023). Hopefully, this means we are not only providing great opportunities for our young people to build a positive experience with movement, but also helping the adults who will influence them to do this too.

My Learning from this Process

Hopefully our experience can support others to adopt a more inclusive approach to PE, where the learning becomes meaningful, valued and truly enjoyable for all young people. So here are some key things to consider:

- Have a clear vision statement that guides all your decisions.
- Ensure you focus on what is common to you all but still meets the national curriculum.
- Define what you teach, especially if you are going beyond the national curriculum to consider more holistic characteristics.
- Only assess what you teach, and students learn – the knowledge, not the sport!
- Don't be precious, having external quality assurance is scary but so valuable.

- Co-create – you do this for young people, and it needs to hold meaning and value for them. Whilst not every lesson can be fun and enjoyable, you should hope that most students, most of the time, enjoy the learning experience.

CHAPTER 1: **DIRECTION**

Chapter 1 Summary

Direction: from Dread to Delight

DREAD

Practice before Purpose:
A PE delivery in schools with no clearly articulated purpose leading to practice that fails to meet needs of students or 'why' of teachers.

Meaningless PE:
Students fail to find meaning in PE and therefore fail to find learning relevant, challenging or fun.

More of the Same:
Teachers face pressure from multiple stakeholders that contradicts their vision.

DELIGHT

Articulate the Intent:
PE teams are clear on why PE exists in their school and communicate this clearly to all. Practice meets purpose.

Meaningful PE:
Students find meaning in PE and teachers incorporate social interaction, fun, challenge, motor competence, personally relevant learning in order to achieve delight.

Physical Literacy Informed:
Students are placed at the centre of planning and delivery, developing competence, confidence and motivation.

Where would you place yourself right now?

DREAD   **DELIGHT**

Reflection Questions
- What is my 'why'?
- Does my current practice meet my 'why'?
- How do the external pressures (such as SLT, parents, society) impact the delivery of PE at my school?
- What do I believe to be the purpose of PE? Is this a shared belief?
- What is my collective PE team/school intent?
- Do students value PE in my school? How do I know?

- Do students enjoy PE at my school? How do I know?
- Am I/my team happy with the Direction for PE in our school? Are we more towards Dread or Delight?
- What are my next steps?

Call to Action

As we conclude this chapter, it's time to reflect on what you've learned and consider how to apply it. The SHIFT mnemonic can guide you through the next steps: a structured approach to transform your insights into meaningful actions. Take a moment to work through the following questions:

S **Summarise** the key takeaway from this chapter that stands out to you.

H **Highlight** how this takeaway challenges or aligns with your current practices.

I **Initiate** a small change or step right now to put what you've learned into practice.

F **Frame** how this change will contribute to achieving your long-term vision for PE.

T **Take** others on the journey—share your new insights and encourage collaboration.

References

Association for PE. (2015). AfPE's position on fitness testing for school-aged pupils. [Online]. Available at: https://www.afpe.org.uk/physical-education/fitness-testing/ [Accessed 13 April 2024].

Association for Physical Education. (2019). Definitions of school sport, physical education, and physical activity. [Online] Available at: https://www.afpe.org.uk/news/624058/Definitions-of-Physical-Education-School-Sport--Physical-Activity.htm [Accessed on 9th Oct 2024].

Barnard Flory, S. (2014). Sociocultural Issues in Physical Education. Rowman & Littlefield.

Beni, S., Fletcher, T., & Ní Chróinín, D. (2017). Meaningful experiences in physical education and youth sport: A review of the literature. Quest, 69(3), 291–312.

Beni, S., Fletcher, T., & Ní Chróinín, D. (2021). 'It's how PE should be!': Classroom teachers' experiences of implementing Meaningful Physical Education. European Physical Education Review, 27(3), 666–683. https://doi.org/10.1177/1356336X20984188

Berkshire, M., Mason, J., & Hardwicke, J. (2024). The continuity of PE-as-sport: Exploring secondary school students' accounts of the meaning and purpose of physical education in England. European Physical Education Review, 0(0). https://doi.org/10.1177/1356336X241256866

Chorley, J., Ribbeck, P., Szybinski, S., & Brenner, J. (2023). The Youth Athlete. Academic Press.

Deci, E. L., & Ryan, R. M. (2000). The "what" and "why" of goal pursuits: Human needs and the self-determination of behavior. Psychological Inquiry, 11(4), 227–268. https://doi.org/10.1207/S15327965PLI1104_01

Department for Education. (2013). Statutory guidance: National Curriculum in England: Physical Education programmes of study. [Online]. Available at: https://www.gov.uk/government/publications/national-curriculum-in-england-physical-education-programmes-of-study/national-curriculum-in-england-physical-education-programmes-of-study [Accessed 22 March 2024].

Department of Education. (2023). Northern Ireland Curriculum. [Online]. Available at: https://www.education-ni.gov.uk/publications/northern-ireland-curriculum [Accessed 22 March 2024].

Durden-Myers, E. J. (2020). Operationalising physical literacy within physical education teaching practice through professional development. PhD Thesis, University of Bedfordshire. Available at: https://uobrep.openrepository.com/handle/10547/624942

Durden-Myers, E. J. and Bartle, G. (2023). Physical literacy enriched physical education: a capabilities perspective. Children, 10(9), 1503. https://doi.org/10.3390/children10091503

Durden-Myers, E. J., Green, N. R., & Whitehead, M. E. (2018). Implications for promoting physical literacy. Journal of Teaching in Physical Education, 37(3), 262–271.

Eather, N., Wade, L., & Pankowiak, A. (2023). The impact of sports participation on mental health and social outcomes in adults: A systematic review and the 'Mental Health through Sport' conceptual model. https://doi.org/10.1186/s13643-023-02264-8

Education Scotland. (2017). Physical education, physical activity and sport. [Online]. Available at: https://education.gov.scot/parentzone/learning-at-home/supporting-health-and-wellbeing/physical-education-physical-activity-and-sport [Accessed 22 March 2024].

Goddard Blyth, S. (2005). The Well Balanced Child: Movement and Early Learning. Hawthorne Press.

International Physical Literacy Association (IPLA). (2017). Definition of Physical Literacy. Accessed online: 3rd of July 2024. Available at: https://www.physical-literacy.org.uk/

MacAllister, J. (2013). The 'Physically Educated' Person: Physical education in the philosophy of Reid, Peters, and Aristotle. Educational Philosophy and Theory, 45(9), 908–920. https://doi.org/10.1080/00131857.2013.785353

Pill, S. (2001). Valuing learning in, through, and about sport – physical education and the development of sport literacy. ResearchGate.

Quennerstedt, M. (2019). Physical education and the art of teaching: Transformative learning and teaching in physical education and sports pedagogy. Sport, Education and Society, 24(6), 611–623. https://doi.org/10.1080/13573322.2019.1574731

Sport England. (2023). Physical literacy consensus statement for England. Accessed Online: 3rd July 2024. Available at: https://www.sportengland.org/news-and-inspiration/physical-literacy-consensus-statement-england-published

Sport England. (2024). Physical Literacy Consensus Statement for England. [Online]. Available at: https://www.sportengland.org/funds-and-campaigns/children-and-young-people?section=physical_literacy [Accessed 30 March 2024].

Sullivan, L. (2021). Is PE in crisis? Leading meaningful change in physical education. Scholarly.

Trendowski, T., & Mays Woods, A. (2015). Seven student-centered principles for smart teaching in physical education. Journal of Physical Education, Recreation & Dance, 86(8), 41–47. https://doi.org/10.1080/07303084.2015.1075923

Trowbridge, M. (2023). "What are we doing in PE today?" PE Scholar [Guest Blog]. [Online] Available at: https://www.pescholar.com/insight/what-are-we-doing-in-pe-today-the-relationship-between-physical-education-physical-activity-and-sport/ [Accessed on 9th Oct 2024].

Welsh Government. (2019). Area of Learning and Experience: Health and Well-being. [Online]. Available at: https://hwb.gov.wales/curriculum-for-wales/health-and-well-being [Accessed 22 March 2024].

Welsh Government. (2020). Curriculum for Wales: Guidance. [Online] Available at: https://gov.wales/curriculum-for-wales [Accessed on 9th Oct 2024].

Whitehead, M. (1993). Physical literacy [Paper presentation]. International Association of Physical Education and Sport for Women and Girls Congress, Melbourne, Australia.

Whitehead, M. E. (2001). The concept of physical literacy. European Journal of Physical Education, 6(2), 127–138. https://doi.org/10.1080/1740898010060205

Whitehead, M. E. (Ed.) (2010). Physical Literacy: Throughout the Lifecourse. London: Routledge.

Whitehead, M. E. (Ed.) (2019). Physical Literacy: Across the World. London: Routledge.
Whitehead, M. (2010). Physical Literacy Throughout the Lifecourse. Routledge.

Chapter 2: Realistic

Lee Sullivan, Professor Liz Durden-Myers, Phil Cocks, Anna Sheppard

Part 2.1 – Insight
Lee Sullivan

In our second chapter, we delve into the tangible outcomes achievable in PE. Amidst a myriad of claims surrounding the benefits of physical activity and sports, there's a need to discern what lies within the realm of feasibility for our subject. With such limited time in front of our students, this chapter will examine what PE can realistically accomplish and delineate the responsibilities that rightfully belong to our subject, distinguishing them from those that may extend beyond its scope.

A Champion is Born
In the heart of New York City, under the bright lights of the Arthur Ashe Stadium, history was in the making. The air was charged with anticipation as young British tennis player Emma Raducanu stepped onto the court, her determined gaze fixed on the prize that lay before her: the US Open title.

Just months earlier, Raducanu had been a relatively unknown name in the world of tennis, a talented but untested player with dreams of greatness. As the tournament unfolded, Raducanu defied all expectations, dispatching seasoned opponents with ease, not dropping a single set.

In the final, she faced off against Leylah Fernandez, another rising star in the world of tennis. From the first serve, Raducanu electrified the crowd with her precision and power, dictating play with a maturity beyond her years. Her opponent fought back fiercely, matching her shot for shot in a gruelling battle that stretched into the night. As the match reached its climax, she unleashed a blistering forehand that left her opponent flat-footed, sealing her victory and etching her name into tennis history. A champion was born.

The following morning on a popular English breakfast television programme, the presenters interviewed the 18-year old's former PE teacher. He reminisced about Raducanu's time in their lessons, highlighting her dedication, athleticism, and positive attitude. They recalled moments when Raducanu showed exceptional skill and determination on the court, demonstrating the potential for greatness even at a young age. Whilst not directly taking all the credit for the young champion's success, the interviewers were offering praise to the teacher as if PE was the sole reason for her achievement.

Whilst PE might have provided a foundation for Radacanu's physical development and potentially instilled valuable qualities like discipline and teamwork, it was just one piece of the puzzle. Raducanu's journey to becoming a champion can't solely be attributed to her experiences in PE. It was the combination of various factors and support systems that propelled her to success. Rigorous training sessions before and after school, guidance from nutritionists to fuel her body for peak performance, psychologists to help manage the pressures of competition, physiotherapists to prevent and treat injuries, and a network of coaches and mentors all played crucial roles in her development. For every Emma Raducanu, there are thousands of students for whom PE should be about personal growth, not athletic perfection.

PE teachers have limited contact time with students, making the expectation that PE alone can create elite athletes not only unrealistic but also impossible. However, government policies, media narratives, and school curricula often emphasise the pursuit of sporting excellence—a goal that is impractical to achieve given the constraints of time and resources. This fixation on excellence can be damaging, especially for the vast majority of students who will not aspire to elite athletic performance. Instead, the true measure of PE should not be the few who rise to elite success but the many who leave school with a lifelong love of movement. Where do you stand? Should PE focus on cultivating elite athletes, or is its core purpose to inspire all students to lead active and fulfilling lives?

Over the years, other assertions have been made regarding the advantages of PE, outside of developing movement competence. Claims asserting that PE enhances health, improves fitness, boosts academic performance, fosters social skills, and cultivates resilience have been particularly prominent. These assertions have largely shaped the perception of our subject from external stakeholders, with little in the way of evidence or even critical considerations behind these bold claims. We must examine more closely what is said in the name of PE and be more realistic as to what we can genuinely achieve through PE.

Part 2.2 – Delve
Lee Sullivan

If PE alone cannot create professional athletes, it becomes imperative to examine the other purported benefits of our subject and assess what can realistically be accomplished within the time frame available with our students. I have fallen foul of thinking the aims of society and the media were the responsibility of PE. I thought it fell on PE to fix obesity, mental health issues, physical health decline and other global issues that needed fixing. My thinking came from a good place but in truth these are complex issues that are not PE's problems to fix. I have learned to be realistic about what we can achieve through PE and what is relevant to PE and what is not.

PE, Health & Fitness

Undoubtedly, there exists a widespread recognition that the unique contribution PE and School Sport offers to a child's education primarily lies within the physical domain. However, the emphasis on the physical aspect of PE has evolved over time. Initially rooted in health-related objectives during the first half of the twentieth century, it transitioned towards performance-oriented goals in the aftermath of the Second World War. More recently, there has been a shift towards addressing concerns regarding the health consequences of sedentary lifestyles (Bailey, Armour, Kirk, 2009). There is limited evidence linking childhood physical activity to significant physical benefits, however, the importance of promoting lifelong physical activity by establishing secure movement foundations from an early age has gained widespread acceptance.

Laura Davies wrote a brilliant blog addressing the myths behind PE and health (2022). The blog reflects on the evolving role of PE and challenges the prevailing beliefs surrounding its impact on health. Davies recounts her early career, buoyed by the notion that PE teachers play a crucial role in promoting health and well-being. However, recent experiences, including parent-teacher conferences, have prompted discomfort with addressing weight-related concerns and questioning the prevailing belief that weight is synonymous with health.

Davies continues to highlight the damaging assumptions and stereotypes surrounding weight in PE, emphasising the need to shift away from deficit thinking and the simplistic idea of PE as a solution to complex health issues. The blog questions the linear relationship between PE and health and cautions against PE being seen as a Band-Aid solution to societal problems. Davies writes *'it is time that we critically reflect upon the true role of, and intentions behind, PE. It is time that we are honest about the biases we hold, and actively work to prevent the harm we are inadvertently causing to our students. Can we teach students ABOUT health? I would say yes – carefully. Can we truly profess to improve the health of our students? I would argue not. Instead, let's focus on making PE a safe space where everyone is celebrated. Let's focus on providing opportunities for exploration, development and growth. Let's focus on helping our students learn to love movement.'* Ultimately, the blog urges PE educators to prioritise students' holistic well-being, focusing on fostering joy in movement and providing opportunities for exploration and growth. It calls for a re-evaluation of PE's place within the broader context of health and emphasises the importance of acknowledging and addressing biases within the PE community.

PE teachers are often in front of their students for 1 to 2 hours per week. To improve physical health and fitness, would require more physical activity time than what we currently offer. The chief medical officer for the UK currently recommends 60 minutes of exercise per day, falling far short of what we can timetable into the curriculum. However, it is widely accepted that there is a positive association between increased levels of physical activity and health benefits. Therefore, if education were to attempt to tackle physical health and fitness, it would need to be done so on a whole-school level.

Given this widely accepted relationship, advocates of this position stress the importance of promoting physical activity in school to enhance the health of young people. Mong and Standal (2022) explored the importance of health education in PE through their action project exploring methods teaching health in PE. The project introduced logbooks as a reflective tool, encouraging students to express their thoughts and experiences in writing—a departure from traditional PE practices. While some students initially perceived this as unconventional, it allowed for a deeper engagement with health-related topics. Despite initial resistance, students showed increased awareness of health issues, indicating a shift towards viewing health as an educational topic rather than a by-product of physical activity.

Paul Sammons and Mark Bowler proposed something similar with a health-based model for PE, which prioritises a comprehensive approach to students' well-being within the PE curriculum. Health-based Physical Education (HbPE) is a progressive approach dedicated to cultivating students' well-being through physical activity, prioritising health and wellness over traditional sports skills, competition, and athletic performance. The model distinguishes itself by embracing a holistic perspective that extends beyond only the physical aspects of physical activity. At the core of HbPE lies the self-determination theory of motivation, as proposed by Deci and Ryan in 2000. This theory emphasises the importance of intrinsic motivation, autonomy, and competence in fostering a lasting commitment to physical activity. Aligned with the principles of the HbPE model, Bowler and Sammon (2019) delineate four essential learning aspirations: Habitual Movers, Informed Movers, Motivated Movers, Critical Movers.

With such clear links between the positive impacts of physical health and physical activity, it is logical to assume that PE should play a central role in promoting physical well-being. However, with limited curriculum time and the evidence of negative experiences of some in PE and the resulting impact that has on long term engagement, it is difficult to build a case that PE has a direct positive influence on physical well-being for all. What is clearer is the opportunity within PE to teach intentionally about health and provide physical opportunities through curricular and extracurricular activities.

PE and Academic Performance

Research into the cognitive benefits indicates a positive association between physical activity and academic performance, with some studies showing small improvements in academic outcomes when time for PE and school sport is increased.

The World Health Organisation (WHO) conducted a review on Physical Activity and Academic Achievement (2020), finding that regular physical activity, increased physical education, and active classrooms improve both school children's health and academic performance. Their review claimed that children in the WHO European Region spend the majority of their school time in sedentary activities, but increasing physical activity positively impacts cognitive, motor, and social skills, as well as academic performance. The review also highlighted the importance of allowing children to have self-directed outdoor playtime, which fosters learning and prepares them for focused indoor activities. They also acknowledged that while it's challenging to measure the direct impact of physical activity on academic achievement due to various influencing factors, evidence claims that increased emphasis on physical education and regular physical activity benefits academic outcomes.

While assertions about the positive impact of physical activity on academic performance are frequently made and often backed by research, the specific role of PE in this context is not as clearly established. This being said, studies that increased the amount of physical activity students were undertaking by the increasing time dedicated to PE did not report any negative impact on student achievement and grades (Lambert, Ford and Jeanes 2022).

While there is promising evidence suggesting that PE and school sports may contribute to improved academic performance, it is essential to view this as a beneficial by-product rather than the primary purpose of PE. Framing PE solely as a means to enhance academic achievement risks diminishing its true value and the broader impact it has on students' physical, mental, and social well-being. However, for schools where PE is under threat or fighting for curriculum time, highlighting its contribution to academic outcomes could be a strategic approach to securing greater support from senior leaders. This dual perspective ensures PE is both valued for its unique benefits and recognised for its potential to enhance broader educational goals.

PE and Personal Development

It has long been suggested that PE's social and educational processes are crucial in effecting behavioural change, often emphasising the acquisition of personal, social, and socio-moral skills. Whether it be from a concept-driven curriculum, model-based practices, highlighting skills inherent in PE, physical activity and sport or other pedagogical approaches, the idea of developing character through PE is nothing new.

Randall, Jess, Parker, et al. published their research article 'The purpose of primary physical education: The views of teacher educators,' (2024) and the educators teaching primary PE unanimously recognised the importance of movement learning and active participation in physical activities. However, they underscored a broader aim, focusing on the holistic development of children, encompassing physical, social, emotional, and cognitive aspects. They viewed primary PE as a platform for children to creatively enjoy movement, solve problems, and grasp broader life lessons beyond sports and games. Their goal was to nurture individuals who appreciate learning, possess decision-making skills, and are self-motivated. While the primary objective remained on physical development, the educators emphasised integrating cognitive, social, and emotional dimensions into PE.

Despite the positive claims around PE and personal development, uncertainties remain regarding the precise impact of PE programs due to challenges in monitoring, evaluating, and attributing observed benefits to specific initiatives. Nevertheless, there is consensus that enough evidence exists to suggest the potential for PE to result in positive social benefits, and sharing examples of good practice can inform the development of future initiatives (Bailey, Armour, Kirk, 2009).

What Can Be Achieved in PE?

Finally, for this part in the chapter we must reflect on what is actually possible in PE. Where time is often limited and expectations are high, it's essential to clarify the core objectives and realistic outcomes. As educators, we strive to make the most of our time with students, aiming to impart valuable lessons that extend beyond the confines of the gym or sports field.

Consider the ABC (and D) of PE – a framework designed to encapsulate the fundamental goals of our discipline and explore how we can enhance our practice.

Figure 4: ABC (and D) of PE

ABC (and D) of Primary PE

Active for sustained periods of time

Build positive relationship with PE/PA & Sport

Competence - able to move well and confident doing so

Develop character, knowledge and understanding through physical activity

A: Active for sustained periods of time
At the heart of PE lies the promotion of physical activity and its numerous benefits. Encouraging students to be active for sustained periods not only contributes to their physical health but also enhances their mental well-being and academic performance. By providing engaging and varied activities, we can instil a lifelong appreciation for movement and foster habits that promote overall health and vitality.

B: Building positive relationships with PEPASS
Build upon a positive relationship with physical education, physical activity, and sport. By creating enjoyable, inclusive, and purposeful experiences, lessons can help students develop confidence, motivation, and a sense of belonging in movement-based activities. When students connect positively with PE, they are more likely to see physical activity and sport as meaningful and worthwhile both in and beyond school.

C: Competence in a range of activities and environments.
One of the primary objectives of PE is to develop students' competence in various physical activities and environments. From traditional sports to outdoor pursuits and recreational games, exposing students to a diverse range of activities fosters a well-rounded skill set and promotes adaptability. By mastering fundamental movement skills and exploring new challenges, students gain confidence in their abilities and develop a lifelong passion for physical activity. Learning must always be at the forefront of any teacher's mind.

D: Developing character, knowledge, and understanding through physical activity.

CHAPTER 2: **REALISTIC**

While the ABCs of PE focus primarily on physical health and skill development, the addition of "D" emphasises the broader educational value of physical activity. Through thoughtful instruction and reflection, PE can serve as a platform for character development, critical thinking, and interdisciplinary learning.

Incorporating the ABC (and potentially D) of PE into our practice requires a balanced approach that prioritises the holistic well-being of our students. By emphasising the importance of physical activity, fostering positive relationships, and promoting competence and character development, we can empower students to lead healthy, active lives both inside and outside the classroom. As educators, let's embrace the potential of PE to inspire, educate, and transform the lives of our students, one letter at a time.

To Sum it Up

While PE holds undeniable importance in promoting physical health and fitness among schoolchildren, its role in addressing broader societal issues such as obesity, mental health, and academic performance is not as straightforward. While uncertainties persist about the precise impact of PE programmes, there is consensus on their potential to promote positive social benefits. We must be careful around the claims we make (I know from experience) and what we aim to achieve through PE. These are complex issues, and whilst I believe that improving experiences within PE can go some way to support the solution to these issues, they cannot and should not be solved by PE alone. In short, they are not PE's responsibility and expecting the subject to serve as a cure-all for multifaceted challenges is unrealistic and misguided.

In every lesson however, we can all look to get children active for sustained periods of time, build a positive relationship with PE, physical activity and sport, develop movement competence and potentially develop character. This is realistic and achievable for every PE teacher. This might lead to positive results in terms of academic performance and improved health and fitness, but these issues are too complex for PE to be solving alone. They are not the responsibility of PE and it can be harmful to the subject to suggest otherwise.

Moving forward, it is essential for PE educators to acknowledge the limitations and complexities inherent in addressing societal challenges through PE alone. By fostering joy in movement, providing opportunities for exploration and growth, and integrating cognitive, social, and emotional dimensions into PE, educators can create a more enriching experience for students.

Ultimately, PE's true value lies in movement and its ability to contribute to a well-rounded education. A singular focus on creating champions in PE overlooks the wider, more profound impact we can have on every student.

Mid-chapter reflection

What new insights have I gained from this chapter so far?

How does this knowledge reinforce or challenge my current beliefs or practices?

Are there areas or concepts I still need to explore further?

Have I identified any gaps in my team's understanding or practice that need addressing?

How can I share or apply this learning to positively influence others in my team or school?

How can I share or apply this learning to positively influence others in my team or school?

Part 2.3 – Experts

Realistic Outcomes of PE
Professor Liz Durden-Myers

Don't get me wrong I love the ambition that we PE teachers have for our pupils and our subject. But often we can fall into the trap of making bold educational claims that if we took a big step back to consider, we couldn't really substantiate.

This is not a new phenomenon, Bailey et al., in 2009 (Bailey et al., 2009) warned the PE profession to be more realistic about the educational benefits claimed in the name of Physical Education and School Sport (PESS). In his recommendations, he outlines that there is evidence to support the physical, affective, cognitive and social benefits derived from PESS experiences, but he argues that many of these benefits are highly dependent on contextual and pedagogic variables.

As such we need to recognise the complexities of teaching, learning and the promotion of a healthy active lifestyle. Therefore, any oversimplified equation of what we can achieve in PE should be avoided and instead, we need to recognise the complexity of realising these benefits and anticipate the potential intricacies and variabilities along the way.

We also need to be realistic by understanding that we live in a world where there is a significant amount of accountability to regulatory bodies such as Ofsted, a requirement to align to the PE National Curriculum, adhere to Safe Practice in PE, as well as being integrated into whole school systems and processes.

Again, this alludes to the complexity of marrying our own philosophy for PE, the vision of the PE department, alongside the requirements of the school community and the wider PE and education landscape, and that is before we have even mentioned the unique and varying needs, wants and desires of our pupils.

So, having acknowledged that PE needs to be cautious in the educational claims we make and understand that realising these benefits are highly contextual and complex, what realistically should we claim to develop in PE? and how can we ensure that PE delivers on these objectives?

All the best strategies to achieve a goal are clear, memorable and inform everyday life and practice. If we overcomplicate or add too many things to our mission, we risk the chance of not doing any of them well, if at all. The first step is to define:

- What is it that you are claiming to achieve within PE?

- How do you know you are achieving it? and, understand
- Why is this important for children and young people?

So, sticking with the ABCD acronym Lee mentioned earlier, but adapting it slightly, this is what I think we need to do to be more realistic about the educational claims we make in PE and more importantly, make good on these claims.

A = Achievable and Accountable

Most PE offers would feature improving engagement in physical activity as a core objective. An example of an unrealistic goal would be to jump to the grand claim that PE increases physical activity and reduces physical inactivity levels in children. A more realistic goal would be to state that PE is designed to optimise physical activity within lessons. This is an achievable aim. The word optimise is also intentional as some lessons are not always designed to be highly physical – there might be an evaluation or analysis task that reduces physical activity time, but the important thing is that physical activity is prioritised and optimised where appropriate.

Another over-ambitious claim might be that PE supports students' health and wellbeing. Again, health both physical and mental and general well-being are not likely to be significantly affected by two 50-minute PE lessons a week. However, PE can expose children to the short-term benefits of exercise and educate children on the benefits of physical activity for health and well-being. PE can help children and young people understand the importance of 60 active minutes a day, a balanced diet, good sleep quality and hydration.

We could go on, listing thousands of aims and objectives but the point is to make and set goals that you can achieve, they then don't become claims but instead become evidence.

Whatever you decide to be your achievable outcomes for PE, make sure you hold yourself accountable to them. So, if you identify a certain area make sure it is consistently observable in your routines and practices. For example, if the holistic development of the child is important to you and your department, make sure it is evident in your planning, lessons and students are aware of their holistic progress.

B = Balance the P and the E

Quennerstedt (2019) highlights the need to balance the P and the E for us to hold our place as a unique educational subject. What this means is PE cannot just be physical or educative, it needs to be both.

If PE is purely physical it risks losing its educational value, I like to call this the 'happy active good' scenario. Where pupils are doing but not necessarily learning. If they are not learning or making progress you might find yourself in a scenario where PE is being removed from the curriculum in favour of more time learning in other subjects. Phil Cocks (Cocks, 2024) in his episode on the PE Insights Podcast stresses this point by highlighting how teachers should plan 'learning not lessons'.

PE being just educative is also problematic as without the physical element it becomes a theoretical subject that could be delivered in Science or Personal, Social, Health and Economic (PSHE) education lessons. We also know that understanding the importance of being physically active (declarative knowledge) is not the same as having the skills and resources to be physically active (procedural knowledge). Not to mention the power of positive lived experiences in shaping habits and behaviours. So, every lesson must carefully balance the physical and the educative elements of PE.

C = Clear and Consistent Communication
So having established your achievable goals in PE, and having balanced the physical and the educative elements you now need to be clear and consistent in communicating these with your pupils, PE team, senior leadership team, parents etc. We often do not communicate enough the purpose, value and why of PE. If we can become better at articulating the importance and back this up with evidence from our practice, we are more likely to be able to bring people on that journey with us. We also don't always clearly explain what we are learning, how we are learning it and why learning this is important. Children and young people deserve to know the answers to these questions and if we can't answer them, I would query whether it is the right thing to be teaching them?

D = Dedicated to Reflexivity
Finally, the military has a saying that 'the best-laid plans don't survive first contact with the enemy'. I'm not implying that the pupils are the enemy, what I mean to say is that a strategy is just a plan, but you must continually reflect, change, pivot and adapt that plan in response to the needs of pupils. Continual reflection evaluating what is and is not working, coupled with reflexivity in trying out new ideas and solutions, will help you to continually evolve your practice to best meet the needs of your pupils. We cannot afford to stand still, we need to continually refine, adapt and change our practice as our young people adapt and change. It is this commitment to continuous improvement that will help you realise your objectives for your young people in PE.

Summary

To coin a traditional cliché 'Rome wasn't built in a day' and neither will you realise the full educational benefits of PE daily for all pupils. But through small steps and 'increments' we can conquer some challenging issues facing children and young people; we can support their holistic growth and development towards a healthy active lifestyle with the potential to unlock further educational benefits. Our job is to remain true to our values, live them out every day, and capture the glimmers of progress along the way.

Part 2.4 – Apply

Outstanding PE?
Phil Cocks

The expectation—whether placed upon ourselves or by others—that teachers must deliver outstanding lessons every single time is both unrealistic and unsustainable. If you want to be successful, you must be consistent. If you are aiming for learning to be outstanding, you should aim to be consistently good. Every lesson, every day, good or better has been my mantra for over 20 years of teaching. Through my personal experience of six Ofsted inspections, transforming poor Key Stage 4 (ages 13-16) and 5 (ages 16-18) outcomes to above national average on all measures, the overarching fundamental has been to deliver consistently good lessons every day.

In Bill Walsh's excellent book 'The score takes care of itself' he states, *"Do all the right things to precision and 'the score will take care of itself,"* (2009, page 2). Walsh won three Super Bowls in the 1980's with the San Francisco 49ers, establishing himself as one of the all-time great coaches and leaders. His relentless discipline and game-planning redefined the way others prepared for their games and seasons. However, throughout his time he never chased glory, riches, or fame. His philosophy focused on the process, professionalism, and relationships. Walsh became known for his approach of 'Just do the job and treat people right,' (page 102). He is famously linked with a statement that holds true for most professions and one that resonates with teaching physical education for me; *"Today's effort becomes tomorrow's results. The quality of those efforts becomes the quality of your work,"* (page 231).

The learning from many great leaders, such as Walsh, is that highly successful people do not set out to achieve one-word accolades. Fundamentally they have a clear purpose or ambition to make or do something better that will influence others. In the many interviews I have conducted for the teaching profession, the responses from the best candidates have always included a moral purpose for inspiring young people and developing other adults. Great teachers and leaders continually strive to strengthen this vision through their own consistent behaviours and inspirational daily practice.

Teaching physical education is no different. Great PE teachers understand and deliver stimulating pedagogy, with a relentless focus on high standards for quality of movement and expectations. They reflect on their practice, evaluate, and adapt, whilst establishing excellent relationships with young people and adults. Their day in, day out commitment, creates positive experiences and fantastic learning environments for young people to thrive.

CHAPTER 2: **REALISTIC**

Over the past two decades, I have been convinced that because the PE teaching community can reach out with ease nationally and internationally, this has significantly improved the impact it has on young people across the world. There are many aspects supporting this, including systematic sharing, an open and genuine desire to provide high quality PE for all students and fantastic individuals who have set up excellent online platforms. However, the most significant factor is that the science for learning has developed so impressively in recent years.

I have had the privilege to see and experience many incredible PE lessons and excellent teaching, in diverse contexts, delivered in a range of styles that best suits the students they are serving. Throughout all these episodes, the 'best' lessons always have remarkably similar pedagogical principles, whether in a practical or a classroom setting, and consistency is always at the heart of the learning.

The lessons always include

1. **Clarity of expectations:** students know exactly what the teacher wants them to learn and do. Often through excellent use of modelling (demonstration) with clear, concise instructions. Without this clarity, lesson time often drifts and students do not make as much progress as they could. Sometimes this leads to students being off task and potentially poor behaviour or disengagement.
2. **Deep-thought planning to meet students' needs:** I am not suggesting unsustainable levels of differentiation, instead these lessons build from previous learning. Teachers plan for misconceptions. Lessons (and curriculums) are well-sequenced; they have elements of recall and build upon, or strengthen, previously taught knowledge to develop to the next stage. A well-planned effective curriculum with considered lesson sequencing is the treasure map to the gold. It provides both novice and experienced teachers with the structure to deliver high quality provisions, whilst ensuring a minimum entitlement for all learners.
3. **The teacher is the subject expert.** In all the 'best' lessons I have experienced, excellent subject knowledge has been vital. It is noticeably clear that when the teacher knows the content they are delivering, they are pedagogically flexible. Teachers who are confident in the content can stimulate learning in a variety of ways; they are adept at observing the best moments to step in and equally step back, to challenge and to enable their learners to flourish.
4. **Routines and expectations:** the important ingredient to unlocking excellent teaching. The consistency of routines allows students to complete tasks with minimal load on their working memory, allowing them to learn more in each learning episode. When teachers have successful routines from the very start of the lesson, students can respond in confidence and can focus on the new learning. Routines allow the teacher to be more creative in their approach. Great learning cannot happen in chaotic, unusual, and unpredictable environments. Students (and teachers) like to know what to do, how to do it and be recognised for achieving and surpassing it. Consistency builds trust and

creates confidence. Consistency establishes momentum, it develops habits. Consistency helps achieve outstanding results. If you want to be an influential PE teacher, deliver the basics well, time and time again. Bill Walsh's lasting word on this was…*'Mastery requires endless remastery. In fact, I don't believe there is ever true mastery. It is a process, not a destination,'* (page 143).

This is not a formula for 'outstanding PE' - I do not think such a thing exists. However, these elements are part of consistently good teaching that becomes outstanding learning.

PE Lesson Purpose
Anna Sheppard

Every PE teacher has the intent to do right by the students. I am yet to meet a PE teacher who does not wish for students to be active. The difficulty is that many PE teachers have the mindset of a sportsperson. I am not sure I know a PE teacher who does not have sport at their core, and it is often that love for sport that they wish to pass on to others.

However, as research shows, not all children are turned on by sport. Physical activity, yes! Movement is innate. Children love to play. Playgrounds and parks are filled with tag games and exploration through, in and over climbing equipment. However it seems they are not always filled by organised and structured sport and when they are it is generally organised by a grown-up.

When I spend time with my non PE teacher friends, some of them cannot comprehend spending time training, going to bed early, sacrificing foods and drinks. They admire the discipline, but make comments like 'yeah but you're good at sport' like I'm some kind of superhuman. These friends are happiest when they are walking in the fresh outdoors, bike riding or maintaining healthy habits through the gym or a fitness class, not on a sports field or court.

For me, this has always questioned the purpose of PE. Why do so many schools spend so many hours in PE lessons teaching children skills such as layups in basketball, javelin throws in athletics and the intricacies of how to score in badminton? Many people never use these skills when they leave school and if they do play some badminton they often interpret the scoring and rules to suit the space they are in and in a much less formal manner. I'm not for a moment suggesting that these activities or sports should not be in a PE curriculum but I am certain that the purpose of PE is physical literacy not the teaching of sport.

'Physical literacy has been defined as the motivation, confidence, physical competence, knowledge and understanding to value and take responsibility for engagement in physical activities for life." IPLA 2017 and more recently defined as the relationship we have with physical activity and movement through life.

Our role as educators within a PE setting is to ensure children develop that positive relationship with movement. This means success, every step along the way. This is building on from the successes that a child has had before they even reach the school environment. The rewards gained from learning to pull up and stand as a baby, learning to crawl to fetch and carry and progressing to walking and running. Our role as PE teachers is to continue to facilitate success.

When looking at curriculum design, I zoom out. I look at the end point and take a backwards-by-design approach. When these young people have left our care, what do we wish for them to have gained? What skills and attitude would we like for them to have developed during their time with us and what experiences have we been able to offer them. Laurence Peter, Canadian educator quoted *'if you don't know where you're going, you'll probably end up somewhere else'*.

When I have facilitated these conversations with PE teachers, no one has ever reflected on individual skills such as mastery of the basketball layup or javelin throw. They have usually stated soft skills such as leadership, responsibility, motivation to stay active, empathy, being a kind person, and most usefully, the confidence to sign up to a club at a university Freshers' Fair. When considering the physical aspect of PE, teachers have declared students should leave school having an understanding of their bodies, injury prevention and knowing what to do if they enter a gym. Quite ironic actually when I see many schools' curriculum maps and continued persistence to offer traditional sports in PE, often duplicating what is offered in their school's sports programme!

I believe PE should be a purposefully planned journey. A learning journey which should take children into adulthood through a wide and varied offering, allowing students to gain positive experiences and a wide range of skills.

In an inspiring blog post from Nathan Walker, he provided principles to guide the journey of meaningful experiences in PE. Three principles in particular that stand out;

Fun, But With Depth: I'm a huge believer that PE lessons should be fun. However fun by itself is not enough, there needs to be learning, hence the depth.

Creating Experiences That Matter: Our time with children is limited; ensure the time you have in PE lessons matters. As Walker rightly says 'meaningful experiences don't just happen—they're crafted'.

Personal Relevance: If physical literacy is the relationship a person has with movement, this relationship is unique for each individual. Students need to be involved in choice and lead what is important to them. I love the questions that Julie Stern poses to students in relation to curricula and lessons; 'How is this learning relevant and significant for me?'

FROM PE DREAD TO DELIGHT

I would argue that every lesson counts. It doesn't take many bad experiences to turn children off PE. Every lesson needs purpose. Every lesson needs a teacher who is making connections with the children, adapting their teaching based on the students in the class. If there is no purpose to the lesson it becomes more difficult to meet the three principles previously outlined. Individual lessons are the final steps in the backwards-by-design approach. Without carefully planned activities, what's the point? The lesson may as well be a collapsed rainy day 'tournament' lesson.

Lesson outcomes are stepping stones in a child's journey; pieces of a puzzle that a child or later adult is able to piece together. PE teachers have the privilege to ignite a child's relationship with physical literacy and nurture this relationship. Sadly though this relationship can be destroyed through negative experiences, poorly selected activities and through lessons that bare no meaning or relevance to a child.

Chapter 2 Summary

Realistic: from Dread to Delight

DREAD

Excellence Expectations:
Unrealistic belief in PE's ability to create professional athletes

Our Responsibility:
Fixation on PE as the sole solution to societal issues

All on PE:
Belief that PE is solely responsible for health and fitness

PE Superheroes:
Unrealistic expectations placed on PE teachers

DELIGHT

Reframe Excellence:
Emphasis on developing personal, social, and cognitive skills in PE

Realistic Responsibility:
Realistic assessment of PE's role in addressing complex societal challenges

Beyond PE:
Understanding that health and well-being are multifaceted and extend beyond PE

Complex Challenges:
Acknowledgment of the limitations and complexities inherent in addressing societal challenges

Where would you place yourself right now?

DREAD   **DELIGHT**

Reflection Questions
- What can PE realistically achieve at my school?
- How does the role of the media/society influence my aims within PE?
- What role should PE play in supporting these wider issues?
- How has my perspective on PE's role in addressing societal issues changed?
- How do I/can I ensure consistently good teaching to inspire young people's learning takes place day to day?
- What actions can I take to prioritise enjoyment and overall well-being in my PE classes?
- How will I promote a broader understanding of health among your students?

Call to Action

As we conclude this chapter, it's time to reflect on what you've learned and consider how to apply it. The SHIFT mnemonic can guide you through the next steps: a structured approach to transform your insights into meaningful actions. Take a moment to work through the following questions:

S **Summarise** the key takeaway from this chapter that stands out to you.

H **Highlight** how this takeaway challenges or aligns with your current practices.

I **Initiate** a small change or step right now to put what you've learned into practice.

F **Frame** how this change will contribute to achieving your long-term vision for PE.

T **Take** others on the journey—share your new insights and encourage collaboration.

References

Association for Physical Education. (2015). AfPE's position on fitness testing for school-aged pupils. [Online]. Available at: https://www.afpe.org.uk/physical-education/fitness-testing/ [Accessed 13 April 2024].

Association for Physical Education. (2019). Definitions of school sport, physical education, and physical activity. [Online] Available at: https://www.afpe.org.uk/news/624058/Definitions-of-Physical-Education-School-Sport--Physical-Activity.htm [Accessed 9 Oct 2024].

Bailey, R., Armour, K., & Kirk, D. (2009). The educational benefits claimed for physical education and school sport: An academic review. Research Papers in Education, 24(1), 1–27. https://doi.org/10.1080/02671520701809817

Barbosa, A., Whiting, S., Simmonds, P., Scotini Moreno, R., Mendes, R., & Breda, J. (2020). Physical activity and academic achievement: An umbrella review. International Journal of Environmental Research and Public Health, 17(5972). https://doi.org/10.3390/ijerph17165972

Barnard Flory, S. (2014). Sociocultural Issues in Physical Education. Rowman & Littlefield.

Beni, S., Fletcher, T., & Ní Chróinín, D. (2017). Meaningful experiences in physical education and youth sport: A review of the literature. Quest, 69(3), 291–312.

Beni, S., Fletcher, T., & Ní Chróinín, D. (2021). 'It's how PE should be!': Classroom teachers' experiences of implementing Meaningful Physical Education. European Physical Education Review, 27(3), 666–683. https://doi.org/10.1177/1356336X20984188

Berkshire, M., Mason, J., & Hardwicke, J. (2024). The continuity of PE-as-sport: Exploring secondary school students' accounts of the meaning and purpose of physical education in England. European Physical Education Review, 0(0). https://doi.org/10.1177/1356336X241256866

Bowler, M., & Sammon, P. (2020). Health-Based Physical Education – A framework for promoting active lifestyles in children and young people. Part 1: Introducing a new pedagogical model. Physical Education Matters, 15(3), 60–63.

CHAPTER 2: **REALISTIC**

Chorley, J., Ribbeck, P., Szybinski, S., & Brenner, J. (2023). The Youth Athlete. Academic Press.

Cocks, P. (2024). Episode 29: Four Mantras for Teaching and Learning. PE Scholar: PE Insights Podcast. [Online] Available at: https://podcasts.apple.com/gb/podcast/pe-insights-pe-scholar-physical-education/id1710712630 [Accessed 4 July 2024].

Davies, L. (2022). Physical Education & The Great Health Myth. PE Scholar. [Online]. Available at: https://www.pescholar.com/insight/physical-education-the-great-health-myth/ [Accessed 19 Jan 2024].

Deci, E. L., & Ryan, R. M. (2000). The "what" and "why" of goal pursuits: Human needs and the self-determination of behavior. Psychological Inquiry, 11(4), 227–268. https://doi.org/10.1207/S15327965PLI1104_01

Department for Education. (2013). Statutory guidance: National Curriculum in England: Physical Education programmes of study. [Online]. Available at: https://www.gov.uk/government/publications/national-curriculum-in-england-physical-education-programmes-of-study/national-curriculum-in-england-physical-education-programmes-of-study [Accessed 22 March 2024].

Department of Education. (2023). Northern Ireland Curriculum. [Online]. Available at: https://www.education-ni.gov.uk/publications/northern-ireland-curriculum [Accessed 22 March 2024].

Durden-Myers, E. J. (2020). Operationalising Physical Literacy Through Physical Education Professional Development (PhD Thesis). University of Bedfordshire. Available at: https://uobrep.openrepository.com/handle/10547/624942

Durden-Myers, E. J., Green, N. R., & Whitehead, M. E. (2018). Implications for promoting physical literacy. Journal of Teaching in Physical Education, 37(3), 262–271.

Durden-Myers, E. J., & Bartle, G. (2023). Physical literacy enriched physical education: A capabilities perspective. Children, 10(9), 1503. https://doi.org/10.3390/children10091503

Eather, N., Wade, L., & Pankowiak, A. (2023). The impact of sports participation on mental health and social outcomes in adults: A systematic review and the 'Mental Health through Sport' conceptual model. https://doi.org/10.1186/s13643-023-02264-8

Education Scotland. (2017). Physical education, physical activity and sport. [Online]. Available at: https://education.gov.scot/parentzone/learning-at-home/supporting-health-and-wellbeing/physical-education-physical-activity-and-sport [Accessed 22 March 2024].

Goddard Blythe, S. (2005). The Well Balanced Child: Movement and Early Learning. Hawthorne Press.

Jess, M., Parker, M., Carse, N., Douglass, A., Keay, J., Martinez Alvarez, L., Murray, A., Pearson, J., Randall, V., & Sweeney, T. (2024). The purpose of primary physical education: The views of teacher educators. European Physical Education Review, 0(0). https://doi.org/10.1177/1356336X241237081

Lambert, K., Ford, A., & Jeanes, R. (2024). The association between physical education and academic achievement in other curriculum learning areas: A review. Physical Education and Sport Pedagogy, 29(1), 51–81. https://doi.org/10.1080/17408989.2022.2029385

MacAllister, J. (2013). The 'physically educated' person: Physical education in the philosophy of Reid, Peters, and Aristotle. Educational Philosophy and Theory, 45(9), 908–920. https://doi.org/10.1080/00131857.2013.785353

Mong, H. H., & Standal, Ø. F. (2022). Teaching health in physical education: An action research project. European Physical Education Review, 28(3), 739–756. https://doi.org/10.1177/1356336X221078319

Pill, S. (2001). Valuing learning in, through, and about sport – physical education and the development of sport literacy. ResearchGate.

Quennerstedt, M. (2019). Physical education and the art of teaching: Transformative learning and teaching in physical education and sports pedagogy. Sport, Education and Society, 24(6), 611–623. https://doi.org/10.1080/13573322.2019.1574731

Ryan, R. M., & Deci, E. L. (2000). Self-determination theory and the facilitation of intrinsic motivation, social development, and well-being. American Psychologist, 55(1), 68–78. https://doi.org/10.1037/0003-066X.55.1.68

Sport England. (2023). Physical literacy consensus statement for England. [Online]. Available at: https://www.sportengland.org/news-and-inspiration/physical-literacy-consensus-statement-england-published [Accessed 3 July 2024].

Sport England. (2024). Physical literacy consensus statement for England. [Online]. Available at: https://www.sportengland.org/funds-and-campaigns/children-and-young-people?section=physical_literacy [Accessed 30 March 2024].

Sullivan, L. (2021). Is PE in crisis? Leading meaningful change in physical education. Scholarly.

Trendowski, T., & Mays Woods, A. (2015). Seven student-centered principles for smart teaching in physical education. Journal of Physical Education, Recreation & Dance, 86(8), 41–47. https://doi.org/10.1080/07303084.2015.1075923

Trowbridge, M. (2023). "What are we doing in PE today?" PE Scholar [Guest Blog]. [Online] Available at: https://www.pescholar.com/insight/what-are-we-doing-in-pe-today-the-relationship-between-physical-education-physical-activity-and-sport/ [Accessed 9 Oct 2024].

Walsh, B. (2009). The Score Takes Care of Itself: My Philosophy of Leadership. London: Penguin Publishing Group.

Welsh Government. (2019). Area of Learning and Experience: Health and Well-being. [Online]. Available at: https://hwb.gov.wales/curriculum-for-wales/health-and-well-being [Accessed 22 March 2024].

Welsh Government. (2020). Curriculum for Wales: Guidance. [Online] Available at: https://gov.wales/curriculum-for-wales [Accessed 9 Oct 2024].

Whitehead, M. (1993). Physical literacy [Paper presentation]. International Association of Physical Education and Sport for Women and Girls Congress, Melbourne, Australia.

Whitehead, M. E. (2001). The concept of physical literacy. European Journal of Physical Education, 6(2), 127–138. https://doi.org/10.1080/1740898010060205

Whitehead, M. E. (Ed.) (2010). Physical Literacy: Throughout the Lifecourse. London: Routledge.

Whitehead, M. E. (Ed.) (2019). Physical Literacy: Across the World. London: Routledge.

Chapter 3: Experiences

Lee Sullivan, Paul Sammon, Kate Reynolds and Shaun Wilkinson

Part 3.1 – Insight
Lee Sullivan

Negative experiences are more powerful than positive ones. The aim of this chapter is to consider how we might prioritise positive experiences in PE and consider the long-lasting positive and negative impact we can have within the lessons we provide.

More than a Meal
In the world of culinary excellence, chefs create experiences that transcend mere fine dining, where a meal becomes a form of storytelling, and their restaurant serves as stages for unforgettable experiences. One such chef is Heston Blumenthal, the visionary mastermind behind the Fat Duck, a beacon of creativity nestled in the small town of Bray, Berkshire. In Blumenthal's restaurant, a meal is not just about satisfying hunger; it's about weaving narratives, invoking memories, and forging deep connections with diners. Each dish tells a story—a tale of tradition reimagined, of ingredients elevated to their fullest potential, and of emotions evoked through every bite.

One example of this was his renowned "The Sound of the Sea," creation. Diners are first handed a card containing questions aimed to inspire and focus conversation between guests. The questions act as a prompt to diners to reminisce about childhood beachside memories ensuring they are in the correct mindset to receive what's next. As the dish is then placed before the diner, their senses are immediately engaged by the stunning visual presentation: a pristine arrangement of sashimi glistens atop a bed of tapioca "sand," while delicate sea foam delicately blankets the plate. The server sprays a gentle sea air mist around the diners that immediately transports them to the coast. But it's not just the sight and smell that captivates guests; the dish comes with a conch shell which hides an individual iPod for each guest. Diners place on the headphones which deliver the ultimate sensory experience: the authentic sound of the sea. Diners are immersed with the sound of crashing waves, distant seagulls, and the faint hum of chatter which heighten the rush of nostalgic memories: carefree days spent on the beach, cherished summer holidays and moments shared with loved ones. This auditory element, combined with the harmonious interplay of taste, sight and aroma, serves to elicit profound emotions, enveloping diners in a multi-sensory journey of unparalleled depth and resonance.

What sets Blumenthal apart is his unwavering belief in the power of these emotional connections to transform not only the dining experience but also the lives of those who partake in it. He believed that even the smallest negative element could overshadow an otherwise stellar meal, emphasising the necessity of crafting an emotional connection that transcends the act of eating itself.

Similarly, in our PE lessons, the activities alone may not suffice to foster a lasting connection. While they may captivate some students, will they be sufficient to evoke a sense of connection beyond those already enamoured with the activity? Engage in a conversation with someone who has endured a negative experience in PE, and you'll quickly realise that their memories extend far beyond a mere dislike of a particular sport or activity. Emotional scars of humiliation and failure, intensified by authoritarian teaching methods, and the discomfort of performing in front of peers often loom large in their recollections. The lingering aroma of damp, sweat-ridden bibs serve as a reminder of past experiences, while the sight of hanging ropes still evokes feelings of dread. These deeply ingrained memories underscore the profound impact that negative PE experiences can have on individuals. Thus, it is crucial for PE educators to consider not only the activities themselves but also the overall experience and environment in order to create positive and meaningful connections with all students. The emotional scars of PE linger long after the lesson ends; we must strive to craft experiences that heal rather than harm.

While it is not suggested that teachers sweep the floors or wash bibs before every lesson, it is crucial to recognise the totality of a student's experience and strive to create an environment that fosters respect, inclusivity, and positive emotional engagement. Just as with Blumenthal's approach, every collective element of our PE lessons—be it the activity, the pedagogy, the environment, method of assessment, opportunities to socialise, succeed and learn —must harmonise to create something truly meaningful and enduring. For many, PE's lasting impact comes not from the activities, but from how those activities made them feel.

Part 3.2 – Delve
Lee Sullivan

The Impact of a Negative Experience
Studies have shown that negative emotional memories, such as feelings of humiliation, failure, and embarrassment, tend to have a stronger and longer-lasting effect on individuals compared to positive experiences. For example, a study published in the Journal of Sport and Exercise Psychology found that individuals tend to remember negative emotional events more vividly and for a longer duration than positive ones (Baumeister, Bratslavsky, Finkenauer, & Vohs, 2001).

Research in psychology has extensively documented the phenomenon known as the negativity bias, wherein negative events and emotions tend to carry greater weight in human cognition and decision-making processes. Furthermore, studies have shown that negative experiences tend to be more memorable and influential than positive ones, shaping individuals' attitudes, preferences, and behaviours. Negativity bias, suggests that negative experiences in PE, such as being singled out by a teacher or experiencing social exclusion during team sports, can leave a lasting imprint on students' perceptions and attitudes toward physical activity and exercise. Additionally, negative experiences may contribute to decreased motivation, self-esteem, and overall enjoyment of PE, and even impact the motivation of an individual to engage in physical activity and sport long after their school years.

Margaret Whitehead (2010) highlights the critical role of individuals' prior experiences in shaping their engagement with physical activity, stating that "establishing and maintaining physical literacy is highly dependent on experiences encountered in relation to their involvement with physical activity." Whitehead further suggests that negative past experiences may discourage continued participation, as individuals may have encountered limited success and found previous experiences unrewarding. Dr. Ekkekakis, et. al. (2018) concurred that memories from PE significantly influence future engagement in physical activity. In their article, titled: "My Best Memory Is When I Was Done with It": PE Memories Are Associated with Adult Sedentary Behaviour' they explored the relationship between memories of enjoyment or non-enjoyment of PE during childhood and present-day attitudes, intentions, physical activity and sedentary behaviour in adulthood. Using a retrospective survey completed by 1028 American respondents aged 18 to 45 years, participants rated their retrospective enjoyment of PE and provided insights into their present attitudes and intentions towards physical activity, as well as their current levels of physical activity and sedentary behaviour. The findings revealed that retrospective enjoyment of PE was positively associated with present-day attitudes and intentions for physical activity, and negatively correlated with sedentary time on the weekend. Their research revealed that the most favourable memories were linked to enjoyment of class activities (56%), feelings of physical competence (37%), and, notably, 7% expressed relief at

CHAPTER 3: **EXPERIENCES**

no longer having to attend PE class or skipping it altogether. Conversely, the worst memories were associated with embarrassment (34%), lack of enjoyment (18%), bullying (17%), social-physique anxiety (14%), injury (16%), and punishment by the PE teacher (2%). It was concluded that childhood memories of PE have a significant impact on attitudes towards physical activity and sedentary behaviour in adulthood (Ekkekakis et al., 2018, p. 1). Negative experiences in PE can become defining memories, shaping a student's lifelong attitude towards physical activity.

We must not underestimate the long-term ramifications that negative experiences in PE can have on an individual's future engagement and consequently, the value that is placed by those in society on our subject.

The 'Hair in the Soup' Mentality

It is easy to think that it is long-term and on-going negative experiences that impact future motivation to engage in PE, physical activity and sport. We must be mindful of the finer details in PE too. It is not just the sport-driven and performance obsessed PE delivery that can negatively impact experiences, it can be the smaller decisions we make as leaders that have negative outcomes.

While Heston Blumenthal stands at the pinnacle of culinary excellence, restaurateurs across all echelons are dedicated to curating a comprehensive dining experience for their patrons. Regardless of the establishment's scale or prestige, restaurateurs strive to attend to every part of your dining experiences. This entails crafting a diverse menu that accommodates a spectrum of dietary preferences, ensuring each guest's individual needs and tastes are met with thoughtful consideration. From extending a warm welcome upon arrival to ensuring your glass remains replenished throughout the meal, restaurateurs are committed to providing attentive and hospitable service. Moreover, they adeptly navigate any mishaps, swiftly replacing dropped cutlery and engaging young diners, all in pursuit of cultivating a positively memorable experience for every guest.

You might frequent a restaurant, consistently enjoying excellent service and delicious meals, prompting you to enthusiastically recommend it to friends. Yet, all it takes is one unfortunate incident to tarnish the entire perception. Consider, for instance, a single visit where a hair is discovered in your soup—a disconcerting and unappetising encounter that overshadows any previous positive experiences. Despite the string of enjoyable visits beforehand, this one negative episode stands out vividly, significantly impacting your overall perception of the restaurant. It may even stop you wanting to dine there ever again.

The discovery of a hair in the soup, regardless of its accidental nature, eclipses all prior positive encounters, profoundly influencing your future motivations and decision-making processes.

One study by Bradley J. Cardinal , Zi Yan & Marita K. Cardinal (2013), titled 'Negative Experiences in Physical Education and Sport: How Much Do They Affect Physical Activity Participation Later in Life?' highlighted a significant correlation between negative early-life experiences in team selection and reduced exercise levels in adulthood. Individuals who were picked or chosen last for a team in their youth reported engaging in fewer exercise sessions per week later in life, compared to those who had never experienced this. The research also revealed that a considerable percentage of participants had encountered negative experiences in physical education or sports, such as being cut from a team or not getting to play. Essentially, what might be considered as a flippant practice of selecting teams can in fact be a considerable 'hair in the soup' moment for many. Just as a single hair in the soup can ruin a meal, one negative experience in PE can ruin a student's outlook on physical education.

In PE, a key aim is to nurture a positive relationship with our subject, physical activity, and sport. This can be achieved by creating meaningful and enjoyable experiences for our students. Yet, even the smallest and seemingly insignificant moments can profoundly shape their overall perception. Whether it's receiving feedback from assessments that feels overly critical, experiencing a sense of failure due to an overemphasis on outcomes rather than the learning process, making mistakes and facing peer reprimands, or enduring ridicule while demonstrating skills in front of peers, these instances can all become the metaphorical "hair in the soup" of our students' PE experiences.

Reflecting on this, imagine the awkwardness or regret of encountering a former student years later who recounts their "hair in the soup" moment—an incident you may not even remember, but which left a lasting mark on how they felt about PE or being active. It serves as a powerful reminder of the vital role teachers play every day in shaping not just skills and knowledge, but the self-esteem and lifelong attitudes of the young people in their care. How often do our actions, however unintentional, become that unwelcome element in our students' otherwise positive journey through PE? How can we ensure we are a source of support and encouragement rather than a "hair in the soup" in the story of their PE experiences?

CHAPTER 3: **EXPERIENCES**

Mid-chapter reflection

What new insights have I gained from this chapter so far?

How does this knowledge reinforce or challenge my current beliefs or practices?

Are there areas or concepts I still need to explore further?

Have I identified any gaps in my team's understanding or practice that need addressing?

How can I share or apply this learning to positively influence others in my team or school?

How can I share or apply this learning to positively influence others in my team or school?

Part 3.3 – Experts

Changing Rooms
Paul Sammon

Totality of the Student Experience in PE

When reflecting on how we, as practitioners, can enhance students' experiences in PE, it is important to consider the experience as a whole. While it is common to focus on curriculum, pedagogy, and assessment, we must also recognise that changing rooms can play a significant role in shaping the overall PE experience, occupying a considerable portion of students' time and impacting their wellbeing. Unfortunately, changing rooms can be a source of negative experiences for many students. Issues such as embarrassment over body image, struggles with gender identity or sexuality, and bullying can create significant barriers to enjoyment, often leading to feelings of dread associated with PE lessons. These negative experiences can overshadow the intended benefits of learning through movement contexts, highlighting the need for a supportive and inclusive environment in changing areas.

Pandemic PE

During the Covid-19 pandemic, many schools allowed students to wear their PE uniform to school on days that they had PE lessons, avoiding the need for crowded changing rooms and helping to maintain social distancing. This approach had clear benefits, such as keeping students safe, increasing time for physical activity, reducing bullying opportunities, and lowering student anxiety. While many schools have continued this practice post-pandemic, others have reverted to their pre-pandemic uniform policies, requiring students to change during lesson time. This inconsistency raises an important question: is using precious PE curriculum time for changing really providing students with the best possible educational experience?

What is the argument against the use of PE curriculum time for changing?

The practice of requiring school children to change clothing during their timetabled PE lessons has been a long established, and often uncontested, expectation in many schools. Recognising this practice, the National Society for the Prevention of Cruelty to Children (NSPCC) recently published guidance recommending that schools should have measures in place to ensure children and young people feel comfortable and are safe when getting changed for PE (NSPCC,

2024). However, evidence has highlighted that changing room environments can lead to young people experiencing negative feelings of comparison, judgement and body dissatisfaction (O'Donovan et al., 2015).

To compound matters, research conducted by Moen, Westlie and Skille (2018) found that many PE teachers do not view the changing room ritual as part of the curriculum experience and consequently not their responsibility to supervise. This is problematic as a lack of supervision can encourage unwanted behaviours, such as rowdiness and bullying, which can lead to feelings of anxiety and dread for some students, often the most vulnerable (Butler, 2022; Gerdin, 2017). Due to the perception that changing time is not effectively supervised, Metz, Zander and Hunger (2024) have reported that some bullied students view PE as a 'state of anarchy', where the teacher has little control over students' interactions.

Together with the potential to negatively impact on students' mental wellbeing, employing changing rooms during PE can also adversely affect their physical wellbeing. National guidelines published by the Association for Physical Education (Harris, 2020) recommend that students should be active for 50-80% of PE lessons, but actual activity levels have been reported as much lower at only 23.8% of lesson time on average (Beale et al., 2021). Further, research by Ofsted (2022) has identified changing time as a key barrier in terms of young people being sufficiently active during PE. Indeed, Sammon and Sullivan (2023) highlight that a third of the allocated curriculum time for PE, equating to around 26 hours over the course of a school year can be lost to changing and stress that time should be maximised to ensure that students are actively learning through meaningful movement contexts. As curriculum PE represents the main (and sometimes only) opportunity each week for some young people to be physically active, it is argued that using this time for changing is totally unacceptable in terms of supporting students' health and wellbeing.

What is the argument in favour of using changing rooms?

To stimulate debate, it is also important to consider some common arguments in favour of using changing rooms for PE, such as promoting good personal hygiene habits. Undoubtedly, following outdoor PE lessons in adverse weather conditions, changing out of wet or muddy PE uniform into dry clothing is essential for student comfort and can also help to keep the school environment clean. A further commonly cited argument is around school image concerns. For example, some schools prevent students attending school in their PE uniforms for fear of looking less smart in public. Other schools have experienced PE uniform policy enforcement challenges such as students wearing their PE uniform to school on days when they do not have timetabled lessons, which has subsequently resulted in a return to the use of changing rooms.

What might teachers consider when deciding whether or not to use changing rooms?

When considering the arguments presented, schools and teachers must balance the perceived importance of hygiene and comfort with the need to create an inclusive, safe and active learning environment for all students. They also need to carefully consider whether the changing ritual represents the best use of precious curriculum time. Before deciding whether to use changing rooms, it is recommended that teachers consult students in order to share their thoughts and feelings on getting changed. For example, how do changing rooms impact on their experience of PE and more broadly, their wellbeing? The COVID-19 pandemic has demonstrated that removing the requirement to change for PE can have many positive benefits for students' wellbeing, such as reduced anxiety, less vulnerability and increased time to be physically active. Finally, teachers must reflect on their own wellbeing, as supervising changing rooms can be a stressful task, resulting in increased workload and feelings of anxiety and discomfort. In an era of serious challenges with teacher recruitment and retention, it is strongly recommended that practices which contribute to teacher workload and stress should be avoided where possible.

CHAPTER 3: EXPERIENCES

Part 3.4 – Apply

Grouping in PE
Shaun Wilkinson

In contrast to the relative privacy of classroom-based subjects, the public nature of the learning environment in PE places students' bodies and abilities on display and thereby prospectively potentially intensifies feelings of scrutiny, inadequacy, and/or failure. This accentuates the importance of considering students' perspectives and experiences of ability grouping practices in PE.

The incidence of ability grouping practices in PE
Ability grouping practices are often at the fore of discussions about curriculum design, teaching, and learning in PE. There remains however, considerable uncertainty about which approach (or combination of approaches) should be preferred and under what circumstances. A recent national survey, for example, revealed that a wide range of ability grouping practices are adopted in PE in secondary schools in England (Wilkinson & Penney, 2023). Mixed-ability grouping was reported as the most common of these practices, particularly in Key Stage 4, although there was a notable increase in setting and a decrease in mixed-ability grouping as students moved through Key Stage 3 (Wilkinson & Penney, 2023). A smaller number of schools reported using alternative grouping strategies in PE at Key Stage 3 and 4, such as streaming, mixed-ability grouping with top or bottom sets, or grouping based on factors like confidence, attitude towards learning, or curriculum pathways (Wilkinson & Penney, 2023). By comparison, mixed-ability grouping is reported as widespread in PE in primary schools in England (Wilkinson & Penney, Forthcoming).

What key research should teachers be aware of?
Previous research indicates that the benefits of setting and mixed-ability grouping are highly contested and varied, although much of this research has focused on classroom-based subjects, particularly mathematics, English, and/or science. Systematic reviews of the existing research show that while setting may benefit the achievement and self-confidence of higher-attaining students in classroom-based subjects, these benefits invariably come at the expense of losses to mid- and lower-attaining students (for example in terms of achievement, self-confidence, and/or engagement with learning) (Slavin, 1987, 1990; Sukhnandan & Lee, 1998). By contrast, mixed-ability grouping has often been found to have neutral to positive effects on the achievement and self-confidence of higher-attaining students and positive effects on the achievement and self-confidence of mid- and lower-attaining students in classroom-based subjects (Sukhnandan & Lee, 1998; Francis et al., 2020).

A small body of emerging research indicates that overall, most students prefer setting to mixed-ability grouping in PE, with this preference most prominent amongst boys, students who identify as high ability, and students who report being taught in sets in PE (Wilkinson & Penney, 2024). The most frequently reported reason for preferring setting is that it enables students to learn at a pace and level of instruction commensurate to their needs (providing a greater level of challenge for higher-attaining students and more targeted support for mid- and lower attaining students, for example) (Wilkinson & Penney, 2021, 2024). Previous research indicates that some teachers pitch resources and teaching strategies at 'the middle' in mixed ability classes, with this tendency resulting in some students being unable to cope with the pace and level of work and others being insufficiently challenged (Boaler et al., 2000; Francis et al., 2020). Other reported reasons for preferring setting in PE include that it ensures that lower attaining students are less exposed to judgement, criticism, and/or surveillance by higher attaining peers, the reduced range of ability creates fairer and more balanced competition, and familiarity with the practice (Wilkinson & Penney, 2021, 2024).

Students who prefer mixed-ability grouping in PE mostly highlight the inclusive and collaborative nature of the practice, including the opportunities that it provides to make friends with others from different backgrounds and ability levels, the benefits of supporting and mentoring others in their learning, and the importance of more able peers in promoting and enhancing learning (Wilkinson & Penney, 2022, 2024). Mixed-ability grouping is also reported as reducing the chances of students being labelled and stigmatised by others in PE as they are not formally allocated to a 'low ability' group, receiving inequitable access to teachers, resources, and/or the curriculum, and avoiding the problems of fairly and accurately allocating students to sets in a multidisciplinary subject area (Wilkinson & Penney, 2022, 2024). Recent research highlights that the abilities being recognised and used as the basis for setting decisions in PE are often invariably narrow, centring on motor-skill proficiency, physical fitness, and/or performance in team games (Wilkinson & Penney, 2021, 2023). Further and relatedly, research in PE and classroom-based subjects has repeatedly indicated that once established, there is relatively little movement between sets (often due to timetabling constraints and/or a lack of monitoring of student progress) (Ireson & Hallam, 2001; Francis et al., 2020; Wilkinson & Penney, 2023). Research also indicates that some students perceive that setting is necessary in activities and learning situations involving direct physical bodily contact (e.g. rugby and football) or individual public performance (e.g. swimming and athletics), whereas mixed-ability grouping is seen as being more suited to recreational and socially oriented activities (e.g. outdoor and adventurous activities) and activities where students are equally inexperienced (such that skill imbalances are minimal) (Wilkinson and Penney, 2022, 2023).

What might teachers consider when deciding how to group students in PE?

It is important to recognise that there is limited empirical evidence to support the use of setting, mixed-ability grouping, and/or any other grouping practice in PE. This area of research is in its infancy and additional studies are required to extend understanding of the impacts and efficacy of different ability grouping practices in the subject. That said, PE teachers are in a prime position to facilitate grouping practices that are equitable and inclusive of all students in PE. To do so, teachers should adopt creative and flexible approaches (rather than a rigid one-size-fits-all approach) to grouping that are responsive to changes in the learning focus, environment, and/or the needs and preferences of students in a specific setting. Teachers should also seek to adopt a student-centred approach (e.g. by consulting with students about grouping practices) that enables students to have choice and voice in the decision-making process. This approach has been identified as a key strategy in fostering students' sense of ownership and has resulted in students feeling more engaged and motivated to learn in PE (Wilkinson & Penney, 2022, 2023).

Fit for Purpose PE Kit
Kate Reynolds

Creating a Safe and Inclusive Environment: Addressing Psychological Safety in PE : Kit and Changing Rooms in an all-girls school

As a PE teacher at an all-girls school in Liverpool with a rich history and tradition, I've witnessed firsthand how something as seemingly simple as getting changed for PE can become a source of anxiety and discomfort for our students and a negative experience from the outset. Our school, once an independent institution with deep-rooted traditions, had a PE kit that reflected those traditions—a fitted collared shirt and pleated skirt that, while emblematic of our school's history, in 2023 did not serve the diverse needs of our current student body.

In recent years, there has been a shift in how we view PE attire and the environments in which students change for these activities. This shift has been influenced by a broader understanding of psychological safety and the importance of inclusivity in schools. Here, I want to explore how we, as PE teachers, can create a more psychologically safe environment for all students, particularly when it comes to changing for PE classes. When making the decision to change our PE kit, I did so based on extensive research, student and parent voice to make sure that this decision was going to be a worthwhile and positive experience for everyone. Here, I share some of my findings and what we did with this knowledge.

The Changing Room Challenge

Changing rooms can be a triggering environment for many students. Research and personal experience have shown that getting changed can be particularly daunting for young people, leading to a dislike for PE before they even step onto the field or court. Several factors contribute to this:

Body Image Concerns: Adolescence is a time of significant physical and emotional change, and many students feel self-conscious about their bodies. Traditional PE kits, like the one our school used to require, can exacerbate these feelings, especially if the attire is form-fitting, ill-fitting or considered outdated by students' standards.

Gender Identity and Expression: As our understanding of gender has evolved, so too has our awareness that not all students identify with the gender assigned to them at birth. We found that for some students who do not identify as female, wearing a traditional girls' PE kit can be uncomfortable and distressing, compounding feelings of exclusion and anxiety.

Peer Judgment: The fear of judgement from peers in a vulnerable setting like a changing room can lead to heightened anxiety. This fear is often exacerbated in environments where privacy

CHAPTER 3: **EXPERIENCES**

is limited, and students feel exposed. Our changing rooms are bright and airy, but very open with only a few toilet cubicles and little space for privacy when changing.

Cultural and Religious Sensitivities: For some students, changing in front of others can conflict with their cultural or religious beliefs, creating additional barriers to participation in PE.

Creating a Safe and Inclusive Changing Environment

To address these challenges, it was crucial to create a changing environment that promotes psychological safety and inclusivity. Here are some strategies that have been effective in our school and could be considered more broadly:

Revisiting PE Kit Requirements: In 2023, we revamped our PE kit to reflect modern standards of practicality, appropriateness, and inclusivity. We moved away from the traditional attire to more flexible options that cater to different body types and preferences. Offering choices in PE attire—such as longer shorts, skorts, leggings, tracksuit pants and a choice of loose-fitting or form fitting tops, as well as a range of outerwear such as fleeces, hoodies and waterproof jackets—can help students feel more comfortable and less self-conscious. Our students helped design the kit that they now choose from giving them a sense of pride in what they are wearing.

Student Voice: When redesigning the kit, this was done through extensive student voice; they would be wearing the kit, so ultimately their voice would be the most important in this process. We obtained a wide range of kit options and vetoed any that were poor quality or impractical. We dressed several mannequins and displayed all the kit options in the corridor inviting students to feedback their thoughts. From this we were able to narrow down the choices to provide options that all students would wear. By giving students a platform to share their thoughts and preferences, we empowered them and made them feel valued in the process. This inclusion not only fosters a sense of ownership and acceptance of the changes but also ensures that the solutions we implement are more likely to meet their needs and be embraced by the entire student body.

Consulting Parents on Kit Changes: It's also essential to involve parents when making changes to the PE kit, especially regarding cost. We know that the financial burden of school uniforms and kits can be a concern for many families. By consulting parents and considering their feedback, we ensured that the new PE kit is affordable while maintaining quality and a sense of school identity. At our school, this meant working closely with a local supplier to keep costs down and provide a convenient, accessible place for families to purchase the kit.

Working with local kit suppliers: Working with a local supplier allowed us to negotiate a price for a PE kit that was affordable whilst not reducing quality. It also gives parents a shop to go to, a place for students to view kit and try it on before they buy, and the community aspect allows parents to set up flexible payment plans. Kit is easily obtained and replaced when needed rather than waiting for online orders to be shipped.

Changing Rooms: We made the radical decision to metaphorically "get rid of the changing rooms". Instead students come to school in PE kit on PE days, something they voted for almost unanimously from our student voice research. The impact has been extremely positive and added to their feelings of psychological safety. If this isn't possible, installing privacy screens or curtains in changing rooms can significantly reduce anxiety for students who feel uncomfortable changing in front of others too. Offering a few individual stalls allows students to choose a changing option that best suits their comfort level.

Encouraging Continued Open Communication: Creating a safe space for students to express their concerns about anything related to PE has helped teachers address issues proactively. Whether through anonymous feedback forms or open discussions, allowing students to voice their feelings can lead to positive changes that improve their overall experience.

Inclusivity Training for Staff: As educators, we must continually educate ourselves about the evolving needs of our student body. Training on inclusivity, gender diversity, and psychological safety can help PE teachers understand the unique challenges faced by their students and how best to support them. I have worked more closely than ever before with our SENCOs, the Culture and Diversity teams and LGBTQ+ groups within school, as well as wider agencies and community groups to make sure as a department we fully understand our student body and their ever changing needs.

Positive Outcomes and Increased Engagement

The impact of these changes on our student experience has been overwhelmingly positive. All students are now in appropriate kit for PE lessons, and not having to change at school has increased the amount of learning time available during lessons. The anxiety around changing has been largely eradicated, which means that students who may have previously avoided PE are now participating regularly. The number of lost PE kit items has significantly decreased, much to the delight of parents. The culture of always being prepared for PE has also meant that students are more willing to borrow kit if needed, reducing any stigma around this.

Most importantly, students feel comfortable in their kit, which has led to an increase in effort and engagement levels during lessons. By addressing the psychological barriers associated with changing for PE and making practical changes to our kit and routines, we have created a more inclusive and supportive environment. PE has become a happier place, and we are proud

CHAPTER 3: **EXPERIENCES**

to see our students more actively engaged in their physical education, feeling safe, confident, and included.

Feedback

Cecilia, Year 9
With our school now allowing us to come in wearing PE kits and changing the kit as a whole, I have found it very beneficial as we lose less time. For students like myself, who really enjoy PE, it used to feel like a great lesson was being rushed. Also, with the new PE kit and a greater number of options, more girls feel comfortable wearing it as it better suits them and their cultures. If all schools offered such variety, there would be a positive change in participation. I've always loved PE, so being in a school with such an amazing PE department—one that listens to students' voices—is something I'm really grateful for.

Alix, Year 12
I always hated getting changed for PE, which is why I used to hide in the toilets or avoid it at all costs, often going to student support instead. However, when the school changed the policy to allow us to come in wearing our PE kits, everything changed for me. I went from refusing to take part to joining in with every lesson during Year 11—right when I needed PE the most before my exams.

Mia, Year 7
We did this in primary school, so it makes sense to continue in secondary school too. I'm so glad we have this option; otherwise, I would probably be really put off PE. It takes me ages to get changed, and I know I would get told off by my teachers for being late to my next lesson.

Anonymous, Year 10
I used to do PE in my uniform. I came out as trans in Year 8, and there was no way I was wearing a skirt. Being involved in the process of designing the new kit meant that students like me now feel comfortable in a less feminine option. There are so many choices available, which is great for people like me.

Parent of a Year 11 Child
My daughter has always loved PE, but she is one of the most forgetful girls on the planet! I was forever buying new kit because she would leave it everywhere— in the locker room, on the bus, even at other schools! Going to school in her PE kit has solved this issue. Being consulted during the kit redesign process also meant that parents could have their say on price. It's great that we can get a full kit for less than £100, especially when my friend's son's school charges well over £300 for theirs.

Looking Forward

These changes have reaffirmed the importance of listening to our students and parents and being willing to adapt our practices to meet their needs. Creating a psychologically safe environment in PE is not just about the physical kit but also about understanding and addressing the emotional and social challenges our students face. By continuing to engage with our school community and make thoughtful, inclusive decisions, we can ensure that PE remains a positive and enriching experience for all our students. I would encourage all Heads of PE to have wide conversions with their student body to find out their views surrounding PE kit and changing. Do you foster an inclusive environment? Does the kit meet the needs of all students? Does it encourage a positive relationship with movement? Is the price point of PE kit reflective of your local community? Do your changing facilities promote psychological safety?

Chapter 3 Summary

Experiences: From Dread to Delight

DREAD

Hair in the Soup:
Small, often unconscious areas of practice or interactions with students that could cause or contribute towards a negative self-perception or experience of PE.

DELIGHT

Positive Experiences:
Consider the totality of the students experiences within PE and do our best to ensure they are as positive as possible for all.

Where would you place yourself right now?

DREAD —————————————————— **DELIGHT**

Call to Action

As we conclude this chapter, it's time to reflect on what you've learned and consider how to apply it. The SHIFT mnemonic can guide you through the next steps: a structured approach to transform your insights into meaningful actions. Take a moment to work through the following questions:

S **Summarise** the key takeaway from this chapter that stands out to you.

H **Highlight** how this takeaway challenges or aligns with your current practices.

I **Initiate** a small change or step right now to put what you've learned into practice.

F **Frame** how this change will contribute to achieving your long-term vision for PE.

T **Take** others on the journey—share your new insights and encourage collaboration.

References

Bailey, R., Armour, K., Kirk, D., Jess, M., Pickup, I., Sandford, R. and BERA Physical Education and Sport Pedagogy Special Interest Group (2009) 'The educational benefits claimed for physical education and school sport: an academic review', Research Papers in Education, 24(1), pp. 1–27. https://doi.org/10.1080/02671520701809817

Barbosa, A., Whiting, S., Simmonds, P., Scotini Moreno, R., Mendes, R. and Breda, J. (2020) 'Physical Activity and Academic Achievement: An Umbrella Review', International Journal of Environmental Research and Public Health, 17, 5972. https://doi.org/10.3390/ijerph17165972

Baumeister, R.F., Bratslavsky, E., Finkenauer, C. and Vohs, K.D. (2001) 'Bad is stronger than good', Review of General Psychology, 5(4), pp. 323–370. https://doi.org/10.1037/1089-2680.5.4.323

Boaler, J., Wiliam, D. and Brown, M. (2000) 'Experiences of ability grouping – disaffection, polarisation and the construction of failure', British Educational Research Journal, 28(5), pp. 631–648.

Bowler, M. and Sammon, P. (2020) 'Health-Based Physical Education – A framework for promoting active lifestyles in children and young people. Part 1: Introducing a new pedagogical model for Health-Based Physical Education', Physical Education Matters, 15(3), pp. 60–63.

Butler, C. (2022) PE kit petition at The Deepings School highlights pupils' anxiety over changing rooms. Available at: https://www.stamfordmercury.co.uk/news/school-s-pe-policy-leads-to-petition-9262623/ (Accessed: 4 July 2024).

Cardinal, B.J., Yan, Z. and Cardinal, M.K. (2013) 'Negative experiences in physical education and sport: How much do they affect physical activity participation later in life?', Journal of Physical Education, Recreation & Dance, 84(3), pp. 49–53. https://doi.org/10.1080/07303084.2013.767736

Cocks, P. (2024) Episode 29: Four Mantras for Teaching and Learning. PE Insights Podcast, PE Scholar. Available at: https://podcasts.apple.com/gb/podcast/pe-insights-pe-scholar-physical-education/id1710712630 (Accessed: 4 July 2024).

Davies, L. (2022) Physical Education & The Great Health Myth. PE Scholar. Available at: https://www.pescholar.com/insight/physical-education-the-great-health-myth/ (Accessed: 19 January 2024).

Ekkekakis, P., Ladwig, M.A. and Vazou, S. (2018) My best memory is when I was done with it: PE memories are associated with adult sedentary behaviour. Available at: https://www.researchgate.net/publication/327118352_My_best_memory_is_when_I_was_done_with_it_PE_memories_are_associated_with_adult_sedentary_behavior (Accessed: 7 February 2024).

Francis, B., Taylor, B. and Tereshchenko, A. (2020) Reassessing 'ability' grouping: improving practice for equity and attainment. London: Routledge.

Gerdin, G. (2017) 'The "old gym" and the "boys' changing rooms": the performative and pleasurable spaces of boys' physical education', YOUNG, 25(4), pp. 36–53.

Harris, J. (2020) Health Position Paper. Association for Physical Education.

Ireson, J. and Hallam, S. (2001) Ability grouping in education. London: SAGE Publications.

Jess, M. et al. (2024) 'The purpose of primary physical education: The views of teacher educators', European Physical Education Review, 0(0). https://doi.org/10.1177/1356336X241237081

Lambert, K., Ford, A. and Jeanes, R. (2024) 'The association between physical education and academic achievement in other curriculum learning areas: A review of literature', Physical Education and Sport Pedagogy, 29(1), pp. 51–81. https://doi.org/10.1080/17408989.2022.2029385

Metz, S., Zander, B. and Hunger, I. (2024) 'The suffering of students in physical education: Unsettling experiences and situational conditions', Physical Education and Sport Pedagogy, pp. 1–13. https://doi.org/10.1080/17408989.2024.2352825

Moen, K.M., Westlie, K. and Skille, E.Å. (2018) 'The changing room in physical education as cross roads between fields and curricula: The experiences of Norwegian students', SAGE Open, 8(4). https://doi.org/10.1177/2158244018818926

Mong, H.H. and Standal, Ø.F. (2022) 'Teaching health in physical education: An action research project', European Physical Education Review, 28(3), pp. 739–756. https://doi.org/10.1177/1356336X221078319

NSPCC (2024) Safeguarding considerations for changing rooms. Available at: https://learning.nspcc.org.uk/research-resources/schools/safeguarding-considerations-changing-rooms (Accessed: 4 July 2024).

O'Donovan, T., Sandford, R. and Kirk, D. (2015) 'Bourdieu in the changing room', in Hunter, L., Smith, W. and Emerald, E. (eds.) Pierre Bourdieu and physical culture. London: Routledge, pp. 57–64.

Ofsted (2022) Research Review Series: PE. Available at: https://www.gov.uk/government/publications/research-review-series-pe/research-review-series-pe (Accessed: 4 July 2024).

Quennerstedt, M. (2019) 'Physical education and the art of teaching: Transformative learning and teaching in physical education and sports pedagogy', Sport, Education and Society, 24(6), pp. 611–623. https://doi.org/10.1080/13573322.2019.1574731

Rozin, P. and Royzman, E.B. (2001) 'Negativity bias, negativity dominance, and contagion', Personality and Social Psychology Review, 5(4), pp. 296–320. https://doi.org/10.1207/s15327957pspr0504_2

Ryan, R.M. and Deci, E.L. (2000) 'Self-determination theory and the facilitation of intrinsic motivation, social development, and well-being', American Psychologist, 55(1), pp. 68–78. https://doi.org/10.1037/0003-066X.55.1.68

Sammon, P. and Sullivan, L. (2023) Is it time to ditch changing during PE lessons? PE Scholar. Available at: https://www.pescholar.com/insight/is-it-time-to-ditch-changing-during-pe-lessons (Accessed: 4 July 2024).

Slavin, R.E. (1987) 'Ability grouping and student achievement in elementary schools: A best evidence synthesis', Review of Educational Research, 57(3), pp. 293–336.

Slavin, R.E. (1990) 'Achievement effects of ability grouping in secondary schools: A best evidence synthesis', Review of Educational Research, 60(3), pp. 471–490.

Sukhnandan, L. and Lee, B. (1998) Streaming, setting and grouping by ability: a review of the literature. Slough: National Foundation for Educational Research.

Walsh, B. (2009) The Score Takes Care of Itself: My Philosophy of Leadership. London: Penguin Publishing Group.

Wilkinson, S.D. and Penney, D. (2021) 'Setting policy and student agency in physical education: Students as policy actors', Sport, Education and Society, 26(3), pp. 267–280.

Wilkinson, S.D. and Penney, D. (2022) '"The participation group means that I'm low ability": Students' perspectives on the enactment of mixed-ability grouping in secondary school physical education', British Educational Research Journal, 48(5), pp. 932–951.

Wilkinson, S.D. and Penney, D. (2023) 'A national survey of ability grouping practices in secondary school physical education in England', Research Papers in Education. https://doi.org/10.1080/02671522.2023.2217819

Wilkinson, S.D. and Penney, D. (2024) 'Students' preferences for setting and/or mixed-ability grouping in secondary school physical education in England', British Educational Research Journal. https://doi.org/10.1002/berj.4000

Wilkinson, S.D. and Penney, D. (Forthcoming) 'An investigation of ability grouping practices in primary physical education in England', Research Papers in Education.

Chapter 4: Assessment

Lee Sullivan, Will Swaithes, Jon Campbell and Will Grove

Part 4.1 – Insight
Lee Sullivan

In this chapter, we dive into the complexities of assessment in PE, exploring how common practices often fall short in meeting the diverse needs of students and teachers alike. We'll examine the prevalence of outdated assessment methods and their limitations, shedding light on the need for a shift in how we approach assessment in PE.

Paving Progress or Proving Proficiency?

There are some things we do in PE that in any other job or industry just wouldn't work. That's not to say they work for PE, they don't always, but we do them anyway. Often because it's the way it has always been done. Despite its flaws and inadequacies in serving the needs of students and teachers, assessment is one such practice that often defies logic or effective practice, simply because it's how it's always been done. I am not suggesting we stop assessing, but we must seriously consider the why, what and how of assessment in PE.

For many years, I followed the same assessment methods that I experienced as a student and observed among my colleagues. As both a PE teacher and Head of Department, I adhered to the customary practice of conducting assessment lessons at the conclusion of each unit of work. I would stand and observe the students in the lesson in drills or a conditioned game, holding a clipboard with their pictures/names printed on a piece of paper. I was assessing only on practical ability while I meticulously recorded whether they could replicate specific skills or movements or not. This would then inform a level, based on some highly wordy criteria (which often had sub-levels), as to the level of physical competence each student demonstrated. I would then transfer my observations from my clipboard into a computerised spreadsheet, which would then be sent home as part of the child's report. This is the method of assessment that was used with me when I was a PE student, it was the method that I had observed when training as a teacher and it was how I assessed for many years, even when a Head of PE.

CHAPTER 4: **ASSESSMENT**

However, upon reflection, I recognised the limitations of this approach and its failure to meet the broader educational needs of my students. The assessment process lacked depth and meaningful engagement, as students were solely evaluated on their practical abilities without any opportunity for feedback or improvement. Moreover, the narrow focus on practical prowess, often aligned with GCSE PE outcomes or elite performance standards, overlooked the diverse interests, abilities, and learning styles of my students.

Essentially, the traditional assessment model served a singular purpose: to inform stakeholders—students, senior leadership, and parents—of a student's proficiency in a particular activity. Yet, it fell short in fostering a culture of learning and growth, as students seldom revisited the same activity and were deprived of the chance to reflect on their performance or receive constructive feedback.

Acknowledging the shortcomings of this approach, I embarked on a journey to redefine my approach to assessment in physical education.

Purpose of Assessment

It is time we reconsider who it is we are teaching and what we are attempting to achieve. We are not trying to create elite sports people; we are attempting to nurture physical literacy for all. We are not an elite education system; we are a mass education system. Therefore, an assessment obsessed with performance is not supporting our intent and likely doing more harm than good.

The AIESEP Position Statement on Physical Education Assessment describes assessment as, 'a process by which information on student learning is obtained, interpreted and communicated, relative to one or more predefined learning outcomes. It serves several educational purposes, such as:
- Guiding and supporting the learning process of students
- Informing teachers about the effectiveness of their teaching and curriculum
- Deciding whether students may progress to a following phase in their learning process
- Providing evidence of student learning for relevant stakeholders (accountability).

(AIESEP, 2020).

Often when we think about an assessment, we think of a test. I think it's time to reframe what that means in PE as we consider what we are hoping to gain from any form of assessment in PE. Assessment should be less about proving proficiency and more about paving the way for student progress.

Figure 5: Purpose of Assessment in Physical Education

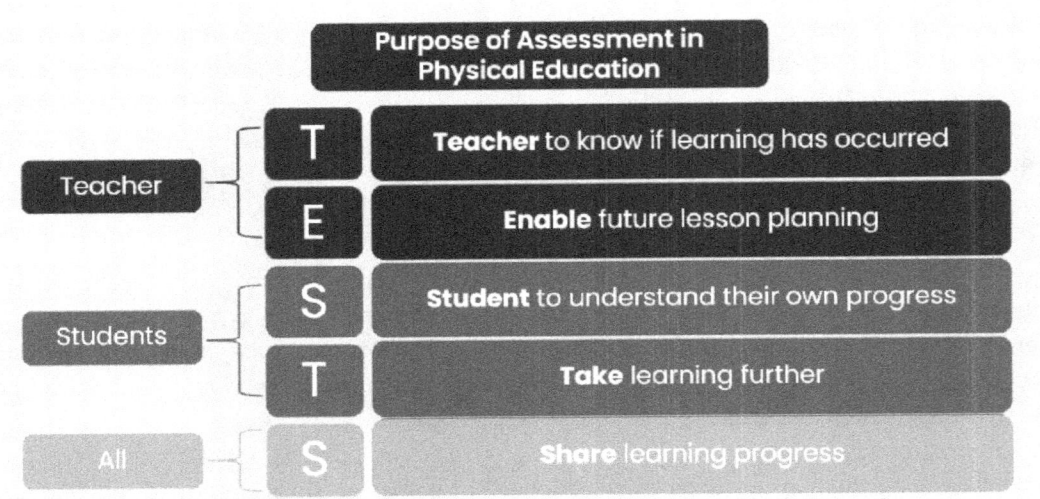

Firstly, the teachers should use their observations to reflect on whether learning has occurred. Do they know what I need them to know? Can they show what I want them to show? If they can then great, we can increase the level of challenge or move on in the scheme of work. If not, then we may need to revisit prior learning or provide more time for practice. Either way, this information should enable and inform future lesson planning.

We must also acknowledge the vital part that students themselves must take in their learning journey. The best assessments in PE not only measure progress but also inspire students to take ownership of their own learning journey. Students should reflect on their own progress. What can they do now that they couldn't before? More importantly. What do they need to do/know to take their learning further?

Finally, it is important to share learning progress with our senior leaders, parents and other key stakeholders. I am often saddened to see the number of schools who will provide summaries of learning progress in every subject but PE. What does this say to the educational value that PE holds in that school and the importance of PE to the children's development?

CHAPTER 4: **ASSESSMENT**

Part 4.2 – Delve
Lee Sullivan

Formative vs Summative

Assessment is often delineated into two distinct forms: summative and formative. Daisy Christodoulou, in her keynote speech for Making Shift Happen (2018), aptly characterised these as follows: "formative assessment is the journey and summative assessment is the destination."

To try to put this into perspective, let's consider two different business people. One, we will call 'X' and the other 'Y'.

Businessperson X is working on the same project. Throughout this project, X has no clear indication of their performance or progress as they will be judged on the success of the project at the time of the set deadline. X's bosses are using a vague but wordy success criteria, focusing only on how the project looks at the time of assessment, that they will use to judge X's performance at the end of the project time. As the project nears completion, X is informed that they will receive a numerical grade based on their overall performance. However, this grade is presented in isolation, without any context or explanation of specific strengths or weaknesses. X receives a low numerical grade, indicating poor performance, but they are left without any understanding of why or how to improve. This lack of feedback and guidance leaves X feeling disheartened and disconnected from the project outcomes. Consequently, they are demotivated to participate in similar projects in the future, lacking confidence in their abilities and unsure of how to progress. Even when forced to complete a project in the future, X is unsure on how to improve their performance.

In contrast, Businessperson Y is also engaged in the project but experiences a different assessment method. From the outset, Y is provided with clear and concise success criteria, outlining the expectations for each phase of the project. They receive regular feedback on their performance, both from themselves and others involved in the project. Y is given time to practise and refine their skills, with opportunities to seek clarification and guidance when needed. Progression through the project is based on mastery of each task and focuses on the project but also how Y has worked with others as well as the attitudes and behaviours they have demonstrated. The criteria ensures that Y fully understands and completes one stage before moving on to the next and if they are unable to do so then the deadlines set are amended. As a result, Y feels supported and empowered throughout the project, knowing exactly where they stand and what areas they need to improve. At the end of the project, Y receives constructive feedback on their performance, highlighting their strengths and areas for development. The final judgements are communicated in a motivational way considering the individual journey that Y is on within the organisation. Armed with this insight, Y feels motivated to continue learning and growing, confident in their ability to tackle future projects successfully.

For PE teachers, the analogy underscores the importance of adopting a balanced approach to assessment, integrating both formative and summative methods. Providing ongoing feedback and support, tailored to individual student needs, is essential for fostering a positive learning environment and promoting student growth and development.

In alignment with Christodoulou's insightful analogy of the 'journey and destination,' formative assessment can be likened to navigating a road trip. It's akin to consulting the map and adapting your route in response to real-time factors like traffic conditions, road closures, and weather forecasts. This dynamic process involves ongoing adjustments to optimise the journey towards your intended destination, ensuring smooth progress and efficient travel.

Summative assessment in a road trip is comparable to setting a target distance to cover within a specified time frame and then evaluating how closely you got to achieving that distance within the allotted time. It's comparative to measuring your progress solely based on how close you got to reaching the predetermined distance within the set time constraints. No matter what happens on the journey, you will not deviate on your route in order to get as close to the destination in the time set as you can. This approach can overlook the quality of the journey, the experiences gained, and the connections made with fellow travellers. It reduces the richness of the journey to a single metric, neglecting the holistic picture of the travel experience. Furthermore, in this analogy, little learning from the journey is taken into account. As a consequence, when embarking on a similar journey in the future, there may be minimal reflection or consideration given to how to improve the experience based on past learnings. This narrow perspective limits the potential for growth and development, both in travel and in education. Just as a road trip is more than the time spent driving, education encompasses more than just the final outcome.

Despite the clear differences between summative and formative assessment, expert Wiliam argues, in The Research Ed Guide to Assessment (2020), that they shouldn't be treated as separate entities. Rather, he suggests that assessment can serve both summative and formative purposes. This notion is reinforced by Christodoulou (2016), who proposes a blended approach termed 'descriptor-based assessment'. This method involves using performance descriptors to assess student progress throughout an entire scheme of work, culminating in a summative grade upon completion.

I am aware I may lose a number of readers during my next comment: I am a Tottenham Hotspur Football Club season ticket holder. Hold on, stay with me, I hope to make a valid point. Let's say if I were to only go to watch one game a season and (as is often the case),

CHAPTER 4: **ASSESSMENT**

Tottenham fail to perform at their best. Or more specifically if focusing on the performance of an individual, maybe our esteemed club captain has an off day (and for the sake of longevity in this book, I'll refrain from naming specific players, knowing full well the ever-shifting landscape of professional football, the player would have likely moved on). If I were to judge the captain solely based on that single match, they might receive a less-than-flattering evaluation. Anyone can have an off day.

However, what if I followed the captain's performance throughout the entire season, observing each game closely? Through this ongoing, formative assessment, a much clearer picture of the captain's competency would emerge, therefore, my assessment would carry more weight and reliability.

In addition to the detrimental assessment practices I've employed in the past, I must also admit to adhering strictly to predefined schemes of work that unavoidably led to summative assessment, regardless of student readiness. I operated with a fixed endpoint in mind, progressing towards it regardless of whether the students were adequately prepared. Lessons were delivered in a predetermined sequence, with minimal opportunity for practice, and little flexibility to adjust based on student needs. Take, for instance, a rugby scheme of work. I would proceed from teaching basic passing skills to passing backwards and then on to tackling, strictly following the scheme of work. Even if students hadn't fully grasped the concept of passing backward or tended to throw the ball randomly when approached by an opponent instead of making a strategic pass, I would move forward with the lesson on tackling nonetheless. Once the tackling session concluded, we would promptly move on to rucking. However, mastering tackling requires time to develop competence and confidence, not to mention the obvious dangers around progressing without a full understanding and experience of safe tackling. Nevertheless, the demands of the scheme of work necessitated summative assessment across multiple skills, prompting me to progress through the content at the expense of student development.

Transitioning to the use of formative assessment to inform summative judgements marked a significant shift in student experience and led to improved learning outcomes. Considering the purpose of assessment, we can use on-going formative assessment to ensure learning is taking place and students are ready to move on. If not, we can pause the scheme of work and spend some time developing the required competence. Take time to respond to the needs of the students. Provide opportunities for them to create, practise, play and embrace the joys of the activity. Every class is different and using formative assessment to enable future planning will provide accessible learning at their own pace.

There is no point having a completed scheme of work but students that lack competence AND confidence and potentially write off that activity completely. That is not why we became a PE teacher, is it?

Ipsative Assessment

As well as on-going formative assessment, we should be considering what exactly we are measuring our students against. Alongside or through formative assessment, ipsative assessment is a type of evaluation that compares a learner's current performance against their previous performances rather than against a standard or the performance of others. The term "ipsative" comes from the Latin word ipse, meaning "self," indicating that the focus is on the individual's progress over time.

This type of assessment often incorporates personal goals set by the learner, making the evaluation more meaningful and relevant to their unique learning journey. Feedback is typically qualitative, focusing on personal development rather than numerical scores or grades, which can enhance motivation and encourage a growth mindset. However, it can also be subjective, relying on personal reflections, self-assessments, or portfolios to demonstrate progress over time.

This form of assessment promotes self-reflection, aims to motivate learners to improve by concentrating on personal progress, and recognises that each learner has a unique journey. Nevertheless, this approach may lack external benchmarking, making it challenging to gauge overall competence or readiness for specific tasks. Additionally, the subjective nature of ipsative assessment can lead to inconsistencies in how progress is perceived and measured.

Fitness Testing

Though still prevalent in practice (Harte, Alfrey, Spray and Cale, 2023), using fitness testing to form the basis of assessment serves only to shame (Alfrey, and Gard, 2019) and can be harmful to the psychological well-being and motivation of students. Fitness testing as a method of learning or assessment should be avoided. That's it, that's the paragraph.

Loud and Clear

At the beginning of the academic year, a Year 7 student approached me to express his belief that he couldn't dance. When I asked if he had any previous injuries, he shook his head. Curious, I probed further to understand why he felt this way. He recounted receiving a low grade in a dance performance in Year 6, which he interpreted as a reflection of his lack of ability. I considered how this perception might affect his willingness to participate in other activities; perhaps he avoided school events with dancing or felt self-conscious during physical education classes. Might a low grade in other activities impact his motivation to ever want to attempt them again. I reassured him that he had the potential to dance, emphasising that he didn't need to be the most skilled dancer but could find joy and self-expression through movement.

CHAPTER 4: **ASSESSMENT**

The recent overhaul of assessment in schools in England, with the removal of levels, was touted as a significant change. Yet, it seems that levels have been replaced by different terminology with similar negative consequences – levels in disguise. Many schools now employ a GCSE 1-9 grading system or categorise students as working below, at, or above expected levels, often based on performance in English and maths. The relevance of such grading systems to PE, with its focus on building positive relationships with physical activity and sport, is questionable. Are these approaches, akin to traditional skill-drill PE delivery, doing more harm than good? This has no relevance to PE and more importantly goes against our intent. We are often forced to assess in the same way that other subjects do, in order to conform, but why? We have very different aims to them. The maths form of assessment doesn't care if students remain active, or probably doesn't even care if they have a positive relationship with maths. English assessment isn't bothered if students build a strong connection with PE, physical activity or sport; it is more focused on providing information to students as to how prepared they are for an exam. This messaging that conforms with the way in which learning is assessed and communicated in other subjects is irrelevant, contradictory and problematic for us in PE.

Equally important is the manner in which we convey assessment information. Some PE departments opt to record students' grades in their planners, while others share attainment levels in a register-style format. Recently, I even encountered a notice board analogy where assessment grades were depicted as participants in a 100-metre sprint, with higher achievers placed closer to the finish line. This begs the question: what message does this send to students who excel and those who, based on performance assessments, do not?

The language we use to communicate progress and the methods employed to convey this information are crucial considerations in promoting positive attitudes towards learning and achievement in PE. Imagine a PE class as a diverse garden filled with different types of flowers. Despite receiving the same instructions and guidance from the teacher, each student progresses at their own pace. Just as some flowers blossom early in the season while others take longer to bloom, in PE, students exhibit varying levels of skill development. For instance, in one class, you may have a county badminton player who excels at the sport, while in the same class, there might be someone who has never picked up a racket before. Each student, like these flowers, requires individual attention and support to flourish and grow in their physical education journey. The messaging from our assessment must reflect the fact that every student is on their own learning journey and developing at their own pace. It should be motivational and aspirational, challenging and holistic. It should be bespoke to your school and the curriculum intent of your department. If you get assessment right, you can better support every child to learn, develop and want to continue to do so for as long as they are with you and beyond.

Mid-chapter reflection

What new insights have I gained from this chapter so far?

How does this knowledge reinforce or challenge my current beliefs or practices?

Are there areas or concepts I still need to explore further?

Have I identified any gaps in my team's understanding or practice that need addressing?

How can I share or apply this learning to positively influence others in my team or school?

CHAPTER 4: ASSESSMENT

Part 4.3 – Experts

Assessment
Will Swaithes

Assessment in PE plays an essential role in measuring students' knowledge, skills and overall development. However, doing it well requires much more than just observing performance in a range of scenarios; it demands a research-informed approach that considers a variety of factors to ensure it is:
- Comprehensive without becoming unwieldy or confusing
- Inclusive and equitable to help close the disadvantage gap
- Supportive of students' holistic growth and not fixated on performance in specific sports

In his great book The Craft of Assessment, Chiles (2020) promotes the idea of:
- **C**ondensing knowledge to support the transfer to our long-term memories for retrieval through effective use of deliberate practice
- **R**eflection opportunities to ensure new knowledge (and skills) stick
- **A**ssessment opportunities to check for understanding and revisit previously learnt material
- **F**eeding forward the outcomes of assessment to inform future teaching and correction of misconceptions
- **T**arget-driven improvement where students are given time to focus on practising specific knowledge gaps.

1. Examples of Practice Seen
I feel very privileged to be able to visit lots of schools to support trainee, new and experienced teachers in a range of settings across primary, secondary and special schools that are state funded but also independent and international schools and as a consequence I feel I have a strong understanding of the landscape. Like elsewhere around the world, there is wide-ranging practice here in England. The Department for Education removed the poorly implemented attainment targets from the national curriculum in 2014, intending to allow "teachers greater flexibility in the way they plan and assess pupils' learning" (DfE 2014,p2). The subsequent era of 'assessment without levels' has led to varied practice. At its best PE teachers have worked carefully and collaboratively over a number of years to fine tune a simple model of assessment that fits whole school systems yet enables them to recognise the importance of holistic development of students in the physical, cognitive, affective and social domains of learning. This is often articulated as 'Hands, Head and Heart' (Orr, 1992; Sipos et al., 2008; Frapwell, 2014; Islam et al., 2022) or the 'Me in PE' (Bowler, cited in Youth Sport Trust, 2017) model, both of which are student-centred. These approaches allow everyone to articulate the

meaning, value and aspects of personal strength to be celebrated, alongside the areas of focus for next steps in learning and what success will look like. Unfortunately, all too often I see PE assessment at its worst. I see the watering down of GCSE Physical Education assessment criteria and attempting to deliver that content to all students with a misplaced belief that this will provide a flightpath onto the GCSE PE course for all students. However, those qualifications are not well-aligned to the needs, motivations or ambitions of core PE for all and, consequently, can do more harm than good. Other examples of poor practice, in my opinion, include half-termly units of work where the teacher wanders around with a clipboard in the last lesson grading every student on their capability to perform in a specific activity (for example, football or gymnastics or athletics) and even end of unit written tests related to sport rules and/or bodily systems to measure declarative knowledge. Is it any wonder that we are currently losing the battle on inspiring more young people to live healthy, active lives and squeezing the joy out of being a PE teacher?

2. The Purpose and Goals of Assessment

Surely the primary goal of assessment in PE is to facilitate greater learning and progress? I fully subscribe to the analogy first described by Dylan Wiliam (2013) that assessment is the bridge between teaching and learning.

Figure 6: Dylan William (2013) Quote

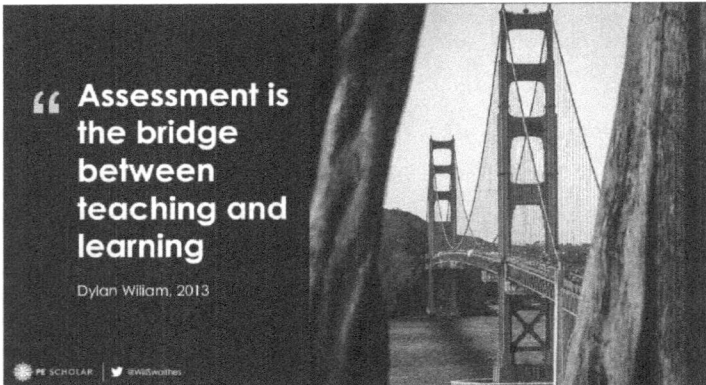

Within PE, assessment must provide insights into students' progress in physical competence, cognitive understanding and social skills related to physical activity. If current participation trends are anything to go by, perhaps the most important piece of the puzzle is the affective domain; we need to find meaningful ways to recognise, reward and set personalised targets in relation to the attitudes, values, emotions and feelings that young people have towards sport, physical activity and movement. Social and Emotional Learning (SEL) has an important place in PE and within education more broadly but so too do the ideas of confidence, motivation and

CHAPTER 4: ASSESSMENT

character development. Research emphasises the need to align assessment strategies with educational objectives, such as promoting lifelong physical activity, developing motor skills, enhancing fitness levels, and fostering positive attitudes towards PE. To achieve this, teachers need to establish clear, specific, and measurable learning outcomes that guide the assessment process and I would encourage the use of a holistic framework such as:

- Move, Think, Feel and Connect strands as identified in Sport England's (2023) physical literacy consensus statement work.
- Hands, Head and Heart (Orr, 1992; Sipos et al., 2008; Frapwell, 2014; Islam et al., 2022).
- 'Me in PE' (Bowler, 2014 cited in Youth Sport Trust, 2017) featuring physical, thinking, healthy, leadership and creative strands.
- Know, Show and Grow as captured in Lee and the team's Concept Curriculum (PE Scholar, 2022)

It has been suggested that a flexible approach to pupil assessment "allows for the development of a more inclusive pedagogy, shifting the focus from teacher-centred
to child-centred, and embracing more diverse learning styles" (McLennan and Thompson, 2015, p32). This reminds us of the essential interplay between curriculum, pedagogy and assessment.

3. Utilising Diverse Assessment Methods

A research-informed approach advocates for using a variety of assessment methods to capture different dimensions of student learning. Traditional methods like knowledge and/or skill tests and fitness assessments should be used with caution and complemented by alternative forms of assessment, such as:

- **Teacher observation** - this is by far our most useful tool and one that requires constant focus to sharpen both the time given to it and the focus of our attention to ensure all domains of learning are given equal merit.
- **Peer and self-assessments** - enabling students to accurately assess their own and their classmates' performance, progress and effort can enhance self-awareness, reflection and support collaborative learning.
- **Portfolios** - in an age of increased digital literacy with Match of the Day style analysis and TikTok montages possible via smartphones there is definitely a place for collecting video evidence of progress and performance … and often students can become really engaged in doing so, but be careful not to let it take away too much from time moving in lessons. Collecting a portfolio of students' work including fitness logs, reflective journals and skill progression records can provide a comprehensive picture of their development over time.
- **Performance-based assessments** - there is no getting away from the fact that examination PE and sport courses at level 2 (GCSE equivalent) and level 3 (A level equivalents) involve students demonstrating their skills in game-like scenarios, which are more authentic and reflective of real-world application. The different awarding organisations provide clear

rubrics for this type of assessment in named activity areas and, whilst it is essential as a physical educator to be able to carry these out in a broad range of activities with objectivity and accuracy, I would strongly discourage utilising these rubrics as standard across core PE.

4. Formative versus Summative Assessment

> *"Formative assessment differs from summative assessment in that the information gathered in the formative process is used to shape improvements, rather than serve as a summary of performances... Studies show that formative assessment is one of the most effective strategies for promoting high student performance. It is also important for improving the equity of student outcomes and developing students' "learning to learn" skills"* (OECD, 2005, p13).

Formative assessment, which is ongoing and provides immediate feedback, is critical in PE. It helps us teachers to identify students' strengths and areas for development, allowing instruction and future teaching to be tailored accordingly. Research supports the use of formative assessment (sometimes referred to as Assessment for Learning or AfL) to motivate students and promote continuous improvement rather than focusing solely on final outcomes. Chng and Lund (2018, p34) flag the importance of identifying the purpose of the assessment and by sharing that with students via simple learning outcomes or success criteria it promotes the idea of visible learning. Perhaps within the category of formative assessment is the idea of diagnostic assessment where we figure out what students already know and can do to inform the pitch, pace and focus of future learning. This diagnostic assessment is crucial if we want to hook learners in, avoid boredom and adapt plans to match what individuals need and not necessarily what the scheme of work says to do next!

Summative assessments, typically administered at the end of a unit or course, should be used much more sparingly to evaluate overall achievement and learning. However, remember even these summative assessments should be carefully designed to reflect the holistic nature of PE, assessing not only physical performance but also knowledge, attitudes and behaviours related to physical activity.

5. Equity and Inclusion in Assessment

UNESCO, the DfE, Ofsted (2022, 2023) and others repeatedly remind us that we must 'level the playing field' and in doing so be more equitable in our assessment practices in PE. As teachers we must consider the diverse range of student needs and motivations, including those with Special Educational Needs and/or Disabilities (SEND), different cultural backgrounds and varying levels of prior exposure to physical activity. Assessments should be adaptable, allowing all students to demonstrate their learning in a manner that is fair and inclusive of them. For instance, modifying tasks or offering alternative activities can ensure that assessments are accessible to all students.

6. Feedback and Reporting

Providing constructive feedback (or feed forward as Dylan Wiliam would call it) is a key component of effective assessment. Feed forward should be specific, timely and focused on both the effort and achievement to encourage a growth mindset. Additionally, assessment results should be communicated clearly to students, parents, and other stakeholders, emphasising progress and areas for improvement rather than merely reporting scores. Perhaps my favourite way to do this is related to circulating the class and plenaries. When students are practising a task, like many, I like to circulate the class to provide hints, tips, motivation where needed, stretch, challenge and maybe even some words of wisdom. The key is in saying less and pinpointing the thing that, with a little nudge in the right direction, will have the biggest impact on progress. Sometimes that means saying nothing at all because often learning is stickiest if we have to figure it out for ourselves. But, if you do share some thoughts then I suggest:

1. Ensuring you reinforce a careful and equal balance of all domains of learning in your lessons. Physical or performance skills are therefore not valued over cognitive, inter- or intra-personal skills such as teamwork or resilience.
2. Carefully considering the different personalities in your class and how your actions, or those of others in the class, will affect feelings, confidence and motivation going forwards.
3. Ensuring you provide opportunities for students to turn your individual feedback into 'feedforward' moments by sharing it with the rest of the group. This achieves a few key objectives:
   - It reduces teacher-talk by getting students to lead mini-plenaries.
   - It provides an opportunity to see if what you said was understood, listened to and if it had impact.
   - It enables other students in the group with similar misconceptions to learn too.
   - Importantly it reduces your cognitive load to remember what you said and to whom.

Conclusion and Takeaways

In summary, assessment in PE should be multi-faceted, inclusive and aligned with educational goals. By incorporating diverse assessment methods, balancing formative and summative assessments and ensuring equity, teachers can create a comprehensive assessment system that supports all students' physical, cognitive, social and affective development. Research-based practices ensure that assessments not only measure performance but also contribute meaningfully to students' lifelong engagement in physical activity.

Part 4.4 – Apply

Creating a Holistic Rubric
Jon Campbell

Big Change – The Curriculum for Wales
The Curriculum for Wales was born out of a clear need to modernise and overhaul the Welsh education system to better meet the needs of today's learners in an ever-evolving society. The traditional content-heavy approach was deemed insufficient to equip students with the skills and capabilities needed to thrive in the 21st century. As a result, the Welsh Government initiated an ambitious reform aimed at creating a more flexible, inclusive, and learner-centred curriculum. The Curriculum for Wales is designed to foster creativity, critical thinking, collaboration, and well-being, underpinned by its Four Purposes (Welsh Government, 2019a), which define the core aims for every learner in Wales: to become ambitious, capable learners; enterprising, creative contributors; ethical, informed citizens; and healthy, confident individuals. This reform is built around six Areas of Learning and Experience (AOLEs)—broad, interdisciplinary areas that focus on equipping students with transferable skills and knowledge. One of these is the Health and Wellbeing AOLE, within which physical education (PE) now finds its place. This new structure reflects the importance of developing the whole person, recognising the connection between physical, mental, and emotional health, and guiding students towards a holistic understanding of their well-being.

The (Need for) Evolution of Physical Education in Wales
For many years, PE in Wales has been synonymous with athletic performance—how fast students could run, how high they could jump, or how skilfully they could play a particular sport. PE teachers had often been tasked with assessing these physical achievements, measuring students against fixed performance criteria and then reporting that back to parents and guardians in the form of a (often meaningless to the student) number. However, within the Curriculum for Wales, PE has found itself undergoing a profound and necessary shift. Many schools are moving away from a narrow focus on physical performance to a more holistic approach—one that places equal value on a child's physical literacy (their relationship with movement and physical activity throughout life), well-being, and personal development.

The Curriculum for Wales represents more than just a change in taught content; it's a transformation of the entire educational philosophy. For PE, pedagogy itself has been placed under the microscope. One of the key drivers behind this reform is the need to create a

CHAPTER 4: **ASSESSMENT**

more inclusive and flexible physical curriculum that considers the needs and affordances of a student's context.

For us as PE teachers, this shift is particularly relevant. Assessment practices need to be tuned to support and inform students' overall physical and emotional well-being, helping them to develop a lifelong love of physical activity, and guiding them to understand how being active can positively impact their health and happiness. This means facilitating and recognising meaningful experiences, not merely participating in a schedule or yearly rotation of different sports.

PE and the Health and Wellbeing AOLE: A New Framework

Under the Curriculum for Wales, the Health and Wellbeing Area of Learning and Experience (AOLE) reflects a broader understanding of how physical activity contributes to overall well-being. This shift emphasises the interconnectedness of physical, mental, and emotional health, moving away from a purely performance-based approach to one that supports the whole child.

At the core of this approach are the What Matters Statements (Welsh Government, 2019b), which define the key areas of development for learners. These statements form the backbone of our planning, helping to shape the PE curriculum in a way that promotes holistic development. The five What Matters Statements within the Health and Wellbeing AOLE are particularly relevant to PE, as they provide a structured framework to ensure that our lessons address not only physical competence but also the emotional, social, and cognitive aspects of learning through movement.

1. **Developing physical health and well-being has lifelong benefits:** This statement highlights the importance of encouraging learners to understand the positive impact physical activity has on their health and well-being. In PE, we need to design lessons that help students develop an awareness of their own physical health and the benefits of movement, such as improved fitness, mental clarity, and stress relief. Teaching them to appreciate physical activity as part of a balanced lifestyle is key to fostering habits that last beyond school. This means moving beyond teaching sports skills alone and incorporating discussions on the value of regular activity and how it supports overall health.
2. **How we process and respond to our experiences affects our mental health and emotional well-being:** This statement emphasises the need for learners to develop emotional resilience and self-awareness. In PE, this means creating opportunities for students to reflect on how physical activity makes them feel, how they respond to challenges, and how they cope with both success and failure. By incorporating reflection, mindfulness, and emotional intelligence into PE lessons, we can help students build mental resilience, which is just as important as physical stamina. Activities like cooperative

games or personal challenges encourage students to process their experiences in ways that strengthen their emotional well-being.

3. **Our decision-making impacts on the quality of our lives and the lives of others:** This statement underlines the role of decision-making and responsibility in shaping our experiences and well-being. In PE, this can be integrated by teaching students how to make informed choices about their health and fitness. It's also about helping them recognise the wider social impact of their actions, such as the importance of teamwork, respect for others, and ethical play. By fostering an understanding of how decisions made during physical activities—like playing fairly or supporting a teammate—affect their lives and those of others, we equip students with skills that extend beyond the PE classroom.

4. **Healthy relationships are fundamental to our well-being:** The social aspect of PE is crucial, as it provides a natural environment for students to learn about relationships and communication. PE lessons often involve collaboration, whether in team sports, partner work, or group challenges. It is important that we consciously create situations where students can develop social skills such as cooperation, leadership, and empathy. These experiences help learners understand the value of building healthy relationships, managing conflicts, and supporting one another in achieving shared goals, which are vital for their overall well-being in school and as part of the wider community.

5. **How we engage with social influences shapes who we are and affects our health and well-being:** Through PE and the experiences it offers, learners explore how social influences can impact their character and world view. Rules, social norms, attitudes and values are created and reinforced through their interactions with the students in their classes and the people in their community. Through PE, we can explore the notion of culture, and how the cultures of others are celebrated through physical experiences. Pedagogies of affect can be used to guide students towards positive behaviours and relationships.

In considering these What Matters Statements, we recognise that PE has the potential to contribute far beyond the development of physical skills (Casey & Kirk, 2021; Campbell, 2023).

By aligning our teaching with these principles, we ensure that PE becomes a key driver in fostering resilience, confidence, well-being, and lifelong engagement with physical activity. Our role as PE teachers is now more important than ever, as we could shape not just physically capable students, but well-rounded, healthy, and emotionally aware individuals.

Shifting Assessment: Moving Beyond Physical Performance

In the past, our assessment practices were largely summative. But let us be honest, these assessment lessons rarely reflected the efforts or progress of all students—especially at the end of a 6-week unit of a particular sport in which the student had no interest. One-off performance is not a strong proxy of learning. As a teacher, I never enjoyed this approach—they were always the least enjoyable lessons.

Now, the focus is on formative assessment, where we are looking to evidence progress in physical literacy rather than simply judge and report upon performance. This means we need to assess not only physical competence but also how students think, feel, and engage with physical activity as individuals and socially. These softer skills are crucial to fostering a love for physical activity that can last well beyond the school years.

Challenging the Physical Education "Status Quo" in Wales

PE teachers – we can be a surprisingly stubborn bunch. Strangely to me, for a subject that professes to foster adaptability, resilience and help set long-term and ambitious goals for our students, many PE teachers seem terrified of change – doing something new or showing a level of conscious incompetence in the admirable struggle to develop one's own practice. The biggest challenge I've experienced within the PE sector in Wales is the misconception that a new way of thinking represents a sudden move away from developing and assessing physical competence – or making PE "unrecognisable". The shift to holistic assessment allows us to better understand and support our students as whole individuals, addressing their motivation for, and relationship with, movement. Therefore, how can we ensure that every child leaves our lessons with a sense of accomplishment, no matter their physical ability? How can we use formative assessment to encourage growth and development in all facets of physical literacy? And how can we ensure that our teaching and assessment practices in PE are contributing meaningfully to the wider Health and Wellbeing AOLE?

The incorporation of 'Know, Show, Grow'

The first step was small. It was about identifying that the current (and almost singular) focus of our curriculum was performance. A simple student voice activity demonstrated that students wished to be assessed more through the affective domain, and this served as the catalyst for change.

FROM PE DRE**A**D TO DELIGHT

Figure 7: The Disconnected Curriculum

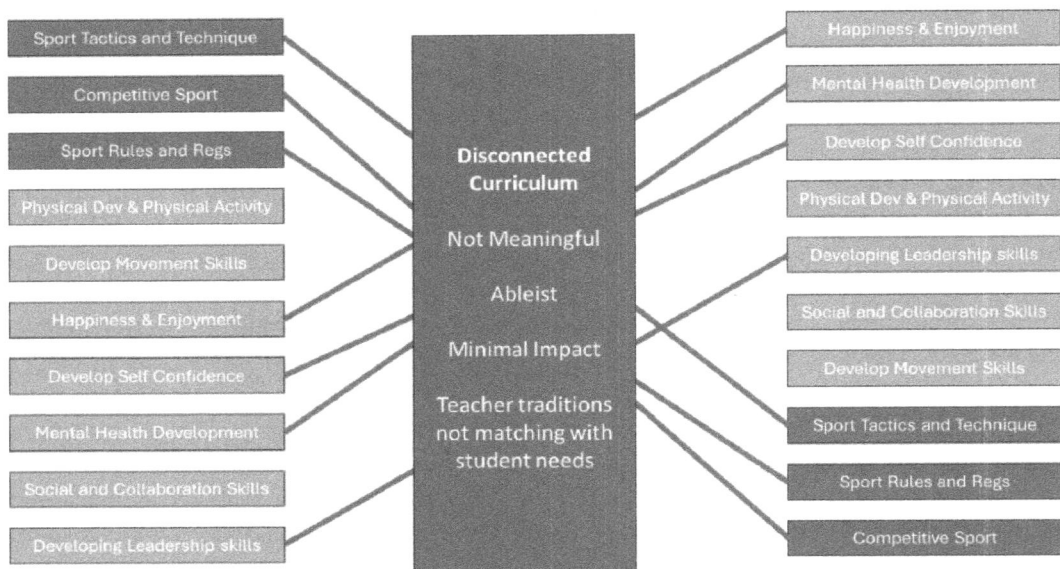

Taking inspiration from Lee Sullivan's (2021) 'Is PE in Crisis?' and Phil Mathe's (2022) 'Happiness Factories', and developing a strong forum with two very forward-thinking Heads of Department from local schools, the value of a 'Know, Show, Grow' approach (as will be discussed in chapter 11) became clear. Trialing it with a selection of classes, and analysing the impact on student engagement and progress gave me the confidence to adopt it as a standardised department teaching and learning approach. Students were arriving to lessons knowing that increasing physical competence was the goal, but it was not the only way to engage successfully with learning outcomes. Immediately feedback to students becomes more tailored and students become more willing to evidence learning and progress in a domain(s) that they connected with through the activity in the moment. Engagement skyrocketed. Could a student perform an efficient and successful lay-up in a lesson using basketball as the vehicle for learning? Perhaps not, but could they show resilience by not giving up, seeking help, and continuing to engage with more able peers to develop their own competence? They sure can. Is this observable change in behaviour the very evidence of learning we are looking for? And if it's there, shouldn't

CHAPTER 4: **ASSESSMENT**

we be celebrating that? A student showing this evidence of personal growth may never perform the perfect technical lay-up. But you can be sure they will eventually discover a technique that feels right to them that will begin to bring success in due course. Nobody would have taught David Beckham to lean so far to the side (at risk of slipping) of his planted foot when crossing a ball or taking a free kick. In fact, in a documentary, he states that some coaches had tried to "correct" this technique to something more in line with traditional coaching points. But through his experiences on the pitch and his resilience in persisting with something he felt he could master he developed a technique that allowed him to develop a level of curl and 'whip' on shot or pass that made him such a unique threat during his career. In PE, assessing a student by getting them all to 'climb a tree', when - in a well-known analogy - your classes consist of monkeys, fish, elephants and dogs, is never going to allow you to represent or guide progress in all students effectively.

Evidencing individual progression is the central tenet of the Curriculum for Wales. Although students evidenced progress in their physical competency through performance and video-based evidence, in my context a student log was created and introduced.

Figure 8: Student Log

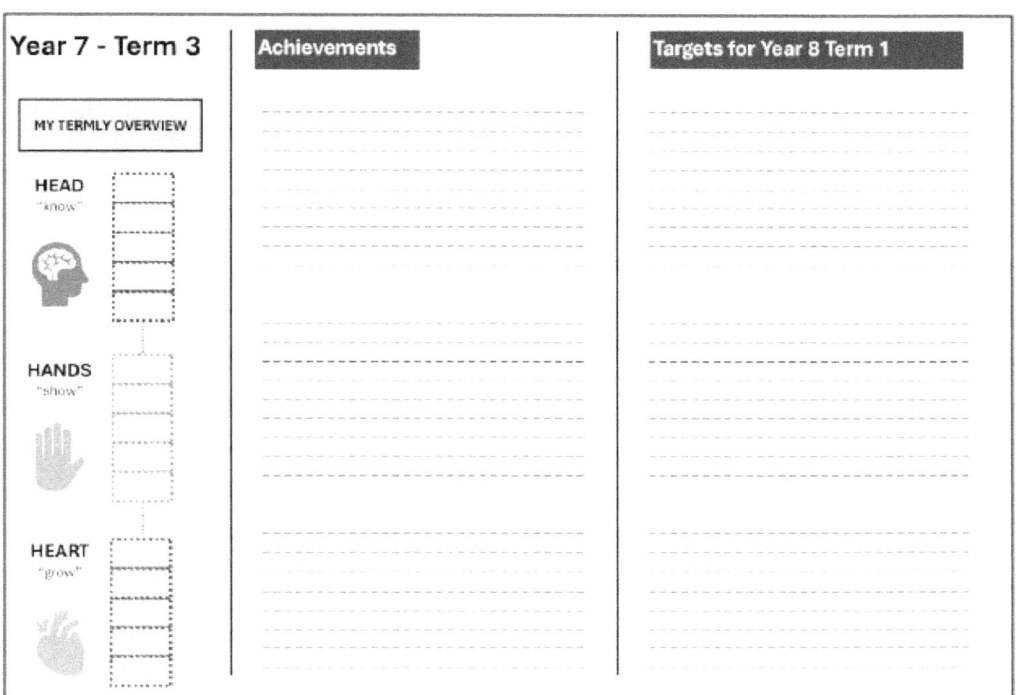

FROM PE DREAD TO DELIGHT

This log is completed termly (3 times per year) in classroom-based Well-being lessons. The log engages students in the subject's 'Know, Show, Grow' learning domains, whereby the 'Emerging, Acquiring, Developing, Securing, Thriving' characteristics are closely mapped to the Progression Steps of the AOLE's What Matters Statements. The descriptors of learning are purposely activity non-specific; this was to ensure that students were able to become familiar with them, and ensure that language used in their evaluations and improvement planning could be understood across their whole-school learning journey. With this, I developed a progress tracker that would take this input and produce a full physical literacy learning journey on a page. This has been key in ensuring a lived-experience of progress for students, but also providing them with a visual and qualitative representation of it in a subject that many students previously felt no connection with.

Figure 9: Progress Tracker

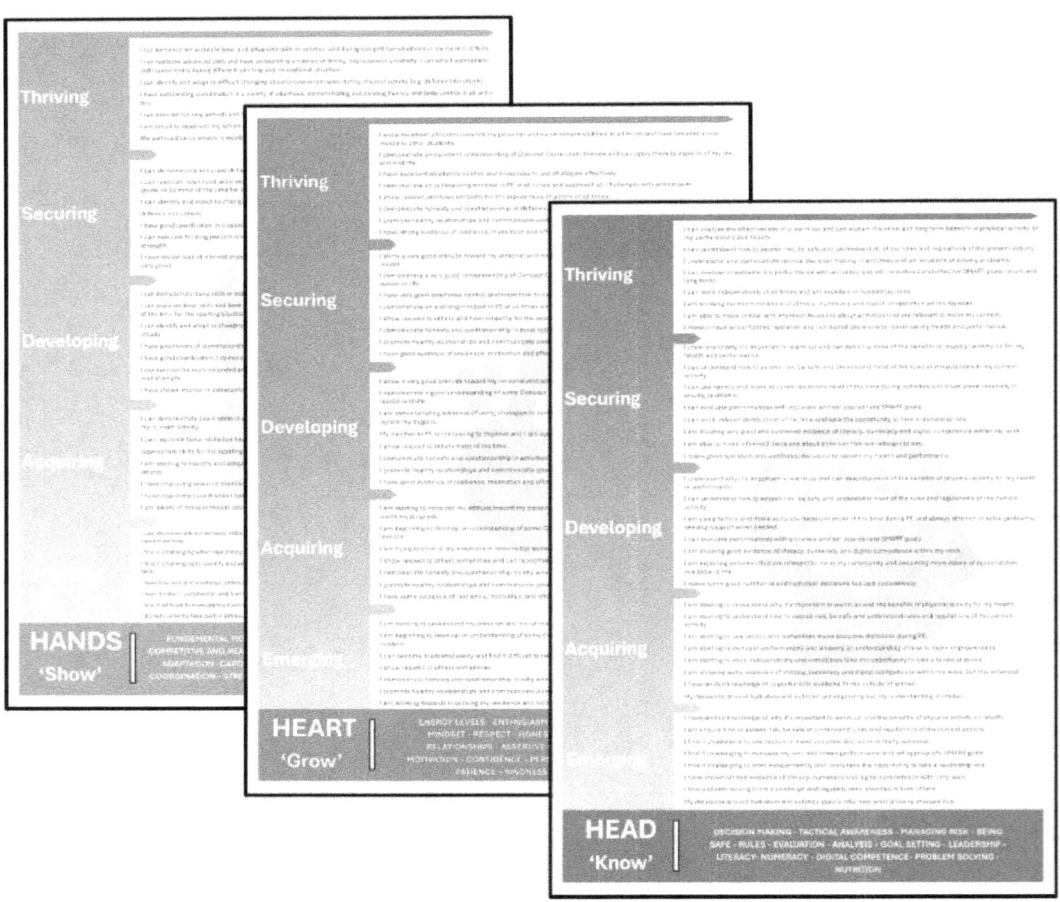

CHAPTER 4: **ASSESSMENT**

One of the most significant changes I've made is incorporating student reflection on the key features of Meaningful PE (Fletcher et al., 2022)—fun, challenge, social interaction, personal relevance, and autonomy—as part of my assessment process. By encouraging students to think about their experiences in these terms, I've been able to gain a deeper understanding of their holistic progress, beyond just physical competence.

Figure 10: Student Reflection

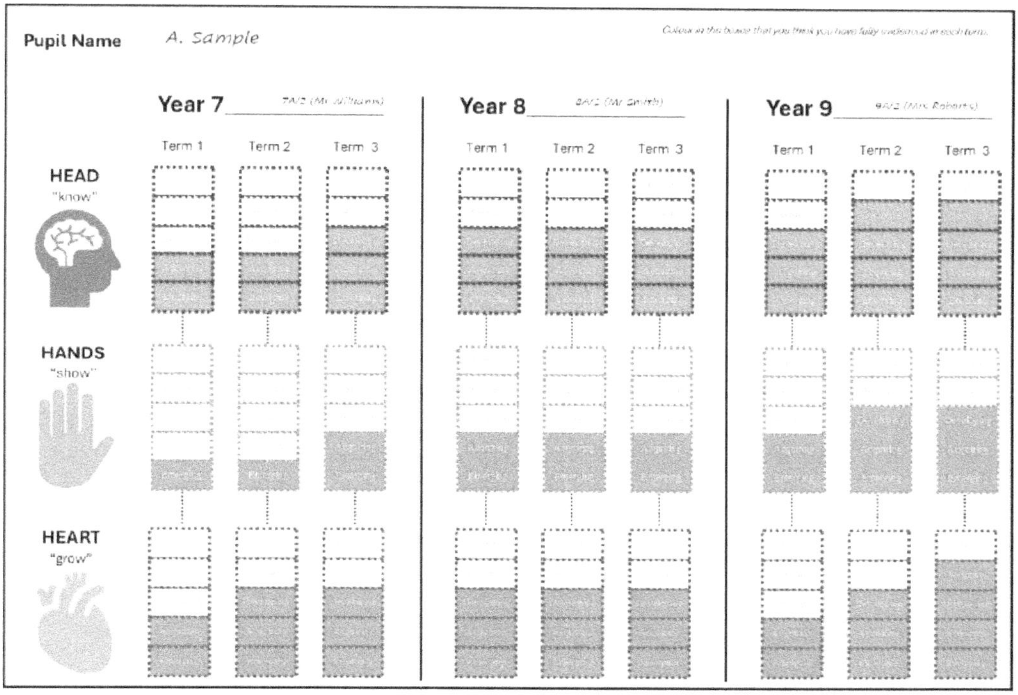

1. **Fun and Enjoyment:** I've found that fun is the hook that keeps students engaged in PE. Now, I regularly ask my students to reflect on what activities they enjoy the most and why. Their answers are often surprising and insightful. Some enjoy the thrill of competition, while others find joy in achieving a personal goal or simply being active with friends. Understanding what makes an activity fun for them helps me tailor my lessons to ensure every student finds something to connect with. This reflection on enjoyment also helps them see physical activity as something positive and enjoyable, rather than just another school subject.

2. **"Just Right" Challenge:** One of the most powerful shifts I've noticed is how my students now reflect on the challenges they face in PE. Instead of just assessing their physical abilities at the end of a unit, I ask them to think about how they've been challenged and how they've responded to that challenge. This reflection helps them recognise that growth isn't just about being the best at a sport—it's about learning to persevere, to try again after failure, and to develop resilience. I've seen students who used to shy away from difficult tasks now embracing challenges because they understand that personal growth is part of the process. It's been incredibly rewarding to see students develop not just physically, but mentally and emotionally as well.
3. **Social Interaction and Collaboration:** PE has always involved teamwork, but now I place a much greater emphasis on the social aspect of physical activity. I ask students to reflect on how they work with others during activities—how they communicate, how they support their peers, and what role they take within a team. By reflecting on these interactions, students have begun to see the value of cooperation and leadership. It's helped them build stronger relationships in and out of the classroom, and I've noticed an improvement in the way they approach group work in other subjects as well. The ability to reflect on social interactions has not only improved their teamwork skills but also fostered a sense of belonging and mutual respect.
4. **Personal Relevance:** One of the key aspects of Meaningful PE is ensuring that what we teach is relevant to students' lives. I encourage my students to think about how the activities we do in PE relate to their own interests, goals, and lives outside school. This has been a game changer in terms of student engagement. Some students now see connections between PE and their hobbies, while others recognise how the lessons we learn in class—like resilience or managing stress—can help them in other areas of life. By making these connections, students are more motivated and invested in their own progress, and I've seen a noticeable improvement in their attitudes towards PE.
5. **Increased Motor Competence:** One of the most transformative aspects of this approach has been giving students more autonomy over their learning and the physical skills they are developing. I've started allowing them more choice in the activities we do and the goals they set for themselves. After each unit, I ask them to reflect on how having control over their participation has affected their experience. Many students have said that having a say in their learning makes them feel more invested and motivated. This has also encouraged them to take ownership of their physical health and well-being, as they begin to understand that they are in control of their own progress.

By incorporating these reflections into my assessment practices, I've seen a dramatic shift in how students perceive PE. It's no longer about achieving a particular score or mastering a specific skill; it's about their personal journey and the meaningful experiences they gain along the way. They're developing not only as physically competent individuals but also as thoughtful, emotionally aware young people who understand the broader impact of physical activity on their well-being.

CHAPTER 4: **ASSESSMENT**

Figure 11: Reflection Assessment Practice

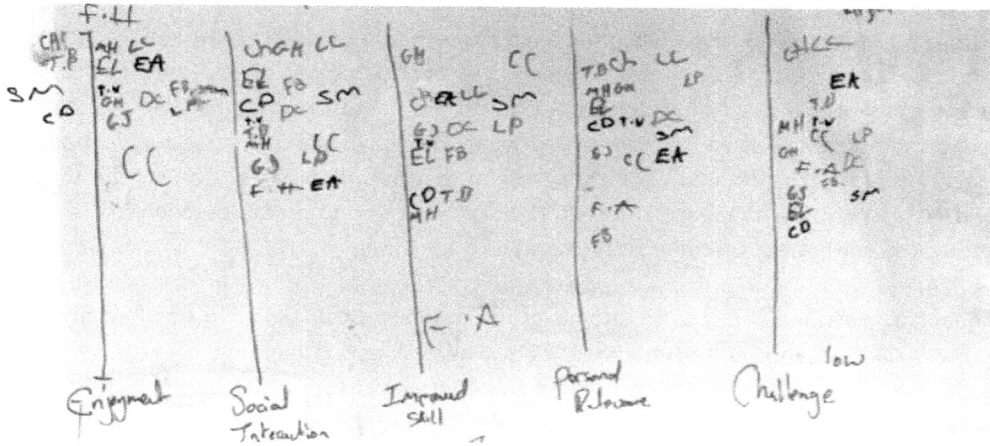

This approach has aligned perfectly with the Curriculum for Wales and the What Matters Statements within the Health and Wellbeing AOLE. I've found that by encouraging students to reflect on these features, I'm helping them progress in areas far beyond just physical competence. I'm contributing to their development as ambitious, capable learners and healthy, confident individuals. This approach has reinvigorated my teaching, and I now feel that I'm making a lasting impact on my students' lives, guiding them not only in their physical literacy but in becoming well-rounded, resilient individuals who can appreciate the full value of movement and physical activity.

Sequential Curriculum Design
Will Grove

Lee has asked some poignant questions to reflect on and has already gone into the reasons why we should spend time looking at our method of assessment. I will share an assessment process which allows us to ensure all stakeholders in PE can use the data collected. When I use the term data here, I'm including quantitative and qualitative means of collecting data. So this starts us off with the question, why do we assess?

Pupils will want to know how well they have done-the classic look at the front page of an exam and chuck it to the side. Then take low numbers as bad, high as good. To avoid this scenario it is key to ask ourselves: 'What do pupils do with their assessment data?' 'How is the feedback delivered to them?' And 'do they know what they have been assessed in?' Then we must decide what makes it meaningful to them and their future choices? Can we flip the narrative with assessment to what happens next, rather than lingering on the percentage, level or other methods of feedback on their assessment?

Teachers, we want to know, or should want to know, if our teaching has had an impact on pupils' learning and, as Lee has explained, where does the learning go next for the pupils? This could be used as a very useful reflective tool after each lesson based on what they have seen and heard to inform the next steps in learning. Based on work undertaken by Professor Liz Durden-Myers, we use a reflective tool (shown here) that helps teachers balance, over a unit of work, the domains that pupils spend their time in during lessons. This assessment allows teachers to decide whether the lesson has been knowledge-heavy so in the next lesson they may need to spend more time in the physical domain.

Figure 12: Physical Education Lesson Reflection

CHAPTER 4: **ASSESSMENT**

Physical Education Lesson Reflection

Cognitive | Affirmative

Physical | Range of Environments

Heads of Department, we want to know the impact of our curriculum and whether pupils are moving towards the curriculum intent. As Myatt (2021) discusses, curriculum is an evolving process; as middle leaders we should take great interest in our assessment of pupils, how teachers use assessment and find opportunities to assess its impact. Let us take as an example our Greenshaw Learning Trust intent, which is adapted for the various contexts:

> *"Nurturing a lifelong commitment to health and physical activity by developing pupils' Physical Literacy, preparing them to take responsibility for their engagement in physical activity at their chosen level"*.

As a Head of Department I would want to assess:
- Where students have the opportunity to take responsibility for their involvement in physical activity (number of students engaging in extracurricular activities, joining clubs outside of school)?
- How do they travel to school?

- What activity do they do at break time?
- What physical activity do they do after school?

This would give me a clear indication as to whether we are moving towards our curriculum intent.

Parents and Senior Leaders, these stakeholders are usually the hardest to reach. The 'why' for most parents is to see if their child is progressing at school, engaging and is well-behaved?. SLT tends to look at the data as an indication of the strength of teaching and learning in a department and possibly looking towards the future GCSE intake.

This takes us to the next question, what do we assess?

All of these questions should form the basis for our curriculum design. Are we still operating an activity-driven curriculum with football for 6 weeks at the beginning of September, assessing pupils' competency using some descriptors based on how they produce football skills? Do we only do this again the following year?

Are we sending messages, perhaps unintentionally, to our students through our actions?
- "Football is very important but only for 6 weeks of the year"
- "For those who are footballers and play six hours out of school, you're good and my lessons show that you are good"
- "For those of you who aren't footballers, don't worry because football isn't your sport. Thanks for the 6 weeks of trying."

This leads into the second question, how do we convert the physical competency in one activity into our school's chosen unit of reporting or assessment? This then creates a potential tick box to put people into categories and then probably some form of manipulated GCSE-type level descriptor to give a grade. Levels without saying it's levels. Then if we must report three times a year and we assess at the end of each activity-driven uni, the progress probably fluctuates. We then tell parents…"Well, they were working above in football, working below in dance and working at the right level in athletics where they had lessons in five different disciplines." This sends the message and probably tells pupils what they already know without taking part in PE, basically whether they are good at that activity or not. Then be ready to be told the same again next year. This type of assessment structure links back to Lee's story of the student whose self-belief in his dancing came from a report he received, this story is echoed in my experience by pupils who opt for other subjects for GCSE and then at the end of year 11 they are either an exceptional athlete or physical activity enthusiast and tell me they wish they'd taken a form of Exam PE but when they chose their options felt due to the assessed activities felt they were not capable.

CHAPTER 4: ASSESSMENT

There are multiple methods to assess curriculum impact and the teaching and learning that is taking place. With summative assessment we give students feedback on what they have learned at the end of a unit or year. Where does this go next and what is actually done with this, except to have a talking point at parents evening?

We are also very quick to forget a thing about children that is highly prevalent in the physical domain and cognitive domain and that is, they grow. They grow at different rates and different times. Lloyd and Oliver (2012) depict this in the Youth Development model where females typically enter their adolescent growth spurt at 10 whereas males do so at 12. Girls tend to grow quicker than boys; if we look at our summative assessment, do we have radical progression early, then plateaus or even regression as they get older, then vice versa for the males? Taking our yearly term one, '6 weeks of football' example, are we truly assessing what our students have learned in that time or are we simply assessing their growth rates? This lends itself well to Sullivan (2021) 'does this make PE meaningful to any of the stakeholders?' Teachers will take it as, 'look at the progress I supported these students to make'; pupils see it as 'I progressed year on year, then it simply stopped?' Parents, on the other hand, see a grade on a report and SLT sees the data with no real meaning behind it. As Head of Department do we use this data to inform curriculum changes or to help us answer the same issues about PE which usually include year 10 and 11 girls engagement, extracurricular numbers and pupils taking exam PE?

Efficient Assessment

Efficient assessment is a term I've used because as teachers we make a big noise about our time. So, if we are taking time to assess, record and report this data, then at least let's make that use of time more beneficial. The assessment should always return to the pupils, to help them understand where they are now, where do they want to be, and how do we help to get them there? Which for us represents itself in the form of curriculum design. In my role as a Trust Lead for PE, I have performed curriculum reviews of PE and experienced varied models from Head, Heart, Hands, to a concept-based curriculum, activity-driven curriculum or a physical literacy based curriculum. I usually find that the method of assessment is a real talking point and usually forms the basis for reporting or because the school requires some form of data. I also get the phrase "well that won't work here". I am a firm believer that if the process is good, the outcome will be good just like a maths equation - if you have the processes correct you are more than likely to get the right answer, or close to it. I say close to it because curriculum design is an evolving process that will never be perfect; we have found following this process enables us to build an effective use of assessment to shape our curriculum for our students.

Step 1: Decide what it is that pupils need to achieve the desired intent.
For example, if your intent is for every student to compete in a sport, then what skills do they need to do so? For us it is the pillars of physical literacy, Whitehead and Murdoch (2006), - pupils need knowledge and understanding so they can make choices and decisions. They need

a level of moderate competency to engage with physical activity at any level. Pupils need the motivation to take part in physical activity and the confidence to take part in physical activity.

Step 2: The data collection process.
How will you assess your students? it is essential that the department collaborate on this so they are on the same page to make it consistent. This links to step 1 as you are deciding how you assess those key areas. We created a matrix with a continuum scoring of 1 to 5 for each area of physical literacy with descriptors of what teachers may see or hear from students to indicate where they are on that continuum. This may slide throughout a unit of learning or across a lesson due to the transient nature of the areas such as confidence and motivation.

When will you assess? PE teachers are constantly assessing when in circulation or from Pastore's Perch (Lemov, 2012), we can see and hear where pupils are finding success and where they are not. Therefore, with a continuum system we can move the scale for students when we notice they are being challenged. We can look at their body language, effort, attitude, success rate in a task and listen to the words they are using. We can note this whether it is individuals or the class we assess, and make a decision to reteach or build the skills which are causing the barriers to learning. During our reflections we can note this down and then adjust our scores appropriately plus give feedback on the curriculum. This can lead to a discussion with the pupils or the class there and then or in our next lesson. Pupils are then involved and lessons become more meaningful knowing that their strife or success are being realised. Creating a safe environment to fail and a positive environment to thrive. Literally from the dread of failing in the physical domain to delighting in it. Of course, I consider that doing this for 30 students each lesson is a challenge but noticing that the class or an individual is struggling can improve our teaching.

Step 3- the most important: Make it efficient.
This step allows us to use the data to inform the pupils next steps, what we tell them, how we tell them and then what we aim to teach them next. For example a student who can tell you everything there is to know about a skill, understands when it should be implemented and when it needs to be manipulated then can't physically carry that out with a level of physical competency. If I look at my assessment I can give them huge positive feedback to say you're 5 out of 5 for these two areas so let's focus on the competency now and practise that. This tells me, as a teacher, that we need practice time. This can take a student from the dread of PE and feeling they cannot achieve to feeling that they have grasped aspects of PE and are yet to grasp others. The key word here when discussing with students is yet.

For a Head of Department I might look back through previous units of work to see where we have missed a skill which means that students can't access that activity. Then if this is a reoccurring issue then we can highlight that unit to make changes either before it or add a lesson in before. I like to highlight lessons within a scheme of learning then discuss them at PE

CHAPTER 4: **ASSESSMENT**

Department CPD meetings to reorganise the curriculum. If we can isolate areas which cause a barrier to pupils accessing that part of our curriculum then we can make adaptations.

Step 4: The 360.
Have a look at other data collected in relation to the department's aims such as the extra curricular activities, activities that are on the playground at lunchtime, pupils choosing exam pe and pupils attending clubs outside of school. This is a superb way to see if your curriculum is having an impact on the pupils and of course if it isn't. Both are good to know. If we are looking for extra curricular attendance or performances, is our rugby team made up of 15 players who attend the local rugby club and play four hours of rugby outside of school then if so what have we contributed to that and can we prove it. Seeing that four students did not play rugby before because they lacked confidence in tackling but after a lesson on grappling, falling and they have improved in confidence now chosen to go to rugby after school, that's a big tick for impact. When we perform pupil voice do they rate PE as meaningful, do they understand the assessment and how it leads into the bigger picture. If they say yes to the latter then it automatically increases the meaningfulness to those students which will motivate them to take part more whether regression or progression is needed.

Step 5: Be adaptable.
This is more of a culture than a step, whatever assessment takes place it needs to be acted upon. Not all at once but in incremental steps to ensure our students get the best experience of PE as we set them up for life. This may mean we need to teach activities which deviate from the norm, we may need to spend time looking at biomechanics, we need to spend time looking at psychology for students who perform at a level which exceeds our knowledge. A great way of building this culture of adaptability is using the PES Model (Cocks). What is the purpose of that lesson or unit of learning, what environment do we need to create to achieve that purpose and then the teaching strategies which allow us to get pupils within that environment to make steps towards the purpose. My favourite example of this is Javelin, the one lesson of Javelin a year which means four lessons at school from year 7-10. On reflection, it's throwing, can we sequence in more throwing opportunities across the year? Most definitely, then when we come to teaching throwing for distance using Javelin as the vehicle for learning the students have already thrown in a multitude of different ways but have the essential skills to throw further. For us, assessing their throwing becomes more important with the level of competence than if they can throw a javelin and make it stick in the ground.

Following this process will lead to a well sequenced curriculum which will support the intent. It will show where pupils have barriers to learning due to missing knowledge, skills or lack of time to practise those skills. If used correctly pupils are positively engaged in the process and enables them to know where they can go next. In our parents evening we discuss varying confidence levels, their pupil may be a formidable football player yet move them to gymnastic they lose their confidence or motivation and can we bridge the gap or ensure the pupils know how the two connect. We can inform our SLT about our pupils' motivation and confidence levels when they have a challenging task set out before them, how they are in the physical environment which is forever changing which causes pupils anxiety which can be discussed with the pastoral team. So can we use the assessment data collected to raise the profile of PE across the school.

CHAPTER 4: **ASSESSMENT**

Chapter 4 Summary

Assessment: from Dread to Delight

DREAD

Summative-Only Assessment: Students are evaluated with final grades without ongoing feedback or opportunities for improvement

No Student Ownership: Assessment used purely to provide a final 'grade', without any student reflection or opportunities to continue and develop learning further.

Demotivating Messaging: Assessment 'grading' in which students leave feeling negative about the activity or their progress in that activity.

DELIGHT

Formative to Inform Summative: Teachers use on-going formative assessment to gauge if learning has occurred and to effectively plan moving forward.

Students Own Learning: Students are able to effectively use assessment to understand progress made and how to progress further, with opportunities to do so.

Motivational Messaging: Assessment language is progressive and motivational, understanding that all students learn and develop at different rates and are therefore on their own learning journey in PE.

Where would you place yourself right now?

DREAD   **DELIGHT**

Reflection Questions
- What is the purpose of the assessment used in PE at my school?
- Does it effectively fulfil this purpose?
- How can formative assessment inform summative judgments?
- Why is it important to move away from numerical 'levels' for assessment in PE?
- What messages might the language used when assessing send to students?

Call to Action

As we conclude this chapter, it's time to reflect on what you've learned and consider how to apply it. The SHIFT mnemonic can guide you through the next steps: a structured approach to transform your insights into meaningful actions. Take a moment to work through the following questions:

S **Summarise** the key takeaway from this chapter that stands out to you.

H **Highlight** how this takeaway challenges or aligns with your current practices.

I **Initiate** a small change or step right now to put what you've learned into practice.

F **Frame** how this change will contribute to achieving your long-term vision for PE.

T **Take** others on the journey—share your new insights and encourage collaboration.

References

AIESEP (2020) AIESEP position statement on physical education assessment. Available at: https://aiesep.org/wp-content/uploads/2020/06/AIESEP-Position-Statement-on-PE-Assessment-FINAL1.pdf (Accessed: 16 March 2024).

Alfrey, L. and Gard, M. (2019) 'Figuring out the prevalence of fitness testing in physical education: A figurational analysis', European Physical Education Review, 25(1), pp. 187–202. https://doi.org/10.1177/1356336X17715361

Bailey, R., Armour, K., Kirk, D., Jess, M., Pickup, I., Sandford, R. and BERA Physical Education and Sport Pedagogy Special Interest Group (2009) 'The educational benefits claimed for physical education and school sport: an academic review', Research Papers in Education, 24(1), pp. 1–27. https://doi.org/10.1080/02671520701809817

Barbosa, A., Whiting, S., Simmonds, P., Scotini Moreno, R., Mendes, R. and Breda, J. (2020) 'Physical Activity and Academic Achievement: An Umbrella Review', International Journal of Environmental Research and Public Health, 17, 5972. https://doi.org/10.3390/ijerph17165972

Baumeister, R.F., Bratslavsky, E., Finkenauer, C. and Vohs, K.D. (2001) 'Bad is stronger than good', Review of General Psychology, 5(4), pp. 323–370. https://doi.org/10.1037/1089-2680.5.4.323

Boaler, J., Wiliam, D. and Brown, M. (2000) 'Experiences of ability grouping – disaffection, polarisation and the construction of failure', British Educational Research Journal, 28(5), pp. 631–648.

Bowler, M. and Sammon, P. (2020) 'Health-Based Physical Education – A framework for promoting active lifestyles in children and young people. Part 1: Introducing a new pedagogical model for Health-Based Physical Education', Physical Education Matters, 15(3), pp. 60–63.

Butler, C. (2022) PE kit petition at The Deepings School highlights pupils' anxiety over changing rooms. Available at: https://www.stamfordmercury.co.uk/news/school-s-pe-policy-leads-to-petition-9262623/ (Accessed: 4 July 2024).

CHAPTER 4: **ASSESSMENT**

Campbell, J. (2023) Using Teaching Personal and Social Responsibility (TPSR) as Pedagogy of Affect to Enact the Health and Well-being AOLE Through PE. PE Scholar. Available at: https://www.pescholar.com/insight/using-teaching-personal-and-social-responsibility-tpsr-as-pedagogy-of-affect-to-enact-the-health-and-well-being-aole-through-pe/ (Accessed: 20 December 2024).

Cardinal, B.J., Yan, Z. and Cardinal, M.K. (2013) 'Negative experiences in physical education and sport: How much do they affect physical activity participation later in life?', Journal of Physical Education, Recreation & Dance, 84(3), pp. 49–53. https://doi.org/10.1080/07303084.2013.767736

Casey, A. and Kirk, D. (2021) Models-based practice in physical education. Abingdon: Routledge.

Chiles, M. (2020) The CRAFT of Assessment: A whole school approach to assessment of learning. London: Hachette UK.

Chng, L.S. and Lund, J. (2018) 'Assessment for learning in physical education: The what, why and how', Journal of Physical Education, Recreation & Dance, 89(8), pp. 29–34.

Christodoulou, D. (2016) Making good progress? The future of assessment for learning. Oxford: Oxford University Press.

Cocks, P. (2024) Episode 29: Four Mantras for Teaching and Learning. PE Insights Podcast, PE Scholar. Available at: https://podcasts.apple.com/gb/podcast/pe-insights-pe-scholar-physical-education/id1710712630 (Accessed: 4 July 2024).

Davies, L. (2022) Physical Education & The Great Health Myth. PE Scholar. Available at: https://www.pescholar.com/insight/physical-education-the-great-health-myth/ (Accessed: 19 January 2024).

Department for Education (2014) National curriculum and assessment from September 2014: Information for schools. London: DfE.

Donarski, S. and Bennett, T. (2020) The ResearchEd guide to assessment: An evidence-informed guide for teachers. Woodbridge: John Catt.

Ekkekakis, P., Ladwig, M.A. and Vazou, S. (2018) My best memory is when I was done with it: PE memories are associated with adult sedentary behaviour. Available at: https://www.researchgate.net/publication/327118352_My_best_memory_is_when_I_was_done_with_it_PE_memories_are_associated_with_adult_sedentary_behavior (Accessed: 7 February 2024).

Fletcher, T., Ní Chróinín, D., Gleddie, D. and Beni, S. (2022) Meaningful physical education: An approach for teaching and learning. Abingdon: Routledge.

Frapwell, A. (2014) A practical guide to assessing without levels. 1st edn.

Gerdin, G. (2017) 'The "old gym" and the "boys' changing rooms": the performative and pleasurable spaces of boys' physical education', YOUNG, 25(4), pp. 36–53.

Harte, N.P.A., Alfrey, L., Spray, C.M. and Cale, L. (2023) 'The if, why and how of fitness testing in secondary school physical education in the United Kingdom', European Physical Education Review, 0(0). https://doi.org/10.1177/1356336X231219937

Harris, J. (2020) Health Position Paper. Association for Physical Education.

Ireson, J. and Hallam, S. (2001) Ability grouping in education. London: SAGE Publications.

Islam, M.A., Haji Mat Said, S.B., Umarlebbe, J.H., Sobhani, F.A. and Afrin, S. (2022) 'Conceptualization of head-heart-hands model for developing an effective 21st century teacher', Frontiers in Psychology, 13, p.968723.

Jess, M. et al. (2024) 'The purpose of primary physical education: The views of teacher educators', European Physical Education Review, 0(0). https://doi.org/10.1177/1356336X241237081

Lambert, K., Ford, A. and Jeanes, R. (2024) 'The association between physical education and academic achievement in other curriculum learning areas: A review of literature', Physical Education and Sport Pedagogy, 29(1), pp. 51–81. https://doi.org/10.1080/17408989.2022.2029385

Lemov, D. (2012) Teach Like a Champion 2.0: 62 techniques that put students on the path to college. San Francisco: Jossey-Bass.

Lloyd, R. and Oliver, J. (2014) Strength and conditioning for young athletes: Science and application. Abingdon: Routledge.

Mathe, P. (2022) Happiness Factories: A success-driven approach to holistic Physical Education. Woodbridge: John Catt.

McLennan, N. and Thompson, J. (2015) Quality physical education (QPE): Guidelines for policy makers. Paris: UNESCO Publishing.

Moen, K.M., Westlie, K. and Skille, E.Å. (2018) 'The changing room in physical education as cross roads between fields and curricula: The experiences of Norwegian students', SAGE Open, 8(4). https://doi.org/10.1177/2158244018818926

Myatt, M. and Tomsett, J. (2021) Huh: Curriculum conversations between subject and senior leaders. Woodbridge: John Catt Educational.

OECD (2005) Formative Assessment: Improving learning in secondary classrooms. Paris: OECD Publishing. https://doi.org/10.1787/9789264007413-en

Ofsted (2022) Research review series: PE. Available at: https://www.gov.uk/government/publications/research-review-series-pe/research-review-series-pe (Accessed: 21 August 2024).

Ofsted (2023) Subject report series: PE. (Accessed: 21 August 2024).

PE Scholar (2022) Concept Curriculum Launch Event. Available at: https://www.pescholar.com/insight/pe-concept-curriculum-2-0-launch-event/ (Accessed: 13 February 2025).

Rozin, P. and Royzman, E.B. (2001) 'Negativity bias, negativity dominance, and contagion', Personality and Social Psychology Review, 5(4), pp. 296–320. https://doi.org/10.1207/s15327957pspr0504_2

Ryan, R.M. and Deci, E.L. (2000) 'Self-determination theory and the facilitation of intrinsic motivation, social development, and well-being', American Psychologist, 55(1), pp. 68–78. https://doi.org/10.1037/0003-066X.55.1.68

Sammon, P. and Sullivan, L. (2023) Is it time to ditch changing during PE lessons? PE Scholar. Available at: https://www.pescholar.com/insight/is-it-time-to-ditch-changing-during-pe-lessons (Accessed: 4 July 2024).

Slavin, R.E. (1987) 'Ability grouping and student achievement in elementary schools: A best evidence synthesis', Review of Educational Research, 57(3), pp. 293–336.

Slavin, R.E. (1990) 'Achievement effects of ability grouping in secondary schools: A best evidence synthesis', Review of Educational Research, 60(3), pp. 471–490.

Sport England (2023) Physical Literacy Consensus Statement for England. (Accessed: 21 August 2024).

Sullivan, L. (2021) Is PE in Crisis?: Leading a Much-Needed Change in Physical Education. Scholary.

Welsh Government (2019a) Developing a vision for curriculum design. Available at: https://hwb.gov.wales/curriculum-for-wales/designing-your-curriculum/developing-a-vision-for-curriculum-design/#curriculum-design-and-the-four-purposes (Accessed: 20 December 2024).

Welsh Government (2019b) Health and Well-being: Statements of what matters. Available at: https://hwb.gov.wales/curriculum-for-wales/health-and-well-being/statements-of-what-matters (Accessed: 20 December 2024).

Whitehead, M. and Murdoch, E. (2006) 'Physical literacy and physical education: Conceptual mapping', Physical Education Matters, 1. Association for Physical Education.

Wiliam, D. (2011) Embedded formative assessment. Bloomington: Solution Tree Press.

Wiliam, D. (2013) 'Assessment: The bridge between teaching and learning', Voices from the Middle, 21(2), pp. 15–20.

Wiliam, D. (2014) Principled assessment design. London: SSAT (The Schools Network) Limited.

Chapter 5: Disengaged

Lee Sullivan, Justen O'Connor, Grace Cardiff and Neil Moggan

Part 5.1 – Insight
Lee Sullivan

The way in which people engage in physical activity is changing rapidly. PE leaders being deaf to feedback and blind to change could result in further disengagement and alienation from PE. Embracing this feedback and adapting our approaches accordingly could be the key to revitalising PE programmes, making them more inclusive, relevant, and impactful for all students. This chapter delves into what the changes in trends are and how we can better listen to our students to ensure our PE curriculum reflects these shifts in engagement.

Deaf to Feedback and Blind to Change

In the heyday of the 1990s, Blockbuster Video was the go-to destination for movie rentals, boasting thousands of stores worldwide. Families and movie enthusiasts alike flocked to its iconic blue-and-yellow outlets, arguing in the aisles, stacked with VHS tapes and later DVDs, on what movie they should rent that evening. Once decided, customers would head home, enjoy the movie, ensure the VHS was rewound ready for the next customer and head back to the store to return the rental. Blockbuster Video has become integrated into the fabric of family weekends at a time when movies were popular and households owned the more accessible VHS or DVD players.

As the 21st century dawned, the landscape of home entertainment underwent a seismic shift. While initially offering rentals by mail, the true game-changer came with the emergence of smart TV's and digital streaming services like Netflix, which fundamentally challenged the traditional rental model. These platforms provided consumers with unprecedented convenience, allowing them to access a vast library of movies and TV shows from the comfort of their own homes.

In a bold move, Netflix's CEO, Reed Hastings, approached Blockbuster with a proposal to join forces and adapt to the changing market. Netflix offered to sell itself to Blockbuster for $50 million, presenting an opportunity for Blockbuster to pivot towards the emerging digital streaming market. However, Blockbuster's leadership, entrenched in the success of their physical rental store model, failed to grasp the significance of the offer. They underestimated the potential of digital streaming, believing it to be a passing fad and doubting its profitability. Furthermore, Blockbuster was hesitant to embrace the subscription-based rental model that Netflix was pioneering, as it clashed with their existing revenue model based on late fees and individual rentals.

As consumer preferences shifted towards the convenience and accessibility of online streaming, Blockbuster remained blind to this fundamental change in the industry landscape. Despite growing dissatisfaction among customers with late fees and limited selection, Blockbuster failed to heed the voice of its patrons clamouring for a more convenient and affordable alternative. The customers' desire for movies remained constant; it was the mode of content consumption that underwent a significant shift. This disconnect between Blockbuster and its customers' evolving preferences would ultimately seal the company's fate, as it struggled to adapt to a rapidly changing market environment.

As Netflix soared in popularity, Blockbuster found itself lagging behind. The company's reluctance to embrace digital innovation and invest in online distribution platforms proved to be a fatal error. By the time Blockbuster attempted to catch up, it was already too late. Consumers had moved on, leaving Blockbuster's once-thriving empire in ruins.

Whilst there were numerous contributing factors, essentially, we can focus the cause of Blockbusters demise on the following two factors:

- Failure to listen to consumers
- Failure to adapt to shifting trends

If PE was a Business

The demise of Blockbuster Video serves as a cautionary tale for PE teachers navigating a rapidly evolving landscape. Just as Blockbuster failed to adapt to changing consumer preferences, PE programmes must remain agile and responsive to shifting trends. This means listening to our students. It means recognising and understanding the evolving motivations, attitudes, and preferences of students towards physical activity.

Young people have been articulating their discontent with physical education through numerous channels, including articles, research papers, and surveys, for quite some time. These expressions consistently highlight a fundamental issue: PE isn't resonating with many students. Instead of feeling empowered and motivated, they often experience feelings of disengagement, exclusion, humiliation, and a lack of confidence within PE settings. These sentiments are not isolated occurrences but widespread among various demographics of students.

Moreover, the repercussions extend beyond the classroom. Despite the government's daily activity targets, dropout rates from physical activity post-school years remain alarmingly

CHAPTER 5: **DISENGAGED**

high. Many young people are not meeting these targets, indicating a systemic failure in fostering a lasting enthusiasm for physical activity. This disconnect between the aspirations of policymakers and the realities experienced by young individuals underscores the urgent need for a comprehensive re-evaluation of current PE practices and a reimagining of how physical education can truly engage, empower, and inspire all students.

Often physical education classes are still solely focused on traditional sports and fitness activities. Though, today's students have diverse interests and expectations when it comes to physical activity. Some may be drawn to team sports like basketball or soccer, while others may prefer activities such as yoga, dance, or martial arts. Moreover, with the rise of technology and sedentary lifestyles, there is a growing need to incorporate innovative approaches to physical education that engage students and promote lifelong fitness habits.

To remain relevant, or more importantly to ensure we offer a meaningful and impactful PE offering that is valued by all, PE teachers must listen to the voices of their students and adapt their curriculum and teaching methodologies accordingly. We must be aware and accommodating of any shift in attitudes, barriers to participation, preferred methods of movement and the availability of movement opportunities locally. This means actively seeking feedback from students about their interests, preferences, and experiences with physical activity. By creating a supportive and inclusive environment where students feel empowered to voice their opinions and ideas, PE teachers can ensure that their programmes resonate with the needs and aspirations of today's youth. Like Blockbuster, failing to adapt risks rendering PE programmes irrelevant and meaningless in the eyes of students, undermining our ability to develop movement competence, build positive relationships with PE, physical activity and sport and ultimately get them active.

We should ask ourselves, if PE was a business, would we still be in business? This reflection prompts us to consider the adaptability and sustainability of our programmes in meeting the changing needs of our students and ensuring the long-term success of physical education initiatives. Are we really listening to the needs of our students? Are we considering the shifts in engagement, motivation and attitudes towards physical activity? Are we offering something that is relevant, meaningful and of value? How do we know?

Every year Sport England releases its data from its Active Lives Survey. In November 2022 their data showed that 47.2% of children and young people (3.4million) are meeting the Chief Medical Officers' guidelines of taking part in sport and physical activity for an average of 60 minutes or more every day. This number is back to pre-pandemic levels however it still highlights that over half of young people in England are not meeting this guideline.

The survey also found that only 47% of young people (ages 7-16) reported enjoying sport and physical activity, 35% felt confident when engaging and only 21% felt competent in sport and physical activity. Whilst there are complex issues that might be considered when unpicking this data, it still makes for difficult reading.

Part 5.2 – Delve
Lee Sullivan

Are we Listening?
For a considerable period, the PE curriculum has been predominantly shaped by teachers. While educators are expected to adhere to national curriculum objectives, the selection of activities and sports within PE lessons has often been influenced by individual teacher preferences and available resources. This approach has resulted in issues of disengagement, an overly sports-centric curriculum, and a lack of personal relevance in the learning experience. Some will engage in PE for the same reasons we did, though lots won't and we need to understand why.

According to Iannucci and Parker (2022), 'Student voice involves and empowers students to be collaborators and decision makers regarding their own educational experience.' Leveraging student voice to drive change in PE is a potent strategy. It helps bridge the gap between leadership vision and student experiences. By involving students in the dialogue and giving them a platform to express their views, we gain valuable insights into their needs, preferences, and aspirations. This knowledge serves as the cornerstone for shaping a PE programme that is relevant, enjoyable, and meaningful for our students.

Moreover, student voice serves as a catalyst for change within the team. It becomes challenging to disregard the collective voice of the students and persist with outdated practices that fail to resonate with them. Student feedback becomes a compelling call to action for the entire team, motivating them to reconsider their approaches, embrace innovation, and strive towards creating a PE programme that genuinely serves the students' interests.

In their 2022 JOPERD article entitled 'Beyond Lip Service: Making Student Voice a Meaningful Reality in Elementary Physical Education', Iannucci and Parker delve into the practical implementation of collecting and utilising student voice. They emphasise the importance of cultivating both students' ability to express themselves authentically and teachers' capacity to listen and respond to their voices effectively, while also fostering a safe learning environment where all children feel empowered to contribute actively.

In "Talking the Talk, Walking the Walk: Six Simple Strategies for Enacting Student Voice in Physical Education," Donal Howley (2022) addresses the implementation of student voice in high school PE settings. While student voice is often advocated for, Howley notes its ineffective practice at times. He stresses that student voice is a social and emotional process, requiring competencies in self-management, self-awareness, social awareness, relationship skills, and responsible decision-making from both teachers and students.

Howley presents six strategies to effectively implement student voice:

1. Full-Value Contract: Collaboratively create rules and expectations relevant to PE, fostering class ownership.
2. Personal Biographies and Timelines: Reflect on personal PE experiences through timelines, promoting self-awareness and social awareness.
3. Digital/Written Reflections: Allow students to reflect on learning experiences online, tailored to class content for engagement.
4. Taster Sessions: Provide varied activities for students to vote on preferences, making the PE curriculum relevant.
5. Cooperative Learning: Foster positive interdependence and interpersonal skills through group discussions.
6. Consultation and Negotiation Classes/Conferences: Allocate time for teachers and students to discuss and decide on the PE curriculum collectively.

These strategies aim to empower students, enhance engagement, and make the PE curriculum more meaningful and inclusive.

While not an exhaustive list, the image below illustrates some of the methods used to collect student voice, along with the limitations to consider when evaluating the information gathered.

Figure 13: Methods used to collect student voice

CHAPTER 5: **DISENGAGED**

Methods of Collecting Student Voice

	Method	Advantages	Limitations
V	Vote	Really quick form of student voice that can be done in lesson to provide students with autonomy and inform in-lesson decision making.	Inevitably, some students will vote against the consensus and have to go along with the majority. Some may vote depending on how peers vote.
O	Opinion Survey	A really effective method of gathering large numbers of opinions. MS Forms, Google Forms, etc. will provide clear results in a number of ways (graphs, percentages, etc.)	Completing the surveys is sometimes difficult, with limited access to devices. Practical time used. Providing anonymity can be difficult when using school systems.
I	Interview	Collecting the opinions of students by speaking to them in person is useful if you want more information or to delve deeper into an area of delivery by asking further questions	Students may be less likely to give you negative feedback if they are talking to you in person.
C	Council	Creating a student council provides opportunities for students with a passion for the subject to volunteer their time and provide constructive feedback in order to improve it.	Often the most engaged students will volunteer to be part of a sports council, therefore giving a biased opinion of PE and not-reflective of the whole student body.
E	Engagement Check	Also known as a pulse check. Can be used at key points throughout the year. Provides a brief update on selected areas of exploration so tweaks can be made immediately.	Ensuring students respond repeatedly to student voice opportunities and do not lose the value in providing their on-going feedback

Grace Cardiff's article, 'Just let them have a say!' Students' Perspective of Student Voice Pedagogies in Primary Physical Education,' underscores the significance of integrating student voice pedagogies in primary physical education to enrich the learning experience. Cardiff's study investigates how student involvement in decision-making and reflection can empower them to shape their PE lessons.

The article outlines several strategies employed to promote student voice in PE:
- **Sharing Learning Objectives and Lesson Outline:** Communicating learning objectives and lesson outlines at the outset of each lesson enables students to grasp the purpose of activities, fostering active participation.
- **Offering Choice:** Providing students with choices in warm-up/cool-down activities, equipment selection, and activity order and duration empowers them and cultivates their voices in the learning process.
- **Groupings:** Offering students the choice between student-selected or teacher-selected groups for games and activities enhances engagement and collaboration.
- Challenge Level: Initially presenting different challenge options for activities allows students to choose their preferred difficulty level, eventually progressing to co-creating challenge levels with the teacher, granting them autonomy over their learning experiences.
- **Personal Practice Time:** Allocating 5-10 minutes for personal practice time at the end of lessons enables students to work on specific skills of their choosing, reinforcing the relevance of PE activities.
- **Self-Designed Games:** Collaboratively designing games based on learned content in small groups encourages decision-making and effective communication.
- **Reflective Pedagogies:** Implementing reflective methods such as goal setting, in-class discussions, and post-lesson reflections through exit tickets and prompts provides students with a platform to express their thoughts and influence future lessons.

The research underscores the broader context of student voice in PE, highlighting how it can foster more meaningful experiences for students. Cardiff underscores the importance of creating a safe space for students to express their voices, illustrating how sharing curriculum objectives and engaging in reflective practices positively impacted learning experiences. Moreover, the article discusses the value of choice in PE activities and groupings, allowing students to collaborate with friends or select challenge levels.

Getting to know our students on a deeper level, beyond their demographic categories, helps us address their specific needs, demands, and priorities.

Using student voice to inform change requires openness and acceptance. Whilst the student voice might not always be easy to accept, accept it we must! The table below provides some examples of where we might look to use student voice to inform change.

Figure 14: ACCEPT Student Voice

CHAPTER 5: **DISENGAGED**

ACCEPT Student Voice to Inform our PE Delivery

A — Assessment
Student voice can be gathered to gain insights into how students experience assessment and what changes might be made to improve the process. Additionally, involving students in co-creating assessment tasks and rubrics can increase their engagement and ownership of their learning.

C — Curriculum
By gathering and using student voice, you can create a curriculum that is tailored to the unique needs and interests of your students, with the aim of increasing engagement. Find out the activities children enjoy most, engage with outside of school and would most like to see on the curriculum.

C — Class
Instead of setting by gender or ability, we can use student voice to inform how our classes are allocated. We can ascertain students attitudes towards physical activity and what motivates them (and demotivates them) when engaging. Classes can be set up to group children with like-minded individual who engage for similar reasons.

E — Engagement
Students are more likely to engage in learning when they can see the relevance of the content to their interests, goals and application to wider life. By gathers and using student voice, you can ensure that your curriculum is relevant to the current interests and needs of your students, which can improve their engagement and progress.

P — Pedagogy
Knowing what motivates our students to engage can also inform our pedagogical approach. Our most competitive students might engage well with the Sports Education model and those that find less relevance with the learning in PE might prefer a concept-driven approach.

T — Tasks
How children engage with the tasks and activities we set can be informed by student voice. Providing autonomy is a powerful tool for engagement. Giving students the options of adding their own rules, selecting various equipment, methods of travel, etc. enable student ownership of their learning.

In essence, seeking and accepting feedback from our students is essential for creating a student-centred learning environment where their voices are heard, valued, and respected. By prioritising student feedback, we can effectively tailor our teaching practices to meet the evolving needs of our students and foster a lasting appreciation for PE, physical activity, and sport.

Shift Happens

O'Connor and Penny (2020) identify the shift in physical activity engagement patterns by presenting the rise of informal sports and the decline of formalised sports. In this study, formal sports are defined as activities conducted within affiliated sports clubs, adhering to established sporting structures. Participants typically pay membership fees, commit to regular training sessions, and often engage in competitive leagues and tournaments. This aligns with the traditional model of PE, where structured lessons are often centred around teaching specific sports skills and rules within the framework of formal sports such as football, cricket, or netball.

Conversely, informal sports encompass activities that are less structured and formalised. These include recognisable traditional sporting forms like cricket, football, and basketball, where participation occurs informally without requiring membership fees or formal affiliations. Informal sports allow for greater flexibility, enabling individuals to participate on a drop-in basis. It can be characterised by its fluidity and diversity, accommodating various levels of competitiveness and individual preferences. For instance, informal cycling groups may range from competitive races to leisurely rides to coffee shops, showcasing the varied nature of participation.

In their 2021 research paper titled 'Informal sport and curriculum futures: An investigation of the knowledge, skills and understandings for participation and the possibilities for physical education' O'Connor and Penny noted that the rise of informal sports signifies a departure from the hyper-competitive, hierarchical, and patriarchal nature of traditional sports. These new forms of engagement respond to societal demands for greater freedom, social connection, and autonomy while challenging the constraints of conventional sports. Activities such as early morning cycling pelotons, park runs, open water swimming, and casual games in community facilities have become increasingly popular, reflecting a diverse range of interests and preferences among participants.

The decline in traditional club-based sports participation among young people is evident, driven by factors such as accessibility, changing interests, and limited resources. Alternative activities like fitness sports and outdoor pursuits are gaining popularity, particularly among younger generations. In the UK, there is a noticeable shift from traditional team sports to individualised lifestyle pursuits, reflecting changing preferences and priorities among participants. While formal sport participation remains popular in childhood, enjoyment and confidence decline as children age, highlighting the need for more inclusive and flexible participation opportunities.

In contrast to competitive sporting clubs, initiatives like parkrun prioritise community spirit and personal challenge, providing supportive opportunities for exercise on participants' own terms. Informal participation blends structure and flexibility to align with individual interests and resources, with physical education playing a crucial role in promoting and supporting these trends.

Additionally, the 2022 study by O'Connor and Penny distinguishes between lifestyle or leisure sporting forms, such as surfing, skateboarding, or parkour, and both formal and informal sports. These activities often emerged independently or in resistance to traditional sporting structures. While they may not be part of the typical PE curriculum, they represent alternative avenues for physical activity and recreation outside of formal sports settings.

Crafting the Classification Categories

Len Almond (1982), proposed a taxonomy of games that categorises them into four main types: invasion, net/wall, striking/run scoring, and target games. This classification system aimed to provide a framework for understanding and teaching different types of games effectively. By grouping games based on common primary rules, learners could better differentiate between game types, facilitating a deeper understanding of their mechanics and strategies. Additionally, this taxonomy assisted physical education teachers in diversifying their curriculum, offering a broader range of game experiences to students.

However, O'Connor, Alfrey and Penny (2022), call for a reconsideration of the current classification framework for games and sports in PE. They suggest that the traditional four-game classification system may no longer adequately represent the diverse range of sports and activities that appeal to young people today. Instead, the authors propose an extended classification system that includes route, rush, action, and rhythmic sports, reflecting contemporary preferences and trends in participation. The authors hope that this reconfiguration will stimulate further research, planning, and advocacy in PE, focusing on sports and participation forms that are relevant and accessible to young people within their communities.

This leads us back to our original question: are we considering the shifts in engagement, motivation and attitudes towards physical activity? It seems that our curriculum has focused on formal sports, however the research now shows that numbers participating in such activities is in decline. Therefore, we must stop and consider if our curriculum is now updated and not true representative of how our students will likely wish to engage in physical activity beyond our PE lessons. If we fail to listen and act now, we might end, like Blockbuster, going out of business.

FROM PE DREA**D** TO DELIGHT

The PE curriculum should be driven by the learning needs of young people, rather than the preferences of adults delivering it.

Part 5.3 – Experts

Informal Sport and Physical Education: Widening understandings of sport participation for a contemporary physical education
Dr Justen O'Connor

People are finding an increasingly diverse range of ways to be physically active. As societal trends continue to shift towards more flexible, inclusive, and participant-centred sporting and movement experiences, there is a need to rethink how physical education can better reflect these changes and support young people to negotiate ever changing notions of sport. In this chapter I draw on a body of research conducted within informal sport settings to challenge rigid understandings of sport and its relationship with physical education. Undoubtedly sport will continue to remain a key focus for physical educators, but I argue for a greater focus to be placed on the negotiation of the sporting experience to tap into more contemporary and informal sporting cultures. Rather than looking to reproduce structured and highly competitive sporting formats, albeit in modified ways, physical education could benefit from an understanding of sport that is more open to participant negotiation of their sporting experience. The chapter will outline societal trends, what informal sport is and what this might mean for student learning in PE.

The role of physical education (PE) in schools has long been influenced by an emphasis on the transferable skills, tactics and knowledge geared towards preparing young people for a lifetime of formal sport (Berkshire et al., 2024; Kirk, 2010). Kirk (2010) points out that "if skills form the basis of participation in games and sports, then transfer of learning will be from the skills learned in school to participation in sport..." (p. 107). Models of physical education, such as Siedentop's (2002) Sport Education, and games-based models are designed to reproduce the formal structures of sport, albeit in modified and developmentally appropriate ways. These models are often implemented based on the idea that through teaching transferable administrative roles, tactical understandings, and prerequisite skills of particular sports or indeed sporting forms (i.e., territory, net-wall, striking fielding, target), that young people will attach themselves to one or more of these sports and play throughout adulthood.

Physical education has been conceived in this light as the foundation piece of a structural pyramid geared towards getting more children into club-based competitive sport (Berkshire et al., 2024; Kirk & Gorely, 2000; Ward, 2014). Yet what we know about lifelong participation is that most people are not that interested in formal competitive sport. In Australia, only 47% of children aged 0-14 years (Ausplay, 2023) and less than 10% of adults (Eime et al., 2019) participate in competitive club-based sport. Only 12% of Europeans engage with sport through a sporting club (Rask et al., 2024). The most popular physical activities remain those with less structure, less overall commitment, and a lower focus on outright ability.

Children are being exposed to club-based sporting models as young as 5 or 6 years of age in often appropriately modified sporting formats. From 10-12 years they transition into structured competitive sport models where they begin to receive quite clear signals about who belongs and what kind of commitment is needed to sustain this belonging (umpires, training, away games, team selection, bench time, league tables, MVP awards). As young people gain the autonomy to influence choices around their leisure-time options, they start voting with their feet. Within Australia participation in club-based sport halves from the 10–14-year age group (46%) to the 15–19-year age group, and halves again to 12% in the 20-24 year age group (Eime et al., 2019). According to Eime, Harvey, et al. (2023) nearly half of sport club participants aged 4–29 years drop out of Australian club-based sport participation within 2 years of starting. Tracked sports in the US also appear to be losing 40% to 50% of participants annually (Aspen Institute, 2023). In Europe, 16 out of 18 sports experience a decrease in participation from U14-U16, with females being four times less likely to participate in organised sport across all age categories and across most sports (Emmonds et al., 2024). Despite the relatively large numbers of young participants sampling formal club-based sport, there remains little evidence that physical education programs play a key role in this and even less evidence that lifelong participation in sport occurs as a consequence of physical education programs (Kirk, 2010). A physical education that dedicates itself towards taking advantage of an opponent in structured competition is likely a misuse valuable resources.

Societal Sporting Trends

Sport is continually evolving. What sport is, gets determined by what society at large says it is and so sport is based on prototypical models. We can look to the pinnacle of sporting competition, the Olympics, to see prototypical sports like the 100m sprint, the Javelin or water polo. We can see that these activities have a level of physicality and skill, that they have a set of sanctioned rules that place limitations on what is possible (and create obstacles to be overcome), there is an agreement for engaging in some sort of contest or ranking to determine a winner. Based upon these prototypes of sport, we might rule out going for a jog, skating in the park or surfing as a sport based upon the lack of agreement for a competition with a clear set of rules. But importantly, we can also modify almost any physical activity and turn it into an Olympic sport through codification of rules and the establishment of criteria for determining a winner. Phrases like lifestyle sport, alternative sport and informal sport, suggest that there is real sport and then there are other things that sit somewhere outside of that. The rise of skateboarding, surfing, sport climbing and break dancing as Olympic sports highlights a reality where the boundaries around sport are in reality quite blurry.

If we considered prototypically what the wider population is doing in the name of sport, then the priority for sport would likely not sit with a narrow focus on club-based scheduled competition with all its structures and sanctioned rules. Indeed, the overwhelming sport participation base engages in more diverse forms of sport that tend to deprioritise the need to clearly rank and compare (scheduled, fixtured, umpired, selected, uniformed). Especially amongst the younger demographic, with participation fuelled by the expansive reach of social media (Cameron et al., 2022), the growing appeal of more fluid, yet often physically demanding sporting forms is becoming quite obvious. These sporting forms leave significant space for features like self-expression, identity formation and aesthetics to exist that can drive belonging alongside any priority for competition (higher, faster, longer, more technical).

In a previous paper colleagues and I pointed out that within Australia, 68% of the top 50 participation 'sports' did not sit within the dominant four-game form classification frame and three of these game forms (net/wall, target, striking, fielding) were represented by just 6 of the top 50 participation 'sports' (O'Connor et al., 2024). Observing suburban sporting fields in Australia, we found almost as many informal sport participants playing team-based sports as formal ones and we did not count the huge numbers of swimmers, runners and cyclists (Jeanes et al., 2024). A key factor in emerging prototypes of sport participation is the capacity of the individual to negotiate their experience.

What is informal sport

Competitors at the Olympics tend to make very few decisions about their experience. What they wear, what time they participate, who they participate against, when they train, how long they participate for and even what they eat gets heavily regulated externally. As with community sporting competitions, a lot of this externally determined governance structure is present to determine a clear winner within a standardised contest (fixtures, age groups, ability groups, rules, umpires, uniforms, official equipment). Yet for most people, this is far from their sporting reality. In moving us away from a binary formal/informal sport divide, Miyashita et al. (2024) challenges us to consider sport in a way that is more sensitive to the "relations among actors and their practices that co-construct the governing processes of sport participation" (p. 5). That is, sport should be understood through considering the negotiations taking place that mobilise resources and establish how the activity is governed (Miyashita et al., 2024). When we define informal sport, we make sure to define it first and foremost as sport and not something that sits in contrast to it. We can then consider the negotiations that take place to establish the terms of the experience. In this case who is making the decisions, tells us something about the level of informality. We define informal sport as:

> *Sport, whereby the experience (including any rules and goals for comparison and competition) is more readily negotiated by the participants, alongside other forms of achievement or expression.*

This definition challenges artificial organised/unorganised, formal/informal binaries that likely only exist in extremes, if at all. We are interested in the negotiation of features of the experience that shape what a particular version of sport is for the particular people playing it. The closer the individual participant is to negotiating most of the parameters of their experience, the more informal the sport is likely to be (modifying the rules, picking teams on the day, turning up if you can, wearing something practical, playing hard or taking it easy). When key decisions are negotiated by committees, bodies, federations, clubs or coaches on behalf of participants, the sport is likely more formal (adopted fixed rules, fixtured schedule of training and competition, umpired decisions, committee sanctions, team selection, positional play, overt focus on competition and ranking, expectations to attend, official equipment). Depending upon what gets negotiated, informal sport can still be a highly competitive, highly complex endeavour or it can be a much more relaxed affair where competition is barely noticeable. Importantly, negotiations in more informal sport are not devoid of power structures, hierarchies and norms, but these tend to emerge more fluidly from within the group as opposed to forming in and around existing hierarchies.

All forms of sport can be exclusionary. Negotiating the sporting experience primarily from within the participant group will always have a complex mix of positive and negative implications amidst different power structures. Without the formal and historical governance structures of the sporting club, access to suitable facilities and equipment can be quite a challenge (Jeanes et al., 2022; O'Connor & Brown, 2010). There might be a lack of policies or insurances potentially leaving participants vulnerable. Groups often form and are sustained (or fade away) on the whims of those who exert leadership and therefore power from within (O'Connor & Brown, 2007). It can be hard to locate informal sporting groups and to infiltrate what looks like an established sporting culture with insider knowledge. They can also be easier to access than formal sporting clubs (Jeanes et al., 2019). More informal sport tends to be either free or low cost, flexible and adaptable and consequently better positioned to suit diverse individual and collective needs. Informal sport is not contained by seasons, is not necessarily predicated on ability and participants can often seek out periodic 'events' that enable them to test themselves in more formal competition without long-term commitment. The potential for individual agency (still within existing power structures) means the terms of the experience might be more readily negotiable instead of historically and hierarchically imposed.

Implications for Physical Education

Through understanding informal sport as a spectrum of negotiated practices and decision making, we can better target a curriculum, pedagogy and assessment that supports young people and their potential to negotiate an informal sporting future, perhaps as practitioners focused on winning, but more likely as participants (those for whom any competition is just one part of the experience). When physical education has as its focus more formal structured forms of competitive sport, it tends to ignore much of the knowledge, skills and understandings required to negotiate the kinds of sporting experiences most people will have access to across their lifespan. It prioritises tactical knowledge needed to advance a ball down the field (or defend it from doing so), it prioritises technical ability to execute a passing shot into open space, and it focuses on knowledge tied to primary and secondary rules (O'Connor et al., 2024). In the case of Sport Education, it might loop in additional knowledge and understandings associated with being on a committee, being a coach, reinforcing particular rules, establishing a fair draw, and updating the league table or ladder, but this tends to mirror the hierarchical decision found in more formal sport.

Our work on informal sport participation suggests an informal sport education requires a much greater emphasis on the spectrum of negotiations needed to engage fully in a sporting experience. Negotiating the places we are in, the facilities and equipment we have access to, the range of abilities we have amongst the group, the balance of individual needs (i.e. level of competition, if at all) and how competitive we want to be are key features of the experience. Informal sport participants must negotiate the rules that matter, the kind of conduct they are willing to put up with and the type of sporting culture they want to propagate. All this needs to happen before worrying about any tactics or skills. How decisions get made by whom in the absence of structural hierarchies requires particular knowledge and skills often overlooked when the focus is on more formal sport (O'Connor & Penney, 2021).

The level of and focus on competition is one of the key features open to negotiation in an informal sport education producing quite different versions of what might be considered the same 'sport'. Informal sport has capacity to accommodate a much wider range of abilities, particularly when participants learn how to subjugate their own optimal experience of sport in exchange for the benefits that come with a sustained and shared group experience.

Informality invites the question 'what will you be willing to give up, so that you can share in this experience together?'. Rather than reaching the top of the ladder, the measure of success is the sustainability of the sporting experience. Many informal sporting groups come and go because of a failing individually and collectively to negotiate an adequate response to this question.

Informal sport approaches in physical education

Word limits here prevent me from providing any elaborate outline for enacting this in physical education. I conclude by saying an informal sport physical education can exist through the adoption and adaptation of a range of existing models or approaches. First I would ask teachers and students to collectively consider a more expansive notion of sport, beyond the 4 game classification framework that seems to have been in operation for some time (see O'Connor et al., 2024). Try not to limit your thinking about what sport is and isn't, instead, teachers and students should consider what is accessible, relevant and negotiable in this context for these students.

An informal sport education also adopts principles of Meaningful Physical Education, particularly through an emphasis on student negotiation of experience (Beni et al., 2017; Fletcher et al., 2021). I can imagine a scenario where three different versions of the same sport are happening in a physical education class, one more formally structured and competitive, one more informal and relaxed and something in between, as negotiated by students.

Teachers can certainly draw on (Quay & Peters, 2012) Creative Physical Education framework which involves students working in small teams to decide the parameters of their sport, trialling their version and testing viable models with the class. Like parkrun, those who build in levels of flexibility will be more likely to sustain the interest of a reasonable portion of the class, allowing individuals to negotiate the experience at their level of need. Finally, the obvious model would be an adaptation of Siedentop's SEPEP model (Siedentop, 2002) where the rigid and hierarchical structures of committees, coaches, umpires, fixtures, ladders and fixed teams get stripped out and replaced with a framework that supports greater participant negotiation at the local level (see O'Connor and Penney, in press).

Conclusion

This chapter has explored the evolving landscape of physical activity, particularly focusing on the growing popularity of greater informality in sports. This is not a discrete category of sport, but rather describes a form of participation where some or all the decisions about playing get negotiated from within the participant group itself, as opposed to being imposed externally. This participant-driven format has the potential to offer young people greater diversity in the ways they might learn about and ultimately engage in sport and draws attention to the myriad of decisions that need to be negotiated when formal club structures are not available. A physical education that reflects informal sport participation through fostering an environment that allows students to negotiate key elements of their sporting experience, can help to unlock contemporary sporting cultures, promote inclusivity and flexibility, and support lifelong participation in physical activity.

Part 5.4 – Apply

Student Voice
Grace Cardiff

The Importance of Student Voice
Children like having a say in their educational experiences. Extensive research on student voice in PE has demonstrated several benefits of the approach, including (a) increased student engagement and participation, (b) stronger relationships between students and teachers, and (c) more meaningful and personally relevant experiences in PE. What's not to like?

Enacting student voice, however, is not as simple as occasionally asking for children's input or handing out an end-of-term feedback survey. For student voice to reach its full potential, many researchers argue that traditional classroom power dynamics need to shift. Student voice requires a collaborative approach to teaching and learning, where power is shared, and teachers and students work together as partners in shaping their educational experiences. In this sense, students need to be actively involved in day-to-day decision-making in the classroom, rather than being consulted as a one-off event. That said, teachers face numerous challenges when trying to incorporate student voice into their daily practice. With limited time and an extensive curriculum to cover, how can this approach be effectively integrated into teaching and learning in PE?

Insights from my Research: Exploring Student Voice in Primary PE
As a primary school teacher responsible for teaching all subjects, I often found teaching PE challenging. I lacked confidence in certain topics, such as dance, and often left my planning until the last minute, prioritising other curricular areas first. Additionally, when I transitioned from teaching early primary to the upper year groups, student engagement in PE became a concern. I struggled with how to make PE inclusive and meaningful for all children in my class. This prompted me to re-evaluate my approach and consider the value of incorporating my students' voices into the teaching and learning process in PE.

In learning to enact student voice in my PE practice, I was guided by the democratic and reflective pedagogical principles of Meaningful PE (Fletcher & Ní Chróinín, 2022) and Lundy's (2007) model of participation. I also drew on research from Iannucci and Parker (2022a, 200b) and Howley and colleagues (2021). I started by creating opportunities for students to express their opinions and share their input at the beginning, during, and after PE lessons. I began each lesson by sharing the learning objectives and a lesson outline with the children and inviting them to make suggestions or offer alternatives to the activities planned. During the lessons, I made a conscious effort to pause and ask for student input, using brief 60-second check-ins during activities. I would ask questions like, "Is this rule working?" "Is the task too easy? How could we make it more challenging?" or "Is your group working well together?" These short pauses encouraged the children to reflect on their experiences and actively shape the lesson, rather than being passive participants in PE. Pausing to reflect also allowed me to gather feedback and enact immediate change to my practice if something wasn't working. For example, during a gymnastics lesson in which I had different stations set up to practice balancing and jumping, the children told me that one station was "a bit boring." As a result, I changed the station in the moment, making it more challenging and distinct from the others. Reflecting with the children at the end of PE lessons also supported them in evaluating the decisions they made during the lesson, and helped us to plan for future lessons.

While reflecting with the children and giving them opportunities to share their views was important, I also wanted to involve students in decision-making during PE lessons. I began by offering simple, closed-choice options, such as:

- **Warm-ups:** "Which warm-up activity would you like to do today? Here are three options to choose from."
- **Groupings:** "Would you prefer to choose your partner for this activity, or would you like me to choose?"
- **Challenge level:** "Here are three ways to complete this skill development task. Choose the level of challenge you're most comfortable with."

Offering the children simple choices in lessons allowed them to develop their confidence in decision-making and helped them to realise the role they played in shaping their PE experiences.

Gradually, as I became more comfortable relinquishing control in lessons and as the children gained confidence in making decisions, I began to facilitate more open-ended decision-making opportunities. The children began to suggest activities for lessons, modify tasks, and adjust the challenge level of activities without prompting. I also introduced "personal practice time", during which the children could choose a skill to practice themselves, within the content area being covered. As we came towards the end of topics/units of work, I provided time for the children to create their own games. They were responsible for designing an activity or game that would review the skills we had been learning. The children took this responsibility seriously, often creating games that became class favourites.

My research illustrated that children value having choices, feeling heard, and being able to direct their learning experiences in PE. While my approach to teaching PE evolved significantly over the course of the research, the content and objectives of my lessons remained largely the

CHAPTER 5: DISENGAGED

same. What changed was how the students were empowered to shape and adapt the lessons to meet their needs and preferences.

Key Considerations for Enacting Student Voice

While the strategies I used in my practice were effective, they are by no means exhaustive. Different approaches may work better for different teachers, so it's essential to find an approach that fits with your practice, rather than trying to fit the strategies to your practice.

In adopting a student voice approach, it's helpful to start small and aim for an "easy win" (Ní Chróinín et al., 2024). For instance, begin by offering simple choices in PE, such as varying the level of challenge of a skill development activity or allowing students to choose who they work with. Starting small enables teachers to gradually become more comfortable with relinquishing control and deviating from lesson plans. It also helps scaffold students' ability to make decisions in PE, particularly for those who may not have had these opportunities before.

In addition, the importance of reflection in PE should not be overlooked. Regularly pausing to reflect with students provides an opportunity for teachers to listen to students' voices, while helping students make sense of their PE experiences. Reflection also enhances students' participation in decision-making by helping them to realise how their choices impact both their own and others' experiences. Ultimately, reflecting with students strengthens their ability to shape their PE experiences and goes hand in hand with student voice.

Trauma Informed Practice
Neil Moggan

The Importance of Trauma-Informed Practice in Physical Education

In recent years, the conversation around trauma and its impact on students has gained significant traction. As educators, it is crucial to understand and integrate trauma-informed practices to foster an inclusive and supportive learning environment.

Why is it so important for PE teachers to be trauma informed?

Physical Education offers a unique environment where the dynamics of physical activity, personal interaction, and emotional vulnerability intersect. For many students, PE can be a source of joy and a vehicle for positive self-expression.

However, for those who have experienced trauma, this setting can trigger anxiety, fear, and disengagement. Understanding the nature of trauma and its pervasive effects on a student's behaviour and learning capacity is vital for several reasons:

- **Creating a Safe Space:** PE classes often involve activities that require close physical proximity, competition, and exposure to potential failure or embarrassment. For trauma-affected students, these situations can be particularly daunting. We need to create an environment where students feel physically and emotionally safe.
- **Developing State Regulation and a Sense of Belonging:** PE can be used to help regulate young people's state and their sense of belonging. For trauma-affected students these can be areas that they particularly struggle with which has knock on effects across the rest of their school life and beyond. We have a golden opportunity that few other teachers have.
- **Building Trust and Relationships:** Trust is a fundamental aspect of any educational relationship. Trauma can severely impact a student's ability to trust others, including teachers. Being trauma-informed helps us approach students with empathy, patience, and consistency, which are crucial for building trust.
- **Promoting Inclusive Participation:** Trauma can manifest in various ways, including withdrawal, aggression, or avoidance of activities. PE teachers who are trauma-informed can recognise these signs and adapt our teaching strategies to ensure all students can participate meaningfully.

How might trauma impact engagement in PE?

Trauma can have profound and varied effects on a student's engagement in PE. These impacts can be both direct and indirect, influencing physical, emotional, and social aspects of participation.

- **Physical Impact:** Students who have experienced trauma may exhibit heightened stress responses, including increased heart rate and muscle tension. These physiological reactions can make physical activity uncomfortable or overwhelming, leading to avoidance or minimal participation.
- **Emotional Impact:** Trauma often leads to emotional dysregulation, where students may struggle with intense emotions such as fear, anger, or sadness. In the context of PE, these emotions can be triggered by competitive activities, fear of failure, or negative body image, resulting in disengagement.
- **Cognitive Impact:** Trauma can affect cognitive functions, including concentration, memory, and executive functioning. Students may find it challenging to follow instructions, remember rules, or stay focused during activities, which can hinder their engagement and performance in PE.
- **Behavioural Impact:** Trauma-affected students might display a range of behaviours such as withdrawal, aggression, or defiance. These behaviours are often misunderstood as laziness or disobedience but are, in fact, coping mechanisms. Understanding these behaviours in the context of trauma is crucial for PE teachers to respond appropriately.

What can we consider to support all students?
Implementing trauma-informed practices in PE requires a deliberate and thoughtful approach. Here are several strategies that we can consider to support all students:

- **Building Strong Relationships:** Foster positive relationships by showing genuine interest and care for each student. Consistent and supportive interactions can help build trust and make our students feel valued and understood. Psychological safety cues such as smiley faces, open body language, active listening and attuned voices are key to this.
- **Creating Predictable Routines:** Establish clear and consistent routines to provide a sense of stability and predictability. Students who have experienced trauma often find comfort in knowing what to expect.
- **Providing Choices and Autonomy:** Allowing students to make choices about their participation can empower them and reduce feelings of helplessness. Offer alternative activities or modify tasks to accommodate different comfort levels and abilities.
- **Mindfulness and Relaxation Techniques:** Integrate mindfulness and relaxation exercises into the PE curriculum. These practices can help students manage stress, improve emotional regulation, and enhance overall well-being. This worked surprisingly well with my Year 8 sporty boys.
- **Professional Development and Training:** Ongoing training in trauma-informed care is essential. We should seek professional development opportunities to understand trauma's effects and learn effective strategies to support affected students.

Integrating Emotional Regulation and a Sense of Belonging: The RISE Approach
We have a unique opportunity to use movement to develop emotional regulation and a sense of belonging among students. This advantage arises from the curriculum time, facilities, and equipment available to PE classes, which other subjects frequently lack.

- **Repeaters:** Repetitive activities such as running, walking, or yoga offer physical benefits and serve as avenues for regulating the nervous system and reducing stress. These activities calm the amygdala, widen the window of tolerance, and help students access their prefrontal cortex, enabling better thinking and learning.
- **Inclusive Teams:** Team sports provide opportunities for social connection and a sense of belonging. As students work together to achieve common goals, they experience the release of oxytocin, fostering feelings of camaraderie and support.
- **Stress Busters:** Many students grapple with pent-up emotions and frustrations. Stress-busting activities like boxing, weight training, contact rugby, or yoga offer outlets for

releasing tension in a safe and controlled way. These activities calm the amygdala, widen the window of tolerance, and help students access their prefrontal cortex, enhancing their ability to think clearly and learn.
- **Energisers:** High-energy activities such as circuit training, skipping or dance invigorate the body and trigger the release of neurotransmitters like dopamine and serotonin, promoting feelings of happiness and motivation. Energisers help students reconnect with the world around them.

The RISE approach provides a wide range of activities that you are already delivering in schools. This allows students to choose activities that excite and engage them, fostering a sense of agency and enthusiasm.

I Invite You To Reflect On These Questions:
- Understanding Trauma: How well do I understand trauma and their potential impacts on my students?
- Creating Safe Spaces: What psychological safety cues do I currently use to make my PE classes feel safe and welcoming for all students?
- Using Movement: Do I teach how movement can help my young people regulate themselves and feel a sense of belonging?
- Professional Development: Would I benefit from additional training to integrate Trauma Informed PE into my practice to support my young people?

Conclusion
The role of PE teachers extends beyond teaching physical skills; it encompasses nurturing the holistic development of students.

By adopting trauma-informed practices, we can create a more inclusive and supportive environment that acknowledges the diverse needs of all students.
As we navigate the complexities of contemporary education, being trauma-informed is not just beneficial but essential in transforming PE from a source of dread to one of delight.

Chapter 5 Summary

Disengaged: from Dread to Delight

DREAD

Stubborn to Change:
Doing things as they have always been done and not considering an alternative.

Not Listening:
Never asking the students about their thoughts on the PE delivery, their likes or dislikes about PE, Sport or physical activity and failing to consider their motivations for engaging.

Blind to the Shift:
Not embracing the emerging and more prominent methods of engaging in physical activity beyond formal sport.

DELIGHT

Open to Change:
Considering other approaches in the understanding that there might be other and more effective methods of PE delivery.

Incorporate Student Voice:
Taking the time to collect student feedback through various means and acting on their responses.

Adaptive Curriculum:
Considering how students and adults are engaging in physical activity beyond the school gates and adapting the curriculum to reflect these shifts.

Where would you place yourself right now?

DREAD   **DELIGHT**

Reflection Questions
- Am I truly listening to student feedback and integrating it into decision-making?
- Does my PE curriculum resonate with students' diverse interests and needs?
- How can I empower students to shape their PE experiences?
- Does my PE curriculum need to reflect the shift towards informal and lifestyle sports?

Call to Action

As we conclude this chapter, it's time to reflect on what you've learned and consider how to apply it. The SHIFT mnemonic can guide you through the next steps: a structured approach to transform your insights into meaningful actions. Take a moment to work through the following questions:

S   **Summarise** the key takeaway from this chapter that stands out to you.

H   **Highlight** how this takeaway challenges or aligns with your current practices.

I   **Initiate** a small change or step right now to put what you've learned into practice.

F   **Frame** how this change will contribute to achieving your long-term vision for PE.

T   **Take** others on the journey—share your new insights and encourage collaboration.

References:

Alfrey, L. & Gard, M., 2019. Figuring out the prevalence of fitness testing in physical education: A figurational analysis. European Physical Education Review, 25(1), pp.187–202. https://doi.org/10.1177/1356336X17715361

Almond, L., 1982. Changing the focus. British Journal of Physical Education.

AIESEP, 2020. AIESEP position statement on physical education assessment. [online] Available at: https://aiesep.org/wp-content/uploads/2020/06/AIESEP-Position-Statement-on-PE-Assessment-FINAL1.pdf [Accessed 16 March 2024].

AusPlay Data Portal, 2024. Australian Sports Commission. [online] Available at: https://www.clearinghouseforsport.gov.au/participation-in-sport [Accessed 25 Sept 2024].

Beni, S., Fletcher, T. & Ní Chróinín, D., 2017. Meaningful Experiences in Physical Education and Youth Sport: A Review of the Literature. Quest, 69(3), pp.291–312. https://doi.org/10.1080/00336297.2016.1224192

Berkshire, M., Mason, J. & Hardwicke, J., 2024. The continuity of PE-as-sport: Exploring secondary school students' accounts of the meaning and purpose of physical education in England. European Physical Education Review, p.1356336X241256866. https://doi.org/10.1177/1356336X241256866

Cameron, A., Bratanova, A., May, C., Reynolds, G., Burgin, N., Menaspà, P. & Burns, S., 2022. The Future of Australian Sport. The second report: Megatrends shaping the sport sector over coming decades. CSIRO. https://www.clearinghouseforsport.gov.au/__data/assets/pdf_file/0020/1082333/The-Future-of-Australian-Sport-Second-Megatrends-Full-Report.pdf

Cardiff, G., Ní Chróinín, D., Bowles, R., Fletcher, T. & Beni, S., 2023. 'Just let them have a say!' Students' perspective of student voice pedagogies in primary physical education. Irish Educational Studies, 42(4), pp.659–676. https://doi.org/10.1080/03323315.2023.2255987

Chiles, M., 2020. The CRAFT Of Assessment: A whole school approach to assessment of learning. Hachette UK.

Chng, L.S. & Lund, J., 2018. Assessment for learning in physical education: The what, why and how. Journal of Physical Education, Recreation & Dance, 89(8), pp.29–34.

Christodoulou, D., 2016. Making good progress? The future of assessment for learning. Oxford University Press.

Casey, A. & Kirk, D., 2021. Models-based practice in physical education. Abingdon: Routledge.

Department for Education, 2014. National curriculum and assessment from September 2014: information for schools.

Donarski, S. & Bennett, T., 2020. The ResearchEd guide to assessment: An evidence-informed guide for teachers. John Catt.

Eime, R.M., Harvey, J.T. & Charity, M.J., 2019. Sport drop-out during adolescence: is it real, or an artefact of sampling behaviour? International Journal of Sport Policy and Politics, 11(4), pp.715–726. https://doi.org/10.1080/19406940.2019.1630468

Emmonds, S., Till, K., Weaving, D., Burton, A. & Lara-Bercial, S., 2024. Youth Sport Participation Trends Across Europe: Implications for Policy and Practice. Research Quarterly for Exercise and Sport, 95(1), pp.69–80. https://doi.org/10.1080/02701367.2022.2148623

Fletcher, T., Ní Chróinín, D., Gleddie, D. & Beni, S., 2021. The why, what, and how of Meaningful Physical Education. In: Meaningful Physical Education: An Approach for Teaching and Learning. 1st ed. Routledge. https://doi.org/10.4324/9781003035091

Frapwell, A., 2014. A practical guide to assessing without levels. 1st ed.

Harte, N.P.A., Alfrey, L., Spray, C.M. & Cale, L., 2023. The if, why and how of fitness testing in secondary school physical education in the United Kingdom. European Physical Education Review. https://doi.org/10.1177/1356336X231219937

Howley, D., 2022. Talking the talk, walking the walk: Six simple strategies for enacting student voice in physical education. Strategies, 35(6), pp.38–40. https://doi.org/10.1080/08924562.2022.2120350

Iannucci, C. & Parker, M., 2022. Beyond lip service: Making student voice a (meaningful) reality in elementary physical education. Journal of Physical Education, Recreation & Dance, 93(8), pp.41–49. https://doi.org/10.1080/07303084.2022.2108177

Islam, M.A., Haji Mat Said, S.B., Umarlebbe, J.H., Sobhani, F.A. & Afrin, S., 2022. Conceptualization of head-heart-hands model for developing an effective 21st century teacher. Frontiers in Psychology, 13, p.968723.

Jeanes, R., O'Connor, J., Penney, D., Spaaij, R., Magee, J., O'Hara, E. & Lymbery, L., 2024. A mixed-method analysis of the contribution of informal sport to public health in Australia. Health Promotion International, 39(3), daae048. https://doi.org/10.1093/heapro/daae048

Jeanes, R., Penney, D., O'Connor, J., Spaaij, R., O'Hara, E., Magee, J. & Lymbery, L., 2022. Spatial justice, informal sport and Australian community sports participation. Leisure Studies, pp.1–15. https://doi.org/10.1080/02614367.2022.2085772

Jeanes, R., Spaaij, R., Penney, D. & O'Connor, J., 2019. Managing informal sport participation: tensions and opportunities. International Journal of Sport Policy and Politics, 11(1), pp.79–95.

Kirk, D., 2010. Physical Education Futures. Taylor & Francis Group.

Kirk, D. & Gorely, T., 2000. Challenging Thinking About the Relationship Between School Physical Education and Sport Performance. European Physical Education Review, 6(2), pp.119–134. https://doi.org/10.1177/1356336X000062002

Lemov, D., 2012. Teach Like a Champion 2.0: 62 Techniques that Put Students on the Path to College. San Francisco: Jossey-Bass.

Lloyd, R. & Oliver, J., 2014. Strength and Conditioning for Young Athletes: Science and Application. Abingdon: Routledge.

Mathe, P., 2022. Happiness Factories: A success-driven approach to holistic Physical Education. John Catt.

McLennan, N. & Thompson, J., 2015. Quality physical education (QPE): Guidelines for policy makers. UNESCO Publishing.

Miyashita, S., O'Connor, J. & Jeanes, R., 2024. Reconceptualising informality in sport participation: Towards understanding informalisation of sport governance. International Review for the Sociology of Sport, p.10126902241270858. https://doi.org/10.1177/10126902241270858

Myatt, M. & Tomsett, J., 2021. Huh: Curriculum Conversations Between Subject and Senior Leaders. Woodbridge: John Catt Educational.

OECD, 2005. Formative Assessment: Improving Learning in Secondary Classrooms. OECD Publishing, Paris. https://doi.org/10.1787/9789264007413-en

Ofsted, 2022. Research review series: PE. [Accessed 21 August 2024].

Ofsted, 2023. Subject report series: PE. [Accessed 21 August 2024].

O'Connor, J. & Penney, D., 2021. Informal sport and curriculum futures: An investigation of the knowledge, skills and understandings for participation and the possibilities for physical education. European Physical Education Review, 27(1), pp.3–26. https://doi.org/10.1177/1356336X20915937

O'Connor, J., Alfrey, L. & Penney, D., 2022. Rethinking the classification of games and sports in physical education: A response to changes in sport and participation. Physical Education and Sport Pedagogy. https://doi.org/10.1080/17408989.2022.2061938

O'Connor, J.P. & Brown, T.D., 2007. Real Cyclists Don't Race: Informal Affiliations of the Weekend Warrior. International Review for the Sociology of Sport, 42(1), pp.83–97. https://doi.org/10.1177/1012690207081831

O'Connor, J.P. & Brown, T.D., 2010. Riding with the sharks: Serious leisure cyclist's perceptions of sharing the road with motorists. Journal of Science and Medicine in Sport, 13(1), pp.53–58.

PE Scholar, 2022. Concept Curriculum Launch Event. [online] Available at: https://www.pescholar.com/insight/pe-concept-curriculum-2-0-launch-event/ [Accessed 13 Feb 2025].

Quay, J. & Peters, J., 2012. Creative Physical Education: Integrating Curriculum Through Innovative PE Projects. Human Kinetics.

Siedentop, D., 2002. Sport Education: A Retrospective. Journal of Teaching in Physical Education, 21, p.409.

Sport England, 2023. Physical Literacy Consensus Statement for England. [Accessed 21 August 2024].

Sullivan, L., 2021. Is PE in Crisis?: Leading a Much-Needed Change in Physical Education. Scholary.

Ward, G., 2014. Learning movement culture: mapping the landscape between physical education and school sport. Sport, Education and Society, 19(5), pp.569–604. https://doi.org/10.1080/13573322.2012.690342

Welsh Government, 2019a. Developing a vision for curriculum design. Hwb. [online] Available at: https://hwb.gov.wales/curriculum-for-wales/designing-your-curriculum/developing-a-vision-for-curriculum-design/#curriculum-design-and-the-four-purposes [Accessed 20 Dec 2024].

Welsh Government, 2019b. Health and Well-being: Statements of what matters. Hwb. [online] Available at: https://hwb.gov.wales/curriculum-for-wales/health-and-well-being/statements-of-what-matters [Accessed 20 Dec 2024].

Whitehead, M. & Murdoch, E., 2006. Physical literacy and physical education: Conceptual mapping. Physical Education Matters, Vol. 1. Association for Physical Education.

Wiliam, D., 2011. Embedded formative assessment. Solution Tree Press.

Wiliam, D., 2013. Assessment: The bridge between teaching and learning. Voices from the Middle, 21(2), pp.15–20.

Wiliam, D., 2014. Principled assessment design. London: SSAT (The Schools Network) Limited.

Youth Sport Trust, 2017. Improving Wellbeing Through Secondary Physical Education.

Chapter 6: Delight

Lee Sullivan, Scott Kretchmar, Jordan Wintle and Rhys Meredith

Part 6.1 – Insight
Lee Sullivan

Darts, once perceived as a dull and pub-like activity underwent a dramatic makeover to become a globally recognised sport with mass appeal. Similarly, PE, long criticised for its outdated methods and lack of inclusivity, is undergoing scrutiny and calls for reform to better serve the diverse needs and interests of today's students. Therefore, this chapter will consider what valuable lessons can PE learn from the extraordinary journey undertaken by the sport of darts, transitioning from minimal engagement to captivating millions of television viewers? More importantly, the chapter will also explore the research around meaningful PE and the concept of 'delight' as it pertains to PE.

From Pub to Popular
Darts, initially confined to pubs, gradually transitioned to larger venues, attracting growing numbers of spectators. Despite its evolution into a televised sport in the 1980s, darts faced significant challenges due to its association with heavy drinking and smoking among players. By the mid-1980s, dwindling TV coverage and waning sponsorship interest signalled a decline in darts' popularity.

Faced with dwindling audience engagement, limited revenue streams, and a tarnished reputation associated with the ridiculed beer-swigging players, darts encountered a crisis of relevance. However, recognising the urgent need for reform, a coalition of promoters, led by Barry Hearn, orchestrated a strategic overhaul to rebrand darts as a mainstream entertainment spectacle.

Central to this transformation was a comprehensive marketing strategy aimed at injecting personality and flair into the sport. They realised that fans had little connection to most players. Therefore, catchy player nicknames were crafted, adding vibrancy to the once-stale image of darts. The incorporation of nicknames and walk-on music in darts enhanced personal relevance by making players more identifiable and relatable, echoing the significance of personal connections between the fans and the players.

CHAPTER 6: **DELIGHT**

Efforts were also made to elevate the production quality of television broadcasts, employing dynamic commentary, multiple camera angles, and on-screen graphics to captivate viewers' attention. Furthermore, efforts were made to enhance the reputation of players by prohibiting alcohol consumption during matches. Darts was recognised as a sport, and thus, athletes were expected to conduct themselves accordingly. The rise in prize money incentivised some to transition to professional status, thereby elevating the skill level of players and resulting in more captivating gameplay. Additionally, fostering rivalries between players generated excitement around specific matches.

Organisers understood that to really capture the attention of the masses they had to distinguish darts from other sporting events. This could be achieved by re-imagining the fan experience. This involved fostering supporter engagement, permitting chants, displaying signs, and embracing fancy dress. Such vibrant and entertaining interactions were pivotal in making darts tickets highly sought-after. Moreover, the communal atmosphere, with groups gathered around tables singing along to 'Sweet Caroline,' propelled darts to become one of the most-watched sports events in the UK.

The success of this rebranding endeavour catapulted darts into the global spotlight, leveraging its newfound television exposure, dynamic production techniques, and active audience participation to shed its pub game image. Today, darts stands as a captivating entertainment phenomenon, transcending its humble origins to captivate audiences worldwide. Just as darts underwent a remarkable transformation to secure its relevance and appeal, PE faces a similar imperative for radical reform to ensure its survival and effectiveness. Both darts and PE encountered challenges stemming from outdated perceptions, limited engagement, and the need for increased excitement and relevance.

Darts managed to shift fans from dread to delight, with fans flocking to Alexandra Palace, amongst other sold-out arenas, keen to interact with others, watch world-class darts from their favourite stars and have a great time. The masterminds behind the darts revival have breathed new life into what was once a stale experience. Fans have embraced the sport with a sense of delight, distinct from mere enjoyment. Scott Kretchmar explains the differences between delight and other concepts by saying 'Delight is different from fun, just as "love" is different to "like" and "excellence" is not the same thing as "competence"' (2006, page 7).

Darts fans don't merely enjoy attending matches; their passion for the sport runs deep. The heartfelt chants of "don't take me home, please don't take me home, I just don't want to go to work" eloquently convey their sentiments. They have forged a profound connection with the sport, finding genuine meaning in their experience. How can we, in physical education, replicate such delight and engagement among our students?

Part 6.2 – Delve
Lee Sullivan

What is Meaningfulness?
In their paper, 'Exploration and creation of meaningful teacher educator practices in physical education teacher education,' Dylan Scanlon, Alex Beckey, Jordan Wintle, and Mats Hordvik explore their work practices which either enhance or diminish meaningfulness in physical education teacher education. They discuss the significance of searching for and experiencing meaning in life as crucial conditions that contribute positively to individuals' quality of life and overall human flourishing. This concept is supported by Frankl (1963) and further explored by Martela and Steger (2016), who highlight that, while having meaning in life does not guarantee positive outcomes, individuals who perceive meaning and purpose in their lives are generally more likely to experience greater happiness and improved health (Steger, 2012).

In order for PE teachers to improve the experiences within PE, we must first understand what ingredients are needed in order to make PE meaningful.

Fletcher and Ni Chronin (2018) draw from Kretchmar's (2007) definition of meaning which 'includes all emotions, perceptions, hopes, dreams, and other cognitions – in short, the full range of human experience' (Page 382). They further explore this concept of meaning considering a tripartite conceptualisation of life-related meaningfulness which involves: (a) purpose as a motivational component, related to goals, aims and direction, (b) feelings of significance as an emotional component involving evaluation of life's inherent value and worth, and, (c) coherence as a cognitive component related to understanding of one's life making sense and being comprehensible (Leontiev 2017; Martela and Steger 2016). Understanding these three aspects of meaningfulness—purpose, feelings of significance, and coherence—can help educators design experiences that resonate deeply with students, motivating them, fostering emotional connections, and promoting a sense of understanding and relevance in their learning journey.

What is Meaningful PE?
The Meaningful PE approach places significant emphasis on prioritising meaningful experiences as a central organising principle for decision-making in PE. Rather than relying on chance, meaningful experiences serve as the principal criterion that informs and guides a teacher's pedagogical decisions within the PE context (Ni Chronin, et. al. 2020). By adopting this approach, educators aim to ensure that every aspect of the PE curriculum and instructional strategies is designed and implemented with the overarching goal of fostering meaningful experiences for students. This intentional focus on meaningfulness not only enhances the

effectiveness of teaching practices but also enriches students' overall learning journey in PE, promoting deeper engagement and long-term retention of knowledge and skills.

Kretchmar's (2006) criteria for meaningful experiences in physical education and youth sport—social interaction, fun, challenge, increased personally relevant learning, motor competence, and delight—serve as guiding principles for designing and facilitating meaningful experiences for learners.

In Beni, Fletcher and Ni Chroinin's (2016) article, titled 'Meaningful Experiences in Physical Education and Youth Sport: A Review of the Literature,' they delved into the significance of movement forms commonly addressed in school physical education and youth sport programs, such as dance, aquatics, gymnastics, and games.

The research found that personal meaningfulness in physical education is constructed through experiences that resonate with individuals, involving a synthesis of past, present, and future interactions. These meaningful experiences are influenced by learners' perceptions of the value and identified learning goals in physical education. The key findings of their research as it pertains to Kretchmar's criteria for meaningful experiences in PE are summarised below:

Table 2: Key Literature Findings of Meaningful PE

Meaningful Experiences in Physical Education and Youth Sport: A Review of the Literature. Beni, Fletcher, Ni Chroinin (2016). Key Literature findings	
Social Interactions	<ul><li>Social interaction plays a crucial role in meaningful experiences within physical education and youth sport contexts.</li><li>Social support from peers and teachers enhances meaningful engagement in physical education.</li><li>Feelings of isolation and gender biases perpetuated by teachers can diminish meaningfulness in physical education.</li><li>Students' preferences for group composition vary, with self-selected groups and teacher-selected teams both having pros and cons.</li><li>Student choice in group organisation positively impacts intrinsic motivation and physical activity levels.</li><li>Student interactions within groups facilitate deeper learning experiences.</li><li>Moments of meaningfulness can occur through personal and private experiences within the context of social interaction.</li><li>Teachers and coaches should consider both social interaction and personal experiences, providing opportunities for individual and group work and managing biases to promote meaningful engagement.</li></ul>

CHAPTER 6: **DELIGHT**

Fun	• Many participants in physical education and youth sport emphasise the importance of fun in meaningful activity experiences. • Secondary students often interpret fun as learning and challenge rather than simply playing games. • Game-centred approaches and Sport Education instructional models contribute to students' enjoyment and meaningful experiences in physical education. • However, an overemphasis on fun, such as allowing unstructured activities, can detract from the meaningfulness of the experience. • While fun is essential, it should not be the sole focus of physical education lessons; instead, it should be integrated as a vital component of meaningful experiences.
Challenge	• Engagement in activities that provide an appropriate challenge is crucial for a meaningful experience in physical education and youth sport. • Students often associate challenge with enjoyment and find physical education more meaningful when they can choose their level of challenge. • Some learners perceive boredom in physical education as a result of inadequate challenge. • Challenges perceived as personally meaningful, such as setting and achieving goals, lead to increased motivation and continued participation. • Competition is a sub-theme that further extends how students perceive challenge in physical education and youth sport.
Competence	• Students' perceptions of their own motor competence significantly influence their experiences in physical education and youth sport. • High perceived motor competence leads to more positive and meaningful experiences, while low perceived competence is associated with reduced enjoyment and participation. • Students' perceived competence impacts their motivation and effort in physical education, with high competence levels correlating with increased effort and low competence levels leading to decreased motivation to participate. • Motor competence contributes to meaningful engagement through executing game skills, understanding performance relative to peers, receiving praise, and responding to classmates' feedback.

Personally Relevant Learning	• Physical education and youth sport experiences are more meaningful when participants recognise the importance of what they are learning and can make explicit connections to their daily lives outside of the school or community setting. • Failure to establish relevance can lead to a lack of meaningfulness in physical education and youth sport experiences. • Pedagogical models such as Game-centred approaches and Sport Education help students make connections between physical education experiences and their lives outside the classroom. • Individualising pedagogical approaches, including offering student choice and input into learning experiences, enhances the personal relevance of activities and increases their meaningfulness. • Personally relevant learning is consistently linked to meaningful physical education and youth sport experiences, and reflection on experiences strengthens the personal significance derived from these experiences.

Prioritising Meaningfulness

In their research article titled "Children's Experiences of Pedagogies Prioritising Meaningfulness in Primary Physical Education in Ireland" (2021), Ni Chroinin, Fletcher, Beni, Griffin, and Coulter aimed to investigate how children aged 9–10 experienced PE when five Irish generalist primary teachers prioritised meaningfulness as the guiding principle for their pedagogical approach.

Teachers implemented strategies to enhance the meaningfulness of PE for children. Firstly, they adopted a shared ownership of learning focus, whereby they shared learning intentions with students before PE lessons. This approach helped children understand the purpose of activities and enabled them to set personal learning goals. By establishing this shared focus, teachers increased children's engagement in PE, which was a notable improvement from past experiences where activities lacked purpose. Additionally, goal-setting and reflection exercises further facilitated children's engagement and progress in PE.

Secondly, teachers prioritised collaboration on learning processes by involving children in decision-making. This included allowing them to adjust tasks, select activities, and contribute to the direction of their participation. By empowering children to take part in these decision-making processes, teachers increased their sense of autonomy and made learning more personally relevant. Moreover, negotiations and compromises among children fostered inclusivity and cooperation during PE activities.

Lastly, teachers paid close attention to the quality of individual experience in PE. They addressed children's preferences and needs to enhance the meaningfulness of their PE experiences. This involved valuing aspects such as social interaction, motor learning, and challenge. Additionally, teachers made efforts to minimise competition and emphasise inclusivity, resulting in more positive experiences for all children, regardless of their skill level. Overall, teachers' pedagogies focused on enhancing individual experiences, which promoted engagement and meaningful learning in PE and ultimately, led to increased engagement and personal relevance for these children.

Delight

In conversation with Andy Vasily in his 'Run Your Life' podcast, Meaningful PE advocate Scott Kretchmar was asked 'what did he used to think PE was and what does he think it is now?' He responded: 'I used to think PE was about teaching skills. Now I realise PE is all about relationships." He goes on to discuss how it's important to realise that as PE teachers we can't do everything and teach every sport. He offers the analogy of an English teacher by saying that they can't teach every classic, it just couldn't be done. The English teacher needs to select three or four great books so that a student wants to keep reading in their own time. Similarly, in PE, the focus should be on cultivating meaningful connections with a select few activities that resonate with students, their own community or context, sparking their desire to continue exploring physical activity outside of structured lessons. We will hear more from Scott Kretchmar later in this chapter, but this concept aligns with the essence of delight in PE – the genuine enthusiasm and eagerness students feel to pursue physical activity beyond the confines of the classroom, driven by the meaningful connections forged during PE lessons. It is the long-lasting satisfaction that can lead to habit formation.

Tim Fletcher concedes that 'Delight is not easily planned for, and as such, a teacher might aim to provide meaningful experiences in physical education such that students may experience delight on their own through engagement with their own personal playgrounds' (Fletcher et. al, 2021, Page 9). Once again, Scott Kretchmar provides valuable insight into the transformative potential of our curriculum units. During an episode of the Physical Activity Researcher Podcast, he shared his approach to introducing table tennis units. Kretchmar begins by inviting students into the unit with a compelling vision, explaining how the upcoming series of lessons could have a profound impact on their lives. He encourages patience, acknowledging that mastering certain techniques will require time and practice, but highlights the possibility that this sport could become a lifelong pursuit. This approach sets a wonderful tone for the start of the unit, instilling students with a sense of excitement and purpose from the outset. It also serves as a reminder that the lessons we deliver, if meaningful, can have a profound impact on intrinsic satisfaction and pleasure that goes way beyond fun.

So, although delight is difficult to plan for and to assess long-term impact, it shouldn't stop us striving for it. By using the guiding principles of meaningful PE in our decision-making, planning and delivery we will be much better placed to create meaningful connections with PE, physical activity and sport, where children seek out further opportunities for activity and genuinely go from PE dread to delight.

Mid-chapter reflection

What new insights have I gained from this chapter so far?

How does this knowledge reinforce or challenge my current beliefs or practices?

Are there areas or concepts I still need to explore further?

Have I identified any gaps in my team's understanding or practice that need addressing?

How can I share or apply this learning to positively influence others in my team or school?

CHAPTER 6: DELIGHT

Part 6.3 – Experts

Finding Delight in PE
Professor Scott Kretchmar

I have always been a fan of play. I define play as an experience that is self-rewarding. Playgrounds are places we want to be just for the sake of being there or things we want to do just for the sake of doing them.

Given these understandings, an initial question that always bothered me was whether a playground is something that is found or grown, come upon or developed, a place that is visited or one that must be dwelled in. The answer, of course, is it can be both.

We find a swimming pool. We come upon a soccer pitch. We visit an amusement park. We call them playgrounds because they are environments that are conducive to play. They invite play. For many of us they whisper or shout, "Come and play here." However, for others they may also whisper or shout, "Better find another place to spend your time."

The science of building a playground can be helpful in extending play opportunities to more individuals. A good playground should be safe. A good playground should be colourful, inviting, and attractive. It should be accessible. A good playground may be constructed to promote interesting challenges and competition, or exhilarating sensory experiences, or opportunities to gamble and try one's luck. Good playgrounds should be complex. They should invite participants to return again and again. Playgrounds must be age-appropriate. They should not present challenges that are too difficult and thus serve to produce anxiety, nor should they present challenges that are too easy and thus serve as a site for boredom.

In short, the science of building a good playground is important. A good playground provides an invitation to play, an introduction to play. However, whether or not it will provide a lasting relationship is an open question . After all, love at first sight is not the same thing as a durable marriage. A first date may also turn out to be a last date.

Durable relationships are actually grown, developed, and cultivated far more than they are found, come upon, or visited. If the player-playground relationship is to endure, we have to pay attention to what happens after introductions are made, after the initial handshake takes place, after the player and playground tell one another their names.

This takes us beyond the science of building good playgrounds into the art of promoting life-long play relationships. Building lasting connections is an art because no two relationships will be exactly the same. It is an art because the play instructor needs to know when to push and when to pull, when to demand more and when to demand less, when to require additional work and when to recommend recovery, when to talk and when to be silent, when to motivate extrinsically and when to let intrinsic motivation take over, how long to keep the pair together and when to let them have some time alone.

Growing play relationships is an art because the instructor cannot automatically or magically transmit the joys of a playground to the learner. The learner has to trust the play instructor. The instructor has to earn that trust. The learner becomes a traveller, the teacher becomes the acknowledged guide.

The journey into any land of joy may take time and effort. The instructor knows the player and playground may squabble from time to time. They may even wonder why they chose to be together. They may even consider an early divorce , but that is when the play guide has to nudge them forward, nudge them over the skill, fitness, or endurance hurdle to the rewards on the other side.

It has always bothered me that we have courses for our majors that would help students teach sport skills, treat a sport injury, or establish a personalised program for physical fitness but not a single course on how to grow a playground. This is both odd and unfortunate, for if we are as serious about promoting physical activity for a lifetime as we often say we are, it would stand to reason that we become serious about how to do just that. Arguably, no better way exists to promote life-long physical activity than to build a movement playground. To accomplish that, we will have to complement the science of introductions with the art of growing relationships . . . durable play relationships between a player and a playground.

CHAPTER 6: DELIGHT

Part 6.4 – Apply

Lifestyle Sports as Meaningful Experiences
Jordan Wintle

Lifestyle sports such as parkour, skateboarding, and BMX have experienced high growth in participation during the 21st century, yet, despite their growing popularity (Gilchrist & Wheaton, 2016), they have struggled to feature heavily in physical education curricula across the globe (Beaumont & Warburton, 2020; Griggs & Fleet, 2021; Wintle, 2022). Given that many young people cite current versions of physical education as lacking relevance (Hemingway et al., 2023; Ladwig et al., 2018), it seems logical that we should try and move with the times in an attempt to improve physical education experiences for our pupils.

To do that, I implemented an action research project, delivering two units of lifestyle sports (Parkour and a CrossFit/Kickboxing hybrid) in two English secondary schools (48 pupils aged 11-13 years old, mixed ability and gender) over an 8-week period, using pedagogies aligned to the meaningful physical education approach (Fletcher & Ní Chróinín, 2022). Data was collected using a multi-mixed-methods approach that included pre- and post-unit pupil questionnaires (aligned to meaningful physical education), reviews of lesson plans and resources used in the units, structured observations by an observing teacher, teacher-researcher reflections on each lesson, post-unit pupil focus groups and teacher-observer interviews. Data analysis of the quantitative questionnaire data was completed through a range of inferential statistics (Pallant, 2020), and the qualitative data was analysed using thematic analysis (Braun & Clarke, 2022).

The analysis of the data revealed some promising outcomes. There was a significant increase in meaning for pupils in the parkour unit, with several features of meaningful physical education showing positive change (competence, fun, challenge, choice). Pupils also rated the meaningful physical education pedagogies (goal setting, democratic approaches and reflection) as being more prominent in the parkour unit. As a result, overall meaning was significantly improved when compared with "normal physical education". The Kickboxing/CrossFit unit, while not as clear in the statistical data, also showed some positive outcomes. Several pupils identified increased meaning in the unit, particularly for girls and those who identified as non-sporty.

Several key themes emerged from the qualitative data that shed further light on the quantitative element; these were - the marmite of "normal" PE, meaningful physical education (as a useful lens to analyse experiences), and diversification of the curriculum.

The Marmite of Normal Physical Education

For context, Marmite is a dark, thick yeast extract spread used on toast and sandwiches; some people love it, whilst others hate it. Unsurprisingly, given what we already know about young people's experiences in physical education, this analogy fits well with pupils' experiences of normal physical education. Reference was made to the competitive nature of most lessons, a lack of freedom and choice and a limited variety of activities on offer. Some key quotes below highlight this:

> "I don't like the uniform, and sometimes I don't like the things [activities] that we do."(Sophie)
> "I love PE... 'Cause I like sports". (Luke)
> "There is, like, a few sports that I'm not sure if I like to do them, like dodgeball. I don't like dodgeball." (Amber)
> "In normal PE, we don't really get to have freedom." (Max)
> "It's just some of the sports I just don't like" (Poppy)
> "We did a survey before at our school and we found that 55% enjoyed PE, 45% didn't. So we were thinking, well, 55% enjoy PE, what about the 45%, that's a huge number" (Rob, Teacher Interview)

With polarising views of normal physical education, the journey from dread to delight could potentially be quite a long one for some pupils, and often, the strong views made during primary and early secondary school are resistant to change.

Meaningful Physical Education

Both the questionnaire, during lessons and subsequent focus groups, and the meaningful physical education framework provided a suitable lens for us to analyse experiences and create a shared language to describe experiences. The established key features resonated with pupils in this age phase, but two key features seemed to resonate more than others:the need for social interaction with peers (and, to some extent, the teacher) and finding an appropriate level of challenge. The latter was supported by providing choices for pupils, for example in the height of the obstacle in parkour or designing their own routines in kickboxing /CrossFit.

> "[it was] meaningful, cause it was fun...and not something we'd normally do as well. And we had, like, the choice to do it so we weren't, like - you didn't have [emphasis] to do the same as everyone else." (Faye)
> "You were with your friends and everything and you could - it wasn't like you had to be quiet and just do it. You could talk while you were doing it and, like, help each other. And that kind of leads into the social and also with the social you spoke to, like, new people [chuckles] that you'd not really spoken to before." (Toby)
> "There's like a set standard in PE that you always have to achieve...but in parkour you, you do what you can do to your own ability." (Lee)

Teaching reflections and observations revealed that using meaningful physical education pedagogies and features to guide decision-making had a positive influence on pupils' experiences.

Diversification of the Curriculum

Pupils and teachers expressed a desire to broaden the range of activities used in physical education. This shouldn't be seen as a call to extend the menu of activities on offer in the curriculum but a re-balance away from a curriculum overloaded with traditional competitive sports. Lifestyle sports offer a contemporary, typically non-competitive, mastery-based approach to physical activity that seems to appeal to many pupils. Teacher feedback suggests that the potential for these types of activities was recognised:

> "Some don't, they don't take to, erm, what we would class as the traditional sports at all, they don't like them, they don't really want to do them, and I think doing something like that [parkour] offers them a way of being physically active…they really enjoyed it" (Amy)
>
> "I think there's, there's a lot on competitive sports, isn't there…but I, I definitely think this kind of non-competitive, erm, environment as such is, is good"

Pupils also expressed a desire to see a greater variety of activities on their curriculum; when asked the one thing they would change about their current physical education experiences, several pupils commented on the activities on offer:

> "More variety in sports and activities" (Megan)
> "Trying different sports or types of sports" (Ross)
> "The variety of sports options" (Jemima)
> "What kind of things we do. I think we should do more different activities more often" (Amir)

The research project made clear the importance of both the activity and the teaching approaches. Manipulating each one on its own could have some positive impact, but combining a new activity with a complementary approach allowed a deeper impact to be seen in many pupils. I would challenge teachers to reflect on both these points: Do you really offer a balanced curriculum, and where could a focus on meaningfulness using the features and pedagogies of meaningful physical education help to move your pupils toward the delight end of the continuum?

CHAPTER 6: DELIGHT

Meaningful PE in Practice
Rhys Meredith

When I was at school and a student myself, in the 1990's, my experiences of PE before the application of meaningful PE was very much teacher-led. The teacher was doing all the talking and leading of the activities. Students would have no voice and would just "do as they are told" and so be less invested and engaged in PE.

There would be little to no differentiation, where the lessons would be pitched for a middle ability student, so not meeting the needs of those who need support or challenge. Games would be two teams on full size dimensions with no accommodations made, where those who were the best would dominate and those who needed support would be disengaged.

Time being active would be consistently wasted either by waiting to play, waiting for a turn or by too much teacher talk.

Meaningful PE resonated with me as it is a more inclusive way of teaching. Students are in charge of their own learning and embarking on 'challenge by choice' during the lessons. With each student being in charge of their differentiation and selecting their own entry point, students feel success in a way which is meaningful to them. Getting regular feedback from students instantly lets the teacher know how the lesson went and enables quality reflection for all. Students can also see that teachers care about their views, they are being asked and the teacher acts on their input where appropriate.

With students making the choice it is less work for the teacher and the students take the lead in choosing what is a meaningful 'Just Right' challenge for them. This encourages the students to be assessment-capable learners who can self-adjust.

Meaningful PE was mainly applied through promoting a student-centered approach. Students have ownership of their learning as they have choice about the challenges that they set themselves during the lesson.

At the start of each unit, students would be asked what games or activities they wanted to do during the unit. All views would be taken, tallied up and shared with the students. Knowing this and following it helps to ensure that the experiences are meaningful for the students.

Students can also choose their challenge when undertaking skill practice. For example in a striking and fielding unit when independently practising throwing and catching skills, students can choose:
- What they throw and catch (ball or other item, size of ball etc.)?
- If they work alone or with others?

FROM PE DREAD TO DELIGHT

- Where they stand (how far from the target or others?)
- The technique that they use (overarm, underarm, high)?
- What target they aim for (another person or a wall)?
- How competitive they make it (keeping scores or points)?

With this consistently being the expectation the students are able to select a task which is meaningful to them and one which is a 'Just Right Challenge'.

Exit tickets and student voice are used each lesson to gather feedback from the students. Examples of potential exit tickets are:

- Establish how the lesson went for the students
- What were the barriers to students achieving full success?
- Were they able to master the skills or want to improve?
- What activities do the students want to do in a unit?

Figure 15: Establish how the lesson went for the students

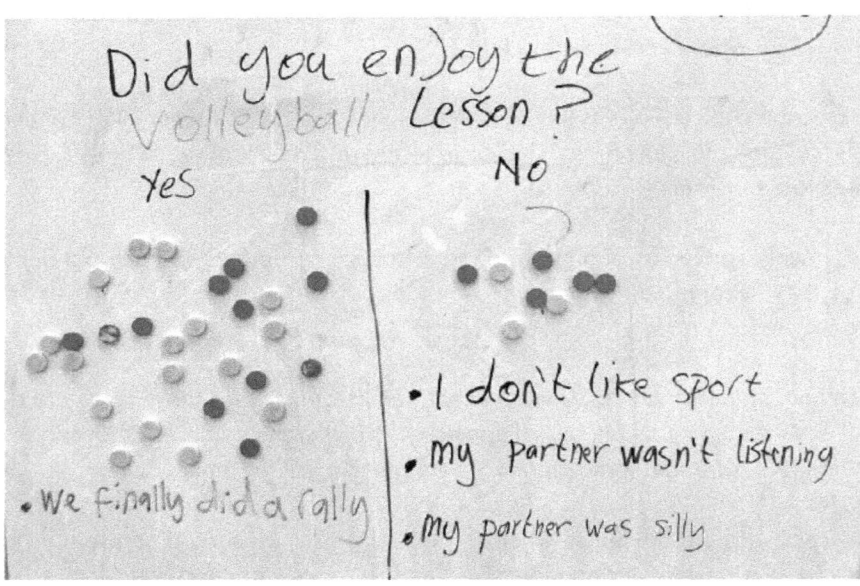

Figure 16: What were the barriers to students achieving full success?

CHAPTER 6: **DELIGHT**

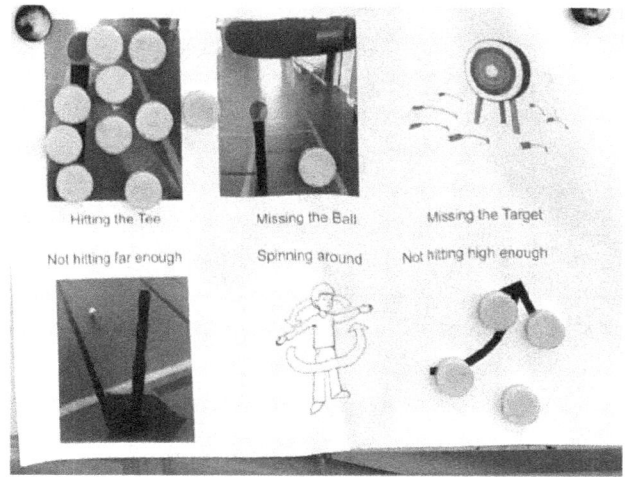

Figure 17: Were they able to master the skills or want to improve?

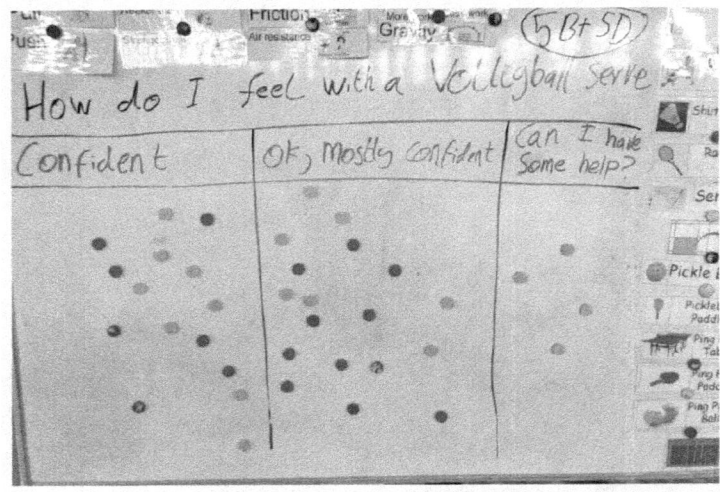

Figure 18: What activities do the students want to do in a unit?

Net and wall games - What students wanted to do

Badminton 85

Volleyball 44

Tennis 43

Ping Pong 25

Rally 5

Pickleball 2

Hit the ball faster 1

Through Meaningful PE the trust and relationship between teacher and student has grown and improved so much.

Firstly, The students see that the teacher is listening and acting on their input. So they feel more invested and engaged in PE as they have the trust in the teacher to enable them to have an involvement in decision-making.

Students are also involved in creating success criteria for how to achieve well in games. This enables them to share their knowledge in child friendly language

They are also responsible for generating agreements around behaviour, how to demonstrate respect in PE and how to celebrate in a respectful way. Involving students in creating these agreements gives them such a sense of ownership and helps to hold students and teachers accountable.

Figure 19: Student Ownership

Respect in PE

What does respect look like in PE?

Win well	9	Be humble	1
Lose well	9	Be flexible	1
Be safe	8	Call for the ball	1
Follow the rules	6	Be active	1
Include others	6	Give space	1
Keep your hands and your feet to yourself	6	Encourage	1
Show sportsmanship	5	Don't argue	1
Listen	5	Take responsibility	1
Help and support others	4	Think of others	1
Play fair	4	Be sensible	1
Be kind	2	Have good manners	1
Be calm	2	Be careful	1
Pay attention	2	Be supportive	1
Try your best	2	Look after the equipment	1
Share	1		
Work as a team	1		

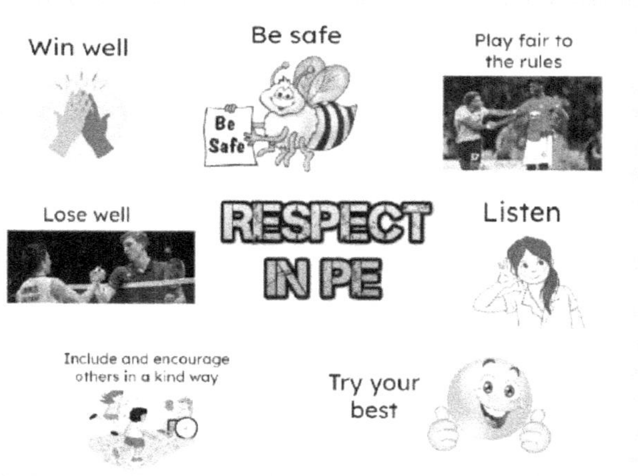

Figure 20: Respectful Celebrations in PE

CHAPTER 7: **EXCELLENCE**

Respectful Celebrations in PE

Say "Good Game" at the end	62
Shake hands/ high 5 or fist bump at the end	20
No bragging if you win	19
No screaming in others faces or boo	18
High five a team mate for something good	15
Say 'Yes' if I score quickly and calmly	9
Say well done to the other team if they do good	6
Get on with the game and have fun	5
Other	5
Clap something good	3
Say 'Unlucky' if someone misses	1
Total	162

Allowing the students opportunities to reflect enables them to independently find strengths and areas of growth, which help to create assessment-capable learners who can self-adjust.

With trust established the students feedback is honest and often critical. This enables the teacher to act appropriately to change and improve future lessons to make them more meaningful.

The exit tickets act as a formative assessment tool for the students providing a snapshot of how they feel they are achieving. If a member of the leadership and management team asks for any data to show progress then the data is authentic and easy to access to show progress.

Chapter 6 Summary

Delight: From Dread to Delight

DREAD

Fun:
Students imitating activity specific skills in isolation repeatedly. Students perceive lessons as dull and boring.

Isolation:
Students receive little social support from teachers and peers, have no choice in group organisation and experience feelings of isolation and bias.

Little or Too Much Challenge:
Students find activities too challenging or too easy and have no opportunities to select their own level of challenge.

Incompetence:
Students fail to improve and have feelings of low competence within activity leading to a sense of frustration or apathy.

Irrelevancy:
Students do not value learning and see no impact on their lives beyond PE.

Dread:
Students have no motivation to seek out further opportunities to be physically active and prefer to avoid it.

DELIGHT

Fun:
Learning is structured to provide appropriate challenge through various instructional models. Lessons are perceived as enjoyable.

Social Interaction:
Students have some choice in group organisation and social support from peers and teachers is prevalent.

Just Right Challenge:
Students have opportunities to select their level of challenge and activities provide the appropriate level of challenge.

Motor Competence:
Learning is demonstrated and students perceive feelings of high competence.

Personal Relevancy:
Students value the learning and reflect on how it can apply to their lives in and beyond PE.

Delight:
Students have a feeling of long-lasting satisfaction and actively seek out further opportunities to be physically active, leading to habit formation.

CHAPTER 7: EXCELLENCE

Where would you place yourself right now?

DREAD   **DELIGHT**

Reflection Questions
- How can I incorporate the tripartite conceptualisation of life-related meaningfulness – purpose, feelings of significance, and coherence – into my PE curriculum to foster deeper engagement and relevance for students?
- How can I ensure that social interaction, fun, challenge, relevance, competence, and delight are addressed in my PE teaching?
- How can I involve students in decision-making to boost their autonomy and ownership in PE?
- How can I adapt strategies to enhance meaningfulness in PE to better suit my teaching context and student needs?
- How can I connect with select activities in PE to spark students' interest in exploring physical activity beyond class, fostering delight and long-term satisfaction?

Call to Action
As we conclude this chapter, it's time to reflect on what you've learned and consider how to apply it. The SHIFT mnemonic can guide you through the next steps: a structured approach to transform your insights into meaningful actions. Take a moment to work through the following questions:

S **Summarise** the key takeaway from this chapter that stands out to you.

H **Highlight** how this takeaway challenges or aligns with your current practices.

I   **Initiate** a small change or step right now to put what you've learned into practice.

F **Frame** how this change will contribute to achieving your long-term vision for PE.

T **Take** others on the journey—share your new insights and encourage collaboration.

References

Beaumont, L. C., & Warburton, V. E. (2020). Lifestyle sports, pedagogy and physical education. In S. A. Capel & R. Blair (Eds.), Debates in physical education (2nd ed., pp. 239–255). Routledge.

Beni, S., Fletcher, T., & Ní Chróinín, D. (2017). Meaningful experiences in physical education and youth sport: A review of the literature. Quest, 69(3), 291–312. https://doi.org/10.1080/00336297.2016.1224192

Braun, V., & Clarke, V. (2022). Thematic analysis: A practical guide. SAGE.

Fletcher, T., & Ní Chróinín, D. (2022). Pedagogical principles that support the prioritisation of meaningful experiences in physical education: Conceptual and practical considerations. Physical Education and Sport Pedagogy, 27(5), 455–466. https://doi.org/10.1080/17408989.2021.1884672

Frankl, V. E. (1963). Man's search for meaning: An introduction to logotherapy. Washington Square Press.

Gilchrist, P., & Wheaton, B. (2016). Lifestyle and adventure sport among youth. In K. Green & A. Smith (Eds.), Routledge handbook of youth sport (pp. 186–200). Routledge.

Griggs, G., & Fleet, M. (2021). Most people hate physical education and most drop out of physical activity: In search of credible curriculum alternatives. Education Sciences, 11(11), 701–712. https://doi.org/10.3390/educsci11110701

Hemingway, K., Butt, J., Spray, C., Olusoga, P., & Beretta De Azevedo, L. (2023). Exploring students' experiences of secondary school physical education in England. Physical Education and Sport Pedagogy, 1–16. https://doi.org/10.1080/17408989.2023.2256771

Kretchmar, R. S. (2006). Ten more reasons for quality physical education. Journal of Physical Education, Recreation & Dance, 77(9), 6–9. https://doi.org/10.1080/07303084.2006.10597932

Ladwig, M. A., Vazou, S., & Ekkekakis, P. (2018). "My best memory is when I was done with it": PE memories are associated with adult sedentary behavior. Translational Journal of the ACSM, 3(16), 119–129. https://doi.org/10.1249/TJX.0000000000000067

Leontiev, D. (2017). Converging paths toward meaning. Journal of Constructivist Psychology, 30(1), 74–81.

Martela, F., & Steger, M. F. (2016). The three meanings of meaning in life: Distinguishing coherence, purpose, and significance. The Journal of Positive Psychology, 11(5), 531–545.

Ní Chróinín, D., Fletcher, T., Beni, S., Griffin, C., & Coulter, M. (2023). Children's experiences of pedagogies that prioritise meaningfulness in primary physical education in Ireland. Education 3–13, 51(1), 41–54. https://doi.org/10.1080/03004279.2021.1948584

Pallant, J. (2020). SPSS survival manual: A step by step guide to data analysis using IBM SPSS (7th ed.). Allen & Unwin.

Scanlon, D., Beckey, A., Wintle, J., & Hordvik, M. (2024). Exploration and creation of meaningful teacher educator practices in physical education teacher education. Sport, Education and Society, 1(1), 1–16. https://doi.org/10.1080/13573322.2024.2417782

Sraithes, W. (2022). Book review: Meaningful physical education – An approach for teaching and learning (2021). PE Scholar. https://www.pescholar.com/insight/book-review-meaningful-physical-education/ [Accessed 5 April 2024].

Steger, M. F. (2012). Experiencing meaning in life: Optimal functioning at the nexus of well-being, psychopathology, and spirituality. In P. T. P. Wong (Ed.), The human quest for meaning: Theories, research, and applications (2nd ed.). Routledge.

Wintle, J. (2022). Physical education and physical activity promotion: Lifestyle sports as meaningful experiences. Education Sciences, 12(3), 181–197. https://doi.org/10.3390/educsci12030181

FROM PE DREAD TO dElIGHT

Chapter 7: Excellence

Lee Sullivan, Emerick Kaitell, Katie Hart, Catherine Fitzpatrick and Vicki Gill

Part 7.1 – Insight
Lee Sullivan

In the first part of this chapter dedicated to Excellence in PE, I seek to unravel the underlying factors that fuel this relentless pursuit for excellence in PE. Ranging from the pressures of academic qualifications to the pervasive influence of professional sports culture, our PE delivery has been impacted to pursue perfection. Whilst I am not naive to the fact that there are many other reasons as to why PE has been distracted by excellence (teachers' own experiences, educational policy, etc.) the following three examples will hopefully outline some of the pressures PE faces and the negative impacts of these pressures. In the second part of the chapter, I consider what excellence is in PE and whether it is what we should be aiming for and whether we might reframe excellence to better meet the aims of what can realistically be achieved.

Pursuit of Excellence One: Led by Elite Sport
For decades, elite sport has played a pivotal role in shaping the landscape of PE delivery. The influence of elite athletes and high-performance sports has led government agendas and educational policies, often positioning sport performance as a key benchmark for success in PE. Key stakeholders frequently point to the achievements of elite athletes as examples of excellence and as aspirational models for students in PE programs. The success of national sports teams, Olympic medallists, and championship-winning athletes are often touted as evidence of a successful PE system. As a result, there is often a strong emphasis on aligning PE curricula and activities with the training methods, skills, and values exhibited by elite athletes.

In the 2022 Women's Football European Championship, the Lionesses won the first ever European trophy for England. Their Euro Championship win not only brought glory to the team but also served as a symbol of progress and empowerment for women in sports.

In the aftermath of their triumph, the Lionesses seized the opportunity to leverage their success for a greater cause, advocating for increased access to football for girls across all levels of education. In their letter to the Prime Minister, they wrote:

CHAPTER 7: **EXCELLENCE**

We have made incredible strides in the women's game, but this generation of school girls deserve more. They deserve to play football at lunchtime, they deserve to play football in PE lessons and they deserve to believe they can one day play for England. We want their dreams to also come true. This is an opportunity to make a huge difference. A change that will impact millions of young girls' lives.

The letter drew a great deal of media attention, with politicians put under pressure to ensure all girls had the same access to football in schools as boys. Whilst the drive for equality was welcomed, ensuring there were greater and increased opportunities for girls to learn and play football, some in the PE community were concerned by PE being driven by elite sport. The desire to have all girls playing football in PE is problematic, as not all girls may have an interest in football or team sports in general. Mandating football in PE for all girls could lead to further PE disengagement and reduced participation among students who do not enjoy or excel in the sport. Though the Lionesses' well-intentioned letter was not implying that all girls must be striving for excellence, it serves as a prime example of how elite sport can often drive PE delivery.

Pursuit of Excellence Two: Drive to Win

One brisk Spring afternoon, our school football fields were a bustling hub of activity as two extra-curricular football fixtures were taking place. On one pitch, the Year 11 team faced off against their opponents, while on the adjacent field, the Year 8 squad engaged in their own match.

In the Year 11 game, with the County Cup final at stake, the game was tense. Players were resorting to aggressive tackles and engaged in unnecessary tussles the longer the game went on. The air was filled with profanity as frustrations boiled over. What was more disappointing was the conduct of the PE teachers on the side-lines, who, instead of fostering a positive environment, were seen shouting at the referee, criticising players for making mistakes and shouting unnecessary comments at the opposition players. Completely undermining the spirit of the game. It was evident that the primary focus was on winning at all costs, neglecting the educational aspect of sportspersonship, teamwork, and personal development. This was a stark departure from how sport should be played in schools, even during extra-curricular activities.

Meanwhile, on the Year 8 pitch, a slightly different scenario unfolded. The game was nowhere near as close as one team took a first half 7-0 lead. I spoke with one manager to see if they might consider ending the official game at half time, mixing the teams up and allowing everyone to play in a more even competition, however I was told that this can't happen as the winning team needed the superior goal difference in the league.

As I reflected on these scenes, I couldn't help but ponder the influence of such win-driven behaviour on young athletes. How does this drive for excellence impact our actions, both on and off the field? Remember, those participating in both games are children that had opted in. No wonder so many had opted out.

Pursuit of Excellence Three: PE Qualification Pressures

One of the biggest mistakes I have made as a Head of PE (and I have made many) was to design my core PE curriculum around examination (GCSE) PE. When I joined my school, GCSE PE grades were weak, uptake was poor, and the subject held little value to most. I considered it my biggest priority to change these outcomes, thinking that a PE department is judged mainly by examination results. My vision for PE focused on the following:

- GCSE PE specification sports on Core Curriculum
- Core practical assessment matched with examination board criteria
- Key Stage 3 taught GCSE specific content
- Lessons focussed on performance

All roads led to GCSE PE

In time, outcomes did improve. Results were much stronger. I felt my leadership was working. Until we conducted a Core PE student voice survey. A majority of students found little value in Core PE and in reality, some really didn't enjoy our lessons at all.

The problem with GCSE PE is that it is prioritised over Core PE and this has therefore negatively affected the quality and true purpose of Core PE. What I realised, after much reflection, soul searching, frustration, ranting, etc. was that I was forgetting that Core PE and GCSE PE should have two very different aims. The purpose for a qualification is clear: to demonstrate a level of knowledge or ability in a particular area to move onto further study or employment (Meyer, 2011). Conversely, the purpose of Core PE, whilst often debated, is to prepare young people for lifelong involvement with physical activity.

There is a clear difference in aims between the two. GCSE PE has no intention of nurturing lifelong engagement in physical activity and Core PE is not out to further careers. Yet, for far too long we have been under pressure to use Core PE to meet the aims and better the outcomes of GCSE PE.

The entirety of practical assessment in GCSE PE is dedicated to performance across a limited number of sports. This practical component of PE predominantly fosters the development of elite athletes, and will do little to engage the disengaged, motivate the unmotivated or

CHAPTER 7: **EXCELLENCE**

build positive connections with physical activity for those that do not already have a positive relationship. Nor does it represent the type of physical activity that some students will go on to engage in. It fails to ignite the emotions required for some to fall in love with an activity and remain in love with it beyond school years. This drive for qualification outcomes has been contributing towards our quest for sporting excellence in Core PE, yet I would guess it heavily contradicts the purpose of PE which aligns to lifelong engagement.

Figure 21: Core or GCSE PE?

FROM PE DREAD TO dELIGHT

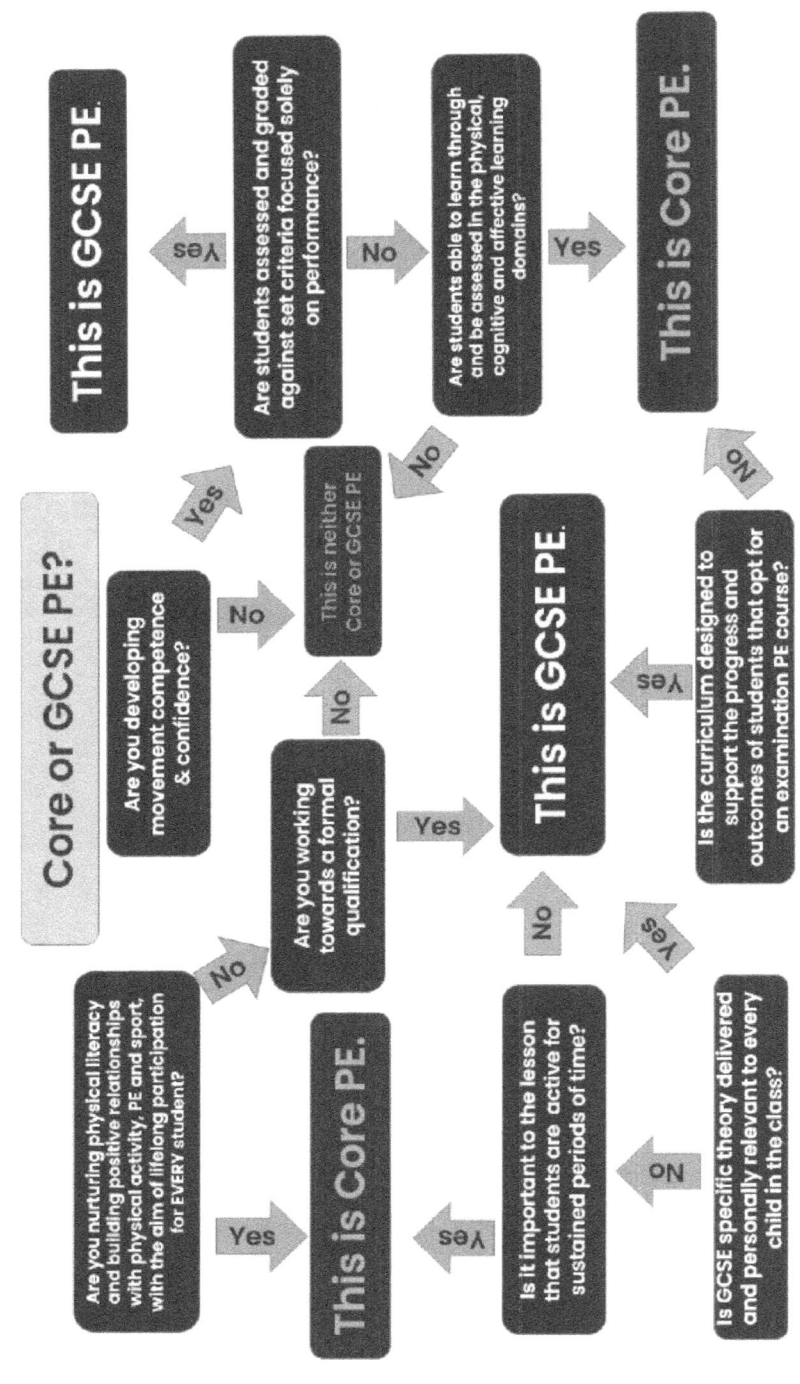

CHAPTER 7: **EXCELLENCE**

Part 7.2 – Delve
Lee Sullivan

Defining Excellence

The ancient Greeks used the word 'aristos' which meant excellent. The word aristos consists of two parts, ar+istos. The first part ar- implies 'join', 'connect', 'fit together'. The last part of the word -istos implies the 'biggest', 'most beautiful', 'fastest' and 'best possible'. Essentially, humans can become excellent when they connect perfectly all the best that they have within themselves (Miller 2004). This includes all human qualities, physical, psychological, spiritual or moral (MacIntyre, 2007).

In ancient Greece, the pinnacle celebration of human achievement occurred at the Olympic Games. These athletes exemplified excellence through their remarkable physical prowess, skill, determination, and passion. This link with excellence and sport has remained resilient as sports have provided individuals with an opportunity to push the boundaries of human potential, inspire others with their feats of athleticism, and unite communities through shared passion and competition.

In modern times, defining excellence in sport seems to be more closely linked to the skills, techniques and understanding demonstrated within the specific sport. Devine (2022) explains that the value of sport resides principally in it providing an avenue by which admirable human skills and capacities can be tested, cultivated, and manifested. He argues that sporting excellence admits four distinct elements:

- **Cluster of Excellence:** refers to the specific set of skills and abilities that a sport is designed to test. Each sport focuses on a particular subset of skills, forming its unique cluster of excellence. Moreover, each sport tests more than one type of excellence: the marathon tests (among other things) speed endurance, technical proficiency, mental toughness, and strategic nous.

CHAPTER 7: **EXCELLENCE**

- **Quantum of Excellence:** the "quantitative" aspect of excellence in sports focuses on the amount of excellence that can be achieved within a sport. Changes to rules, norms, or practices can either increase or decrease the level of excellence attainable. For instance, the transition from amateur to professional sports often results in higher levels of play due to increased resources and training opportunities, leading to an increase in the quantum of excellence.
- **Clarity of Excellence:** refers to the perceptibility of sporting excellence and the degree to which it can be distinguished from other factors affecting performance. In sports like gymnastics or figure skating, where judging plays a significant role, clarity is essential for accurately evaluating performances. It ensures that spectators, judges, and officials can discern excellence from non-excellence, allowing for fair assessment and rule application.
- **Balance of Excellence:** refers to the hierarchical relationship among the various skills and abilities within a sport's cluster of excellence. It emphasises that while all skills within the cluster contribute to performance to some extent, some should be more significant than others.

If we were to transfer this idea of sporting excellence to PE we could consider the following: The concept of 'Cluster of Excellence' could translate to the specific set of physical, cognitive, and social skills that a PE curriculum aims to develop. Just like in sports, each activity or unit within PE focuses on specific skills and competencies, such as agility, coordination, teamwork, and problem-solving. The 'Quantum of Excellence' in PE would relate to the depth and breadth of skills and knowledge students acquire through PE. Changes in teaching methods, resources, and curriculum design can impact the level of excellence achievable by students. 'Clarity of Excellence' in PE emphasises the importance of clear assessment criteria and feedback mechanisms to ensure that students, teachers, and evaluators can accurately perceive and recognise excellence in physical performance and understanding. Finally, the 'Balance of Excellence' in PE might refer to the proportional emphasis placed on different components of physical education, such as motor skills, fitness, knowledge of health concepts, and social development.

The Excellence Mirage

One must apply the concept of sporting excellence to PE with extreme caution as the growth of high-performance elite sports has raised questions about how we define excellence and ability within PE (Kirk, 2010). Perhaps the misconceptions around the purpose of PE or the fact that we can't universally agree on what success looks like in PE, means that so many have attached PE to the concept of excellence in sports. Often, PE only seems significant when it serves as a means to replicate athletic triumphs or produce more accomplished athletes.

Croston (2013) argued that policy has merged educational and sporting targets, which has resulted in a shift in focus away from educational objectives towards supporting elite development. Dawn Penny further explored this relationship between PE and sporting excellence (2000) and argued that the prevailing view of high performance within PE remains narrowly focused on acquiring physical attributes associated with elite-level performance in specific sports. As a result, curriculum planning and teaching often prioritise the development of motor skills and it seems that the key reference points for recognition of learning are visions of elite sport performance.

Chasing excellence in PE can be likened to chasing a mirage in the desert. Just as a traveller in the desert may become fixated on reaching a mirage, teachers in PE may become consumed by the pursuit of perfection. Whilst the water mirage might seem close and achievable, the traveller will become lost and disorientated. The more we chase the excellence mirage in PE, the more we may lose sight of our original goals and intentions.

For some, excellence is synonymous with victory, while for others, it signifies consistently high performance or meeting extremely high expectations. However, regardless of the interpretation, the term "excellence" in PE can carry unintended consequences that may undermine the holistic goals of the discipline. Striving for sporting excellence in PE is selling PE short. It must come to the point where we as individual practitioners, whether this concept of sporting excellence aligns with our 'why', our department's curriculum intent and if not, consider what the alternative to excellence in PE might be.

Modest Competency

Speaking on the Physical Activity Researcher Podcast, Scott Kretchmar defiantly suggested that 'most of us will never achieve anything in sport. However, this was not to say that we couldn't find meaning in our own involvement in sport, but our engagement is often unremarkable.' Furthermore, in his article 'Sport as a (mere) hobby: in defence of 'the gentle pursuit of modest competence' (2019) Kretchmar was arguing that there is more to sport than just those at the elite level, there is a version that is 'quiet, personal, local, and thus too, far less brassy and visible than its perfectionist counterpart. Its players set no records, receive no headlines, and rarely worry about winning any championships. They vary in age from youngsters still learning their game to senior citizens hoping to maintain their skills or slow their rate of decline. Yet, all of them have one thing in common…a hard-to-explain love affair with a game, a relationship that brightens their lives in measurable ways,' (Kretchmar 2019, Page 368).

What Kretchmar is reassuringly suggesting is that whilst we may not go on to achieve sporting greatness or play at the highest level, we can still find our movement experiences meaningful in whatever level or form we engage. If we want our students to engage in physical activity now and beyond, we need to give them the tools to be able to do so. What is excellence to Emma Radacanu is to win the US Open, what is excellence to me is winning a single game or going a game without a double fault. Therefore, it is highly unlikely I would have or even need the tools to win the US Open, however to engage in tennis at a recreational level with friends, I would only need moderate competency.

By aiming for moderate competency we are not lowering our expectations for the few but raising our expectations for the many. We must consider what we can realistically achieve as physical educators and what we are in the profession for. If we are aiming to create that elite athlete, possibly our services might be better served as one of the many brilliant coaches working with the high ability youth sport athletes. That is not to say that PE teachers shouldn't challenge and develop our most able pupils. However, what we as educators should be aiming towards is for every child to leave us with the tools and motivation to remain physically active in whatever method they choose and to achieve personal bests along the way.

Sport is Not a Dirty Word

PE is not sport! But that doesn't mean sport is the problem. The issue lies in how sport has been delivered through PE. When it comes to PE, sport is like a blank canvas – it has the potential to deliver meaningful learning, but how it's presented determines whether it engages or alienates. Too often, sport within PE has been painted with broad, rigid strokes that focus almost exclusively on competition, performance, and a win-at-all-costs mentality. This can create negative associations with physical activity. But sport doesn't have to be painted this way. Just as a blank canvas can become a masterpiece in many different styles and forms, sport can be shaped to serve different purposes. When sport in PE is framed not as a test of ability but as an opportunity for learning, growth and fun we can create far more positive associations.

PE should strive to enhance the transfer of learning from students' physical activities in school to their experiences beyond the school environment and throughout their adult lives. In this pursuit, it is crucial for physical educators not to disregard sport as a community of practice. Instead, we must frame PE with an appropriate model and 'be clear about the aspects of sport we wish to reproduce in schools on the basis of their educational worth,' (Kirk, 2006, page 192). It's essential to reframe the concept of excellence in PE to encompass a broader spectrum of outcomes and experiences. True excellence in PE should encompass not only one's physical personal best, but also personal growth, resilience, perseverance, and a lifelong commitment to health and well-being.

FROM PE DREAD TO dElIGHT

What Does Excellence in PE Mean to You?
Renowned athletics coach, Frank Dick has been celebrated for his transformative impact on athletes worldwide. In a now famous interview that underscores the essence of coaching and teaching, he shared an insightful anecdote about a 9-year-old girl's experience in a 100-metre race. This illuminating story serves as a powerful reminder for PE teachers about the importance of prioritising learning and personal growth over mere outcomes, especially in PE.

Coach Dick recounted how the 9-year-old girl had run the 100m race only to finish last in a time of 18 seconds. She walked up to Coach Dick and, not hiding her disappointment, she expressed how poorly she had performed. However, rather than dwelling on the final result or offering empty consolation, he chose to redefine the concept of excellence for the young girl. Coach Dick pointed out that this was in fact this girl's best over time, making it her personal best, praising her accomplishment and highlighting the progress she had made. Coach Dick recounts how in the next race, when beating her time of 18 seconds, despite not finishing first, the girl's experiences will have changed from one of defeat to personal pride. Her own win.

Frank Dick ends the interview by re-defining winning. He says "That is what winning is, winning is being better today than you were yesterday. Every day."

This book is all about prioritising the needs of our students, therefore, when considering excellence in your teaching, consider focusing on the 4 R's:

- **Reframe:** Instead of solely focusing on winning, comparing what excellence might look like in elite sport and then applying it to our students, shift the focus to the process rather than the outcome of excellence. The journey can be more rewarding than the destination.
- **Rethink:** Start by considering the 'who' and the learning environment and what excellence might mean to them. Excellence doesn't have to be winning the world cup, it can be making personal improvements, overcoming obstacles and achieving a personal best.
- **Relevancy:** Try as we might, an overwhelming majority of our students will not make it to the elite level. Therefore, consider how relevant the learning is to their lives and whether it meets their motivations to engage in physical activity. By pursuing perfection, we might be making many of the learning opportunities irrelevant and meaningless.
- **Role Model:** Consider who we use as the role models for our students and how we conduct ourselves in competitive contexts. Play to win but behave to educate. If we truly value the learning from our subject then we must truly embrace it.

Coach Dick's anecdote serves as a poignant reminder for PE teachers everywhere. In a culture that often places undue emphasis on excellence and winning, it is crucial to shift the narrative towards growth, learning, and personal development. By fostering a supportive and nurturing environment, educators can empower students to embrace the journey of self-discovery and

CHAPTER 7: **EXCELLENCE**

cultivate a lifelong love for physical activity and sports. The true measure of a PE teacher's success is not in the medals won, but in the hearts inspired and the movers motivated and truthfully, you may never know the full impact you had as a teacher unless you meet former students many years down the line.

Part 7.3 – Experts

Excellence in Teaching
Emerick Kaitell

I awoke with a start, sweating, and my heart rate elevated and disorientated after another day of teaching. The Ghost of Teacher Past visited me, reminding me where I was at the start of my learning-teaching journey. Many questions fell upon me: how many children engaged in the learning? How do I know that they learnt? How did the children interact? How did the children solve the challenges? And more questions flooded my mind. The emotional responses remind me of the Almond Effect, and that I am making sense of the past (Bassot, 2016:62). As my physical responses come to mind from my teaching, I can recount what was said, how it was said and recognise the impact of my presence upon the children's learning.

Moreover, using the Cultural Circles of problem-posing, critical dialogue, problem-solving, and action, as discussed by Souto-Manning (2007), enables one to reflect and review to improve future teachings. The concept of lifelong learning comes to mind, recognising that continual learning can improve performance as we aim to develop all pupils in our care. The ability to act upon reflections, experiences and learning that requires knowing oneself, knowing who you are teaching, knowing a range of pedagogical approaches, and knowing the content with the context. Remembering, competition, sport and exams are not the outcome, they are pathways for the pupils to choose.

Meanwhile, I doze off again to muse over the past, consider how I am now, and identify what stages of development I underwent. Senge's Personal Mastery (Bassot, 2020:119) indicates the need to continually review what is essential and where we want to be as practitioners, enabling us to move away from a reactive to a creative viewpoint. It is not a problem; it is an opportunity. The term excellence is personal, and for the discussion, excellence requires consideration of the pupils' experiences and feelings, the pedagogical approaches used and not used, the context of the school's curriculum and the national expectations (standards) that impact me and how I embody the experiences. In this place, all sections interlink to indicate excellence. The Ghost of Teacher Present ensures that reflective practice is core to my practice.

The skill required to make sense of reflection needs to develop. Criticality practices require embracing pupil feedback on how and what they learn as part of our thinking process as professionals. Moreover, gaining feedback from peers, alternative others and us brings awareness of inward and outward inputs that can assist in our continual professional development. Bassott (2020) provides an overview of the reflective development processes

CHAPTER 7: **EXCELLENCE**

that enable us in becoming more effective educators. The reflection process revolves around thinking as a learner and professional, where we gain a deeper understanding of teachers' expectations from a national, local and personal perspective. Reflectivity comprises analysing and evaluating specific aspects of our professional practice, where we aim to take charge of the narrative of our development. Reflexivity requires understanding our biases and the power relationships that can influence our practices. The power of the national policies, school policies, departments, children, parents, subject organisations, and ourselves, as well as how we interact with each other, has implications for the quality of teaching and learning for our pupils. The need to be anti-discriminatory is critical to ensuring that all pupils learn through teaching experiences in physical education.

The Ghost of the Teacher Future allows me to identify the components of developing my professional self and delivering high-quality learning experiences for all students. Previously in this book, the discussion around sport, examination (measure against set standards), and competition provided a landscape that is ever present in our profession. However, to deliver a curriculum for all, we need to review our current practice and identify the next steps that enable us to achieve our purpose of teaching all pupils and allowing them all to improve and develop.

Several processes can assist in our professional development, and they are dynamic. Firstly, we must review our curriculum and teachings and identify how to decolonise our processes. Undertaking the task and amending the curriculum can amend previous discussions around sports, examinations, and competitions. Using the TRACC model (Tan, 2022), reviewing the questions on teaching approach, relationships, activity and assessment, and content can develop a new, exciting experience for all pupils.

Reflecting on our values, purposes, and practices can help us identify our biases, which can aid in decolonising the curriculum. We all have them, and the challenge is determining how ours impacts all pupils' learning in our lessons. The first task is to identify, then review and then amend, always considering the pupils throughout the process.

Figure 22: Freire, teaching, and learning: Culture circles across contexts

FROM PE DREAD TO dElIGHT

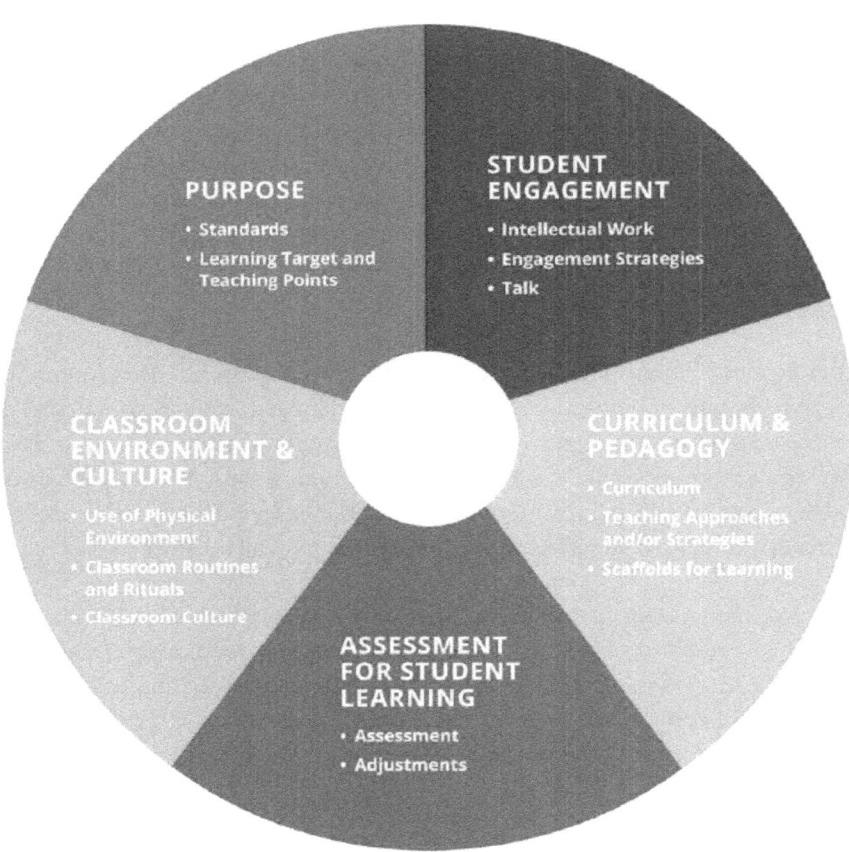

To aid self-review, we can consider the Broffenbrenner ecological system, which involves reviewing the influences upon your practice. Micro influences indicate continual and high influences, while Macro influences are not directly related to your practice, though they influence your role as a teacher.

Figure 23: Bronfenbrenner's Ecological Systems Theory

CHAPTER 7: EXCELLENCE

Chronosystem
Changes Over Time

Macrosystem
Social and Cultural Values

Exosystem
Indirect Environment

Mesosystem
Connections

Microsystem
Immediate Environment

CHILD

FROM PE DREAD TO dELIGHT

Part 7.4 – Apply

The Sports Day Shift
Catherine Fitzpatrick and Katie Hart

Sports Day, a long-standing tradition in many schools, is often centred around athletics, particularly track and field events. While this model may work well for students who are naturally athletic, competitive, or already have a positive relationship with physical activity, it often fails to meet the needs of all students. This dominant format can unintentionally alienate and even embarrass those who feel uncomfortable in competitive environments or participate in front of others. For many, Sports Day can become an exercise in humiliation rather than a celebration of participation and achievement.

By focusing on a more inclusive, student-centred approach, schools can foster a positive experience that promotes physical activity, builds confidence, and encourages a lifelong engagement with movement. The experiences shared in this part of the chapter will offer insights, at a local and national level, into how rethinking Sports Day can create an environment where every student feels valued, included, and empowered to enjoy physical activity, regardless of their skill level or competitive nature.

Katie Hart – Primary PE Teacher

I joined a school that was working hard to embed a focus on learning behaviours across the curriculum. I was delighted, as our curriculum PE lessons provided a wealth of opportunities to develop independent thinking, focus, courage, collaboration, cooperation and support for others. However, as Sports Day approached and I found out more about how this had been organised previously, it was hard to see where many of these attributes would be encouraged, recognised and rewarded. Previous itineraries for the day included a long list of track races with a focus on the fastest and the best. This format resulted in lots of waiting around for pupils and the need for adults to be allocated to 'crowd control'. When pupils competed in traditional field events, they lined up head-to-head against peers in the same year group and direct comparisons were made between pupil performance. Highest points were awarded to the furthest throw or jump with limited opportunities to try again and improve. This format led to emotional dysregulation for some pupils and it appeared that we would suspend all thoughts of our learning behaviours for the day. This seemed incongruous with the school ethos, the curriculum intent and everything we had been working on in our PE lessons throughout the year.

So we designed a Multi-Sports Day that could shine a spotlight on these learning behaviours. Parents and adults were gently guided towards our approach through the words of Mahatma Ghandi *"Satisfaction lies in the effort, not in the attainment, full effort is full victory."* Careful thought was applied to an equitable scoring system that enabled pupils from reception to Year

CHAPTER 7: **EXCELLENCE**

6 to earn points for their efforts and school staff were ready to reward all learning behaviours on display throughout the event.

In our new format, our multi-Sports Day, pupils would now work in mixed-age, house groups, cheered on by their parents. They would carousel around a range of multi-sports that require teamwork, collaboration and collective and individual effort and they would continue to apply the learning behaviours expected in all subjects within the curriculum. On the day itself, our older pupils quickly realised that by taking a leadership role and helping the younger students, they were able to make the most of the ten-minute time allocation at each activity and could accumulate more points for their house. They forgot to compare themselves to their peers and focused on their own effort and improvement. Our younger pupils excelled through the examples modelled by their older peers and adopted similar positive behaviours. They forgot to worry about whether their parents were watching and immersed themselves in the feeling of being part of a team (most of the time). Our pupils with specific needs were nurtured by those around them. With careful and considered support, they could better regulate their emotions and were able to participate in more of the activities than in previous years. What a reward it was to see some pupils participate, who had previously stayed at home on Sports Day due to anxiety and stress.

The equipment that schools have access to will vary but with careful planning of dates and the sharing of equipment I would recommend a selection of the following activities to be included in any multi-Sports Day carousel:

Table 3: Multi-Sports Day Carousel

- Tri-Golf
- Boccia
- Vortex throw
- Speed bounce
- Croquet
- Speed stacks
- Kurling
- Archery
- Egg n Spoon relays
- Hurdles
- Team relays
- Agility ladders
- Balancing tracks
- Seated volleyball with beachballs

I have found it works best when school staff stay at one allocated station on the carousel. They have the opportunity to interact with all pupils in the school throughout the day and each complete a score sheet to record the house, points accumulated and names of students who demonstrate stand-out examples of the learning behaviours. After each rotation, this is sent to the Headteacher who enjoys the role of central scorer and timekeeper and he rings the traditional school playground bell with gusto every ten minutes to signify the time to move on to the next challenge.

We no longer need to consider 'crowd control' roles because pupils are actively engaged in physical activities for extended periods of time, with limited waiting around. Instead, school staff play a positive role in recognising effort and personal achievement. Parent spectators are incredibly encouraging of all pupils in their collective efforts and as Paul Dix highlights "When the adults change; everything changes". The shift in adult behaviour helps to create a safe environment where we see confident pupils, giving their best effort and participating wholeheartedly.

To conclude the event, we celebrate the house that has accumulated the most points as well as all the children who have been recognised by school staff for displaying the learning behaviours. And finally, of course we all enjoy a picnic on the field!

My final note and personal favourite point to note, is that after introducing this format in two different Primary Schools, the first Multi-Sports Day has been won by the house 'that never do well on Sports Day'. My hope is that this phrase disappears from school life, along with the parents' race!

Catherine Fitzpatrick – Director of Physical Education at Complete PE

Hearing Katie's story and learning how Sports Day underwent a meaningful transformation only reinforces the ambition that many of us share on a national scale: to drive change and refocus Primary PE, Physical Activity, and School Sport. As Director of Physical Education at Complete PE, my role is to work with schools and teachers across the UK, to build confidence and enjoyment in teaching High Quality Physical Education.

We are paving the way through PE by embedding a holistic approach to learning. All of the training we use at Complete PE and the resources on our platform focus on whole child outcomes and celebrating learning across the 4 domains. The impact of this approach in schools drastically increases pupil enjoyment in PE and therefore their attainment. Throughout the year, I have the privilege of working with remarkable Primary PE Leaders across the country through the various courses and workshops I lead. We discuss the importance of celebrating our pupils' successes in PE physically, cognitively, socially and emotionally. Together, we devise strategies to ensure that all teachers feel confident and equipped to deliver high-quality PE, creating positive experiences for every pupil. So, how does Sports Day fit into this?

In my experience, working in a number of schools across England, Sports Day is the only major "celebration of sport" in a school year. But what is its real purpose? If we are teaching pupils to value skills like resilience, self-belief, integrity, and respect in their PE lessons, how can Sports Day reflect this ethos?

Instead of focusing solely on the sporting success of a few, we should be celebrating the progress and learning of every pupil.

Katie's approach mirrors a format I used for many years as a PE leader in various schools and it is one that we now share with schools across the country. In this model, pupils work

CHAPTER 8: **LEARNING**

in house teams within their class, rotating around a carousel of events that align with the skills and knowledge they've gained throughout the year. The events often have an athletic focus like sprinting, jumping, and throwing, but instead of competing once and being judged individually, pupils have multiple attempts, earning points for their house team. There's no embarrassment in coming last, as that's never the outcome. Every child remains engaged and active throughout.

Teachers move around the carousel with their class, supporting and observing their pupils' participation. At the end, scores are combined to form a team total for each house. Importantly, every pupil's efforts are recognised, and they receive certificates linked to the four domains of learning. Pupils can earn their certificates for thinking creatively or solving problems, their ability to collaborate or show respect, their resilience or integrity.

Every child is celebrated, and they understand exactly why they've earned their award. While we still recognise the winning house, we also ensure that we celebrate the individual success and unique contributions of every pupil.

This format isn't limited to athletic events, it can be adapted to celebrate achievements across all areas of the curriculum, making it a truly inclusive and meaningful experience for every child. In addition, the format could be used multiple times throughout the year and not just limited to sports day. The success of this format still allows for the right amount of competition and challenge, enabling those pupils who thrive in this environment to still do so. The difference is, those that would truly disengage in other, more traditional formats, now thrive too and isn't that the most incredibly powerful outcome we could hope for?

In our mission to ensure all pupils have a positive relationship with movement and choose to seek healthy active lifestyles, simple modifications to the format of sports day in school can really make a big impact.

FROM PE DREAD TO DELIGHT

Swimming as a Life Skill
Vicki Gill

Every summer we hear the devastating news of a child who has drowned in the ocean, a river or lake, there is no debating that the ability to swim or at the very minimum be confident in the water is an important life skill.

Swimming is the only physical activity taught within schools that has the potential to save your life. Swimming ability is dependent upon when adults provide access to the required resource - a swimming pool. Walking and running together with the vast array of sporting skills linked to football, basketball, athletics for example, can all be improved and developed on a daily basis, with very limited or no equipment. However, if the school has not prioritised swimming how does a child improve their swimming and water safety skills?

The English National Curriculum at Key stage 1 & 2 provides three outcomes that all pupils must demonstrate by the end of Year 6;
- Swim competently, confidently and proficiently over a distance of at least 25m
- Use a range of strokes effectively [for example, front crawl, backstroke and breaststroke]
- Perform safe self-rescue in different water-based situations

When planning a swimming curriculum, schools face various considerations. Schools with their own pools avoid transportation challenges but incur significant operating costs, particularly for indoor facilities, while outdoor pools may only be usable in summer. Schools using community leisure centres must navigate public changing areas and potentially share space with general users. Additionally, leisure facility operators may keep lanes open for paying members, reducing available swimming space. This limits options for non-swimmers and those unable to swim widths, complicating efforts to meet the 25-metre swimming requirement.

Swimming is an open skill, the moving environment and changes in depth of the pool create numerous considerations for the swimming teacher. Swimming is vastly different to the sports field, where we can ask our students to stop, stand still and look at the positioning of their hands. In a swimming pool, it's not possible to just stop, especially if you are not a confident swimmer, your brain is thinking more about the potential impending actions of your head moving under the water than the shaped pathway your hand should be pulling through the water. With swimming, while it may be possible to give some visual feedback in the moment, the majority of feedback is given at the sides of the pool and when the swimmer has their ears above the water!

Many people teaching swimming comment on the varied behaviours of children in the water. As a child in a world of continual stimulation, the silence found from under the water can be both intriguing and enticing, a place of silence and for some total calm. Why would you want

CHAPTER 8: **LEARNING**

your head above the water in the hot, noisy, smelly indoor swimming pool? The tranquillity and silence of the underwater world is just centimetres away, yet some may not fully understand the dangers of submersion or not hear safety information. For others the thought of the underwater world feels like the end of the world, coloured by a previous bad experience, stories told of what may occur if you go under the water, or simply a new experience in an already daunting environment. Children have a real sense of freedom from not being constrained by their school uniform - the release from the itchy shirt or the tightness of their tie - so is behaviour affected by nerves, anxiety, excitement or past experiences? As teachers, do we always take these factors into account? Even the changing rooms, a topic of so much discussion in PE lessons, can be an influence on learning.

Swimming is perceived as a very skill-based activity; certainly some elements such as diving, when there is a safety component, require essential skills to be progressed through before linking together in the 'dive'. The traditional swimming lesson format of warm up, skill development through the whole – part – whole concept and concluding activity is still commonly seen on poolsides across the country. Replacing traditional 'BLABT' - Body Position, Leg Action, Arm Action, Breathing and Timing - teaching approaches with fun challenges, opens swimming lessons up, for both the learner and the teacher, to a more enjoyable and meaningful experience.

There is a common agreement that we learn best when the experience is fun and meaningful. Gaining water confidence comes from fun, what better way is there than play? Once the swimmers are confident in the water – there is a huge opportunity to make this experience meaningful, for the majority of readers I would hasten to guess that their experience of meaningful swimming was wearing their pyjamas to the swimming pool for a couple of weeks during their personal survival lessons.

For the youngest of swimmers, harnessing their imagination in the swimming pool can be the key to a meaningful experience – bringing their classroom activities and learning into the pool – including toys. Plastic dinosaurs love being on the bottom of the swimming pool! A little creativity goes a long way – balls and hoops, swim noodles and more. Noughts and Crosses with coloured rings or laminated pictures to help identify the animals and their movements that children can imitate through the water. Travelling on rockets to new galaxies, or even bringing story books to life. How many children's books include a journey? Rarely is the story in one location for the entire duration of the book - the Room on the Broom Journey – suddenly the streamlined rocket ship shape created by the most fundamental body position in swimming takes more meaning. "Can your body be long and straight like a Broom?" "Can you fly through the water on the broom?" The frog on the broom links to the breaststroke frog leg action, or the simultaneous jumps across the pool. The cat moves in a freestyle / doggie paddle action across the pool.

FROM PE DREAD TO DELIGHT

All of the home nations have their own version of a school Learn to Swim Framework built around the aquatic FUNdamentals of balance and buoyancy, coordination and control, travel, streamlining, breathing, floatation and rotation, entries and exits to develop physical literacy within the water, delivery of which should embrace learning through play – yet it is only in England that swimming is a compulsory part of the National Curriculum! The sense of growth and personal excellence achieved within a short 30-minute swimming lesson for some students can be life-changing and even lifesaving. Progressing from "I can not do that Yet!" to "I can do that sometimes, most of the time or even all of the time!". Altering their self-perception from "I am a non-swimmer!" to "I am a swimmer!" and no longer the exception in the class. When this achievement is also reflected by a physical change in their swimming group (if schools have enough teachers to group by ability) this movement loudly shouts to everyone in the class "I can do this!"

Swimming is so much more than just four competitive strokes it is such an important life skill, these few words barely scratch the surface…

Chapter 7 Summary

Excellence: From Dread to Delight

DREAD

Elite Sport Influence:
The pressure to emulate elite sport success can lead to a narrow focus on specific sports and disregard for individual student interests and abilities.

Drive to Win:
Overemphasis on winning can result in negative behaviours such as aggression, disrespect, and a lack of sportspersonship, both from players and coaches.

PE Qualification Pressures:
Prioritising GCSE PE outcomes over the broader aims of Core PE can undermine the quality and purpose of physical education, neglecting lifelong engagement in physical activity.

Misconceptions of Excellence:
The relentless pursuit of sporting excellence in PE may overshadow the holistic goals of the discipline, leading to unrealistic expectations and disengagement among students.

DELIGHT

Personal Growth Perspective:
Shifting the focus from winning to personal growth and improvement fosters a positive learning environment and encourages students to embrace the journey of self-discovery in physical activity.

Reframing & Rethink Excellence:
Redefining excellence to encompass individual progress and achievements promotes a more inclusive and meaningful approach to physical education.

Relevant Learning Opportunities:
Tailoring learning experiences to students' interests and motivations ensures the relevance and meaningfulness of physical education, promoting sustained engagement in physical activity beyond school.

Role Modelling:
Modelling positive behaviours and emphasising the educational value of PE helps cultivate a supportive and nurturing environment in physical education.

Where would you place yourself right now?

DREAD ⟵⟶ **DELIGHT**

Reflection Questions
- What does excellence in PE mean to me?
- How do external pressures influence my approach to excellence in PE?
- How can I reframe excellence in PE to align with broader goals?
- Am I effectively modelling positive behaviours to inspire students beyond excellence?

Call to Action
As we conclude this chapter, it's time to reflect on what you've learned and consider how to apply it. The SHIFT mnemonic can guide you through the next steps: a structured approach to transform your insights into meaningful actions. Take a moment to work through the following questions:

S **Summarise** the key takeaway from this chapter that stands out to you.

H **Highlight** how this takeaway challenges or aligns with your current practices.

I **Initiate** a small change or step right now to put what you've learned into practice.

F **Frame** how this change will contribute to achieving your long-term vision for PE.

T **Take** others on the journey—share your new insights and encourage collaboration.

References:
Bassot, B. (2020). The reflective journal (2nd ed.). Macmillan International.

Bolton, G., & Delderfield, R. (2018). Reflective practice: Writing and professional development (5th ed.). SAGE.

Bronfenbrenner, U. (2005). Biological perspectives on human development.

Busch, B., & Watson, E. (2019). The science of learning: 77 studies that every teacher needs to know. David Fulton Books.

Croston, A. (2013). A clear and obvious ability to perform physical activity: Revisiting physical education teachers' perceptions of talent in PE and sport. Physical Education and Sport Pedagogy, 18(1), 60–74. https://doi.org/10.1080/17408989.2011.631001

Devine, J. W. (2022). Elements of excellence. Journal of the Philosophy of Sport, 49(2), 195–211. https://doi.org/10.1080/00948705.2022.2059489

Jess, M., Atencio, M., & Carse, N. (2018). Integrating complexity thinking with teacher education practices: A collective yet unpredictable endeavour in physical education? Sport, Education and Society, 23(5), 435–448.

Kirk, D. (2004). Framing quality physical education: The elite sport model or Sport Education? Physical Education & Sport Pedagogy, 9(2), 185–195. https://doi.org/10.1080/1740898042000294985

Kretchmar, S. (2019). Sport as a (mere) hobby: In defence of 'the gentle pursuit of a modest competence'. Routledge.

MacIntyre, A. (2007). After virtue (3rd ed.). University of Notre Dame Press.

Meyer, L. (2011). The value of GCSEs. Centre for Education Research Policy. https://filestore.aqa.org.uk/content/research/CERP-RP-LM-01062011.pdf

Miller, S. G. (2004). Arête: Greek sports from ancient sources. University of California Press.

Penney, D. (2000). Physical education, sporting excellence and educational excellence. University of Tasmania. Sage Publications.

Souto-Manning, M., & Dice, J. L. (2007). Reflective teaching in the early years: A case for mentoring diverse educators. Early Childhood Education Journal, 34, 425–430. https://doi.org/10.1007/s10643-007-0151-1

Tan, D. (2021). Decolonizing university teaching and learning: An entry model for grappling with complexities. Bloomsbury.

The Physical Activity Researcher Podcast. (2022). Scott Kretchmar (Part 1): In pursuit of modest competence. https://pod.link/1479340829/episode/9662a6a0337e4618f86abf84f5d67210 [Accessed 19 February 2024].

Chapter 8: Learning

Lee Sullivan, Professor Ash Casey, Ryan Parker and Nathan Walker

Part 8.1 – Insight
Lee Sullivan

In this chapter, we confront the prevalent but flawed skill-drill approach, drawing from personal experiences and research that illuminate its limitations. This chapter aims to confront the reality that common methods of PE delivery often fail to inspire competent, confident, and motivated movers.

The Demise of the Skill-Drill Approach

My daughter was 6 at the time, and after watching my attempts at playing tennis in a local recreational club, had announced that tennis looked like fun and she would like to give it a try. I was delighted, as this was the first physical activity that she had ever expressed an interest in beyond those my partner and I had suggested. We had tried football and dance which she firmly told us she didn't enjoy and she was learning to swim though it was sometimes a battle getting her into the pool. To this point, the only movement opportunities she would willingly leap into involved soft play or trampoline parks which although brilliant, were too costly to do every week.

My daughter and I enjoyed an hour or two in the park balancing a tennis ball on a racket and throwing balls over the net in various themed games, but I wanted her to learn with other children. So, I managed to book her into a tennis session run by a well-known franchise that offers various sports specific sessions for young children. I wish I hadn't. After a warm welcome from the coaches, the 5- to 7-year-old children stood with rackets in hand and were taught the techniques of a forehand. The children were unable to throw and catch a ball, let alone connect with a moving ball using a racket that was practically the same height as they were. Children practised dropping the ball and attempting the swing and hit it back to their parents for a good 15 minutes. As I looked around the court, the parents were panting and sweating, as they had to run and chase the tennis balls that inevitably went nowhere near the desired destination. The coaches then set up nets and got the children into a line, explaining that they wanted them to each hit the ball over the net using the forehand shot that they had just practised. One by one the children would make their way up to the net, receive a poor feed, swing and miss the ball and return to the back of the line to await their turn again. I timed 2 minutes and 15 seconds between turns. My daughter was standing in line bored and then failing when it was finally her turn. The session ended with a call to practise at home. After three sessions, she told me that Tennis was too hard and boring.

A similar experience had occurred with my 4-year-old son. Following some enjoyable garden kick abouts, I took him to some football sessions arranged by a local coach. He started his sessions by scattering cones and asking the children to collect specific colours and perform various actions with them (hop, jump, balance the cones on their heads, etc.). Often it would be themed to space or animals so my son would be flying in his spaceship or howling like a dog with a huge smile on his face. However, the mood would shift as soon as the footballs came out. Instead of maintaining the playful atmosphere, the coach would line up the children and focus solely on repetitive drills like passing or dribbling. The themed fun was abandoned, and the session took on a serious tone. My son wanted nothing to do with this part of the session and I don't blame him. Both experiences ended with my children not wanting to return.

From these experiences I learned some valuable lessons when it came to my own children when learning through the physical domain:
- They must always be active
- They must experience success
- It must always be fun
- There must be opportunities for explorative play without adult interference

All of the above are seldom achieved through what has been labelled the skill-drill approach, a method focused on repetitive practice of isolated skills without contextual understanding or meaningful application.

Whilst the experiences with my own children happened outside of school, I have been to many lessons before and after that follow the same pattern: explain the skill, demonstrate the skill, students replicate the skill, repeat the skill in isolation numerous times, repeat. I know this is not unique to my observations or a new problem as David Kirk has been campaigning against this skill-drill and sport technique focused teaching for decades and certainly since his Physical Education Futures book (2009). Harris and Cale (2019) make the point that, for many students, especially girls, school sport and PE serves as the only opportunity to participate in physical activity. The focus on sport specific and often complex skills and competition could make a child feel like they are 'no good' or even a failure. If children's only opportunity for physical activity is with us, and they leave feeling the way my own children felt after their respective tennis and football sessions, then they won't want to participate in the future either.

When considering this common form of delivery, it's essential to reflect on what we aim to accomplish. Are we seeking to groom students for the adult version of a particular game? Is this approach truly effective for learning that game? And most importantly, do these methods contribute positively to the overall motivation for students to want to continue playing that game beyond our lessons?

We must also explore the importance of learning in PE and what exactly students should be learning. Mainsbridge, Iannucci, Pill and Williams (2024) argue that studies on PE experiences suggest that many students remember PE primarily for sports and physical activity, often lacking structured learning opportunities. This can result in negative experiences such as embarrassment, bullying, and social anxiety.

Learning or Languishing?

The United Nations Educational, Scientific and Cultural Organisation (UNESCO) established PE as a fundamental right and a crucial element of lifelong education. However, PE has often been promoted for its benefits to other subjects or public health rather than as a subject with its own body of knowledge. This has led to a debate about whether PE should be seen primarily as physical activity or as an educational subject that necessarily involves physical activity.

In PE, learning can be defined as the 'process of change within a learner's intrinsic dynamics (i.e. inherent tendencies/characteristics of each learner's movement repertoire),' (Chow, Davids, Button and Ranshaw, 2016, page 46). Reflecting on the learning to be acquired and the appropriate strategies to use to facilitate learning is vital for all PE teachers when planning their curriculum.

Mikael Quennerstedt aired his concerns about the future of PE in his 2019 paper titled 'Physical education and the art of teaching: transformative learning and teaching in physical education and sports pedagogy'. He said that 'It seems as though the E in Physical Education, the E in PE, is under attack, and has been so for a while.' He argues there is a risk of PE losing its educational importance with an emphasis on heart rate levels or activity time. He also argues that the 'physical' is also under attack' as assessment and grading are prioritised. These trends risk transforming PE into mere sports participation, fitness instruction, or theoretical knowledge without fostering true education. In Judith Placek's 1983 study, she argued that PE teachers often viewed success as students being "Busy, Happy, and Good"—active, enjoying the activities, and well-behaved. This focus on participation and discipline over learning has been criticised in PE research for decades.

The concern lies in whether this long-standing mindset is genuinely educational and aligned with the core purpose of education.

For a number of reasons, many schools place a significant emphasis on team games and sport-specific skill acquisition, as opposed to lifetime activities. This is still the dominant approach taken today. Education seems to be stuck in a game, skills-based and sport-techniques structure (Kirk, 2010). So it seems the 'Education' in 'physical education' is deemed to mean sport techniques, if the dominant form of delivery is anything to go by. However, as cited in Kirk (2010 page 44), Lounsberry and Coker (2008, page 257) 'there is little evidence to suggest that physical education has made strides in developing more successful or skilled performers.' Too often, the focus in PE is placed on the specific sport or activity rather than on what students are actually learning. The emphasis needs to shift towards fostering meaningful and relevant learning experiences that go beyond the activity itself. Moving from activity driven PE to outcome driven PE.

Not only are a large number of young people choosing not to be physically active, they also find the education offered irrelevant. The cherry on this catastrophic cake is that the evidence shows that the education we are claiming to provide, actually doesn't seem to be working. Students are not developing their movement competence in PE. We are aware that PE isn't working and there is no going back from that awareness. Students are not feeling more competent, confident and evidence proves a clear lack of motivation to engage in physical activity beyond our lessons. Therefore, we must consider the 'what' and 'how' of PE, because if we keep doing what we've always done, we will keep getting what we've always got and what we've always got will lead this subject to extinction.

Part 8.2 – Delve
Lee Sullivan

In the second part of our chapter dedicated to learning in PE, firstly I will focus on what the learning is (content) and then how the learning is or can be delivered (pedagogy) in PE lessons. While this section will specifically delve more heavily into learning within the physical domain, I am confident that forthcoming chapters will address essential insights pertaining to the cognitive and affective domains. In this segment. It would be unfeasible to cover all conceivable PE content and pedagogical methods within this chapter. Nonetheless, I have opted to introduce those that I believe could be beneficial and encourage further research beyond that presented in this book. It is also important to state that more rigorous research is needed to better understand and validate learning in PE. This is crucial to address confusion about the educational value of PE and to defend its importance as a school subject (Mainsbridge, Iannucci, Pill and Williams. 2024).

Learning in PE: The What (Content) and the How (Pedagogy)
'Helping young people want and know how to be physically active through school physical education involves two foundational issues: content and pedagogy,' (Barnard Flory, Tischler, Sanders, 2014, Page 9). Content is referring to what is taught and pedagogy refers to how it is taught.

The content is frequently constrained by factors such as available time and space, class size, teacher expertise, and the entrenched perception of what constitutes "traditional" PE. Consequently, sports have become the focal point of PE instruction. The pressure to evidence student 'progress' and the practical constraints of providing full context versions of various sports have resulted in a reliance on isolated drills as the chosen form of pedagogical method. These drills are simpler to organise, afford the teacher greater control, are more straightforward to teach, and often reflect the teacher's own experiences. Due to PE teachers' connection with the subject, the curriculum is designed for 'mini-me's' or effectively students with the same attitudes towards sport, physical activity and PE as the teachers in charge. The curriculum in PE around the world is dominated by sport and a multi-sport approach, in which select sports are offered for a set number of lessons before moving on to a new sport. Each sport is delivered using the same isolated drills approach and that it seems is resistant to change.

As mentioned earlier in this chapter, Judith Placek's 1983 study argued that PE teachers often viewed success as students being "Busy, Happy, and Good". Mikael Quennerstedt, Dhillon Landi and Ashley Casey identified in their 2024 paper titled 'Busier, Happier, and Good(er) – 40 Years on from 'Busy, Happy, and Good' as Success in Teaching Physical Education' that he terms "success" and "effective teaching" are subjective. They depend on broader educational goals. Success in teaching should not just be about achieving lesson objectives,

CHAPTER 8: LEARNING

like increasing physical activity or sports skills, but also about how these contribute to societal and educational goals. In PE, the focus should go beyond just "Busy, Happy, and Good" (participation, enjoyment, and discipline) and consider learning across multiple domains—psychomotor, cognitive, affective, social, and cultural. PE uniquely provides holistic learning through movement, addressing these interconnected areas to help students positively engage with and understand diverse movement cultures. The authors offer a new take on Placek's work, with the 'Busier, Happier and Better' framework. The authors state that 'The aim of our framework is thus that students are busier learning about different movement cultures, happier whilst engaging in the complexities of these different movement cultures, and ultimately better able to engage, create, and sustain different forms of movement in a range of movement cultures.'

The What (Content): The Building Blocks

'Movement is the very expression of life. Long before a child develops spoken language, her feelings and thoughts come to spontaneous expressions through the medium of movement – which is therefore her very first language,' (Goddard Blythe, 2011, page 6). I love this quote because it perfectly articulates the profound connection between movement and human existence. As educators, we play a pivotal role in nurturing and guiding children through their movement journey. Our interactions, guidance, and encouragement shape not only their physical development but also their emotional and cognitive growth. By fostering a supportive and enriching environment, we empower children to explore, experiment, and express themselves through movement. Through our guidance, they learn to navigate their bodies, discover their capabilities, and cultivate a lifelong appreciation for physical activity. As facilitators of their movement journey, we have the privilege of witnessing their growth, resilience, and joy as they embark on this fundamental aspect of human experience.

Fundamental Movement Skills (FMS) serve as the foundational elements for movement and are crucial for mastering more complex physical activities later in life. 'The primary years provide the most appropriate context for children to develop competence in a range of basic body actions. It is a key time for movement skill development within travelling, object control, balance and coordination categories of movement,' (Randall, Griggs, 2022). Proficient FMS acquisition during childhood is vital for overall development, minimising frustration and facilitating the learning of advanced skills as the child gets older. Developing these skills early on significantly influences a child's enjoyment of physical activity and their likelihood of remaining physically active into adolescence and adulthood. . As discussed by Vicky Randall (2022) 'the development of fundamental movement skills can provide the foundation from which children move with increasing complexity, variety and versatility in a range of activity areas. Whilst developing these skills children are also able to build on social, affective and cognitive learning opportunities.' By acknowledging the multifaceted nature of learning in

PE, we can explore alternative approaches that prioritise the physical, cognitive as well as the holistic and affective growth of students, beyond mere quantifiable achievements.

Figure 24: Primary Concept Curriculum, Lee Sullivan (2023). PE Scholar.

CHAPTER 8: LEARNING

The What (Content): Specific Sports and Activities

As previously presented in chapter 5, competitive sport takes up a majority of the PE curriculum, however formal sports participation is falling. Sport is not the enemy.

When selecting sports and physical activities for inclusion in the curriculum, it's essential to consider not only the popularity of the sport and activity but also its accessibility, relevance to students' lives, and potential for lifelong participation. Additionally, it's crucial to incorporate lifestyle sports and activities alongside traditional ones to cater to a diverse range of interests and preferences.

It is also important to consider the sequencing of content and learning that is vital for fostering skill development, progression, and a deeper understanding of movement concepts. By structuring learning experiences in a logical sequence, educators can scaffold students' learning, building upon previously acquired skills and knowledge. This sequential approach ensures that students develop a solid foundation before progressing to more complex movements or activities. Moreover, sequencing learning allows educators to introduce skills and concepts in a manner that aligns with students' developmental stages and abilities, maximising learning outcomes and engagement.

The What (Content): Swimming

Whilst it is not for me to suggest the specific sports or activities that should form the scope of your curriculum, it's imperative to highlight the significance of swimming education. Beyond the development of competence and the promotion of lifelong participation, swimming holds the potential to save lives—a crucial consideration for any educational programme.

In England, the National Curriculum mandates swimming instruction for Key Stage 1 and 2 students, aiming for competency in swimming a distance of 25 metres. However, concerning statistics from Swim England and Sport England's Active Lives Survey (2023) reveal concerning shortfalls. Nearly a quarter of children leave primary school unable to meet this standard, with disparities more pronounced in deprived areas. Moreover, a substantial percentage of primary schools offer no swimming lessons at all.

The rising costs of building, running, hiring and travelling to swim facilities as well as the perceived lack of confidence of teachers to teach swimming and water safety are compounding this issue further. In response, Swim England has advocated for the integration of a swimming programme of study into the national curriculum review, alongside increased funding and exploration of alternative facilities.

Prioritising swimming education is paramount, not only to address these alarming statistics but also to equip children with essential life-saving skills. It is incumbent upon educational

CHAPTER 8: LEARNING

stakeholders to ensure that every child has access to comprehensive swimming instruction, safeguarding their well-being and fostering a culture of water safety from an early age.

The What (Content): In, Through and About

Movement is central to how we perceive and interact with the world around us, with perception and cognition playing significant roles. From birth, humans are naturally drawn to movement and seek to engage with their surroundings (Costas, 2019). Movement also allows individuals to affect their environment, whether through manipulating objects or adapting to changing situations. Infants use movement to explore and understand their world, highlighting the innate nature of movement in learning.

Arnold's distinctions between learning in movement, learning through movement, and learning about movement provide frameworks for understanding how movement contributes to learning. Learning in movement occurs when individuals acquire new knowledge while participating in activities, such as adjusting climbing techniques based on terrain. Learning through movement involves gaining deeper understanding and knowledge through participation in activities, such as learning psychological coping strategies during performance. Learning about movement involves studying and participating in activities to develop greater understanding, such as learning about the effects of dehydration on athletic performance. These distinctions underscore the multifaceted role of movement in facilitating learning across cognitive and physical domains.

The How (Pedagogy): Skill Development

One significant critique of the skill-drill approach is its compatibility with the objective of nurturing intelligent, autonomous performers within sporting environments. In sport, skilled behaviours emerge from the dynamic relationship formed between a performer, the environment and the task (Chow, Davids, Button and Renshaw, 2016, page 37). Emphasising repetition without incorporating variability fails to challenge students to adapt to diverse situations, hindering their ability to develop problem-solving skills and adaptability crucial for success in real-world sporting scenarios.

In his book 'How We Learn to Move: A Revolution in the Way We Coach & Practice Sports Skills', (2021) Rob Gray also provides a compelling argument against the long-held belief that repetition is the key to learning new sporting skills. He reassuringly speaks about his frustrations when seeing static, isolated and choreographed drills in usually dynamic and exciting sports. Gray presents the idea that skillful movers 'do not achieve their goals by moving the same way every time' (page 12). He reviewed experiments that highlighted the variability of movements by comparing performers, thus highlighting the point that aiming to repeatedly imitate a flawless model isn't an effective method for learning, especially in high-pressure situations like competitive matches. Gray suggests that there must be a more effective approach to teaching and learning. One potential method involves encouraging exploration by manipulating various constraints. He advocated for allowing performers to self-organise by giving them time to find their own solutions, often small-sided games exemplify this approach.

Gray presents Newell's Constraints Model (page 46), which offers a framework for understanding how various factors influence motor development in children. Newell's model emphasises three types of constraints that shape movement behaviour: individual constraints, environmental constraints, and task constraints.

- Individual constraints refer to the inherent characteristics of the child, such as height, weight, strength, speed, flexibility, and coordination abilities. These factors influence the child's physical capabilities and movement potential. For example, a child with greater strength may be able to execute certain movements more powerfully or with greater precision compared to a child with weaker muscles.
- Environmental constraints encompass the external factors in the surroundings that influence movement, such as wind, gravity, temperature, lighting, surface conditions. These environmental factors can either facilitate or hinder the performance of motor skills. For instance, windy conditions may affect the trajectory of a thrown ball.
- Task constraints are the specific requirements or parameters of the activity or task being performed. This includes the rules of the game, equipment used, complexity of the task, and available time. Task constraints shape the movement solutions that children employ to achieve the task objectives. For example, the rules of a game may dictate how a child dribbles a ball or the strategy they use to score a goal. The teacher has the most control over this constraint and can manipulate it where required.

Together, these three types of constraints interact to shape the movement behaviour of children in physical education settings. PE teachers play a crucial role in understanding and navigating these constraints to facilitate optimal motor development. By creating an environment that considers individual capabilities, adapts to environmental conditions, and provides varied task challenges, PE teachers can support children in developing diverse movement skills and problem-solving abilities.

Gray proposes that our responsibility as educators and coaches should centre around cultivating problem-solving abilities and adaptable players rather than solely emphasising the provision of a single "correct" technique solution.

The How (Pedagogy): Play On

The United Nations Convention on the Rights of the Child (1989) Article 31 1. states 'the right of the child to rest and leisure, to engage in play and recreational activities appropriate to the age of the child and to participate freely in cultural life and the arts,' Though it has become less common in recent years, play is now becoming fashionable again as children spend more time indoors and in front of screens than they did in previous generations. It refers to the use of structured and unstructured activities that engage students in movement exploration, creativity, and enjoyment. Play in PE can take various forms, including games, challenges, imaginative activities, and free exploration of movement. It often involves elements of competition, cooperation, problem-solving, and creativity, providing students with opportunities to learn through trial and error, experimentation, and discovery. Creativity is an important aspect of play and it is this 'process of exploration, discovery, problem solving and practice' (Pickard and Maude, 2014, page 1) that provides children with the freedom to express themselves, cultivate resilience, and foster a sense of joy and curiosity that extends beyond the playground.

In her 2022 article titled 'Teaching Fundamental Movement Skills Through Play-Based Pedagogy', Rachael Jefferson-Buchanan passionately promotes a play-based approach to physical education delivery. Jefferson-Buchanan wrote that 'motivational qualities of play have been recognised across all types of play, whether it be physical, expressive or involving games with rules' (page 30). She also acknowledges the links between play and high levels of involvement and intrinsic motivation that can stimulate and empower students, bringing them joy and giving them a sense of ownership.

Scotland's Curriculum for Excellence also placed great emphasis on play in their 'Play Pedagogy' article (2020) as they recognised 'the need for children to have a curriculum that ensures sufficient time for children to play uninterrupted' (Page 2). The Play Pedagogy was introduced to put play experience as central to learning, giving pupils the flexibility to find their own solutions to both new and existing problems.' Further to Jefferson-Buchanan's point, the article reaffirms that 'play engages children in personally meaningful activities, learning about themselves and others, and encourages autonomy and motivation'. The aim is to facilitate experiences where each student determines their learning goals within the Curriculum for Excellence framework.

As we get older, the inclination towards play often gives way to more formalised and goal-oriented endeavours in PE. This shift may stem from the necessity to assess or showcase measurable 'learning' progress. Alternatively, it might arise from the pressure to prepare students for adult versions of sports and activities. Regardless of the rationale, departing from playful approaches in PE entails forfeiting numerous avenues for both learning and enjoyment.

The How (Pedagogy): Pedagogical Approaches

A great PE teacher doesn't just teach skills; they ignite a passion for movement that lasts a lifetime. It would be impossible to cover every possible pedagogical approach in this book.

However, in order to support teachers to consider other opportunities to provide learning in, about and through PE, then the summary below might pique interest for further exploration:

Table 4: Pedagogical Approaches

Pedagogical Approach	Insight into Approach
Models Based Practices	Overview: Models-based practices in PE draw upon various theoretical frameworks and pedagogical models to structure learning experiences that prioritise skill development, critical thinking, and holistic development. By incorporating models-based practices, PE educators can create dynamic learning environments that empower students to engage actively in their physical, cognitive, and socio-emotional growth.
	Cooperative Learning: Cooperative Learning (CL) in PE enables students to collaborate in small groups to achieve shared goals, enriching their learning experiences and fostering vital social skills. By empowering students to take responsibility for reciprocal learning and engage in peer coaching, educators enhance engagement and learning potential. In this model, the teacher transitions to a facilitator role, offering guidance while allowing students greater autonomy in their learning journey.
	Cooperative learning environments facilitate the development of teamwork, communication, and interdependence skills, as students actively participate in the learning process. The holistic nature of CL ensures that physical, cognitive, social, and emotional learning are seamlessly intertwine within the same educational unit.
	Direct Instruction: The Direct Instruction PE Model is a teaching and coaching approach rooted in a traditional, teacher-led instructional style. This method, akin to the command style outlined in Mosston & Ashworth Spectrum of Teaching Styles (check out chapter 10), has been a prevailing method since the late 19th century and well into the 1970s. Embracing a systematic approach, it often employs a 'skill and drill' format, emphasising the accurate replication of techniques before application in competitive scenarios, such as small-sided games. Popularised by Rosenhine in 1979, this model focuses on the teacher delivering information and leading activities to ensure students can perform them accurately and safely.

CHAPTER 8: LEARNING

Models Based Practices	Game-Based Approaches: The games-based approach to delivering PE is an instructional method that focuses on using games and game-like activities as the primary means of teaching. This approach aims to make the learning experience enjoyable and engaging whilst developing knowledge and skills. Teachers often employ 'whole, part, whole', modified games, allowing children to create their own or utilising lesson time to analyse and discuss aspects of the game to effectively deliver learning through games.
	Health-Based PE: Health-based Physical Education (HbPE) is a progressive approach dedicated to cultivating students' well-being through physical activity, prioritising health and wellness over traditional sports skills, competition, and athletic performance. The model distinguishes itself by embracing a holistic perspective that extends beyond only the physical aspects of physical activity. At the core of HbPE lies the self-determination theory of motivation, as proposed by Deci and Ryan in 2000. This theory emphasises the importance of intrinsic motivation, autonomy, and competence in fostering a lasting commitment to physical activity. Aligned with the principles of the HbPE model, Bowler and Sammon (2019) delineate four essential learning aspirations: Habitual Movers, Informed Movers, Motivated Movers and Critical Movers.
	Sport Education: Developed by Daryl Siedentop, Sport Education views physical education as a means to educate students about sport in a holistic manner. In the Sport Education model, students participate in a season-long, thematic unit centred around a specific sport. Throughout the season, students take on various roles such as players, coaches, referees, and team managers, allowing them to experience different aspects of sports participation. The Sport Education model aims to create a more meaningful and engaging PE experience by mirroring the structure and dynamics of real sports seasons
	Teaching Personal and Social Responsibility: Crafted by Don Hellison in the late 1970s, Teaching Personal and Social Responsibility (TPSR) is an educational approach that utilises physical activities not merely for the acquisition of physical skills but as a means to nurture personal, social, and moral development. Emphasising values and goals pertinent to real-world scenarios, this methodology aims to instil qualities such as self-esteem, responsibility, resilience, pride in accomplishments, non-judgmental attitudes, respect for others, teamwork, empathy, temper control, and the demonstration of emotional intelligence. Despite its focus on the social and affective domains, TPSR underscores the importance of concurrently supporting students in becoming more competent, knowledgeable, and physically fit. Hellison's TPSR model delineates five levels of responsibility, progressing from respect for the rights and feelings of others to self-motivation, self-direction, caring, and the application of learned principles beyond the confines of the gym.

Athletic Skills Model	The Athletic Skills Model (ASM), developed by Rene Wormhoudt and Prof. Geert Savelsbergh, offers an approach to PE that goes beyond traditional skill instruction. In ASM, the focus is on developing a broad base of athletic skills that underpin various sports and physical activities. Instead of teaching sports-specific techniques in isolation, ASM emphasises the acquisition of 10 fundamentals (balancing and falling, romping and fighting, moving and locomotion, jumping and landing, tumbling and turning, rolling, throwing, catching, hitting and aiming, kicking, shooting and aiming, climbing and scrambling, swinging and music in motion) . These basic movements form the foundation for more complex athletic abilities. By mastering these fundamental skills, students develop a versatile movement repertoire that can be applied across different sports and activities.
Constraints-Based Approach	The constraints-based approach to skill acquisition in physical education, as advocated by Newell (1986), highlights the interaction between individual, environmental, and task constraints in shaping movement behaviour. Unlike traditional teaching methods that primarily focus on technique instruction, the constraints-based approach recognises that learning occurs within a context that includes both internal and external factors. PE teachers employing this approach create environments that manipulate constraints to encourage adaptive movement solutions. Individual constraints, such as a student's physical abilities and preferences, interact with environmental constraints like space and equipment availability, as well as task constraints such as rules and objectives. By carefully manipulating these constraints, teachers facilitate learning experiences that promote skill acquisition, problem-solving, and decision-making.
Non-Linear Pedagogy	Non-linear pedagogy, as outlined by Chow, Davids, Button, and Renshaw (2016), proposes a dynamic approach to skill acquisition in PE. Unlike traditional linear methods that emphasise step-by-step progression, non-linear pedagogy acknowledges the complex and adaptive nature of learning movement skills. In this approach, teachers create environments rich in variability and opportunities for exploration. Rather than focusing solely on correct technique, non-linear pedagogy emphasises the development of adaptable and creative movers who can effectively respond to the unpredictable demands of real-world movement situations.

Whilst only a very brief insight, each model offers unique insights and strategies aimed at enhancing student engagement, skill development, and overall learning outcomes. By embracing new approaches and delving deeper into the theories behind them, PE teachers can expand their toolkit, ultimately enriching the educational experience for their students.

In Summary

In PE, there's a growing recognition of the limitations inherent in the dominant skill-drill approaches. These methods often fail to engage students effectively, lacking in relevance, inclusivity, excitement, and fun. Evidence also suggests that this approach actually fails to improve competence for the majority of students. Instead, there's a call for a shift towards more dynamic and experiential teaching practices. This involves prioritising the development of fundamental movement skills, embracing play as a valuable learning tool, and considering holistic student development. The aim is to create learning environments that cater to diverse student needs and interests, fostering a lifelong appreciation for physical activity and movement. PE teachers have the power to turn the mundane into the extraordinary, showing students that movement can and should be joyful, not just exercise.

Mid-chapter reflection

What new insights have I gained from this chapter so far?

How does this knowledge reinforce or challenge my current beliefs or practices?

Are there areas or concepts I still need to explore further?

Have I identified any gaps in my team's understanding or practice that need addressing?

How can I share or apply this learning to positively influence others in my team or school?

Part 8.3 – Experts

Models Based Practices
Professor Ash Casey

Models-based practice (MbP) - Big M, hyphen, little b, space, big P– refers to a form of practice in physical education (PE) which is models-based. This means that models (in this case pedagogical) sit at the heart of MbP. They are, as David Kirk and I have suggested (Casey & Kirk, 2024, 2021), the organising centre of PE.

But why?
The argument is that PE is broken. Not as a subject – there are loads of great things that can come out of PE, Phys-ed, Health and physical education, physical education and health, HPE, PEH etc. It's that the dominant approach to PE is broken. The 'one size fits all' approach. The one with traditional sports as the organising centre and where the focus is on sports techniques. This is what's broken. Research tells us – time and time again and in research dating back 50 years – that this doesn't engage all children and certainly doesn't create the learning experiences that lead to lifelong physical activity and movement that so many teachers report to aspire for. Yes, there are exceptions. Great teachers with an incredible passion and drive for engagement can have some impact but not as much as we might hope. Yes, we might inspire some children – just look at most of those who go on to become PE teachers themselves – but not enough.

So, what can we do?
Well, we could ignore Einstein's advice about doing the same thing again and again and expecting different results or teaching fish to climb trees which, to be fair, seems to have been the usual response, or we could do something different. MbP is one of those things we could do which is different. It's not the only thing but it is something that has been tried, tested, refined, and redeveloped, and is out there for you to find. There are thousands of resources on the web that could help you and lots of teachers are using the individual pedagogical models that serve as the operating centre of MbP. Why not have a look?

So, what's a pedagogical model? Or more accurately, what are they?
A pedagogical model is a culmination of years of work by individuals and groups of people. In those years there is a period of thinking and theorising. Most pedagogical models have a theoretical underpinning. Sport Education, for example, is founded on play theory, while cooperative learning is built on social interdependence theory. This theorising has led to

CHAPTER 8: LEARNING

a conceptualisation process and then to some prototype models. These have then been used with teachers in schools and have been reconsidered and refined. Teaching Games for Understanding, for example, was used by PE teachers in Loughborough and Coventry and their action-research work sits at the heart of Bunker and Thorpe's (1986) seminal work. Similarly, Siedentop worked with his doctoral students and other cooperating teachers in Ohio for years prior to the release of Sport Education in 1982.

This means that pedagogical models are the culmination of years of work both in terms of thinking and doing. This is important when we start to think about changing the way we teach.

Research is all well and good but why would you choose a pedagogical model and/or MbP?

The key point, to me at least, is what pedagogical models offer you and your programme. They change the organising centre (if you let them). They each have a main idea, and it's this that can then be used to guide your curriculum. Let's imagine that you have a curriculum that is built around games, sports, and activities. You block your timetable around these activities and try to give each an equal amount of time. Experience of working with hundreds upon hundreds of aspiring and practising teachers tells me this is very common. Six to eight weeks of basketball, of gymnastics, or of tennis for example. I even wrote a paper once called "I just remember rugby" which represented one of my pupil's memories of PE as basically rugby. I understand.

Instead of this let's imagine that the organising centre becomes MbP and you decide to use three pedagogical models in your curriculum for 11 year olds. You choose Sport Education, Cooperative Learning and Health-based physical education. So, your organising centre shifts to focus on developing competent, literate, and enthusiastic sports people, pupils learning with, for and from each other, and valuing the physically active life. The layup and the forward roll lose focus as the outcomes of PE and competence, social interdependence and movement take centre stage.

But why is this important?

MbP asks PE to move away from its skills base and focus instead on developing the child. We want children to understand why movement is important, to be confident and literate enough to move and value what others are doing in the same way as they value what they do. We're not so interested in the specific skills of the layup. Balance, eyes, elbow and follow-through (BEEF) are far less important than scoring? Does it matter if my elbow is in the wrong place if the ball goes in and I have the competence and confidence to play a game of pick-up basketball?

I would say absolutely not.
For me, the dominance of sport-specific skills in PE doesn't help young people to engage in PE and learn. Does it matter if I can play the perfect drop shot if I don't understand the way to

manipulate an opponent to create the space for such a shot? Besides, the last time I played badminton was in my back garden and the fun was in beating my adult children and the dropshot was only part of that.

MbP is a way – not the only one – but a robust and well-established way of changing the core of PE and finding new ways of doing what PE does. It takes one step. One model. And time.

CHAPTER 8: LEARNING

Part 8.4 – Apply

Sport Education
Ryan Parker

Why did I opt to employ Sport Education?
While studying part-time for my Master's at the University of Bedfordshire and working as a PE teacher in a primary school in a deprived area of East England, I decided to implement my first Sport Education unit. Whilst learning about the model in more depth, it became clear to me that the students in my Key Stage 2 cohort could benefit from the potential successes that comes from Sport Education. For a 3 form entry school, such a small percentage played organised sport outside of the school gates and the potential to foster affiliation and a sense of belonging within PE sparked my interest as a way to engage and support my students. I had also noticed that there had been years of embedding undesirable behaviours from within PE lessons -arguing with each other, accusations of cheating, lack of respect for their peers, were just a few examples. Their experience had also been rooted in the 6 week, multi-sport unit rotation of 'warm up- skill- game' pedagogies. Learning how different models could be used to achieve similar objectives whilst offering unique properties, I opted for the Sport Education model to start a journey of healthy competition which allowed the students to feel part of a team in PE and develop a secondary identity in depth for the first time, through various roles, such as Team Captain or Referee, to show them that PE could stand for Powerful Education too. There are many reasons why the Sport Education Model can be the right model for your cohorts and this is one of the biggest reasons why I decided to explore the model the first time in practice.

How did I plan and deliver sport education?
Ensuring teams are heterogeneous is vital when planning for a successful unit. Teams must see that the teams are fair and have been placed together to provide every team and every individual the opportunity to succeed. Units tend to last around 12 lessons in total, however, the length of the unit can change if students require more time in the pre-season phase to become more comfortable and established with their wider roles and responsibilities. Competitive season rotations can vary depending on class sizes. In my practice, smaller teams will always be considered over larger teams. Whilst delivering Sport Education lessons, I make it clear that bonus points (for respect, effort, kindness etc.) are prioritised over points earned within the games. In my games leagues, I offer 3 points for a win, 2 for a draw and 1 for a loss and if two teams are tied post-season, it is the team with the most amount of Bonus Points that win. I also ensure that the season has a clear culminating event to work towards. I tend to plan for

an award ceremony, where you can present awards that go beyond the physical (for example most improved, players' player, team spirit).

What were my key considerations when utilising this model?
I strongly believe in a message I once heard from PE Advisor Ian Roberts: we should teach children what they need to learn, not just what we want to teach. I would add to this notion that we should also teach children how they need to be taught. The Sport Education model is an impeccable approach when considering the social, cognitive and (often neglected) affective domains. When matched carefully with the physical, Sport Education can unlock seminal moments of children's school careers. We must firstly consider the national curriculum itself and ask 'What is it that I want these children to learn?'. In my opinion the 'how' is the next consideration. What do the children need to experience in that moment? This is where an array of models could come into play to facilitate the original unit objectives. Sport Education could be selected if you wish to promote physical development through healthy competition, respect for peers and cultures, cognitive autonomy through tactical awareness and empathy through roles and responsibilities. Personally, I believe the sport and/ or physical activity should be tertiary in the process of designing a meaningful curriculum. The sport in question should be the driver to accelerate the curriculum criteria (and could come from the tail end of a 'Games Making' unit driven through the Cooperative Learning model). The national curriculum also suggests that sports can have their rules modified where appropriate. Inclusion and accessibility are essential when adapting rules to support all players. For example, in a football season, implementing a rule where players cannot score twice in a row can prevent individuals from dominating gameplay—a consideration that aligns with Daryl Siedentop's original goals for the model. The Unit Lead should select activities that engage, inspire, and motivate students, helping each one to reach their potential.

What has the impact been?
Recently, a college student I taught in Year 5 spoke passionately about her Sport Education experience, vividly recalling her role, the team dance routine they created during playtimes, and how much she wished they had continued this approach in high school. She even credited this experience as the inspiration for her interest in a teaching career! Sport Education can be that seminal moment for students for different reasons. When delivering Sport Education 'seasons' to cohorts for the first time, I am always blown away by the enthusiasm as it peaks towards the latter stages of the unit. Students become invested and take pride in their wider roles and often seek out when they will go through the seasons again. Students see physical education as more than just dribbling around cones and playing full-sided games; they see that they have an identity to excel within PE lessons. It gives them something to look back on with positive memories which will inspire them to continue seeking out independence and leadership opportunities in the next stages of their school lives. I firmly believe that physical

education makes children's lives better and Sport Education can become a pivotal point they value beyond their school days.

Constraints Led Approach
Nathan Walker

Applying a Constraints-Led Approach in Physical Education

The Constraints-Led Approach (CLA) in physical education is a strategic framework that leverages the manipulation of constraints to achieve desired learning outcomes. Teachers familiar with the STEP model (Space, Task, Equipment, and People) often use the term 'conditions' to describe this approach. By altering these conditions, teachers can introduce new rules and structure to facilitate learning. This method is prevalent in PE teaching, with conditioned games being a common tool. However, the CLA extends beyond basic manipulation by emphasising principles that ensure perception-action coupling and other elements of Nonlinear Pedagogy (NLP), which foster search and exploration within a representative learning environment.

To effectively implement CLA, teachers must focus not just on what changes they make, but why they make them. This reflective practice ensures that the adaptations serve the educational goals. For example, the manipulation of task constraints—such as changing the size of the playing space to increase opportunities for players to experience one versus one contexts in Hockey or Lacrosse, or telling a defending team in Football or Rugby to over-commit to create space for the attacking team—can prompt students to engage with related affordances and explore novel movement solutions and strategies (Renshaw et al., 2019). These interventions must be purposeful and aligned with the desired learning outcomes to be effective.

The key to successful constraint manipulation lies in the teacher's ability to observe and understand the emergent behaviours of students during activities. Sound subject knowledge and keen observation are crucial. Recognising the inherent constraints within a task, such as the rules of a game, helps ensure that the activities match the students' capabilities. For instance, the complexity of Handball or Tchoukball might be overwhelming for beginners, so modifying the game or choosing a different activity that aligns with their skill level is essential. This initial mapping of appropriate games to student abilities sets the stage for systematic constraint manipulation, promoting both motivation and learning.

Research on the manipulation of constraints, such as in basketball, highlights the systematic and random adjustments that can be made. Systematic changes are planned and structured, whereas random manipulations can introduce variability once students have mastered the basic task, encouraging further exploration of movement solutions. This adaptability and responsiveness to student readiness are hallmarks of the CLA.

CHAPTER 9: **INCLUSION**

Figure 25: Newell's Constraint Model (1986)

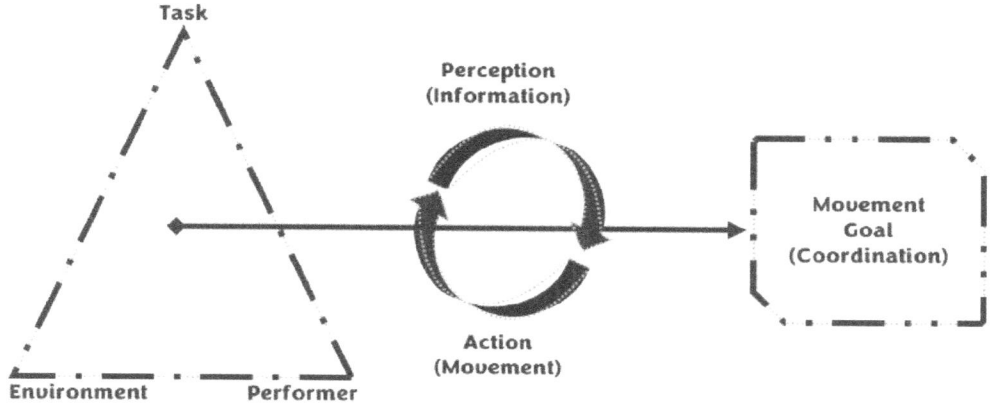

Newell's Constraint Model (1986) reinforces that learning new skills is influenced not just by the student's capabilities but also by the nature of the task and the environment. Individual differences mean that progress varies among students, and adopting a CLA allows teachers to tailor their approach to each student's needs. This student-centred methodology places individual differences at the forefront of planning and teaching, ensuring a more inclusive and effective learning experience.

The Role of the PE Teacher in a CLA: Planning and Teaching

The implementation of a CLA requires thoughtful planning and execution. Teachers must integrate guiding principles that support this approach. Here are some key principles:

1. **Simplify Rather than Decompose:** Simplification involves presenting the entire task or skill from the start, rather than breaking it down into isolated parts. This holistic approach allows students to engage with the task's inherent complexity and develop a comprehensive understanding. Simplifying means adjusting the task's difficulty without distorting its essence, encouraging natural skill development and transfer to various contexts. An excellent example of this in action is illustrated by Moy and colleagues (2014), this study explored coaches who have adopted a constraints-led approach who were working with hurdle athletes with various levels of confidence and competence. In an attempt to simplify the task, the coaches adapted their activities to meet the needs of individuals by changing

the height and distances between each hurdle whilst maintaining the same distance of the race and the nature of competing in a race environment.
2. **Constrain to Afford:** This principle involves using constraints to guide learning toward specific outcomes. Constraints can be external, like modifying the playing area, or internal, such as altering cognitive cues. By intentionally manipulating these constraints, educators create environments that encourage exploration of different solutions. For example, reducing the playing area size can foster quick decision-making and positioning skills. Constraints thus shape learners' behaviour, promoting adaptability and creativity.
3. **Align to Intentions:** Alignment ensures that constraints and tasks match the learning objectives of the curriculum. Tasks that mirror real-life situations make learning more meaningful and applicable. Aligning constraints with objectives ensures that skills developed are transferable to everyday life or specific sports, enhancing the educational value of PE. Teachers should emphasise 'knowledge of the environment' alongside 'knowledge about the environment,' supporting the principles of nonlinear pedagogy. One common mistake is that teachers can add too many layers of conditions or constraints that the task and environment becomes unrealistic and often strays away from the learning objective.
4. **Repetition without Repetition:** This principle focuses on promoting variability through repeated exposure to tasks with subtle differences. Rather than repeating the same task, learners encounter variations that challenge them to adapt and adjust. This approach helps develop a broader skill set, encouraging learners to generalise their learning and apply it to diverse situations. This variability enhances cognitive flexibility, problem-solving, and adaptability, crucial for successful skill execution in dynamic environments. For example, rather than a basketball player repeating shots from a similar location on the court, receiving a similar feed/pass before shooting, and under no pressure from a defensive player, a repetition without repetition approach would encourage the player to move to different location after every shot, it would also encourage the feed/pass before the shot to be high in variety (distance, speed, height, timing), and would also introduce pressure and non-pressure at different occasions which encourages the performer to adapt to the environment.

Evidence of Impact and Knowledge of the Environment

Research supports the efficacy of a CLA in fostering skill development and adaptability. Studies in sports like basketball demonstrate how systematic and random manipulations of constraints can enhance learning outcomes. Evidence shows that such approaches help students develop a deeper understanding of their environment, promoting both 'knowledge of the environment' and 'knowledge about the environment.'

The CLA's focus on individual differences and tailored learning experiences aligns with contemporary educational goals, emphasising inclusivity and student-centred learning. By understanding and applying these principles, PE teachers can create engaging, effective learning environments that foster exploration, adaptability, and holistic skill development.

In conclusion, the Constraints-Led Approach offers a robust framework for PE teaching, combining strategic constraint manipulation with guiding principles that promote meaningful and transferable learning experiences. Through thoughtful planning, observation, and alignment with educational objectives, teachers can leverage CLA to enhance student engagement and skill development in physical education.

Chapter 8 Summary

Learning: From Dread to Delight

DREAD

Skill Drill:
Overemphasis on sports and skill drills, limiting students' exposure to diverse movement experiences.

Inactive:
Students stood around waiting for their turns in isolated drills.

Adult Led:
Irrelevant content delivery in PE lessons, leading to disengagement and boredom among students.

DELIGHT

FMS:
Emphasis on fostering fundamental movement skills acquisition during childhood to lay the foundation for lifelong physical activity participation.

Everyone Involved:
Use activities in which all children are involved (no lines, no 'outs' and lots of play).

Play:
Adoption of a play-based approach in PE delivery, providing students with opportunities for movement exploration, creativity, and enjoyment.

Where would you place yourself right now?

DREAD ⟵——————————————⟶ DELIGHT

Reflection Questions
- How can I incorporate play-based teaching methods to boost students' motivation and participation?
- Am I providing varied opportunities for students to develop fundamental movement skills for lifelong physical activity?
- How can I adapt my teaching methods to accommodate individual differences and environmental constraints in PE?
- Could I/my department trial any of the pedagogical models mentioned ?

Call to Action

As we conclude this chapter, it's time to reflect on what you've learned and consider how to apply it. The SHIFT mnemonic can guide you through the next steps: a structured approach to transform your insights into meaningful actions. Take a moment to work through the following questions:

S **Summarise** the key takeaway from this chapter that stands out to you.

H **Highlight** how this takeaway challenges or aligns with your current practices.

I **Initiate** a small change or step right now to put what you've learned into practice.

F **Frame** how this change will contribute to achieving your long-term vision for PE.

T **Take** others on the journey—share your new insights and encourage collaboration.

References

Barnard Flory, S. (2014). Sociocultural issues in physical education. Rowman & Littlefield.

Bowler, M., & Sammon, P. (2020). Health-based physical education – A framework for promoting active lifestyles in children and young people. Part 1: Introducing a new pedagogical model for health-based physical education. Physical Education Matters, 15(3), 60–63.

Chow, J. Y., Davids, K., Button, C., & Renshaw, I. (2016). Nonlinear pedagogy in skill acquisition: An introduction. Routledge.

Costas, B. (2019). Learning in, through and about movement – Teaching research methods and research skills, engaging the imagination to develop creative and reflective thinkers. University of Hertfordshire. https://www.herts.ac.uk/link/volume-4,-issue-1/learning,-in,-through-and-about-movement-teaching-research-methods-and-research-skills,-engaging-the-imagination-to-develop-creative-and-reflective-thinkers [Accessed 10 April 2024]

Goddard Blyth, S. (2011). The genius of natural childhood: Secrets of thriving children. Hawthorns Press.

Gray, R. (2021). How we learn to move: A revolution in the way we coach & practice sports skills. Perception Action Consulting & Education LLC.

Griggs, G., & Randall, V. (2022). An introduction to physical education. Routledge.

Hamilton, J., & Wood, J. (2020). Playful pedagogy: A guide to getting started. Play Scotland.

Harris, J., & Cale, L. (2019). Promoting active lifestyles in schools. Human Kinetics.

Hendry, D. T., & Hodges, N. J. (2018). Early majority engagement pathway best defines transitions from youth to adult elite men's soccer in the UK: A three time-point retrospective and prospective study. Psychology of Sport and Exercise, 36, 81–89.

Jefferson-Buchanan, R. (2022). Teaching fundamental movement skills through play-based pedagogy. Journal of Physical Education, Recreation & Dance, 93(8), 28–33. https://doi.org/10.1080/07303084.2022.2108171

Mainsbridge, C. P., Iannucci, C., Pill, S., & Williams, J. (2024). Is there education in physical education? A narrative systematic review of research in physical education and learning. Sport in Society, 1–25. https://doi.org/10.1080/17430437.2024.2368628

Moy, B., Renshaw, I., & Davids, K. (2014). Overcoming acculturation: Physical education recruits' experiences of an alternative pedagogical approach to games teaching. Physical Education & Sport Pedagogy, 21(4), 386–406.

Newell, K. M. (1986). Constraints on the development of coordination. In M. G. Wade & H. T. A. Whiting (Eds.), Motor development in children: Aspects of coordination and control (pp. 341–360). Martinus Nijhoff.

Ofsted. (2018). Research review series: PE. Department for Education. https://www.gov.uk/government/publications/research-review-series-pe/research-review-series-pe [Accessed 7 April 2024]

Pickard, A., & Maude, P. (2014). Teaching physical education creatively. Routledge.

Pickard, A., & Maude, P. (2021). Teaching physical education creatively (2nd ed.). Routledge.

Quennerstedt, M., Landi, D., & Casey, A. (2024). Busier, happier, and good(er) – 40 years on from 'Busy, Happy, and Good' as success in teaching physical education. Quest, 1–21. https://doi.org/10.1080/00336297.2024.2393624

Randall, V., & Griggs, G. (2022). An introduction to primary physical education. Routledge.

Renshaw, I., Davids, K., Newcombe, D., & Roberts, W. (2019). The constraints-led approach: Principles for sports coaching and practice design. Taylor & Francis.

Ryan, R. M., & Deci, E. L. (2000). Self-determination theory and the facilitation of intrinsic motivation, social development, and well-being. American Psychologist, 55(1), 68–78. https://doi.org/10.1037/0003-066X.55.1.68

Sport England. (2023). Active Lives Children and Young People Survey: Academic year 2022–23 report. https://sportengland-production-files.s3.eu-west-2.amazonaws.com/s3fs-public/2023-12/Active%20Lives%20Children%20and%20Young%20People%20Survey%20-%20academic%20year%202022-23%20report.pdf [Accessed 20 April 2024]

Swim England. (2017). Swim group review of curriculum swimming and water safety lessons: Recommendations to ensure all children leave primary school able to swim. https://www.swimming.org/swimengland/swimming-water-safety-schools/ [Accessed 8 April 2024]

Sullivan, L. (2023). Primary Concept Curriculum. PE Scholar.

The United Nations. (1989). The United Nations Convention on the Rights of the Child. https://www.unicef.org.uk/wp-content/uploads/2016/08/unicef-convention-rights-child-uncrc.pdf [Accessed 23 March 2024]

Wormhoudt, R., & Savelsbergh, G. (n.d.). The Fundamental 10 from the Athletic Skills Model.

CHAPTER 9: **INCLUSION**

Chapter 9: Inclusion

Lee Sullivan, Shrehan Lynch, Simon Scarborough and Faith Newton

Part 9.1 – Insight
Lee Sullivan

In this chapter, we will explore the important issue of inclusion and ensuring that every student feels valued and safe. We will delve into social justice and trauma-informed PE and the impact that a negative PE space can have on an individual. 'Trauma can be a short- or long-term emotional response to a stressful or disturbing occurrence. Examples include bullying, physical or emotional abuse, rape, neglect, grief, poverty, war, discrimination, etc.' (Lynch, Walton-Fisette, Luguetti, 2022, page 60). Trauma, whether short- or long-term, can lead to a range of emotional and behavioural responses. By fostering trauma-informed spaces, PE educators can better support the well-being and learning of our young people.

Unlike previous chapters, which begin with a narrative designed link with a contemporary PE issue, this chapter takes a different approach. We begin with the personal testimony of Will, a 15-year-old student from England who has graciously agreed to share his experiences. No part of his account has been changed and is published exactly as received. His story serves as a poignant reminder of the complexities and realities that many students encounter in PE classes, offering valuable insights into the impact of the environment on individual well-being and engagement.

Will's Story
From a young age, I have always had a passion for dancing. I remember dressing up to watch Strictly Come Dancing every Saturday night, and it being one of my favourite things to do. Now, as an older secondary student, I am a dance prefect for my school's dance club and have been doing ballroom and Latin dance since primary school. I love the freedom of expression dance gives me and the way it makes me feel alive inside. Dance has led me to create many amazing friendships throughout my life as well. Overall, I would say my dance is one of the most important things in my life.

FROM PE DREAD TO DELIGHT

In addition to dance, I also swim. My parents have taken me to swimming lessons since I was a baby and from there grew my love for the sport. I am now part of my local swimming club. Like dance, it is an important part of my life; it helps me clear my mind, improve my mental health, and socialise with the friends I have made at my club. A few months ago, from the time of writing this, I was competing in my district's county championships, which is a goal I have had for a long time. I would say that I am not an extremely competitive person, but when I'm in the pool, it gives me confidence to compete and improve upon my personal bests.

My experiences with PE and school sports are vastly different from my accomplishments in the pool and on the dance floor.

Ever since my first experiences of PE in primary school, I have always felt uncomfortable or out of place. On the playground, I found football too rough and intimidating, I would've much rather played dress up or create imaginary games with my friends. I remember the one time I tried to play football with the boys, and I hated how they turned so aggressive and competitive, shouting at me when I didn't do the right thing with the ball. My PE lessons were just the same, I just did not enjoy or feel comfortable in that competitive environment, where I was forced to play games of sports, I did not understand with a group of children that did not have the emotional intelligence to accept that some people didn't really care about winning. My PE coaches seemed to not care about my struggles, so I silently survived those primary school lessons.

At secondary school, my relationship with PE worsened even more. Secondary school brought with it its own challenges outside of the subject, like friendship issues and fitting in. I had come out as gay and was experiencing homophobia a lot in school. The boys all seemed to be homophobic, intimidating and just generally unpleasant. The culture at that school was very elitist, the teachers favoured the boys and there was no option for those who didn't enjoy PE (one of those being me) but suffered. A mixed gender group was created when I was in year 8 which I joined, however I did not get along with my teacher. He was the most non-understanding toxic masculine teacher in the department. I also despised the changing rooms. Any time I was in them, I was always wary of receiving homophobic abuse, which did happen on several occasions. I like to describe the boys' changing rooms as the 'festering pits of toxic masculinity', where these boys' attitudes go noticed but unchallenged by PE teachers.

Due to the extreme toxic culture of that school, in Year 9, I moved to another school. Here, I was hoping my experience with PE would be slightly better. And to an extent, it was. I was no longer at such a high risk of homophobia, and my teachers were more understanding. But still, I struggle. I am in an all-boys group, and I don't feel comfortable in it. Every nerve, bone and muscle in my body dreads going to PE. My teacher likes to think his group 'learns through gameplay', whilst I'm on the astro-pitch desperately trying to avoid the football being kicked around wishing to be anywhere else. The only thing it's teaching me to do is hate PE more.

CHAPTER 9: **INCLUSION**

I feel invisible and ignored. Dodgeball is one of the worst, in a room full of boys hurtling balls in my direction I feel trapped and panicked, like a deer in headlights. My teacher asks me why I am not participating, and I tell him it's because I physically can't. My survival instincts, built up from all my years of negative experiences in the subject, force me to panic and feel immensely unhappy and uncomfortable whenever I am forced into an environment like that.

I feel unseen, unheard. PE shouldn't feel like a constant battle to survive for students like me. The culture in schools needs to shift to a more caring one, where those who aren't comfortable or don't have the skills playing/ doing certain sports are nurtured and not ignored.

Social Stressors

Individuals who identify as LGBTQ+ (or other social categories as specified in part 2 of this chapter) may encounter trauma beyond the confines of the physical education classroom. Despite assertions by many, including those within the profession and policymakers, as well as stakeholders external to it, that PE and sports can yield positive outcomes, they may inadvertently contribute to trauma rather than serving as a place to relieve it. Through Will's story we can start to understand how PE can cause trauma. The stress that PE causes Will can be better understood by exploring the Social Stressors Theory. Stress can be defined as any condition that triggers the individual's adaptive response (Dohrenwend, 2000).

Stress researchers have identified individual and social stressors, including traumatic events, chronic stress, and daily hassles. Social stress considers the impact of social environments, such as prejudice and discrimination, on mental and physical health. This concept suggests that stigmatised social categories, like race, gender, or sexuality, may experience heightened stress due to societal biases. Furthermore, the minority stress theory suggests that negative social experiences, like stereotypes and prejudice, can harm mental health. This stress is unique, chronic, and socially rooted, stemming from broader societal structures rather than individual events (Meyer, 2003). For instance, research on minority stress among LGBTQ+ individuals show how sexual prejudice can lead to mental health issues.

In PE settings, minority stress may manifest through biased treatment or lack of inclusivity, contributing to chronic stress rooted in societal structures. Connections to professional sports culture may unconsciously reinforce negative stereotypes and biases among PE teachers. These individuals, influenced by their own positive experiences with physical activity and sports in such environments, may inadvertently recreate toxic dynamics in the PE setting. This perpetuation of harmful norms and attitudes, whether through unconscious bias or conscious choice, can contribute to minority stress within the educational context. Thus, understanding and addressing social stressors in PE is crucial for promoting the well-being of minority groups.

Trauma-Causing PE

Will's narrative sheds light on the potential trauma that PE classes can induce. His recount illustrates how the competitive and sometimes hostile environment of PE, exacerbated in Will's story by issues such as homophobia and toxic masculinity, can deeply impact students. Will's experiences highlight the importance of creating a safe and inclusive space within PE, where students feel respected, understood, and supported. This trauma can have far-reaching consequences, impacting students' engagement, self-esteem, and self-identity. When students endure such negative experiences in PE, they may develop aversions to physical activity altogether, leading to long-term disengagement from exercise and sports.

Everything we are hoping to achieve in PE is lost when some students are subjected to these harmful experiences. Thus, it is imperative for educators to address and rectify these issues to ensure that all students can benefit positively from their PE experiences.

CHAPTER 9: **INCLUSION**

Part 9.2 – Delve

Understanding our students' likes, backgrounds, and potential traumas is crucial in shaping effective PE delivery. The second part of this chapter will focus on socially just and trauma-informed PE. Social justice is a difficult topic to talk about. Teachers often want to know more about it but are afraid to ask in case they offend or say the wrong thing. Therefore, by delving into these important topics, we can equip educators with the necessary insights to create inclusive and supportive PE environments for all students.

What is Social Justice?

As explained on the Taylor & Francis Insights website ("What is Social Justice?", 2024), Social justice refers to the fair and equitable distribution of resources, opportunities, and rights within society, with the aim of ensuring that all individuals, regardless of their background or circumstances, can access the same benefits and opportunities. It involves addressing systemic inequalities, discrimination, and oppression to create a more just and inclusive society

To understand social justice, it is important to understand the differences between: inequality, equality and equity.

Inequality: the unequal access where some people get more, and some get less.
Equality: everyone gets the same distribution or assistance.
Equity: the funnelling of resources to those that need it, some people use their advantages to help others, no one goes without; instead tools are designed to support inequitable situations and circumstances and fairness for all groups to be successful. (Lynch, Walton-Fisette & Luguetti, 2022, pages 1 & 2).

In our blog titled 'Visualising Social Justice Terminology in PE: Clarifications and Insights', Shrehan Lynch and I present a PE specific visual analogy, adapted from the 100m sprint analogy described in Pedagogies of Social Justice in Physical Education, Lynch, Walton-Fisette, and Luguetti (2022).

Figure 26: Visualising Social Justice Terminology in PE

FROM PE DREAD TO DELIGHT

CHAPTER 9: **INCLUSION**

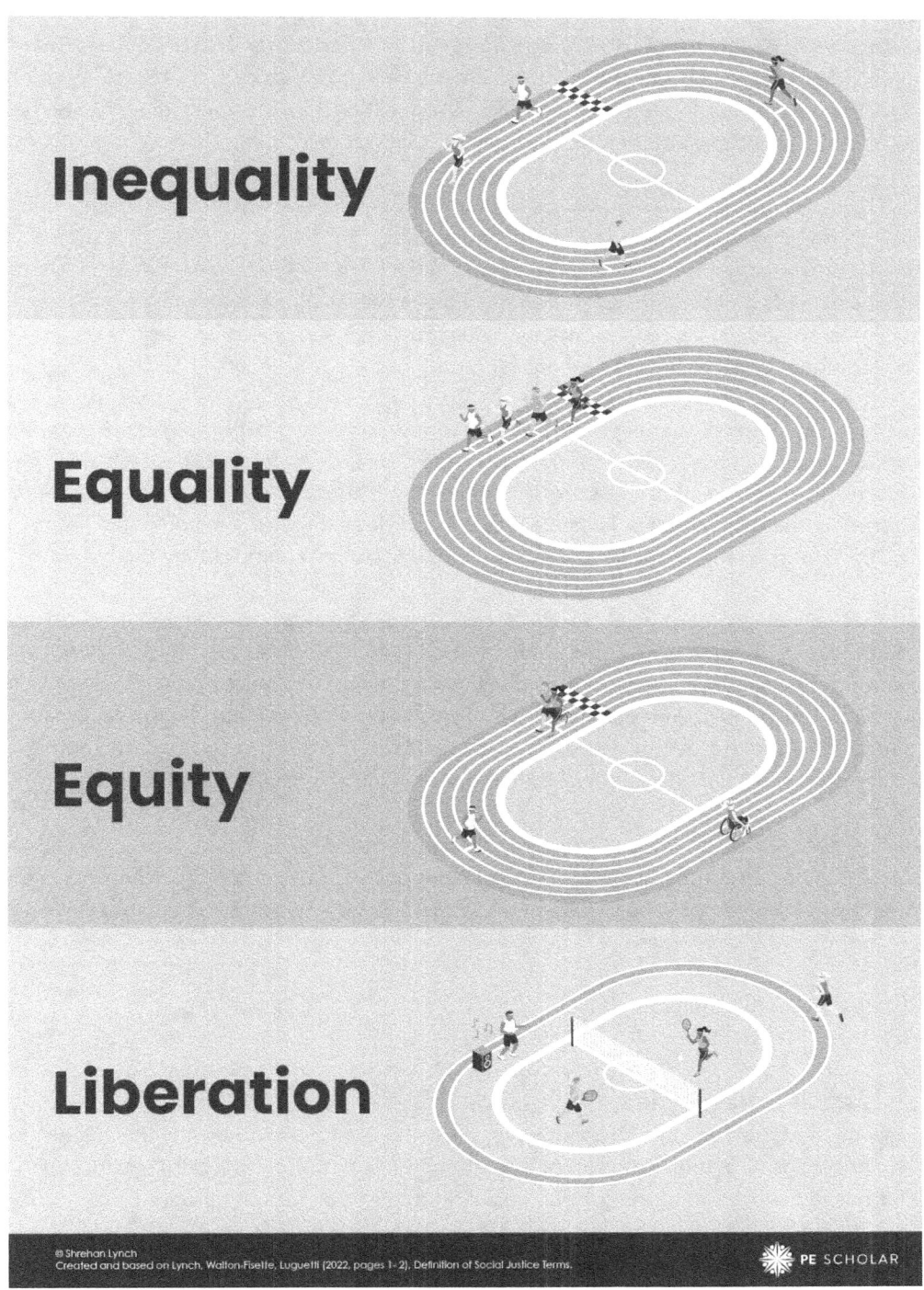

251

Inequality: This illustration depicts individuals beginning at different points on a track, symbolising how people start life with varying levels of opportunity. It highlights systemic disparities in resources, opportunities, and treatment based on factors such as race, gender, and socioeconomic status. In the context of physical education (PE), inequality may manifest as unequal access to facilities, equipment, or extracurricular opportunities.

Equality: Here, all individuals are shown starting from the same point on the track, representing the idea of providing the same resources or opportunities to everyone. While this approach aims for uniform treatment, it can be problematic in PE because it assumes that all students have identical needs and starting points. For example, while all students may receive the same running shoes, some may lack experience with doing up their shoe laces, an understanding of running technique, or even the physical ability to run.

Equity: This illustration emphasises the need to recognise different starting points and provide resources and opportunities tailored to individual needs, ensuring comparable outcomes. In PE, this might involve offering adaptive programs or additional support to marginalised students to guarantee fair participation. For instance, this could include utilising pupil premium funds to provide PE kits or sponsoring students to attend a sports summer camp during the holidays.

Liberation: The final illustration, which ideally should be open for interpretation by the individuals depicted, suggests that by removing barriers and dismantling oppressive structures, we can create environments where everyone has the freedom to make choices and thrive without systemic hindrances. In PE, liberation would not only address immediate disparities but also involve rethinking and restructuring the system to eliminate inherent injustices. For the purpose of this illustration, we have depicted individuals engaging in an activity of their choosing.

In many schools, PE it could be argued, has been providing unequal access to active opportunities. Often the most 'talented', fit or experienced students are afforded the most opportunities to play competitively (particularly if the outcome of extra-curricular activities is prioritised) and so the gap widens.

We must be striving for equitable PE.

Social Justice Pedagogies

Social justice pedagogies entail recognising inequalities and empowering individuals or groups to enact social change. In physical education, these pedagogies aim to address social inequities based on factors such as gender, sexuality, ethnicity, or socio-economic status, rather than perpetuating marginalisation. By emphasising inclusion, democracy, social justice, and equity, they prompt students to critically examine and challenge existing power structures and dominant narratives. Ultimately, they can lead to advocacy and community action. Transformative learning occurs when students develop awareness of their own perspectives and gain new insights into the world around them. This process relies on pedagogies that foster reflection on values, social norms, and assumptions (Gerdin, et. Al. 2020). In essence, it is the staff who establish the prevailing culture within a school. When staff members are socially just and aware, they foster a culture of inclusion through their deeper understanding. For instance, when staff advocate for transgender students, it promotes acceptance and support within the school community. Conversely, when staff lack awareness, they may overlook alternative accommodations, resulting in the continued suffering of marginalised students, as highlighted in Will's experiences.

In their paper 'Social Justice Pedagogies in School Health and Physical Education—Building Relationships, Teaching for Social Cohesion and Addressing Social Inequities', (2020) Gerdin, Larsson, Schenker, Linnér, Mordal Moen, Westlie, Smith and Philpot explore and recommend three key themes that embody social justice pedagogies: relationships, teaching for social cohesion, and addressing social inequities through explicit teaching and action. They are presented in a deliberate order, as building relationships often precedes teaching for social cohesion, forming the groundwork for addressing social inequities. Their study found the following relating to each theme:

- **Relationships:** Teachers across diverse cultural contexts emphasised the need to understand students' backgrounds and everyday experiences. Strategies such as learning students' names, establishing connections with their families, and employing caring teaching approaches were highlighted. Consistency in positive interactions and leveraging knowledge of students' abilities and interests to design inclusive activities are also emphasised.
- **Teaching for Social Cohesion:** In this section, the participant teachers emphasised the significance of fostering relationships and inclusiveness as fundamental aspects of teaching for social cohesion in PE. They highlighted the importance of understanding students' backgrounds and everyday experiences, using strategies such as learning students' names and connecting with their families. Culturally inclusive pedagogies were also employed, with some teachers incorporating indigenous languages and values into their lessons. Furthermore, the teachers prioritised cooperative activities and discussions aimed at promoting teamwork and understanding of diversity. Additionally, they focused on fostering personal and social responsibility among students, providing opportunities for independent decision-making and self-reflection.
- **Addressing** Social Inequalities through Explicit Teaching and Action: Across different countries, teachers made exceptions to rules, such as PE uniform requirements, to ensure inclusion, especially for students from lower socio-economic backgrounds. Additionally, they actively promoted marginalised groups by incorporating cultural elements and providing extra support where needed. Moreover, teachers addressed social inequities by raising awareness through discussions about gender, ethnicity, and cultural identity in

sports participation. Critical reflection on teaching practices, considering power dynamics and prioritising student safety and well-being, was also evident.

Isms

In their book 'Pedagogies of Social Justice in Physical Education', Shrehan Lynch, Jennifer L. Walton-Fisette and Carla Luguetti provide a much-needed explanation of key areas of social injustice. I have written a brief outline of each, from this book, in the following table:

Table 5: Outline of Key Areas of Social Injustice

	What is it?	**How Can I Teach it?**
Healthism & Fatism	• Healthism centres around the conviction that individuals bear full responsibility for their health, placing significant emphasis on the physical aspect of their bodies. • Fatism is discrimination against individuals perceived as overweight or fat, stemming from societal norms regarding body image and health standards.	• Use diverse images of sports figures or individuals engaged in physical activity for discussions on perceptions of health, fitness, and stigma associated with body image. • Engage in readings and discussions about fitness testing, digital technologies, and societal messages regarding health, emphasising critical perspectives and questioning the impact on emotional well-being.
Ableism and Elitism	• Ableism: Belief that disabled individuals are oppressed by societal norms favouring 'normal' productivity and livability standards, leading to constant comparison and marginalisation. • Elitism: Hierarchical dominance of certain groups, like able-bodied individuals, linked to ableism, influencing cultural assumptions and perceptions of bodies in movement spaces.	• Use sports and activities to highlight historical inequities, prompting students to explore exclusions and understand the importance of inclusivity in movement spaces. • Incorporate disabled sports into the curriculum thoughtfully to challenge traditional notions of sport and inclusivity. Offer a variety of disability sports to broaden students' understanding and enjoyment of different games.

CHAPTER 9: INCLUSION

	What is it?	**How Can I Teach it?**
Genderism and Sexism	• Genderism, also known as gender binarism, asserts that there are only two distinct genders, male and female, inherently tied to the biological sex assigned at birth. • Sexism predominantly impacts women and girls, often associated with stereotypes and traditional gender roles. It encompasses the notion that one sex or gender is inherently superior to another.	• Introduce yourself with your social identities and pronouns to signal support and inclusivity. Teach students inclusive language and key terms related to gender while exploring sports and activities. • Involve students in deconstructing gendered curricula to foster inclusivity. Allow them to co-create a curriculum that challenges the gender binary, encouraging critical thinking and meaningful participation for all. • Championing girls and women by creating safe spaces where they can participate, thrive, and reach their full potential.
Heterosexism	Heterosexism presumes heterosexuality as the societal and cultural standard, alongside the biassed notion that heterosexual individuals, commonly known as "straight" people, hold social and cultural superiority over individuals within the LGBTQI+ spectrum.	• Teach young people terminology related to sexual identities and reflect on societal perceptions and power dynamics. Discuss ways to create inclusive spaces, such as wearing symbolic items like rainbow lanyards or pride trainers. • Encourage critical analysis of media images and sporting experiences to explore assumptions about sexuality and inclusivity. • Utilise role play activities, such as dance, to challenge gender and sexuality stereotypes in sports. Provide opportunities for students to perform and discuss typical gender roles within these activities.

	What is it?	How Can I Teach it?
Racism	Racism entails prejudice or discriminatory actions aimed at individuals or groups due to their belonging to a marginalised racial or ethnic community.	• Educate young people on terms such as racism, white supremacy, and allyship to understand their role in perpetuating marginalisation. Stress the importance of correctly pronouncing classmates' names to honour their identities. • Review the PE curriculum for racial and ethnic inclusivity. Consider if it represents all students' identities and historical contexts, taking into account the impact of systemic racism. • Analyse racial representation in sports and examine barriers preventing certain groups from participation.
Classism	Classism is the practice of prejudice and discrimination rooted in social class, where individuals or institutions utilise their privileges to marginalise others.	• Arrange small groups of students to produce a concise news report discussing PE and sports within their local area, children's involvement in sports, and their vision for an ideal PE/sport programme. • Assign reading of "The Pencilsword: On a Plate" by Toby Morris and prompt students to maintain a diary reflecting on their privileges. Discuss how the comic illustrates the impact of upbringing on life outcomes, sparking conversation about privilege and meritocracy.

CHAPTER 9: **INCLUSION**

	What is it?	**How Can I Teach it?**
Linguicism	Linguicism refers to discrimination based on language against linguistic minorities across various levels, including language use, accent, dialect, repertoire, and speech.	• Have students create a timeline of their PE and/or sporting experiences, highlighting critical incidents that influenced their motivation. Encourage the use of their first language to provide insight into their cultural and linguistic backgrounds. • Organise students into groups based on their preferred music genre to compile a list of songs representing their community. They can choose songs in their first language. Then, task them with using the lyrics to craft a new song reflecting their community's identity.
Religionism	Religionism refers to discrimination or prejudice directed towards individuals based on their religion or religious beliefs.	• Present students with a scenario about proposed changes to the school calendar, rotating holidays across different religions. Facilitate group discussions to explore reactions and observations about religious accommodation and dominance. • Ask students to individually or in small groups write down words or phrases related to religion. Examples include religion, God, Christianity, Islam, atheist, church, etc. Collect the responses and use them as a reference point for discussion on religious perceptions and associations.

	What is it?	How Can I Teach it?
Colonialism	Colonialism signifies a historical legacy of suffering and devastation, where one nation exerts dominance over another through the establishment of colonies.	• Engage in reflective diary writing to examine your own cultural background and positionality in relation to your teaching. Challenge biases, assumptions, stereotypes, and prejudices by asking questions such as "Who am I?" and "How does my identity influence my pedagogy?" • Integrate non-Western knowledge into PE programs to celebrate indigenous perspectives and cultural richness. Explore indigenous health knowledge and traditional games, considering how to incorporate them respectfully into the curriculum.

What is trauma-informed?

Trauma-informed practice in PE (and beyond) acknowledges the significant impact of trauma on individuals, groups, and communities. It prioritises understanding how trauma influences neurological, biological, psychological, and social development. The UK Office for Health Improvement and Disparities report titled 'Working Definition of Trauma Informed-Practice' (2022) identified three key areas of trauma-informed practice:

- **Realise that trauma can affect individuals, groups and communities:** Trauma-informed practice recognises the wide-ranging impact of trauma on individuals, groups, and communities, understanding its effects on neurological, biological, psychological, and social development.
- **Recognise the signs, symptoms and widespread impact of trauma:** It increases awareness among practitioners of the signs, symptoms, and pervasive impact of trauma, aiming to foster safe environments and trusting relationships within health and care services.
- **Prevent re-traumatisation:** It seeks to avoid re-traumatisation which is the re-experiencing of thoughts, feelings or sensations experienced at the time of a traumatic event or circumstance in a person's past.

ACEs

CHAPTER 9: **INCLUSION**

Adverse childhood experiences (ACEs) are 'events during childhood that are stressful and may impact upon mental and physical health having effects in childhood and future adulthood,' (Scott, 2020).

Neil Moggan, author of 'Time to Rise Up' (2024) summarises the types of traumas that can cause ACEs (page 226):

ACEs can range from Big 'T' Traumas such as:
- Child physical abuse
- Child sexual abuse
- Child emotional abuse
- Emotional neglect
- Physical neglect
- Mentally ill person in the home
- Drug addicted or alcoholic family member
- Witnessing domestic violence
- Loss of a parent to death or abandonment by parental divorce
- Incarceration of family member

To small 'T' traumas such as:
- Moving house
- Birth of a new sibling
- Failing at an exam
- Friendship issues
- Illness/injury
- Loss of opportunity

Moggan adds 'The key thing to remember is that all of us process trauma differently so what might have a significant impact on one person may not have such an impact on another,' (page 227).

Trauma-Informed PE

Understanding the foundational link between philosophical principles and educational practices is essential. Trauma-informed practices are not merely theoretical concepts, but integral components woven into the fabric of your practice and the educational experiences offered. When considering your trauma-informed approach, you may want to consider the following:

- **Safe Environment:** Create a safe space for all students.
- **Active Empowerment:** Empower students to use their voice and take responsibility for their learning.
- **Foster Equity:** Foster an equitable learning environment through restorative practices.

- **Embedded Philosophy:** Ensure that trauma-informed and restorative approaches are embedded into educational programs and consistently lived out.

By embracing trauma-informed and restorative approaches, educators create environments where every student can thrive.

The Inclusive Curriculum

When considering the content of our curriculum, Barnard Flory, Tischler and Sanders (2014) offer these four points of guidance:

- **Diversity:** Due to the varying backgrounds, interests, skills, etc. diversity should be a key consideration. This does not mean only considering a range of different team sports, but consider a range of active opportunities like outdoor, indoor, competitive, non-competitive, group, individual, social outcomes, and medium to high levels of physical activity.
- **Culturally Relevant Activities:** These activities resonate with students' family and community identities. We must get to know and understand the backgrounds of the children we teach and how that might impact the activities students engage with outside of school. Educators must also consider the opportunities available in their local community for students to engage with. There is little point in students being taught a sport or activity, if there are no clubs or ways to engage with it for miles. We must maximise the chances of further engagement.
- **Popular Physical Activity Culture:** A good way to get students active is to consider what is popular at that time. It can help PE connect with the young people we teach. Embrace the change and whilst the popularity of some activities are only temporary, the opportunity to build programs around youth culture can excite and engage students.
- **Adult Activity Trends:** The authors insist that 'in order for PE to remain relevant, it must do better in aligning its curricular with adult physical activity trends,' (page 13). There is a clear disconnect between what students are taught in PE and how adults engage in physical activity. If we are truly aiming for lifetime engagement, then we must also consider preparing them for how adults choose to remain active.

These principles not only enhance the effectiveness of physical education but also foster inclusivity and help to prepare students for sustained engagement in physical activity beyond their school years.

Mid-chapter reflection

What new insights have I gained from this chapter so far?

How does this knowledge reinforce or challenge my current beliefs or practices?

Are there areas or concepts I still need to explore further?

Have I identified any gaps in my team's understanding or practice that need addressing?

How can I share or apply this learning to positively influence others in my team or school?

Part 9.3 – Experts

Social Justice
Dr Shrehan Lynch

I am an Associate Professor at the University of East London with over a decade of dedication and passion for promoting social justice in physical education and youth sports. It wasn't until my PhD studies that I truly developed a deep love for reading, inquiry, and a particular thirst for justice. Over the PhD years, through various courses and readings on sociocultural issues, I realised that many of the mistakes I made as a practising physical education teacher were valuable learning experiences. These experiences remind me that while perfection in teaching doesn't exist, striving for it is essential. It's that goal at the top of the mountain we all aim for, but as social justice issues evolve, achieving true justice in society remains an ongoing pursuit.

In our own movement spaces, my recently published book, Pedagogies of Social Justice in Physical Education and Youth Sport, serves as a great starting point for any physical education teacher or coach. Written in accessible language, it offers an overview of contemporary issues in physical education, including racism, sexism, classism, heterosexism, ableism, and colonialism, and discusses what we can do as educators to address these social justice challenges within our spheres. While it would be ideal to eliminate these issues from society altogether, it's also unrealistic. In place of you reading another book in more detail right now, I want to offer you five practical tips that you can implement immediately and ponder within your physical education departments:

1. Support the Psychological Needs of All Students
Ensure your lesson objectives include an affective component. For example, ask students: "What are the ways my body enjoys moving?" or "Rank your enjoyment in this activity (on a scale of 1-5, or using smiley faces for younger students)." Encourage students to write three words that describe their feelings towards the lesson or activity. Use this feedback to inform your planning. If a student indicates limited enjoyment, check in with them as they leave the lesson to gather insights and adjust your approach.

2. Ensure the Safety of All Students
Create a safe environment, from the changing rooms to the lesson locations. Consider whether your spaces are inclusive. For example, is there a policy for accommodating trans or gender nonconforming students? Are your facilities wheelchair accessible? Do your spaces affirm or exclude marginalised groups? The PE office has traditionally been a space dominated by hegemonic masculinity, and over the years, I've heard countless stories from trainee teachers about unsettling experiences in these environments. What rules does your department have

CHAPTER 9: INCLUSION

in place to ensure that all staff feel safe and authentically themselves in these spaces? Are students allowed in these spaces and if so, do they feel safe?

3. Show Love Through Care, Empathy, and Commitment
Love, often neglected in education, should not be reserved only for parents or guardians. As bell hooks, a renowned African American scholar, novelist, and academic, explains, love encompasses care, empathy, kindness, commitment, and honesty shared among individuals. Teachers should embody these qualities towards their students. For example, ask students: "What do you love about moving independently or as part of a team?", "What do you love about physical education at this school?", or "What do you love (or hate) about your physical education teacher?". I am certain asking some of these questions under the right circumstances will bring you honest and reflexive results!

4. Promote Belonging for Every Student
Foster an environment where students feel respected, seen, heard, and represented. Do the posters on your walls reflect the diversity of your students? Are all members of society represented in your curriculum materials? Do you always emphasise football, or do you explore your students' varied sporting interests? Building belonging can be as simple as engaging with students on shared interests, such as discussing a popular show like Strictly Come Dancing with a student who is passionate about it such as Will who shared he was in his biography would have made an immense difference. Additionally, when exploring dance in the curriculum, consider asking students about the dance forms that represent their culture and try to incorporate a diverse range of styles, such as urban dance, hip hop, house, street, and funk, rather than just traditional contemporary dance.

5. Enhance Students' Esteem by Promoting Autonomy
Give students a sense of freedom, control, voice, choice, and responsibility. Academic literature provides many examples of how to do this in PE classes, some of which are further explored in my book. As a starting point, ask students what they would like to see in their PE lessons, how they want them set up, and who they prefer to be taught by. Provide opportunities for anonymous feedback where appropriate. For instance, some students may prefer mixed classes, while others might feel more comfortable in single-gender groups – this example will need to be named feedback if you want to act upon it. Years ago, I tried a negotiated curriculum with a Year 10 group of disengaged girls. I asked them what they wanted to do for the year, and we created a 'Tough Mudder' course using old tyres donated by a local mechanic. This co-created curriculum transformed their attitude towards PE, turning reluctance into excitement. Give your students the choice to experience joy in an area of their choosing – you are more likely to foster delight in physical education this way.

I hope these tips offer you some immediate ways to adapt your curriculum, rethink your approach, or at least encourage you to step out of your comfort zone in your ideas, beliefs, curriculum, or pedagogical methods. Social justice matters are an ethical and moral imperative for all teachers. The safety and well-being of our students are within our control, and small changes to our curriculum or pedagogy can have a significant impact. Wishing you all the best in this endeavour!

CHAPTER 10: **GUIDES**

Part 9.4 – Apply

Tackling Homophobia and Transphobia
Simon Scarborough

I strongly believe that Leaders of Physical Education (PE) make strategic decisions about their provision in the best interests of their students. Creating a safe and inclusive environment for all students has been at the heart of my decision making for over two decades. However, I have become aware that some of my decisions and behaviours as a leader will have inadvertently generated anxiety and stress for students who identify as LGBTQ+. Why? Because I was ignorant about the unique challenges that they face growing up.

I started my teaching career in 2002 under Section 28; a law that effectively banned schools from talking or educating young people about homosexuality, which may explain part of my ignorance.

Without the knowledge of the lived experiences of students that identify as LGBTQ+ (or any other protected characteristic that someone may possess) it is understandable that there is a lack of any purposeful advocacy. Taking action to develop an understanding of the issues LGBTQ+ students face in PE, school and the wider community is key to building empathy and becoming a more compassionate educator.

Figure 27: The Ally Continuum

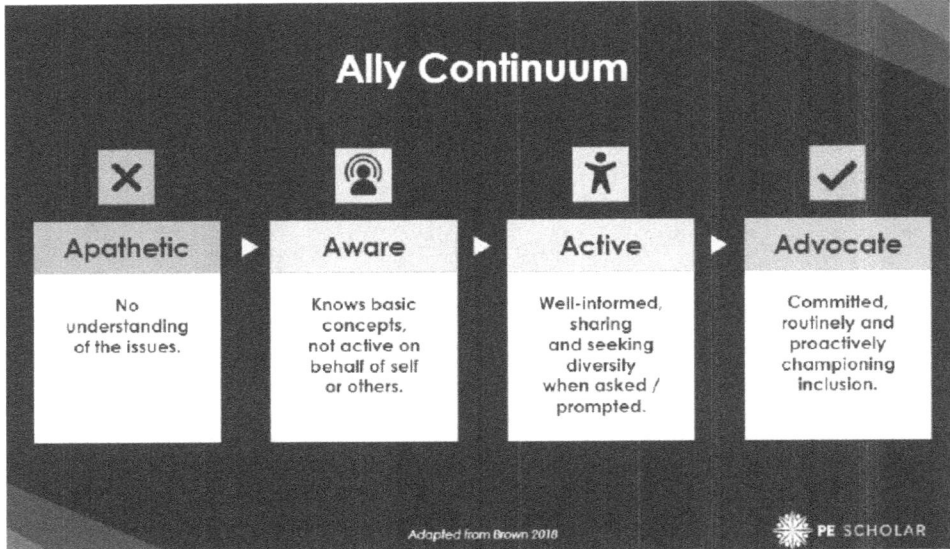

The following five A's of allyship to support the LGBTQ+ community in PE are outlined below:

Awareness about LGBTQ+ is very important. Understanding the LGBTQ+ community and their lived experiences, being knowledgeable and educated on the issues, facts, laws, policies and culture of the LGBTQ+ community, will help the PE profession to create more inclusive environments.

In my experience, local charities that support the LGBTQ+ community are eager to offer their help and support. Schools often have a LGBTQ+lead (unpaid) who stays up-to-date with the changing landscape, organises staff training and advocates for their LGBT students, perhaps through an LGBTQ+ club. Working closely with these staff will develop a better understanding of the challenges that LGBTQ+ students in your setting face and how the PE department can best support them.

Advocacy or, in other words, being seen as a safe person and place for students to be who they are without judgement. Although staff may be in support of the LGBTQ+ community, how would this be obvious to all students in the school? Without this public display of support, LGBTQ+ students can worry about how they will be judged if and when they come out; a constant fear for many.

Wearing an LGBTQ+ pin badge (or similar) is a small gesture that sends an important message to all students. As does more obvious actions such as posters and flags proudly displayed in and around the department. The messaging says we are supportive, we understand the struggles you may be facing, you are safe to be your authentic self in our department.

It is vitally important that PE Departments proactively advocate for all students, modelling respectful language and behaviours to all of our students, particularly when the wider sporting culture (beyond schools) continues to deal with problems of homophobia, transphobia and sex-discrimination.

Adjustments to our language and environments can be made so that we are more inclusive and less binary. Using gendered language, changing facilities, curriculum planning and PE kit are all factors that are worthy of reconsideration. The use of changing rooms should be carefully discussed, demonstrating sensitivity to the needs of both transgender students and other students. We also see from Will's experience that changing rooms can be a difficult place for all LGBTQ+ students, not just those that are questioning their gender. There should be no need for schools to stipulate what students should wear for PE based on their gender. Instead, it is more important that students can choose to wear what they feel most comfortable in. Where students express discomfort with changing arrangements, we accommodate this on a case by case basis, asking the student what they are most comfortable with, which might be changing in a nearby accessible toilet or in a partitioned section of the changing rooms.

Activities should also be gender-neutral, avoiding stipulations that girls take part in netball and hockey while boys take part in rugby and football. Activities are just that, not activities for boys or activities for girls. This also extends to extra-curricular clubs and wider opportunities – all students should be able to attend, regardless of their gender. There are some complexities around this; for example, some students may want to participate in single-sex groups, such as a girls' football club. However, there must be an opportunity for all students to access all activities, so a combination of both single- and mixed-sex groups may be appropriate.

Acceptance of all students and who they are is important. It is the extent to which the LGBTQ+ community, or anyone for that matter, are seen in ways that are positive and inclusive. All young people have faced adversity and challenge in recent years, with unprecedented disruption to their education and restrictions on their social opportunities. Therefore, compassion, empathy and acceptance are key to supporting our young people.

Trans and gender fluid students need compassion and support as much as any minority group or individual and feeling accepted for who you are is important. Being socially and publicly accepted for who you are is tremendously powerful. It highlights that this environment is a safe place for you to be who you are. Leading whole-school events such as a "rainbow run" (colour run) can help to promote diversity and acceptance of all students, regardless of their differences.

FROM PE DREAD TO DELIGHT

Summary
It is important to stress that making changes toward achieving a more inclusive offer does not have to mean that provision is compromised for students. The opposite is true. A fairer and more just provision can support all students, regardless of their background and experience, to develop compassion and consideration for others and embrace difference and diversity. I have long believed that, as a PE practitioner, I am in a privileged position. We have an opportunity and a responsibility to ensure that all students find their passion for physical activity in a safe, supportive and inclusive environment

CHAPTER 10: **GUIDES**

SEND
Faith Newton

PE for SEND Students is Just Good PE

When you read this chapter, you may be thinking about the few students in your class(es) who have SEND. Let me stop you there. There are probably a lot more needs and differences in your class(es) than you are aware of. After all it is estimated that 10-20% of the population is neurodivergent; 1 in 12 boys is colour blind and up to 55% of children may be hypermobile. Due to budget cuts and huge waiting lists there are many young people who will wait years for a diagnosis, if they ever get one at all.

With this in mind, we want to make PE inclusive for all students, whether they are identified as having SEND or not. After all, research shows that teaching that is good for SEND students, is good practice for all students.

The first thing to consider is the unique demands that PE places on students. Whereas a child's performance in history, or maths, is largely private, in PE their skill or lack of it, is visible for everyone to see. Not only that, but PE requires complex physical, communication, and emotional regulation skills in a context that is often competitive and full of sensory stimuli. Add in difficulties that students may have with coordination, or understanding non-verbal communication or colour blindness and you can glimpse some of the challenges students face.

As PE teachers you are fully aware of the benefits of physical activity, but it's important to remember that PE can also provoke negative emotions and experiences. I still remember the shame I felt when I was last to be picked for a team, and the groans that went up from my team mates when they realised I was joining their team. Kind selection practices are crucial. Many teachers avoid letting students pick their own teams to avoid scenarios like the one I experienced, but have you thought about how students select a partner? A study of 114 students age 9-15 found that the least popular girls in the class and the least sporty boys were consistently picked as a partner last. To avoid the humiliation of being actively rejected by their peers these students tended to wait around until the end rather than looking for a partner.

It's vital that all students feel included and safe in PE. Inclusion can be defined as 'a sense of belonging' and 'being included within a group'. You can foster a sense of belonging by listening to your students' voice. It's important to find out what activities your students enjoy and what their anxieties about PE are. In the previous section Will describes his love of dance and swimming, how might PE have been changed for Will if his teacher had known about his accomplishments outside of school and had understood his fears of homophobia. Similarly, parents have told me that their children, who never did PE at school, went on to become Paralympic champions.

Give Them Choice

Another thing that can help PE to be more inclusive is by giving students as much choice as possible. You can give students choice about what equipment to use. Instead of a certain child with SEND having special equipment what would happen if you gave all students access to a range of equipment? This would enable all students to pick equipment that would, through experimentation, give them the right mix of success and challenge. A student with DCD (Developmental Co-ordination Disorder) who finds hitting a ball challenging, could use a wider bat, as could a student without a diagnosis who also struggles with this activity. Can you give students more ownership of how much they push themselves, encouraging them to listen to their bodies to know when to take a break and when to try and beat a personal best? Similarly, can you offer instructions on how to make each activity easier or more challenging, just like a Pilates instructor at the gym or on YouTube does? This can help all students feel included whatever their skill level.

Normalising Sensory and Emotional Needs

When we think of autistic and ADHD students we often think about sensory and emotional regulation. Indeed, as an Occupational Therapist, this is something I am often brought in to help with. However, just as choice about equipment, pacing and tasks can help all students, so can developing their skills in these areas. After all we all have sensory needs, and we all experience a range of emotions. School can be a challenging experience for students with SEND. Some students will have experienced a lot of stress and difficulty before they arrive at your lesson. In what ways can you acknowledge this? Could you model language around your sensory and emotional regulation to make it OK for students to identify their needs?

The STEPS Framework

When designing inclusive PE lessons, the STEPS framework (Youth Sport Trust, 2002) can be a valuable tool for ensuring all students, whether identified with SEND or not, have an opportunity to succeed. The STEPS framework emphasises the importance of adapting Space, Task, Equipment, People, and Speed (or time) to meet diverse needs.

Space: Adjusting the physical environment can either challenge or support students. Reducing space in games like football (soccer) can intensify play, encouraging quick decision-making and tighter control, while increasing space allows for more freedom and exploration. Think about whether the space allows all students to move freely and whether changes might help make activities more accessible.

Task: Adapting the task can make activities more achievable or challenging. By modifying rules, such as requiring a certain number of passes before scoring in football, or adjusting choreography in dance, you can ensure tasks are accessible to all skill levels while still providing challenges for advanced students.

Equipment: Appropriate equipment can enhance engagement and safety. For example, larger or slower-moving equipment in badminton, like oversized shuttles, gives students more time to react, ensuring more success. Offering a variety of equipment choices can give students the autonomy to find what works best for them.

People: Grouping and interactions between participants play a crucial role in the PE environment. Consider mixed-ability pairing to foster peer support and collaboration, ensuring everyone has a positive experience.

Speed (Time): Adjusting the pace of activities ensures students have time to practice and improve. While timed challenges may enhance fitness, skill-based tasks might benefit from longer periods for feedback and refinement.
Using the STEPS framework creates a more inclusive, adaptive environment that supports the needs of all students, helping everyone feel successful and engaged in PE lessons.
Final Thoughts

My final piece of advice in making PE inclusive for SEND students is to be curious. Everyone's needs are different but you will find some common strands. So, ask your students, ask their parents and learn from adults who have these neurotypes or conditions.

Reflection
- Think about a physical activity that you teach. Can you break it down into all of its different demands? Think about what demands it makes in the following areas: physical, sensory, communication and interaction, cognitive and learning, and social, emotional and mental health.
- Can you provide a space where students can go for a few minutes to regulate if they need to?

Chapter 9 Summary

Inclusion: from Dread to Delight

DREAD

Lack of Inclusivity:
PE environments that fail to accommodate diverse backgrounds, interests, and abilities can create feelings of exclusion and discomfort among students.

Ignoring Trauma:
Failure to recognise and address the potential trauma induced by negative PE experiences perpetuates a cycle of disengagement and aversion to physical activity among students.

Inequality:
Disparities in access to resources such as equipment, facilities, and coaching opportunities based on factors like socio-economic status or school funding exacerbate feelings of inequity and disadvantage among students.

DELIGHT

Inclusive Programming:
PE programs that embrace diversity and offer a wide range of activities cater to the varied interests and abilities of students, fostering a sense of belonging and participation for all.

Trauma-Informed Practices:
Implementing trauma-informed approaches that prioritise safety and empowerment. Laying the foundation for positive physical activity experiences.

Equity:
Ensuring equity in all aspects of PE, including access to resources, opportunities, and support, regardless of socio-economic status or other factors, promotes fairness and equal opportunities for all students.

Where would you place yourself right now?

DREAD ←——————————————————→ DELIGHT

Reflection Questions
- How does my current approach to physical education align with the principles of social justice and trauma-informed practice discussed in the chapter?
- In what ways can I actively promote inclusivity and equity in my PE curriculum, considering the diverse backgrounds, interests, and abilities of my students?
- What are the main characteristics of diversity in my context? Who is in need of the equity?

- How can I create a safe and supportive environment in my PE classes to mitigate the risk of trauma for my students?
- Do I have any unconscious biases, that I was previously unaware of, that have been brought to my attention?
- What steps can I take to address any biases or inequalities present in my PE teaching practices?
- How can I integrate the concepts of social justice, trauma-informed practice, and equity into my ongoing professional development and reflective practice as a physical education teacher?

Call to Action

As we conclude this chapter, it's time to reflect on what you've learned and consider how to apply it. The SHIFT mnemonic can guide you through the next steps: a structured approach to transform your insights into meaningful actions. Take a moment to work through the following questions:

S **Summarise** the key takeaway from this chapter that stands out to you.

H **Highlight** how this takeaway challenges or aligns with your current practices.

I **Initiate** a small change or step right now to put what you've learned into practice.

F **Frame** how this change will contribute to achieving your long-term vision for PE.

T **Take** others on the journey—share your new insights and encourage collaboration.

References

Barnard Flory, S. (2014). Sociocultural Issues in Physical Education. Rowman & Littlefield.

Dohrenwend, B. P. (2000). The role of adversity and stress in psychopathology: Some evidence and its implications for theory and research. Journal of Health and Social Behavior.

Gerdin, G., Larsson, L., Schenker, K., Linnér, S., Mordal Moen, K., Westlie, K., Smith, W., & Philpot, R. (2020). Social justice pedagogies in school health and physical education: Building relationships, teaching for social cohesion, and addressing social inequities. International Journal of Environmental Research and Public Health, 17(18), 6904. https://doi.org/10.3390/ijerph17186904

Grimminger, Elke. (2014). Getting into teams in physical education and exclusion processes among students. Pedagogies: An International Journal, 9(2), 155-171. https://doi.org/10.1080/1554480X.2014.899546

Hooks, B. (2001). All about love: New visions. Harper Perennial.

Leisterer, Sascha, and Darko Jekauc. (2019). Students' emotional experience in physical education: A qualitative study for new theoretical insights. Sports (Basel), 7(1). https://doi.org/10.3390/sports7010010

Lynch, S., Walton-Fisette, J. L., & Luguetti, C. (2022). Pedagogies of Social Justice in Physical Education and Youth Sport. Routledge.

Meyer, I. H. (2003). Prejudice, social stress, and mental health in lesbian, gay, and bisexual populations: Conceptual issues and research evidence. Psychological Bulletin, 129(5), 674–697. https://doi.org/10.1037/0033-2909.129.5.674

Mogan, N. (2024). Time to RISE Up: Supporting Students' Mental Health in Schools. Scholary.

Newton, F. (2023). Inclusive PE for SEND Children. p. 40-41.

Scott, K. (2020). Adverse childhood experiences. InnovAiT. Retrieved from https://journals.sagepub.com/doi/full/10.1177/1755738020964498 [Accessed 28 April 2024].

Taylor and Francis. (2024). What is social justice? Retrieved from https://insights.taylorandfrancis.com/social-justice/what-is-social-justice/# [Accessed 30 April 2024].

UK Government Office for Health Improvement and Disparities. (2022). Working definition of trauma-informed practice. Retrieved from https://www.gov.uk/government/publications/working-definition-of-trauma-informed-practice/working-definition-of-trauma-informed-practice [Accessed 25 April 2024].

Webster, E. (2022). The impact of adverse childhood experiences on health and development in young children. Global Pediatric Health. https://doi.org/10.1177/2333794X221078708

Chapter 10: Guides

Lee Sullivan, Professor Shane Pill and Ben Shields

Part 10.1 – Insight
Lee Sullivan and Professor Shane Pill

In the initial segment of this chapter, we explore the fundamental aspects of leadership within PE, considering the importance of varying our approaches depending on what we hope to achieve. I aim to highlight the paramount importance of understanding and implementing diverse leadership and teaching approaches that are tailored to specific objectives. We will then explore the various teaching styles available to us in PE and when best to employ them.

Lessons in Leadership

Before taking on the role of Head of Department in Physical Education, I (Lee) served as a pastoral leader responsible for Year 11 students. My initial cohort presented significant challenges; over 40% were classified as disadvantaged, necessitating numerous meetings with parents regarding behaviour concerns. I forged strong relationships with local law enforcement, often collaborating with them following incidents of misconduct in the community. While my teacher training hadn't prepared me for these challenges, I am grateful for the seven years spent in pastoral leadership as it provided invaluable lessons in managing and leading people.

During this time, I had the privilege of learning from a remarkable individual named Trevor O'Neil, a senior leader and PE teacher. While he may not appreciate public acknowledgment, his impact on me was profound. Trevor epitomised teaching for the right reasons. Though he rarely relied on textbook strategies but instead, addressed each individual before him with empathy and intuition. His approach prioritised positive outcomes for all involved, emphasising the importance of understanding and working effectively with diverse individuals to motivate and support them towards achievement.

One particular incident that left a lasting impression on me was when Trevor was called upon to address an escalated behaviour situation involving a group of girls following a fallout. It was remarkable to witness his approach as he engaged with each individual separately, carefully tailoring his responses to address their unique perspectives and needs. With one individual, he expressed his disappointment calmly and firmly, emphasising the importance of accountability. With another, he conveyed his frustration in a measured manner, avoiding the need for raised voices or harsh words. With another individual, he encouraged collaboration, urging her to play a role in addressing and rectifying the situation, fostering a sense of ownership and responsibility. This nuanced and empathetic approach not only defused the immediate conflict but also paved the way for constructive dialogue and resolution.

He knew that beyond students, we were working with humans. Understanding the complexities and individuality of each person was paramount to him. Trevor recognised that effective teaching and leadership required more than just imparting knowledge; it demanded empathy, adaptability, and a genuine connection with those he interacted with.

Trevor treated his interactions with staff in much the same way. He discerned those with whom he could collaboratively establish goals, allowing them the autonomy to figure out the path forward, and those who required more ongoing guidance. He was indifferent to the approach taken, as long as it led to the desired outcome.

He rarely referred to himself as a leader. Trevor wasn't against the concept of leadership and understood his leadership responsibilities, but he believed the majority of his role was to work as a guide. He understood there were many crossovers between a leader and a guide, but considered it his job as a guide to:

1. Inspire passion and motivation in others
2. Help all to achieve the desired outcome/vision
3. Ensure everyone has the necessary support and resources to reach their goals.

He believed that every teacher was a guide. It was our jobs to ignite a passion in others through our lessons, effectively deliver the learning to achieve the curriculum objectives and ensure every student was supported to reach and surpass their potential. Furthermore, he believed students should take ownership of their learning and support others where they could too. Lessons were rarely 'chalk and talk' with Trevor. Everyone, staff and students, hung off his every word and went above and beyond for him, because you bought into his leadership, or should I say guidance.

Emergence of Leadership Styles

The idea of utilising various approaches when working with others is nothing new. Though, the study of leadership traces its roots to ancient civilizations, where leaders were often viewed as possessing divine or heroic qualities, wielding authoritarian power over their subjects. As societies evolved, particularly during the Industrial Revolution, leadership models shifted towards bureaucratic hierarchies, giving rise to the autocratic style, where decisions were made without consulting subordinates.

However, the understanding of varying our approach when leading others to illicit differing outcomes was about to change forever. Kurt Lewin stands as a prominent figure in the history of social psychology, hailed as the pioneer of experimental social psychology. His study, conducted in the late 1930s, continues to exert a profound influence on leadership research and practice today, serving as a cornerstone in social psychology and leadership studies.

Initiated in 1938 at Iowa University by Ronald Lippitt under Lewin's supervision, the study focused on two groups of eleven-year-old children, predominantly boys, participating in mask-making sessions after school. Acting as a 'democratic' leader with one group, Lippitt encouraged children's participation in decision-making. Conversely, with the other group, he adopted an 'authoritarian' style, dictating decisions without their input. Trained observers closely monitored the children's behaviour throughout the sessions. In a subsequent experiment conducted by Ralph White and Ronald Lippitt, the initial study expanded to include three different leadership styles: democratic, authoritarian and laissez-faire. Each group of boys experienced multiple leaders, each employing one of these styles (Billig, 2014).

- **Democratic Leadership:** In Kurt Lewin's experiment, democratic leadership involved significant autonomy and participation in decision-making among group members. This style fostered cooperation and valued input. Despite lower productivity compared to authoritarian groups, the quality of contributions was notably higher. Lewin found that democratic leadership enhances motivation and creativity by engaging members in decision-making processes.
- **Authoritarian Leadership:** Lewin's experiment depicted authoritarian leadership as characterised by clear directives and tight control from the leader. Decision-making was predominantly top-down, with minimal input from group members. This approach resulted in less creative decision-making and decreased motivation among members.
- **Laissez-faire Leadership:** In Lewin's study, laissez-faire leadership saw minimal guidance from the leader, with group members exhibiting little cooperation or independence. This style yielded the least productive outcomes, with unclear roles and low motivation. Groups lacking direction blamed each other for mistakes and made minimal progress. Lewin's findings underscored the importance of clear guidance and structure in leadership to maintain focus and productivity.

Overall, the findings from the second experiment highlighted the significant influence of leadership styles on group behaviour and performance. Different styles elicited varying responses from group members, underscoring the importance of leadership flexibility and adaptability in achieving desired outcomes. Despite the authoritarian style, at the time, being commonly associated with effectiveness, the study revealed that democratic leadership could lead to more positive outcomes. This revelation revolutionised conventional thinking in the field of leadership.

Moreover, the study's relevance extended beyond academia. Conducted with schoolchildren participating in after-school activities, it offered practical implications for educational settings. Educators and administrators could glean valuable insights to optimise leadership practices and cultivate positive group environments in schools.

Shane (chapter co-author) also has a background in curriculum and school leadership, in his 18 years of school teaching having been a Head of Department, Year Level Coordinator and Sport Coordinator before becoming a Deputy Principal. He has keen interest in education leadership from doing a Masters in Educational Leadership. In particular, he is interested in leadership for learning. Given the global interest in teaching for effective learning through quality teaching practices (see UNESCO Quality Physical Education (QPE): Guidelines for Policy Makers as an example) he believes it is necessary that physical educators give attention to the design of quality learning environments. Drawing on the work of Delors (1996), Shane suggested the physical educator is a leader of learning when they are authentically the 'first learner' in the class. This entails the physical educator knowing their physical education pedagogical identity - what they 'stand for' and how they 'go about it'. Physical educators must therefore be as concerned with the process, or pedagogy, of their endeavours with students as they are with the task or activity selection through which they aim to help students become physically educated (Pill, 2007).

No One Style Fits All

As the study of leadership has progressed over time, so has our understanding of teaching styles in PE. Similarly, to how the diverse leadership styles observed in Kurt Lewin's experiments resulted in varied responses from group members, different teaching styles can profoundly impact student learning and engagement in PE and sport.

The research article by Hao Jin et al. (2022), titled "Effects of leadership style on coach-athlete relationship, athletes' motivations, and athlete satisfaction," delves into the advantages and drawbacks of specific coaching styles, particularly autocratic and democratic approaches. Autocratic coaching, with its emphasis on the coach's authority, offers quick problem-solving but may constrain athletes' freedom and motivation. On the other hand, democratic leadership involves sharing responsibility and empowering athletes, fostering positive psychological outcomes while potentially leading to conflicts. The article also explores the concept of 'situational leadership' theory, which highlights the need for coaches to adapt their leadership style based on various factors such as athlete characteristics, competition level, and the nature of the sport. There is no one-size-fits-all leadership, coaching or teaching style, and effective coaching requires flexibility to tailor the approach according to a number of factors.

Leadership style is not to be confused with teaching style (pedagogy), however, as alluded to earlier a physical educator's pedagogy is an expression of what they believe is valuable in the learning process. Each PE lesson requires a tailored mix of teaching styles based on the curriculum standards and learning objectives for the year group, considering students' readiness to learn and the nature of the activity used to achieve the objectives. For example, when teaching javelin, safety is paramount due to the inherent risks involved. In this case, a more directive 'leadership' approach would be necessary to ensure that students understand and follow safety procedures rigorously. Suited to this leadership approach, requiring students to be under direct timing and pacing control of the teacher, would be the combination (cluster) of Style A-Command with Style B - Practice style pedagogy (SueSee et al., 2020). On the other hand, when facilitating a game or team sport activity where the learning objective is to explore tactical possibilities, a facilitative leadership style enabling a more student-centred approach might be more appropriate. In this scenario, the teaching styles might include Style G-Convergent Discovery, using targeted questioning to guide student thinking and shape in-game actions, and Style B-Practice, as students apply the answers to those questions during the game. If the activity focus is not only on exploring tactical possibilities but also on developing teamwork, decision-making skills, and fair play/good sporting behaviour the teacher would encourage students to actively participate in decision-making processes which may be suited to a Style H-Divergent Discovery teaching episode. If the focus was on collaboration with their teammates a Style C-Reciprocal and/or Style E-Inclusion teaching episode may be suited, and if the teacher was wanting students to take ownership of their learning the teacher may use a Style D-Self-check teaching episode or Style I -Learner-designed teaching episode style (SueSee et al., 2020).

Part 10.2 – Delve
Lee Sullivan and Professor Shane Pill

Spectrum of Teaching Styles in PE
Research indicates that the success of PE programs can hinge on the teaching methods employed by the teacher. While the content imparts physical and behavioural skills to students, the manner in which it is taught is vital for sustaining student motivation to participate (Wallhead, 2024).

In 1966, Muska Mosston introduced the Spectrum of Teaching Styles (STS), which now comprises eleven distinct teaching styles, each identifiable by a specific name or letter (Ashworth, 1995). STS stands as a unified theory that offers educators a comprehensive framework for understanding and implementing effective pedagogy. The STS is a philosophy, a model, and a practice. The STS philosophy is non-verses in that it recognises all teaching styles have purpose. Teaching styles each bring distinctive purpose and therefore learning outcomes with students. The pedagogical skill of the physical educator lies in matching the learner's need related to the activity learning outcome to the teaching style most likely to enable that alignment. In this way, the STS delineates teaching–learning options. It equips teachers with the necessary knowledge for developing a repertoire or 'toolkit' of instructional behaviours (SueSee & Pill, 2018) that embrace all the 'objectives' (social, emotional, cognitive, physical) needed to connect with the readiness to learn of students. In summary, fundamental to the structure of the STS is that all teaching styles are beneficial for what they can accomplish; none is more important, or more valuable, than another (Mosston & Ashworth, 2008, p5).

The STS is a model that encompasses a pedagogical range – the teaching styles, each tailored to meet different educational objectives and student needs. At one 'end', Style A is where the teacher leads pre-teaching planning, teaching impact and post-teaching evaluation and reflection. At the other 'end', Style K is where the learner leads pre-teaching planning, teaching impact and post-teaching evaluation and reflection. The STS styles are:

- In the **command style** (a), the teacher assumes full control, making decisions before, during, and after the lesson. Tasks are performed in response to cues such as a whistle.
- In the **practice style** (b), the teacher demonstrates the task and allows students to practise independently at their own pace. Feedback is provided as students engage in practice.
- The **reciprocal style** (c) involves students working in pairs, taking turns to observe and provide feedback to each other based on predetermined performance criteria.
- Similarly, in the **self-check style** (d), students work independently but assess their own performance against set criteria.

- The **inclusion style** (e) offers tasks of varying difficulty levels, allowing students to choose tasks that best match their abilities and interests.
- **Guided discovery** (f) employs questioning techniques to lead students towards predetermined responses or solutions.
- **Convergent discovery** (g) tasks students with finding a single correct response to a specific problem or situation.
- **Divergent discovery** (h) challenges students to generate multiple solutions to a given problem.
- In the **learner-designed individual program** (i), students take charge of designing, developing, and presenting a series of tasks tailored to their personal learning goals.
- The **learner-initiated style** (j) places the learner in control, allowing them to determine the learning objectives, procedures, and assessment criteria.
- Finally, in **self-teaching** (k), the learner assumes both the teacher and learner roles, making decisions throughout the learning process.

The Spectrum's significance lies in its acknowledgment of the complexity of teaching and learning. It recognises that no single teaching style is universally superior and emphasises the importance of tailoring instruction to suit diverse learning objectives and student characteristics (Zeng, et. al. 2012).

The STS model groups the teaching styles into two clusters. Styles A to E in the STS are considered Reproduction approaches. In these styles, the teacher takes on a predominant role in pre-teaching planning, teaching delivery, and post-teaching evaluation and reflection.
Styles F to K are characterised as Production cluster with more student autonomy, active participation, and independent learning. Students are encouraged to explore, discover, and problem-solve on their own or in collaboration with peers. The teacher's role in these styles is often that of a facilitator or guide, supporting students as they engage in self-directed or self-initiated learning experiences.

The practice of the STS is mobility ability within the STS. Mobility ability is the matching of teaching style or combination of styles to the learner readiness for learning and task learning requirements. When working with the STS you recognise that lessons are a series of episodes and therefore one teaching style will not meet the multiple learning requirements and for the range of outcomes planned for the lesson. You work within the STS not along the teaching styles continuum from A to K.

Leaders as Guides

In the context of PE, leadership has been identified as an important factor that can support, guide and facilitate effective PE (Gazali, 2022). Leadership for learning in this example is the intentional alignment of learner readiness-task requirement-learning outcome. It would be apparent to the reader by now that when a teacher is not locked into 'one model' or one 'way' of teaching and able to employ different teaching styles, students learning will benefit. And, contrarily, it is potentially detrimental for student learning when a teacher consistently chooses the same teaching style from lesson to lesson as this means the teacher is not giving due consideration to student need and readiness for learning (e.g., learning outcomes, learning needs) (Bradford, Hickson and Berg, 2020; SueSee and Pill, 2018).

'For learning to occur, teachers require knowledge of the subject area content being taught and pedagogical expertise to support students' understanding and knowledge acquisition (Bradford, Hickson and Berg, 2020, p152). The STS provides the support that has been found to be particularly needed for generalist teachers in elementary (primary) schools to enhance their understanding of PE delivery. The confidence levels of generalist teachers when delivering primary/ elementary PE is often low and generalist teachers are faced with a number of challenges when it comes to teaching PE. However, generalist teachers must grasp the importance of knowing how different teaching styles aid student learning in PE. Adjusting their teaching style can also impact the kind of learning taking place. Therefore, Bradford, Hickson and Berg (2020) created the Teaching Continuum.

Given that generalist teachers have responsibilities extending beyond PE, fully implementing complex theoretical frameworks into their practice can be challenging. Therefore, the Teaching Continuum offers a modified interpretation of The Spectrum's theoretical underpinnings in a generalist teacher-friendly manner. The Teaching Continuum sought to simplify the utilisation of teaching styles in this context and includes three teaching styles: Teacher as a Guide, Shared Guides, and Student Self-Guide.

In PE, specific learning outcomes often necessitate direct instruction due to safety concerns or limited room for exploration. The **Teacher as a Guide** style involves the teacher making all decisions in the learning environment, providing thorough demonstrations, and assessing student learning based on predetermined criteria.

For learning outcomes that allow for collaboration between teachers and students, such as performing a gymnastics sequence, the **Shared Guides** approach fosters a partnership where students can make decisions while the teacher maintains influence over certain aspects of the learning.

In instances where students have room to explore and create, such as in creative movement, the **Student Self-Guide** style empowers students to plan activities, discover ways to perform them, and assess their learning based on predetermined criteria. This approach promotes independence and problem-solving skills among students.

CHAPTER 10: **GUIDES**

In a PE setting, students can take on leadership responsibilities, contributing to the overall success of the class and their own development. We can encourage peer support among students, especially during physical activities and foster collaboration and teamwork skills through group cooperation and interaction (Xiao, 2024). This inclusive approach to leadership acknowledges that everyone, both teachers and students alike, plays a role in fostering a positive and productive learning environment.

Guides and Teaching Styles

In the STS, certain styles are primarily teacher-guided, while others involve shared guidance or are self-guided. This can be observed in the following table, which is a modification of Bradford et al 2020 based on our understanding of teacher and student responsibility at pre-impact planning, impact-implementation, and post-impact reflection. The table correlates each teaching style with a specific form of guidance in PE:

Table 6: Form of Guidance with Teaching Styles

Type of Guide	Teaching Styles
Teacher Guides	Command style (A), Practice style (B)
Shared Guides	Reciprocal style (C), Self-check (D), Inclusion (E), Guided discovery (F), Convergent discovery (G), Divergent discovery (H), Learner-designed individual program (I), Learner-initiated style (J)
Self-Guides	Self-teaching (K)

To illustrate with a relevant example, the following is each teaching style applied to the teaching of Dance as reflected in Mosston and Ashworth's explanation of each style (2008):

Teacher Guides
- **Command style** (a): The teacher directs students to perform specific dance moves in time with verbal commands or cues, such as "begin with a forward step, followed by a spin to the right." With this style the teacher leads in pre-impact, impact and post impact aspects of the lesson.
- **Practice style** (b): The teacher demonstrates (impact) a choreographed (pre-impact) dance routine, breaking down each step and allowing students to practise independently at their own pace. Teachers will provide feedback and guidance as students refine their movements (post-impact).

Shared Guides

- **Reciprocal style** (c): Students work in pairs or small groups to practise dance sequences. They take turns performing while their partners observe and provide feedback on technique, timing, expression, etc., using explicit criteria provided by the teacher. This approach involves the teacher in the pre-impact phase for planning, both teacher and student in the impact phase for demonstrating, explaining, and practising, and again both teacher and student in the post-impact phase for evaluation.
- **Self-Check** (d): In the pre-impact phase, the teacher plans a detailed checklist and a clear mental representation of the expected performance. During the impact phase, both the teacher and student engage in the process, with the teacher demonstrating and explaining the routine while the student practises independently. The student uses mirrors or video recordings to self-assess their performance, comparing their movements to the instructor's demonstration. In the post-impact phase, the student evaluates their areas for improvement based on the predetermined criteria, reflecting on their progress and identifying steps for further development.
- **Inclusion** (e): Learners with varying degrees of skill participate in the same task by selecting a level of difficulty that matches their abilities. In the pre-impact phase, the teacher plans the task and outlines different levels of difficulty. During the impact phase, both the teacher and students engage in the process, with the teacher demonstrating and explaining the task while students practise and choose roles that fit their skill levels. In the post-impact phase, the teacher and/or students evaluate the performance, ensuring that each student actively engages with the task at a level that suits their abilities, fostering inclusivity by accommodating diverse skill levels within the lesson.
- **Guided discovery** (f): The teacher poses pre-planned questions to students about different dance styles, historical influences, or thematic elements. Through guided discussions and exploration, students uncover the cultural significance and artistic choices behind the dance they are learning.
- **Convergent discovery** (g): Students are presented with a specific dance challenge or question, such as incorporating a particular dance move into their routine. They experiment with different ways to seamlessly integrate the move until they find the most effective solution.
- **Divergent discovery** (h): Students are given creative freedom to explore various interpretations of a dance theme or concept. They brainstorm and experiment with different movements, expressions, and formations to develop unique choreographic ideas.
- **Learner-Designed Individual Program** (i): Students design their own dance routines, selecting music, choreographing movements, and arranging formations based on their personal artistic vision and dance goals. They present their creations to the class, showcasing their creativity and individuality. This approach involves both the student and teacher in the pre-impact planning phase, the student and teacher during the impact

phase for support and guidance, and both the student and teacher in the post-impact phase for evaluation and feedback.
- **Learner-Initiated Style** (j): Students take the lead in planning and executing a dance workshop or performance event. They collaborate with peers to determine the theme, choreography, rehearsal schedule, and performance logistics, empowering them to take ownership of their dance experience. This approach involves both the student and teacher in the pre-impact planning phase, both student and teacher in the impact phase for coordination and facilitation, and both student and teacher in the post-impact phase for assessment and reflection.

Self- Guides
- **Self-teaching** (k): Student's research different dance techniques, styles, and cultural traditions independently, using online resources, books, and instructional videos. They experiment with new movements and combinations, refining their skills through self-directed learning and practice. This approach involves only the students in the pre-impact planning phase, the impact and the post-impact phase.

In summary, the STS offers a diverse teaching toolkit and the Teaching Continuum helps clarify the degree to which the teacher and student lead pre-impact planning, impact-implementation, and post-impact evaluation and reflection. By understanding the diverse teaching styles available and their corresponding approaches to guidance to learner outcomes, teachers can tailor their pedagogical work to meet the unique needs and learning objectives of all of their students. Whether adopting a teacher-guided, shared guidance, or self-guided approach, educators can create inclusive and effective learning environments.

Part 10.3 – Experts

Spectrum of Teaching Styles
Professor Shane Pill

The STS can be used to illuminate the pedagogical necessities of instructional models (e.g., a Tactical model (Metzler, 2017) or otherwise known as Game -Based approach (GBA) such as Teaching Games for Understanding (Bunker and Thorpe, 1982), which are often described in simplified terms. For instance, using the example of a GBA, resources often describe a GBA as a discovery or a guided discovery approach. This is most likely because a core pedagogical emphasis of a GBA is for the teacher to ask questions rather than provide students highly directive information and prescribed answers (SueSee, Pill and Edwards, 2016).

A GBA is not a 'game-only' model it is an active and reflective approach that nuances whole-part-whole practice by including active reflection and problem solving by 'playing with purpose' (Pill, 2013, p.7). No teaching style is 'ruled in or ruled out' by a GBA however a GBA is distinctive by the lesson having a focus on game play and focussing on player thinking and shaping of player attention through the purposeful use of well-considered teacher questioning. However, the use of well-considered teacher questioning does not necessarily lead to a discovery or guided discovery teaching episode. Here I will use an example from my own work (Figure 28) to illustrate what I mean.

Figure 28: Learning Episode

CHAPTER 10: **GUIDES**

Game: Defensive Depth *Activity based on an example provided in Pill, (2013, p41)*

Applications
Touch, netball, basketball, football codes, lacrosse, team handball

Problem-solving
Work together to progress the ball across the playing area in the quickest possible time; make defensive position to delay time, block space to force a turnover.

Playing Area
Mark out a grid divided into 3 equal sections. One defender/ interceptor stands in each section (N=3 defenders in total) and must remain there.

Task Conditions
3 attackers begin with the ball behind the line at one end. The aim is to progress the ball across the playing area and over the other end-line without the ball being touched by the opposing team, intercepted, hitting the ground or out of play. If so team swap roles.

Example Key Questions
- How do interceptors work together to pressure the team with the ball?
- Where is the best place for interceptors to position themselves inside their grid?
- How do the team in possession work together to get the ball across the grid as quickly as possible?

In the learning episode, the teacher has decided the concept in focus (defensive depth). The teacher will decide 'how' to play the game in so far as they may use netball (no travel), basketball (travel by bouncing), or rugby (must pass backwards) rules if the episode was within a sport specific unit of work. When the learning episode is mapped using the STS:

- **Pre-impact planning:** The teacher has decided all subject matter
- **Impact – implementation:** Students will move and pass the way they know how. There is no instruction to 'discover' or 'create' a way to solve either the defensive problem (stop the ball getting across the grid) or offensive problem (get the ball to the other end of the grid)
- **Post-impact reflection:** the teacher has decided the questions and most likely what answers are wanted from the students.

If the teacher provides the play conditions and sets the objective of the game within the context of the learning focus, then playing the game is the students practising what they have been asked to do (Style B-Practice). If the students were asked to create a solution, then the cognitive behaviour expected of the students is creativity. That creativity would occur before 'Impact' because playing the game is the mechanism for testing whether the creative endeavour – e.g., create a solution that enables you to get the 'ball' to the other end without the ball being intercepted or the player in possession being tagged with the ball, is successful. That is, the idea works. If working as a group of 3 to create the solution, then the teaching style may be Style C-Reciprocal. If the teacher has distributed a more knowledgeable player of the game designated to help 'coach' the team in their creative endeavour, then the teaching style is likely Style E-Inclusion.

While the example (Figure 28) includes suggested focus questions for the teacher to ask, it does not provide the inquiry strategy. Let us assume that the teacher wants the defenders to learn a particular strategy related to defensive depth, such as 'delaying the play'. The teacher has prepared a series of questions which converge on an answer, 'a way' to defensively delay the play, and the questions will be used after the defensive team has had a few attempts at the task of defending the attacking play. The learning episode is then a cluster of teaching styles, Style B - Practice + Style G – Convergent Discovery.

If the game Defensive Depth is the opening activity of the lesson introducing a new concept to the students, after the teacher has set the conditions of play and the learning intention the teacher will observe the students playing the game and wait for the students to experience the 'teachable moment' (Launder, 2001) in the game related to the learning objective. At this moment the teacher stops play and using a production cluster teaching style, for the purpose of the example, Style G – Convergent Discovery. During this inquiry the students suggest they need to practise an element of play outside of the complexity of the game dynamics, so the teacher pauses the game-form play and implements a 'skill' focus task. When the teacher feels the students 'have got it', the teacher returns the students to the game-form play. In this GBA approach I have described the cluster of teaching styles is:

Style A-Command (demonstrate and explain) + Style B – Practice (game-form play) + Style G – Convergent Discovery (questions) + Style B – Practice (skill practice) + Style B – Practice (game-form play).

The main teaching style used in the GBA approach of the lesson is Style B – Practice.

What has been demonstrated through the examples just provided is that describing a GBA and similar models as 'discovery' or 'guided discovery' is, from a pedagogical lens', and over-simplification and even a miss-representation. The examples often used to illustrate a GBA are possibly more likely to be Style B-Practice Style pedagogy and not a teaching style from the production cluster of the STS. When we look at a lesson adopting a GBA, from a STS lens we see the lesson as episodic and therefore a cluster of teaching styles.

Part 10.4 – Apply

Teachable Moments
Lee Sullivan

Teaching isn't solely about how, what, or why you communicate with your students; the timing of your delivery is equally crucial. After observing several PE lessons, it became clear that while PE teachers were highly engaged, moving tirelessly between groups and students to provide guidance, there was often a lack of strategic pause for observation or the implementation of planned interventions. Many teachers being observed fell back into their comfort zones or preferred teaching styles, leading to a reactive and heavily teacher-led approach. This tendency to revert to familiar methods underscored the importance of effective planning and the ability to step back and observe. Without these practices, crucial teachable moments may be overlooked. To truly maximise learning opportunities, we must integrate thoughtful planning and observation into our teaching practice.

Teachable moments (Sullivan, 2021) are times within a lesson that the concept can be embedded further, or coaching can be provided to enable practical progression. Teachable moments often emerge when teachers can identify and act upon pivotal moments in lessons. For instance, if using a practice style, these moments might involve prompting students to retrieve and apply specific knowledge. In a reciprocal teaching style, teachable moments might occur when students, assigned as 'coaches,' lead discussions or debates based on teacher questions. In a convergent discovery style, these moments might be anticipated through the design of activities that are meant to provoke specific responses or solutions during gameplay. Connecting back to teaching styles ensures that teachable moments are strategically used to enhance learning rather than simply reacting to classroom dynamics.

Teachable moments come in two forms:
- **Targeted learning:** feedback provided to an individual or small group regarding the concept, key techniques, or sport specific information.
- **Discussion points:** Feedback provided to a class to highlight key learning or address common misconceptions.

Good teachers anticipate teachable moments as part of their planning, ready to respond with a teaching style matched to the learners' needs. They wait for these moments to occur, then step in seamlessly without diverting students' attention from the learning objective. Instead of stopping the game or activity, which can lead to cognitive dispersal, they maintain cognitive focus by subtly guiding the students. If no teachable moments arise immediately, the teacher

CHAPTER 11: **HOLISTIC**

stands back, keeps the students active, and continues to observe, ensuring the learning environment remains dynamic and focused.

Alex Beckey's (2022) chapter within the Meaningful PE book inspired me to consider the notion of teacher reflection in-action. Realising he spent much of his time focusing purely on motor competence and circulating the entire class offering as much technical feedback as he could, Beckey reflected on the need to see the bigger picture of our subject 'to value and engage in a physically active lifestyle' (p54). He presents an 'Equaliser' metaphor to highlight how teachers can and should stand back to make tweaks to a lesson through the meaningful PE lens. Picture a sound equaliser with different dials that control the various volumes and tones of a sound. With so much going on in a lesson and with so many different decisions a teacher has to consider, teachers are able to tweak the 'tone' of their approach through the pedagogical 'dials' available to them by considering potential cues.

If we apply this metaphor to our understanding of the STS, it suggests that if the pre-impact planning wasn't accurate and an activity needs a challenge point change or some other adjustment during the lesson, the teacher can modify their approach accordingly. Otherwise, the 'buttons' are adjusted based on the pre-impact planning.

Beckey goes on to consider the potential cues one might look for in students and how a teacher might act with that information considering his Equaliser framework. Inspired by Beckey's analogy and to embed the idea of teachable moments with my team, I asked them to imagine a control panel situated within their lesson. If they were to stand at this panel, it would give them the perfect view of everything that is happening. The teachable moments control panel concept is designed with precision, featuring three distinct buttons:

- **Adaptive Teaching Strategies:** This button serves as a crucial tool for educators to fine-tune their approach in response to what they observe. By stepping back and observing with a clear purpose in mind, teachers can pinpoint moments when adjustments to the level of challenge or rules are necessary. It's about being attuned to the nuances of student engagement and skill acquisition, ensuring that every aspect of the lesson aligns with the desired learning outcomes.
- **Targeted Learning:** The second button, 'Targeted Learning,' embodies the essence of focused instruction. By keenly observing specific individuals or groups within the class, teachers can identify opportunities for quick coaching to enhance performance. It's not about constant interference but rather judiciously stepping in when a student's development can benefit the most. Observation, therefore, forms the scaffolding upon which targeted learning is constructed, allowing for precise and impactful interventions.
- **Discussion Points:** The final button, 'Discussion Points,' represents a broader approach to addressing common misconceptions or highlighting key learnings to the entire class. Here, observation plays a pivotal role in recognising patterns, both in mistakes and exemplary

practices. When teachers step back and observe they can identify moments when a collective discussion will enrich the learning experience for the entire group.

PE teachers have the ability to press any of these buttons at any time, but they should do so only if the pre-impact planning wasn't accurate and an activity needs a challenge point change or some other adjustment during the lesson. Intervening should be done thoughtfully, as it impacts activity time. Therefore, when pressing one of these buttons, it needs to be for a compelling reason based on the needs of the students and the situation at hand. Otherwise, the 'buttons' are adjusted according to the pre-impact planning.

They may observe a game where the level of challenge is insufficient, suggesting that a rule could be introduced to increase difficulty. Alternatively, if a student is not actively participating or if the overall enjoyment of the game seems lacking, the teacher might need to make adjustments. In such cases, the teacher should consider pressing the 'Adaptive Teaching Strategies' button to modify the activity. For example, they could implement Style E - Inclusion, which involves tailoring the game to accommodate varying skill levels and roles, ensuring that every student is engaged and included. By making these necessary tweaks, the teacher addresses the issues effectively, enhancing both participation and enjoyment.

The teacher might observe a group or an individual student from behind the control panel, identifying an opportunity where quick coaching could enhance performance. If this situation arises, the teacher can press the 'Targeted Learning' button and employ Style A - Command. This approach involves stopping the group or individual to provide specific, direct instruction or corrections. By doing so, the teacher can address immediate needs and guide the student or group towards improved performance with clear, authoritative guidance.

Finally, a teacher may plan using the Divergent Discovery (Style H) teaching style by creating a learning environment that encourages exploration of multiple solutions discovered by the players. The teacher might pre-plan a moment to address key learning with the entire class, particularly if they anticipate common misconceptions or areas where students might struggle. In such cases, the teacher can strategically plan to "press the 'Discussion Points' button," pausing the class to review essential concepts or share effective practices. This preparation ensures that the lesson remains focused on important learning objectives while still promoting student-driven discovery and engagement.

The main purpose of the teachable moments control panel was to get my team to consider how many times they stopped students being active, genuinely consider their planning and application of teaching styles, and ensure that they were not missing opportunities to deliver really meaningful teaching and guide their students more effectively. Feedback from the PE teachers has highlighted the positive impact this tool has had on their lessons. They reported feeling more mindful of how they structure and pace their sessions, ensuring students remain engaged and active for longer periods. The control panel has also encouraged them to reflect on their interactions with students, enabling them to use these teachable moments more intentionally to reinforce key skills, develop game understanding, and foster a positive learning environment. This has not only improved lesson flow but also helped to create a culture of purposeful teaching that enhances both student participation and learning outcomes.

Planning Teaching Styles
Ben Shields

My name is Ben Shields, and I am currently the Head of Primary HPE and Sport at a co-ed, PYP school in Brisbane, Australia. I have had the pleasure of teaching PE in the UK, UAE, and Thailand for over 13 years. The context I find myself in has always shaped my teaching approach, with a focus on understanding and meeting the needs of my students

In my role at this Australian co-ed school, which follows the Primary Years Programme framework, I've been working to integrate various teaching styles into my physical education lessons, especially as I'm new to the school. This approach has helped me connect with the students in my care, allowing me to adapt my teaching methods to best support their learning. I've started with a teacher-centred approach, gradually moving towards a more student-centred one. By blending different teaching styles, my goal is to address both the developmental needs of the students and the objectives of the PYP framework, while also incorporating the key focus areas of the Australian Curriculum. It's quite a complex balancing act! Ultimately, it's all about context and ensuring that we meet the needs of the students—both mine and yours.

A recent unit titled 'Strike, React, Rally' provided an excellent opportunity for reflection. When planning the unit, I focused on my ultimate goal: enabling students to play a modified version of volleyball that allowed them to collaborate with both teammates and opponents, build resilience, understand the rules, and officiate a game. Simple, right? I also wanted to ensure the unit was personally relevant and meaningful. Handball (four square) is almost like a religion here in Australia, making it an ideal starting point for discussing the similarities and differences between the games and the skills they require. Since playground handball games can get very intense, I wanted to use this as a springboard to discuss social connections, build resilience in competitive settings, and emphasise the importance of fairness in games.

To be perfectly honest, before I began in my current role, I had the preconception that a PYP school was 'just' about guided discovery and open-ended exploration—but I was wrong. While these elements are certainly important, as discussed earlier in this chapter, the variety of teaching styles is vital. I quickly realised that incorporating a range of approaches throughout the unit would be essential to achieving our intended goals.

The "Guided Discovery" style (f) was indeed a key part of my pre-impact strategy. I posed open-ended questions to encourage students to think about different ways to approach the game, such as, "How can we modify the rules to make the game more inclusive for everyone?" and "How can we compare this game to handball?" This method allowed students to explore and develop their understanding of games in an engaging and thought-provoking way. We discussed changing the number of bounces and touches of the ball. For example, most students enjoyed playing 'one touch, one bounce' volleyball, which created some fascinating games.

The "Command" style (a) also had its place, in short bursts, particularly at the beginning of the unit when introducing key vocabulary, specific skills and activities. To create a safe learning environment, the command style is vital to set clear expectations and instructions. Students do switch off though if there is too much 'teacher talk'.

I used a "Convergent Discovery" (g) teaching style when exploring the serve. I wanted students to explore various serving techniques in small groups. Each group experimented, noting the ease, accuracy and/or power of each serve. We then came together as a class to share our findings, which was extremely powerful. This collaborative feedback helped students converge on the best serving method for them.

I used the "Reciprocal"(c) and "Practice"(b) styles, often in partnership to foster peer interaction, create opportunities for feedback and ultimately practice. In this approach, students worked in small groups to try volleyball skills, build rallies and play mini games. This allowed students to take turns to perform and provide constructive feedback based on success criteria we created as a class. This prompted leadership skills among the students, and these styles were integral to building communication skills and ensuring that students were actively engaged in both giving and receiving feedback.

During the lessons, the different teaching styles had a noticeable impact on student engagement and learning. The "Guided Discovery"(f) and "Inclusion"(e) styles allowed students to explore skills and strategies in ways that were both enjoyable and developmentally appropriate. However, a small minority of students needed more structure, so I provided them with a suggested framework through a blend of "Command" and "Self-Check"(d). Overall, by encouraging students to devise their own solutions and modifications, I observed increased enthusiasm and creativity. For instance, when tasked with adapting the rules of the game, students proposed innovative ideas that made the game more inclusive and enjoyable for everyone. Involving students in decision-making about the game and its modifications fostered greater buy-in and ultimately created a more meaningful experience.

I also incorporated the "Self-Check" and "Convergent Discovery" styles to encourage self-assessment. We used a whiteboard for students to assess themselves using a success criteria bingo board. The board featured a selection of tasks or skills, such as umpiring a game, giving a partner feedback on their serve, scoring a point with a spike, and building a rally of five within their team. This approach allowed students to independently gauge their progress and identify areas for improvement whilst exploring various skills. It was gratifying to see students take ownership of their learning process, actively engaging with the criteria, and making adjustments based on their reflections. Additionally, this method helped students track their progress throughout the unit, reflect on their performance, and set goals for the remainder of the unit.

On reflection, I would have liked to "let go" even more during the unit. Next year, I plan to have students completely design their own net and wall unit—somewhere between a learner-designed individual programme and a learner-initiated style.

Throughout my 13 years of teaching, I have explored various teaching styles, often incorporating elements of student autonomy. However, being new to this school, I saw an opportunity to push this further, particularly given the emphasis on inquiry-based learning. My previous experiences showed me the benefits of structured progression, but I wanted to experiment with a more student-driven approach to see if it would have a greater impact on engagement and learning. This unit has reinforced the value of that shift, and I will continue refining it for future cohorts. The cycle continues!

Chapter 10 Summary

Guides: from Dread to Delight

DREAD	DELIGHT
Over Reliance on Authoritarian Leadership: Adopting an authoritarian leadership style in PE classes may stifle students' creativity, motivation, and autonomy, ultimately hindering their overall learning experience.	**Inclusive Teaching Practices:** Implementing inclusive teaching practices in physical education that cater to diverse learning needs and abilities, fosters a supportive and empowering learning environment where all students feel valued and included.
Lack of Adaptability: Teachers who consistently employ the same teaching style, without considering the specific context or learning objectives, may miss opportunities to optimise student engagement and learning outcomes.	**Adaptive Learning Styles:** Varying learning styles in PE to accommodate diverse student preferences, activity requirements and learning aspirations.
Teacher Only Guides: Neglecting to incorporate a variety of guiding styles (teacher as a guide, student guide, and self-guide) in PE lessons can restrict students' opportunities for autonomy, collaboration, and self-directed learning.	**All Can Guide:** Incorporating a variety of guiding styles (teacher as a guide, student guide, and self-guide) in PE lessons provides students with diverse opportunities for autonomy, collaboration, and self-directed learning, enhancing their overall learning experience.

Where would you place yourself right now?

DREAD ←————————————————→ DELIGHT

Reflection Questions

- How can I ensure a balanced mix of teaching styles to meet the diverse needs of my students?

- How can I integrate varied learning styles to enhance student learning outcomes in physical education?
- How can I promote autonomy and collaboration through different guiding styles in PE activities?
- How can I adapt teaching and guiding approaches to create an inclusive learning environment?

Call to Action

As we conclude this chapter, it's time to reflect on what you've learned and consider how to apply it. The SHIFT mnemonic can guide you through the next steps: a structured approach to transform your insights into meaningful actions. Take a moment to work through the following questions:

S **Summarise** the key takeaway from this chapter that stands out to you.

H **Highlight** how this takeaway challenges or aligns with your current practices.

I **Initiate** a small change or step right now to put what you've learned into practice.

F **Frame** how this change will contribute to achieving your long-term vision for PE.

T **Take** others on the journey—share your new insights and encourage collaboration.

References

Becky, A., Fletcher, T., Ní Chróinín, D., Beni, S., & Gleddie, D. (2022). Meaningful Physical Education: An Approach for Teaching and Learning. Routledge.

Billig, M. (2014). Kurt Lewin's leadership studies and his legacy to social psychology: Is there nothing as practical as a good theory? Journal for the Theory of Social Behaviour, Vol.

Bunker, D., & Thorpe, R. (1982). A model for the teaching of games in secondary schools. Bulletin of Physical Education, 18(1), 5–8.

Delors, J. (1996). Learning: The treasure within. A report to UNESCO of the International Commission on Education for the Twenty First Century, pp. 13-15. UNESCO Publishing/Australian National Commission for UNESCO.

Gazali, N., Saad, N., Cendra, R., Kamaruzaman, S., & Ripa'i, R. (2022). Leadership in physical education: Systematic review of the last five years. Jurnal SPORTIF: Jurnal Penelitian Pembelajaran, vol, pages.

Jin, H., Kim, S., Love, A., Jin, Y., & Zhao, J. (2022). Effects of leadership style on coach-athlete relationship, athletes' motivations, and athlete satisfaction. Frontiers in Psychology. https://doi.org/10.3389/fpsyg.2022.1012953

Launder, A. (2001). Play practice. Human Kinetics.

Li, X. (2024). Middle school students' leadership skills and their PE class participation. Journal of Education and Educational Research, 7, 221-234. https://doi.org/10.54097/kttcnj44

Metzler, M. (2017). Instructional models in physical education. Taylor & Francis.

Mosston, M., & Ashworth, S. (2008). Teaching physical education: First Online Edition 2008. [Online] Accessed at: https://spectrumofteachingstyles.org/assets/files/book/Teaching_Physical_Edu_1st_Online.pdf [Accessed on 23 April 2024].

Pill, S. (2007). Leadership for learning in physical education. Healthy Lifestyles Journal, 53(1), 21–25.

Pill, S. (2013). Play with purpose: Game sense to sport literacy. ACHPER Australia.

SueSee, B., Pill, S., & Edwards, K. (2016). Reconciling approaches – a game-centred approach to sport teaching and Mosston's spectrum of teaching styles. European Journal of Physical Education and Sport Science, 2(4), 1–28.

SueSee, B., & Pill, S. (2018). Game-based teaching and coaching as a toolkit of teaching styles. Strategies, 31(5), 21–28.

SueSee, B., Hewitt, M., & Pill, S. (2020). The spectrum of teaching styles in physical education. Routledge.
Thompson, J., Camp, J., Trimble, J., Langford, S., & Riggio, R. (2020). Leadership styles. In Leadership (pp. 499–504). https://doi.org/10.1002/9781119547181.ch347

UNESCO: United Nations Educational, Scientific and Cultural Organization. (2015). Quality Physical Education (QPE): Guidelines for policy makers. Author.

Wallhead, T., & Buckworth, J. (2004). The role of physical education in the promotion of youth physical activity. Quest, 56, pages. https://doi.org/10.1080/00336297.2004.10491827

Zeng, Z. H., & Gao, Q. (2012). Teaching physical education using the spectrum of teaching style: Introduction to Mosston's spectrum of teaching style. China School Physical Education, 2012-01, 65–68.

Chapter 11: Holistic

Lee Sullivan, Vicky Randall, Kate Clough and Megan Lockett

Part 11.1 – Insight
Lee Sullivan

This chapter will attempt to navigate the shift towards holistic PE, contrasting ancient Spartan militarism with Athenian intellectualism to question modern PE's alignment. This chapter will advocate for a shift beyond only the physical domain, emphasising a holistic approach that nurtures social, emotional, and cognitive development too. We will explore strategies for making PE personally relevant and bridge the gap between PE curriculum and students' lives, proposing a concept-driven approach to explicitly integrate holistic learning into physical education.

Spartan or Athenian?
In ancient Greece, two prominent city-states, Sparta and Athens, emerged as influential powers. Sparta, renowned for its militaristic society, placed paramount importance on physical prowess and military excellence. From a young age, Spartan citizens underwent rigorous physical training in a demanding educational system. In contrast, Athens fostered a culture that celebrated intellectual pursuits, philosophy, and the arts, valuing the development of the mind and individual expression.

In Sparta, the life of a soldier was meticulously structured from childhood to old age, with each stage of life dedicated to specific forms of training and preparation for military service. Beginning at the age of seven, boys were removed from their families and entered into the agoge, a state-sponsored educational system focused on instilling discipline, physical prowess, and loyalty to the Spartan state. During this initial phase of their training, boys received a basic education that included reading, writing, and rudimentary arithmetic, alongside physical conditioning aimed at developing endurance and strength. As they reached adolescence, typically around the age of twelve, Spartan boys transitioned to a more intensive phase of physical training. Endurance running, wrestling, boxing, and other martial arts formed the core of their training regimen, with an emphasis on developing agility, coordination, and combat skills. Upon reaching the age of eighteen, Spartan youths officially entered military training, embarking on a path towards becoming full-fledged soldiers in the Spartan army. They underwent gruelling physical challenges and simulated combat scenarios to prepare them for the rigours of warfare. Spartan women were not exempt from physical training as they were trained in athletic skills such as running, jumping, wrestling, and javelin throwing. This emphasis on physical education was deeply rooted in the Spartan belief that robust physical fitness in women was vital for ensuring the birth of healthy offspring.

Life in Athens diverged significantly from life in Sparta. Athenian society placed a high value on education, intellectual prowess, and artistic expression in addition to physical training. Unlike the rigorous and lengthy military-focused education of Spartan boys, Athenian boys from affluent families pursued a more balanced education aimed at nurturing both their physical and mental faculties. They often delved into subjects such as philosophy, geometry, astronomy, and public speaking. This comprehensive training prepared Athenian youths for active participation in civic life, including engagement in the Athenian assembly.

These ancient educational systems had very different aims. Spartan education primarily aimed to produce resilient soldiers capable of safeguarding their city-state. Conversely, Athenian education sought to cultivate a society where every individual could actively contribute.

What are we preparing our students for in PE today? There is often a recognition of the importance of physical fitness, skill development and the desire to prepare students for adult versions of specific sports. Essentially developing only the physical assets of our students, similar to the Spartan emphasis on training strong soldiers ready for war. However, for some time there has been an increasing acknowledgment of the need for holistic education, resembling the Athenian focus on developing well-rounded individuals. This is a growing shift towards promoting not only the physical but also social, emotional, and cognitive development of our students.

How closely does your PE curriculum align with the educational goals of Sparta or Athens?

Sporting Christians

The understanding that we can develop children through more than just the physical through physical activity and sport, is nothing new. Anyone that has taught sociology as part of the A Level PE specification will have heard of the term muscular Christianity. Proponents of muscular Christianity argued that engaging in sports and physical activities could cultivate virtues such as discipline, perseverance, teamwork, and fair play. They believed that participation in sports not only improved physical health but also fostered qualities of good citizenship and moral strength. This ideology gained traction in schools, churches, and youth organisations, influencing educational practices and shaping attitudes towards physical education and sport.

CHAPTER 11: **HOLISTIC**

Benefits Behind Bars

The educational opportunities provided by sport have been used beyond traditional schooling too. The August 2018 report "A Sporting Chance: An Independent Review of Sport in Youth and Adult Prisons" by Professor Rosie Meek highlights the increasing recognition of physical activity's role in rehabilitation within prison systems. The report reaffirms that participation in sports offers inmates an alternative to offending behaviour, fostering positive self-identity and providing access to pro-social networks and role models. Additionally, PE staff working with inmates find that sports have enabled them to support conflict resolution and build positive relationships.

More Than Higher, Faster, Stronger?

Even in the Olympic Games, we are witnessing a profound shift from celebrating sheer physical prowess to embracing the holistic spectrum of human expression and achievement. Once solely a showcase of strength, speed, and height, the Olympic stage now welcomes disciplines that epitomise creativity, innovation, and courage. Take, for example, the inclusion of breakdancing in the Olympic line-up. This dynamic art form not only demands physical agility and strength but also celebrates creativity and self-expression. Similarly, the addition of skateboarding to the Olympic roster exemplifies innovation and adaptability. This shift is crucial for the Olympics to remain relevant in a rapidly evolving world, where diversity of talent, reasons for engagement and methods of expression are increasingly valued.

Is it PE's Responsibility?

As discussed in chapter 2 focusing on what PE can realistically achieve, the sole purpose of PE should not be to create more resilient students, nor is it to build stronger leaders, better listeners or more employable workers. Though we hope this might happen, as we will explore in the next part of this chapter, we are unable to evidence this impact. Other subjects can also have an aim to develop character, but it is movement and the opportunity to physically interact with our environment that makes PE unique. It would be unfair and irresponsible to place more pressure on the already heavy shoulders of PE teachers to have the responsibility of creating stronger employees and better humans. We can however provide opportunities to find success and learning that students believe is important in their lives, we can motivate students to want to engage within our lessons and attempt to connect learning beyond PE. Hopefully, this will support students to develop competence, confidence and character in and through movement. PE is best placed to use the wide-ranging learning opportunities available in physical activity and sport in an attempt to develop the whole child.

Part 11.2 – Delve
Lee Sullivan

Introducing Holism

In his 1926 book 'Holism and Evolution,' military leader and philosopher, Jan Smuts introduced the term 'holism' to describe a philosophical concept that emphasises the interconnectedness and integration of parts within a whole system. Smuts proposed that the universe and all its components, including living organisms and social systems, should be viewed as unified wholes rather than mere collections of separate parts. Smuts refers to the holistic nature of man comprising matter and spirit, or in other words, body and mind. 'The ideal personality only arises where mind irradiates body and body nourishes mind, and the two are one in their mutual transfiguration.' (Page 261). In other words, when the mind is engaged and active, it energises and uplifts the body, and conversely, when the body is nourished and cared for, it enhances the capabilities and well-being of the mind.

The Swiss humanitarian Johann Pestalozzi, alongside American transcendentalists like Thoreau, Emerson, and Alcott, as well as progressive education pioneers Francis Parker and John Dewey, all emphasised the importance of education as a holistic endeavour. They believed in nurturing all dimensions of a child's development – moral, emotional, physical, psychological, and spiritual. Known as holism, this approach aims to embrace and integrate diverse layers of meaning and experience, rejecting narrow definitions of human potential based solely on standardised test scores.

Learning Domains

Historically, PE has been viewed primarily as a means to achieve health-related outcomes, but there's a growing recognition that it also plays a crucial role in fostering holistic development among children and youth. Studies by Bailey (2006) highlighted the potential benefits of PE across physical, affective, social, and cognitive learning domains. This study suggested that PE has the potential to make contributions to the development of children's fundamental movement skills and physical competences, which are necessary precursors of participation in later lifestyle and sporting physical activities. They also, when appropriately presented, can support the development of social skills and social behaviours, self-esteem and pro-school attitudes, and, in certain circumstances, academic and cognitive development.

UNESCO's Quality Physical Education Guidelines for Policymakers (2015) further underscored the significance of high-quality PE in developing the whole child: 'a quality PE curriculum promotes movement competence, to structure thinking, express feelings and enrich understanding. Through competition and cooperation, learners appreciate the role of rule structures, conventions, values, performance criteria and fair play, and celebrate each other's varying contributions, as well as appreciating the demands and benefits of teamwork,' (2015, page 14).

Frapwell, in collaboration with the Association for Physical Education (AfPE), published "A Practical Guide to Assessing Without Levels" in 2015. This guide introduces the Head-Heart-Hands framework, which organises content and criteria for assessment. The framework encompasses three key areas: Physical, Cognitive, and Social/Emotional development. Frapwell identified the connection between each aspect of development and their connections to physical activity, and what each individual should be or be able to do:

Head (cognitive domain). The thinking physical being:
- Decision maker
- Analytical – deep understanding
- Confident
- Tactician

Heart (affective domain). The feeling physical being:
- Social and emotional
- Involvement and engagement
- Attitude
- Character and values
- Healthy active lifestyle

Hands (psychomotor domain). The doing physical being:
- Physically competent
- Growth and development
- Physically active
- Competitive

PE, sport and physical activity are so much more than skills, techniques, winning, losing, rules and competition. They are opportunities to interact, learn from mistakes, build resilience, foster teamwork, see and demonstrate leadership qualities, and promote positive conflict resolution. All of this can happen whilst engaging in physical activity, not sitting in front of a board, reading definitions and trying to apply it to wider life. They can be immersed in these learning opportunities, experiencing them first hand.

Social Pedagogy in PE

In their 2025 book Social Pedagogy in Physical Education: Human-Centred Practice, Aspasia Dania and Claudio Farias make a compelling case for a more human-centred approach to PE. They argue that social pedagogy builds on individuals' previous experiences to foster relationship-centred learning, care, health, and well-being (p. 17). Describing it as a "values-led approach to supporting the development of youth" (p. 8), they emphasise the importance of integrating social and emotional development into PE, placing the well-being of students at the heart of teaching practices.

This pedagogy prioritises the holistic development of students, taking into account their individual needs, experiences, and well-being rather than focusing solely on skill acquisition. Central to this is fostering collaboration, mutual respect, and supportive bonds between students and teachers. Social pedagogy is grounded in principles such as care, inclusion, and social justice, aiming to nurture empathy and cooperation. Additionally, it encourages community engagement and the exploration of social and cultural dimensions of physical activity, promoting both personal growth and active citizenship.

Personally Relevant Learning

With methods of engagement shifting, drop-out rates increasing and levels of dissatisfaction consistently high, students are constantly showing us that the learning gained from PE is irrelevant. It might seem obvious, but students want lessons that are safe, relevant, well-informed, inclusive, exciting, and fun. The physical activity opportunities provided in PE are seen by many as traditional, irrelevant, boring, and far from fun (Harris and Cale, 2019).

During a basketball lay-up shot lesson, a student posed a challenging question that left me stumped. They expressed frustration at the difficulty of mastering the lay-up shot and asked, "Sir, when will I ever need this?" It was a tough question to address because, realistically, unless the student pursued basketball as a lifelong pursuit, the lay-up shot might not have practical relevance in their future endeavours. Kirk suggests that we must ask two questions when planning our curriculum (Kirk 2010, page 21):

- How does the learning that occurs within the schools relate to the life beyond the school gates?
- How does school physical education and adolescence relate to the needs of adulthood?

Ash Casey summarised, in his blog from 2018 on Meaningful Experiences in Physical Education and Youth Sport: 'When young people could recognise the importance of what they were learning and make connections to life outside of the situation – either in the present or future – they came to see their experiences as meaningful. On the contrary, failure has the effect of reducing or removing meaningfulness. The connectivity of experience (or the lack of it) to their broader lives was an indicator of meaningfulness'. This is potentially what the inclusion

CHAPTER 11: **HOLISTIC**

of holistic learning opportunities can aim to do, ensure the relevancy of the learning for all so that a stronger connection to our subject and a longer term positive relationship with physical activity is nurtured.

For so many students, the physical learning objective alone, especially when specifically focused on the replication of a complex sporting skill is found irrelevant to their lives. They leave the lesson having not accomplished this skill and therefore also leave feeling a sense of failure. Thus having built little to know connection with our subject, failure to see the value in the learning and no intention of pursuing the activity in their own time.

Effective Affective

It's fair to say that the idea of character development through PE is controversial due to the 'lack of understanding about what affective learning is and does, and how to teach it' (Casey et al. 2019, Page 2). This lack of understanding poses a significant challenge for educators seeking to integrate character development effectively into PE curricula.

Jamie Jacob Brunsdon explored the idea of character education in PE in his paper: Toward the virtuous mover: a neo-Aristotelian Interpretation of physical education (2022). The paper suggests that despite its importance in teaching and teacher education, a lack of agreement among professionals on the emotional domain has hindered teachers' ability to teach morals effectively. This lack of consensus, coupled with misconceptions and stereotypes, has made it challenging for character education in physical education to progress beyond experimental stages. Brunsdon offers five critiques of character education within PE. One of which suggests that character education in schools and physical education is often sidelined, with activities like teambuilding not fully addressing the development of virtues in youth. It suggests that character education should be integrated into core teaching to promote moral development and transferable learning. Therefore, physical education has the potential to nurture various important qualities in students.

The idea of life skills was also considered in the research paper 'A Qualitative Investigation of Teachers' Experiences of Life Skills Development in Physical Education' by Lorcan Cronin et.al. (2022). The study sheds light on teachers' perspectives regarding life skills development and transfer in PE. It reveals that teachers acknowledge the importance of PE in fostering a variety of life skills in students. Furthermore, the findings emphasise the necessity for teachers to cater to individual student needs and employ effective strategies for enhancing life skills within PE. Additionally, teachers recognise the potential for life skills learned in PE to be transferred to other areas of students' lives, advocating for deliberate discussions and practice to facilitate this transfer process.

Essentially, if choosing a character education approach in PE, it should be clearly articulated, integrated into core teaching practices, and delivered using effective strategies.

Tenuous Transfer

The ultimate goal of educators is to equip students with skills and knowledge that extend beyond the classroom, seamlessly integrating into various aspects of their lives. However, the challenge lies in demonstrating the transferability of learning, particularly in character development within PE. The notion of transfer has posed a significant obstacle. Research into transfer is murky at best. However, despite these challenges, educators remain hopeful and committed to the idea that character development in PE can indeed lead to transferable skills. By continually refining teaching approaches, fostering deeper connections between lessons and real-life scenarios, and embracing innovative strategies, there is optimism that the goal of enhancing students' holistic development through PE can be achieved.

A Concept-Driven Approach

David Kirk recognised that PE teachers have gone above and beyond, making the very best of what they have been given. Many PE teachers have become 'skilful operators of a hidden curriculum that uses the technique practices merely as a vehicle to communicate the values and joys of physical activity, or to facilitate for students the practice of responsibility for self and respect for others' (Kirk, 2010, p.4). PE teachers have, for years, advocated for the character development traits that PE can deliver, though this learning was seldom written into the curriculum or explicitly linked to the learning objectives, assessment or even intent of the delivery. If this learning is happening anyway, why not make it explicit?

In 'Is PE in Crisis' I advocated for the inclusion of a concept within our PE lessons and the consideration of a concept-driven approach to PE planning and delivery. A Concept-driven approach to curriculum design is one that moves away from subject-specific content and instead emphasises "big ideas" that span multiple subject areas (Erickson, 2007). Introducing concepts can lead to a significant shift in the perception of a subject (Chambers et al. 2021). It was time to make that holistic learning explicit, planned and the learning from PE relevant to all.

Lynn Erickson (2007) highlights the importance of using concepts in education in order to formulate knowledge, understand the world, and succeed in life beyond school. She argues that concepts:
- Create connections to students' prior experiences.
- Bring relevance to student learning.
- Facilitate deeper understanding of content knowledge.
- Act as springboards for students to respond to their learning.

CHAPTER 11: **HOLISTIC**

In embracing a concept-driven approach to PE, educators have the opportunity to elevate the holistic learning experiences offered to students, making explicit the character development traits inherent in physical activity. Moreover, aiming to foster deeper understanding, relevance, and connection to students' experiences.

The Concept Curriculum

The Concept Curriculum presented in 'Is PE in Crisis?' has evolved to better address the needs of the teachers delivering it and the students receiving it. The purpose of the Primary and Secondary Concept Curriculum is not to create resilient individuals, strong leaders or effective communicators. Although I hope this might happen, the purpose is to provide personally relevant, PE-specific learning that engages every learner and enables all to build strong relationships with PE, physical activity and sport.

This book is not an advertising space for the Concept Curriculum; however, I will provide a brief overview in order to illustrate its evolution and demonstrate its potential to deliver explicit holistic learning within PE:

Lesson Objectives

The lesson aims in the Concept Curriculum are structured around three key objectives: Know, Show, and Grow, introduced by co-author Becky Bridges. The 'Know' objective targets cognitive development, emphasising understanding of safe and effective movement, rules, strategies, and health concepts. The 'Show' focuses on physical skills, encompassing fundamental movement and activity-specific abilities. Lastly, 'Grow' centres on affective development, aiming to foster holistic growth through an overarching concept. Together, these objectives aim to provide a comprehensive framework for enhancing students' cognitive, physical, and emotional development in physical education.

Lesson Framework

This has evolved to use the LEAD lesson framework, standing for: lesson introduction, energise, explore and link, activity and discovery.
- **Lesson Introduction:** At the start of the lesson, by introducing the concept it opens the opportunity to focus the learning and explore its application within our PE context.
- **Energise, Explore and Link:** Once students have understood what is meant by the concept, get them active as quickly as possible and encourage them to explore and make connections with the physical activity we are engaging in. At the end of the activity, ask the students link questions to support understanding and link the learning to the activity.
- **Activity:** The most important part of any PE lesson is the opportunity to be physically active. Create engaging and challenging activities for students to demonstrate their understanding of the concept, develop their competence and confidence with the physical

activity and have plenty of time to practise the skills and techniques required to engage with a variety of activities.
- **Discovery:** The final stage of the L.E.A.D Model is to discuss the discoveries we have made in the lesson and how this learning could be applied elsewhere. Here we encourage students to consider what they have learnt, how they have demonstrated this learning and where else this learning might help them in PE and beyond.

Using an idea given to me by Will Swaithes, picture a lesson where students are awarded bands - blue for Know, green for Show, and pink for Grow - based on their achievement or progress towards specific learning objectives. In a lesson concentrated solely on the physical domain, some students earn Show bands by accurately replicating a skill, while others, including possibly a few more, gain Know bands by articulating how to perform the skill. However, there are students who consistently leave the lesson without any band, experiencing a sense of failure and inadequacy, which can lead to a diminished self-perception of their abilities in that activity and subject. By introducing a Grow objective, the learning experience becomes more inclusive, providing additional opportunities for success and fostering relevant learning that extends beyond the immediate context. Teachers who have implemented this approach in their concept-driven lessons have observed a shift in focus, recognising attributes in students that were previously overlooked in the physical-only focused lessons. This holistic approach not only enhances skill acquisition but also promotes a more positive and empowering learning environment, where every student can thrive and apply their newfound knowledge and abilities to other aspects of their lives.

Providing clear opportunities for students to identify, experience, connect, reflect, discuss and consider application of learning within the lesson is essential for fostering holistic development and empowering students to thrive both in and potentially beyond the PE context.

The Concept Curriculum can be used alongside a number of models-based practices or the non-linear pedagogy approach. Applying this approach to the resilient skill-drill form of delivery, whilst it might make some of the learning more relevant to more learners, will do little to change the dull and boring perspectives of many towards PE.

All learning (Know, Show and Grow) should be sequenced and age appropriate. In Early Years the learning is delivered through immersive stories and games in which the fundamental movement skills are developed in fun and engaging ways. As students advance through the year groups, the complexity and depth of the learning experiences evolve to align with their developmental stages and readiness levels. Through this approach, the Concept Curriculum provides a flexible framework that can adapt to the changing needs and capabilities of students as they grow and develop in their physical education journey.

CHAPTER 11: **HOLISTIC**

Whether you adopt the Concept Curriculum suggested in this book, one of your own, or none at all, it is becoming crucial for PE teachers to explore and embrace the holistic learning opportunities available in physical education.

Part 11.3 – Experts

Child Centred Holistic Pedagogy
Vicky Randall

> "Physical education' may not be permanently regarded as a satisfactory term. In the past, the study of man led to an analysis which split him up into body, mind, and spirit; at the present time we are becoming increasingly aware of his wholeness and of the interdependence of those processes that we have been accustomed to describe as physiological or psychological. It may not be long before we realize that the term' physical '- in relation to humanity-has a very limited meaning."

You might be surprised to learn that this passage comes from the 1952/53 Ministry of Education, *Physical Education in the Primary School Part 1: Moving and Growing*. At the time, the term "Physical Education" was still relatively new, yet it had already sparked debate about whether, and how, the body could be separated from the mind in the teaching of the subject.

Since the syllabus of 1952, Physical Education has continued to be recognised for the important role it plays in a child's learning; one that extends far beyond the functional use of the body and the broader physical domain. To move is to be human, and a physically educated person cannot exist without a connection to the mind, the environment, and the people around them. Even if we tried, we could not segregate our body from our being in the world. Consider how many ways children move. Their movement intention might be for the purpose of play, leisure, travel, or functionality, but there is always a constant invitation from the environment to make decisions about how, what, where, and with whom movement will occur. Each moment evokes a different purpose and a different emotional response. Even when sedentary, the body still has a life-preserving desire to move through the internal mechanism of breath.

The term 'holism' or 'holistic' pedagogy has resulted in other domains of learning within Physical Education to be separated out from the physical context of the activity. This may have emerged due to concerns that the subject struggles to locate its purpose in a congested curriculum space where subjects, such as literacy, science, and mathematics, are held in higher esteem. In many physical education curricula, we see objectives for learning explicitly foregrounded around whole-person engagement, extending beyond what the body can do. For example, objectives that focus on the cognitive domain (strategies, planning, evaluation, decision-making) or the social domain (cooperation, following leadership, shared ideas, and trust-building). However, in reality, is it possible to 'be' in physical education without being cognisant? I have been guilty of explicitly highlighting objectives for learning that are social, emotional, and cognitive in my own practice to reinforce to senior leaders, colleagues, and pupils that physical education supports learning beyond the physical. I would often highlight scientific terminology in lessons or link mathematical ideas when teaching more arts-based activities; for example, awarding a 0.2 tariff score for every quarter turn when evaluating a partner's performance. Was this good practice, or merely a justification of physical education's place in the curriculum that demanded respect? I wonder how many of my maths or science colleagues returned the favour and used a more movement-based pedagogy to enhance their teaching? This is not to say that being granular in our understanding of the teaching and learning process is a bad thing. It can provide clarity that supports a wider picture of a child's understanding in physical education. My point here is that when we ask a child to engage physically in Physical Education, the mind and body will always be connected, regardless of what we put in a lesson plan.

Over the course of my career in physical education, I have been influenced by the work of Rudolf Laban. Reflecting on holism for this chapter has led me to revisit his work. Laban (1879–1958) was a dance artist and theorist who is widely regarded as one of the most influential figures in the field of movement. His work has since influenced the design and development of physical education programs worldwide, offering a whole-person perspective on movement. In his own words, Laban (2011:1) recognises that we "move to satisfy a need," and movement is ultimately a desire toward something of value to us. The reasons why we move, therefore, exist beyond the physical and can hold far greater meaning in our lives when meaning and connection is made. Laban's (1966) work has led to the development of a movement analysis framework that prompts an awareness of the actions of the body through effort, space, and shape.

- **Body:** What are the actions or skills of the body?
- **Effort:** How is movement performed?
- **Space:** Where in space is movement occurring?
- **Shape:** How does our movement respond to the environment and the relationships we have within it?

If you applied each of the four areas above to a physical education context, what differences would you observe? How does the environment, where the lesson takes place, impact how the body moves? How would a lesson in the water create different opportunities for the body (and mind) compared to being in an open field or inside a gymnasium with apparatus?

As curricular frameworks change over time, one constant remains—the child and their body. As physical educators, when we turn our gaze to the importance of holism, perhaps it is not about creating any dramatic change in our practice. Instead, it asks us to focus on making more explicit connections for children, fostering an awareness of how movement makes them feel, how and why they move, and how movement can help navigate the many personal relationships they will encounter.

FROM PE DREAD TO DELIGHT

Part 11.4 – Apply

The Concept Curriculum
Kate Clough

After taking on the role of Head of Department, I knew that change was needed. My school was delivering a curriculum that didn't look too dissimilar to the PE I experienced over 20 years ago. After the life-changing pandemic we all experienced, it was becoming more apparent to myself and my department that we had increasing numbers of students who were becoming disengaged in our subject. Even with targeted interventions from initiatives by the Youth Sport Trust and local clubs, it was becoming a common reflective conversation within the department that students were demonstrating a real lack of effort and resilience. Staff were also questioning why there were reduced numbers attending extracurricular training and fixtures. It was evident something needed to change our curriculum.

At the heart of this curriculum change was developing something in line with the Department Vision; creating a curriculum that supported students' ability to access physical education and develop a love sport and physical activity that they would take with them and apply once leaving education. This curriculum development needed to be right for our students, its community and the school's location. It needed to be underpinned by research, evidence and would ultimately get 'buy in' from my department to drive this forward.

I initially liaised with schools within my Trust and region as well as reaching out to PE teachers on social media. After much research, I purchased the initial Concept Curriculum from PE Scholar. Throughout this process I was supported by my line manager and was able to strategically address any potential issues that may have occurred when initially launching this curriculum change. It was important to be measured in my approach.

I launched this curriculum development to the PE Department with my "Why", highlighting the process that had informed me to get to this point. With the team on board and in agreement that change was needed we initially looked at the purchased Concept Curriculum. Knowing our context, it was agreed this fantastic resource needed to be streamlined to support the department's implementation and students' access. We also agreed that we would carry out a trial during the Summer Term of the Academic Year. We would deliver a traditional curriculum to one half of Year 7 and our developing Concept Curriculum to the other half. With department input we agreed we would carry out student voice interviews, student and staff questionnaires and data from our diagnostic homework to inform the trial.

CHAPTER 12: **TRAINING**

This gave me and my Second in Department (Sophie) a term to create our own proformas, change some of the language and the structure to fit the Trust's Learning Cycle model. During our department's weekly briefings, we updated staff on what we were doing and made sure we discussed key areas such as the language of our weekly focus; this was imperative as staff were a part of this journey and the developments being made. It made the implementation easier as staff understood the Concept Curriculum was not taking away from the physical but underpinning a more robust curriculum. The trial highlighted that, when delivering the Concept Curriculum, staff were more consistent in their delivery and use of language, students were able to articulate what the focus of the lesson was, and many students highlighted how they had enjoyed the delivery of their lessons.

I reached out to PE Scholar after our trial, as I wanted to make them aware of the impact their resource was having on our students. After a Zoom call from Lee and Liz Durden-Myers, Sophie and I were given guidance, feedback, and support and from this point forward I was able to liaise with Lee about our next steps. Their passion, knowledge, and guidance along with the growing community of like-minded professionals really did support our implementation and next steps.

With the resounding success of the trial, it was agreed that the implementation and development of our Concept Curriculum would be the PE Department's focus for the next Academic Year. I informed my Line Manager throughout our developments and was able to present to SLT and the Trust with the process and proposal moving forward. It was agreed with the PE Department that regular feedback would be provided through learning walks during our implementation, along with honest reflections during our weekly briefings as well as sharing of good practice and student voice. In my leadership role I feel this brought my team together, we had a common goal and the impact it was having during our lessons was becoming more evident throughout the year. Our trainees and Early Career Teachers (ECT) commented on the consistency they were seeing in all staff's lessons, and the engagement levels of our students.

Throughout the Academic Year we amended the content from each Learning Cycle ready for the next year. This was a working document which worked well. Learning walks initially showed me that staff had bought into the Concept Curriculum and students could articulate what the focus of the lesson was. Throughout the year it highlighted key areas to work on, such as the developing of "Why" we were focusing on the concept in the lesson and how its application could support the skill development. With these adaptations after the first Academic year, we really did feel like we had started to embed our curriculum and were excited to see how the changes would benefit our students moving forwards.

It would not have been possible to implement the Concept Curriculum without developing and working with my department. We truly became a team who grew to become like- minded. Our "why" was always made clear and we never lost sight of why changes would be implemented, for our students.

My biggest takeaways
- Research and liaise with the PE Community. Social media provided so much support with this.
- Clear communication and clarity. This supported staff buy-in and meant staff were a part of journey.
- Start small. By carrying out a trial I was able to collate data, act on feedback and make appropriate adaptations where needed.

A Concept Curriculum has created a more consistent delivery of PE to our students. It has taken away the fear and judgment some students felt when arriving to our lessons, it has made us more reflective in our practice and provided different experiences for our students. We are now three years into our Concept Curriculum, and I am excited to continue on our journey to deliver meaningful and relevant PE to our fantastic students.

Concept-Driven PE
Megan Lockett

Implementing a Concept-Based Approach in Physical Education at New International School Thailand (NIST)

Evolving Physical Education at NIST: Aligning Curriculum with Mission, Vision and Values

Curricula, much like the learning processes they underpin, are subject to evolution. In 2021, under a new school leadership, the entire school began a journey of curriculum articulation. This period was an invaluable opportunity to look at our existing PE curriculum, prompting a thorough reassessment of our underlying motives, our "why", and ensuring these motives aligned with the school's mission, vision and values. My "why" as a physical education teacher is to create positive learning experiences and inspire students to make active life choices. I love hearing when students practise cycling in the park with their family, join the Mini-Volleyball team because they enjoyed it in class, or feel proud playing 3v3 Streetball because they feel included. I agree with Kirk (2013) that there is no "one-size-fits-all" approach and that students can gain different outcomes from their learning. This adds to the complexity of our subject area but also its beauty.

Implementing the Concept-Based Approach

Our Director of Teaching and Learning has continuously supported us throughout the PE curriculum articulation process. Several frameworks, including the Primary Years Programme (PYP), Middle Years Programme (MYP), Ontario Curriculum, Australian Curriculum, Assessment

CHAPTER 12: TRAINING

and Reporting Authority (ACARA), and SHAPE National PE standards, were reviewed. These frameworks share key principles, emphasising holistic development across physical, cognitive, emotional, and social domains, and student-centered learning that caters to individual needs, interests, and abilities. Inquiry-based learning is central to the PYP and MYP, encouraging exploration and problem-solving. The emphasis on promoting an active lifestyle and developing fundamental and specialised motor skills are a priority. The curricula advocate for integrating physical education with other subjects and real-life experiences, incorporating assessment and reflection to track progress and foster growth. They also highlight inclusivity and equity, ensuring opportunities for all students and incorporating global perspectives to appreciate diverse cultures and practices in physical activity. This analysis allowed department leads to work closely with the Director of Teaching and Learning to develop three key strands for learning in PE at NIST, covering physical, cognitive, social, creative, affective, and spiritual domains (adapted from Bailey, 2006), in, about, and through movement (Arnold, 1979).

Holistic Development PE Strands
1. **Active Living:** This strand emphasises the appreciation of how involvement in physical activity can enhance quality of life. It provides opportunities for reflection, enabling students to discover their passions and determine the next steps for maintaining an active lifestyle. Our aim is to develop a desire for lifelong participation in physical activities.
2. **Movement Competence (Land-Based and Water-Based):** This strand focuses on fundamental and specialised movement competencies essential for participating in physical activities on land and in water. Through movement, students acquire and refine specific skills, developing confidence as they apply movement concepts and strategies to enhance their own performance and support others.
3. **Personal and Social Attributes of Movement:** This strand highlights the personal and social skills that can be developed through physical activities. Key skills include communication, decision-making, problem-solving, critical and creative thinking, and cooperation. Students develop these skills by working individually, in small groups, or on larger teams to perform movement tasks or solve movement challenges.

Our PE curriculum goes beyond the "physical" to embrace a holistic approach, addressing cognitive, social, creative, affective, and spiritual domains. Holistic learning is integral to our philosophy, as it ensures that students develop as well-rounded individuals equipped with the skills and attributes needed for life beyond school.

Cognitive Development
Through our curriculum, students engage in critical thinking and problem-solving activities that enhance their cognitive abilities. For example, strategy-based activities and adventure

challenges require students to plan, make decisions, and evaluate outcomes. These activities help students develop a growth mindset and resilience, essential for personal development.
Social and Affective Growth

Physical education at NIST focuses on social and emotional growth. Activities like cooperative games and team activities foster emotional intelligence, empathy, and interpersonal skills. Students learn to manage their emotions, handle conflicts, and build positive relationships with peers. These experiences contribute to their emotional well-being and prepare them for collaborative environments in the future. This approach aligns with the NIST Attributes, which are informed by and align with the International Baccalaureate Learner Profile and the IB Approaches to Learning. Through the skills we teach and the dispositions we cultivate—such as self-management, caring, self-awareness, and being principled—students develop into well-rounded individuals ready to engage with the world.

Creative Expression

The curriculum encourages creative expression through movement. Dance, for instance, allows students to explore and convey ideas, emotions, and stories through various dance styles. By integrating technology, students can also create digital dance advertisements, enhancing their digital literacy and creativity. These opportunities for creative expression build confidence and self-esteem, empowering students to express themselves authentically.

Spiritual Development

Spiritual development in physical education at NIST involves fostering inner peace, self-awareness, and a connection to something greater than oneself through physical activity. This is explored by integrating mindfulness activities to promote self-awareness and emotional regulation, encouraging reflection on physical experiences to understand personal motivations and growth. Despite being in the bustling city of Bangkok, we try to provide students with more opportunities for outdoor activities, fostering a sense of appreciation for their environment and connection with nature. Helping students find purpose and meaning in their activities through personal goal-setting and understanding their broader impact is also essential. Emphasising teamwork and cooperation fosters a sense of belonging and connection to others. Initially, when the concept of spiritual development in PE was introduced to me, I was sceptical. However, as I observe its impact on student learning, I find myself intrigued by the idea of the "spirit of PE." By incorporating these ideas into physical education, we aim to support students' spiritual development, helping them become balanced, self-aware, and connected individuals.

Curriculum and Implementation

CHAPTER 12: **TRAINING**

We examined our program offerings from these strands, recognising that we were attempting to cover too much. Consequently, we standardised our units to six land-based and 2 water-based per year (we are discussing whether this is still too much). We have five PE lessons in a 10-day cycle, which is divided equally between land-based and water-based activities. Our units include adventure challenges/individual pursuits, movement challenges, games, and fundamentals/health-related fitness, along with personal survival, lifesaving, and stroke development. This structure maintains fluidity, allowing units to interlink, such as incorporating adventure challenges or fitness activities in the water.

We then reviewed how learning progressed from early years (EY) to Year 11, striving to build more progressions and variations in disciplines and assessments across the year levels rather than repeating the same ideas. For instance, in dance, we previously split into small groups to produce a 'final product' performance at every year level. Our approach now introduces expression, form, change, and rhythm through various dance styles, such as Interpretive, Percussion, or Disco. Students can explore and express ideas, emotions, and feelings, contribute individual 'jigsaw pieces' to a collective class Disco performance, or use technology to create a dance advertisement for a student-selected product. These activities allow students to imitate movements, engage in structured choreography, and exercise their creative choices. Students also follow their choreographic process, demonstrating how they crafted and produced their dance. This concept-driven approach is justified by its focus on helping students understand and apply fundamental dance concepts. By exploring concepts such as expression, form, change, and rhythm, students develop their ability to convey complex ideas and emotions through dance while also fostering creativity, teamwork, and digital literacy.

Our collaborative efforts extended to working with aquatics, gymnastics, and football directors to develop progressive skills and assessments covered within each curriculum area. One of my favourite parts was collaborating as a team to craft our unit overviews, providing snapshots of student learning for each unit. These overviews are shared with our entire school community and displayed as unit posters outside our office, fostering engagement and interest.

Example: Are You Ready to Rock? (Year 6 Adventure Challenges)
As the first unit of the year, students will have opportunities to build relationships through cooperative activities, to develop problem-solving skills and build connections that enable them to take on leadership roles and support each other. This unit is designed so that students can challenge themselves through a number of adventures that include rock climbing, bouldering, archery and cycling. Throughout the unit, students will be provided with choices in regard to challenges they face in order to push their boundaries outside of their comfort zone. The question now is… *Are YOU Ready to Rock?*

PYP Key Concepts

- **Connection** - Students will build strong relationships with their peers by emphasising connection through cooperative games, rock climbing, bouldering, archery, and cycling. These shared experiences encourage teamwork, trust, and open communication, creating a sense of community and belonging. As students work together to overcome challenges, they form connections to support one another during the unit and beyond.
- **Responsibility** - Students are encouraged to take ownership of their learning and personal growth. By making choices about the challenges they would like to complete, they develop a sense of accountability for their actions and decisions. This empowers them to step into leadership roles, guiding and supporting their peers while navigating their comfort zones. Emphasising responsibility helps students understand the impact of their actions on others, fostering a culture of mutual respect and cooperation.

Related Concepts: Growth, Relationships, Community.
Our unit planners, which are shared and accessible to all team members, are dynamic working documents. We continuously connect, share ideas, and reflect on the lessons and units we deliver, taking into account the unique needs of our students and the ever-changing environment. Flexibility is crucial. As our school grows, our lesson delivery has evolved to become more adaptable to our whole school's shared facilities. For instance, what was once a single activity like "T-Ball" is now "Happy Hitters," recognising that classes and individuals may be at different stages of learning. This shift allows for tailored modifications to better meet individual developmental needs and skill levels. It ensures developmental appropriateness and provides broader skill-building opportunities. We now offer more student voice and choice opportunities, ensuring that our units accommodate diverse learning needs. This flexibility supports inclusivity, personalised learning, and adaptability, creating a more supportive and effective learning environment for elementary students.

Insights and Challenges in Curriculum Evolution

The curriculum transformation process has been highly collaborative, and allowing extended time for extensive changes has been crucial. Since beginning in 2021, we have recognised the need for ongoing adjustments and evolution. Our diverse team, with various teaching styles and backgrounds, is united in promoting active living. Challenges such as creating genuine transdisciplinary connections amidst shared facilities, balancing conceptual understanding with movement time, and addressing misconceptions about PE being solely sports-related persist. Students sometimes question the absence of traditional sports like "proper" Football, while parents occasionally express concern over lower grades despite their child's involvement in school teams. Additionally, PE classes are occasionally interrupted for other school activities. We advocate for integrating physical activity and well-being options into the schedules of Year 12 and Year 13 students to support their health and active lifestyles. As with any curriculum, there are always areas for growth.

Impact of the Change

The changes have significantly enriched our approach to physical education. We now offer greater clarity within our community regarding the "why," "how," and "what" of PE at NIST. This shift has introduced enhanced fluidity and flexibility in student learning, contributing to a more unified understanding of the PE curriculum. Students enjoy more choices and personalised learning experiences, along with a clearer connection between their activities and learning. While a strength of the department, staff now benefit from a more cohesive and transparent approach to unit planning, alongside enhanced communication about the units. Meanwhile, the broader school community actively engages in and celebrates physical education through participation in PE events that showcase student learning and promote an active lifestyle.

Summary

Implementing a concept-based approach in physical education at NIST has been a transformative journey, deeply aligned with our commitment to holistic learning. This evolution has enriched our curriculum, encompassing physical, cognitive, social, creative, affective, and spiritual development. By integrating diverse educational practices and frameworks, we aim to provide a comprehensive learning experience. Continuous collaboration, reflection, and adaptability are vital, as the process is inherently non-linear. Ongoing adjustments are necessary to navigate the complexities of embedding these holistic principles into our practice, ensuring our approach remains responsive to student needs and the broader educational context.

FROM PE DREAD TO DELIGHT

Chapter 11 Summary

Holistic: from Dread to Delight

DREAD

Spartans:
Learners are only prepared for war.

Obsessed with Physical Skills:
The only focus is on developing sport specific skills which for many are irrelevant.

Irrelevant Learning:
Students constantly experience failure and make little or no connection with learning to life beyond PE.

DELIGHT

Athenians:
Learners are prepared to be active citizens.

Holistic Development:
PE curriculum emphasises the holistic development of students, nurturing physical, social, emotional, and cognitive skills.

Relevant Learning:
Lessons are designed to be practical and relevant to students' lives, enabling them to see and make the connections between what they learn in PE and their experiences outside of PE.

Where would you place yourself right now?

DREAD ⟵⟶ **DELIGHT**

Reflection Questions:
- What are my thoughts on taking a holistic approach in PE?
- Do students find the learning in PE relevant to their lives? How do I know?
- Are there any areas where my curriculum could be adjusted to better incorporate social, emotional, and cognitive development alongside physical skills?
- Do my lesson objectives clearly articulate the cognitive, physical, and affective learning outcomes I aim to achieve?
- How do I ensure that my PE lessons are relevant and meaningful to students' lives beyond PE?

CHAPTER 12: **TRAINING**

Call to Action
As we conclude this chapter, it's time to reflect on what you've learned and consider how to apply it. The SHIFT mnemonic can guide you through the next steps: a structured approach to transform your insights into meaningful actions. Take a moment to work through the following questions:

S **Summarise** the key takeaway from this chapter that stands out to you.

H **Highlight** how this takeaway challenges or aligns with your current practices.

I **Initiate** a small change or step right now to put what you've learned into practice.

F **Frame** how this change will contribute to achieving your long-term vision for PE.

T **Take** others on the journey—share your new insights and encourage collaboration.

References

Arnold, P. (1979). Meaning in movement, sport and physical education. Portsmouth, NH: Heinemann Educational Publishers.

Bailey, R. (2006). Physical education and sport in schools: A review of benefits and outcomes. The Journal of School Health, 76(8), 397–401.

Brunsdon, J. J. (2022). Toward the virtuous mover: A neo-Aristotelian interpretation of physical education. Physical Education and Sport Pedagogy. https://doi.org/10.1080/17408989.2022.2135693

Casey, A. (2018). Meaningful experiences in physical education and youth sport. Retrieved from https://peprn.com/2018/10/meaningful-experiences-in-physical-education-and-youth-sport.aspx [Accessed 1 April 2024].

Casey, A., & Fernández-Río, J. (2019). Cooperative learning and the affective domain. Journal of Physical Education, Recreation & Dance, 90. https://doi.org/10.1080/07303084.2019.1559671

Chambers, F., Aldous, D., & Bryant, A. (2021). Threshold concepts in physical education: A design thinking approach. Routledge.

Cronin, L., Greenfield, R., & Maher, A. (2023). A qualitative investigation of teachers' experiences of life skills development in physical education. Qualitative Research in Sport, Exercise and Health, 15(6), 789–804. https://doi.org/10.1080/2159676X.2023.2222774

Dania, A., & Farias, C. (2025). Social pedagogy in physical education: Human-centred practice. Routledge.

Erickson, H. L. (2007). Concept-based curriculum and instruction for the thinking classroom. Corwin.

Frapwell, A. (2015). A practical guide to assessing without levels: Supporting and safeguarding high-quality achievement in physical education. Coachwise.

Griggs, G., & Randall, V. (2022). An introduction to physical education. Routledge.

Kirk, D. (2013). Educational value and models-based practice in physical education. Educational Philosophy and Theory, 45(9), 973–986.

Laban, R. (1966). The language of movement. Great Britain: Macdonald and Even Ltd.

Laban, R. (2011). The mastery of movement (4th ed.). Alton, New Hampshire, United Kingdom: Dance Books Ltd. (Original work published 1950).

Meek, R. (2018). A sporting chance: An independent review of sport in youth and adult prisons. Ministry of Justice. Retrieved from https://assets.publishing.service.gov.uk/media/5b6d5ddeed915d311c8f5e32/a-sporting-chance-an-independent-review-sport-in-justice.pdf [Accessed 23 March 2024].

Ministry of Education. (1952). Physical Education in the Primary School Part 1: Moving and Growing. HMSO: London.

Smuts, J. C. (1926). Holism and evolution. The Gestalt Journal Press Inc.

UNESCO. (2015). Quality physical education (QPE): Guidelines for policy makers. Retrieved from https://en.unesco.org/inclusivepolicylab/sites/default/files/learning/document/2017/1/231101E.pdf

Chapter 12: Training

Lee Sullivan, Ryan Ellis, Ben Holden and Sue Pye-Beraet

Part 12.1 – Insight
Lee Sullivan

The Evolution of the PE Teacher

In the very first session of my teacher training, our lecturer Tony McFadyen captivated our attention by showing a clip featuring a PE teacher from the iconic film 'Kes'. Before pressing play, he prompted us to reflect on the actions of the PE teacher in the scene and how PE has changed since the film's release in 1969.

Directed by Ken Loach, 'Kes' tells the story of Billy Casper, a 15-year-old lad hailing from Yorkshire. In the midst of a challenging environment rife with bullies both at home and in school, Billy is struggling to find his way in life. In the iconic scene played to us, the timid and PE-averse Billy is reluctantly thrust into the role of goalkeeper during a football PE lesson, under the supervision of the perpetually irate teacher, Mr. Sugden. As captain, referee, and participant in the match, Mr. Sugden's true focus is on reliving his own footballing dreams rather than teaching his students. The PE teacher bends the rules to his advantage, even awarding himself a penalty kick (which he misses and retakes, blaming the goalkeeper for unfair movements). Throughout the game, Mr. Sugden's authoritative presence allows him to dominate the field, both physically and mentally, as he bullies and belittles his young pupils into playing out his football fantasy.

Meanwhile, Billy Casper remains disinterested in the game, spending much of the time distracted by the cold weather or climbing on the goal frame.

During the video, the group of teacher trainees laughed at the comical representation of the PE teacher, however, following the video we reflected back on our own PE experiences and realised there were quite a few commonalities. From the sport-dominated curriculum to the emphasis on winning at all costs, the scene mirrored the competitive atmosphere that often overshadowed the joy of physical activity. Although exaggerated, the authoritarian PE teacher resembled PE teachers we had seen in our own childhoods. We recalled the disinterested students on the side-lines, forced to participate in activities that held little relevance to their lives outside of school.

The role of the PE teacher has had to evolve alongside the evolution of the subject. Our subject has previously focused on sport-specific skills, improving fitness or preparation for war. And so, teachers would adopt a military style approach of 'I say, you do'.

In more recent times, with a sport-driven obsession, the subject knowledge required by a PE teacher meant that teachers would often attend National Governing Body coaching qualifications to add to their sport-specific repertoire. There can be no doubt that teaching PE requires a huge amount of subject knowledge. Teaching a sport or physical activity well requires a deep level of understanding, knowledge and experience. This becomes more challenging when we consider the breadth of activities on offer.

With PE undergoing a significant evolution, so has the subject knowledge required. Students worldwide are expressing their disinterest, and their motivations to engage in physical activity are changing. The growing necessity for a more comprehensive approach to PE, one that equips young people for a physically active life rather than just preparing them for elite sports, has become increasingly apparent. Consequently, the subject knowledge of a PE teacher must adapt accordingly. This doesn't negate the importance of activity-specific knowledge; it remains essential. However, the focus is now shifting towards pedagogy and understanding the most effective methods to deliver PE, what it means to move well, moderate competency, physical literacy, meaningful PE and ensuring relevance and engagement for all students.

Mr. Sugden's approach to PE delivery should become a relic of the past as we strive for more innovative methods to align with the evolving and more relevant objectives of our subject.

Tony McFadyen ended the session by offering us a reflection: What type of PE teacher do you want to be? This is a question we must all ask ourselves.

From Trainee to Teacher

CHAPTER 12: TRAINING

During my initial training, I was equipped with a diverse set of tools designed to deliver PE in innovative and engaging ways. I learned about incorporating different types of physical activities, adapting lessons to meet varied student needs, and employing creative strategies to foster a love for movement. This training instilled in me a sense of excitement and possibility, as I envisioned myself making a meaningful impact on my students' PE experiences.

However, when I began my placements at various training schools, I quickly encountered a stark contrast between theory and practice. The established routines and rigid expectations at these schools often blunted the tools I had been so eager to use. Instead of encouraging creativity and innovation, the environment demanded adherence to 'traditional' methods. Any deviation from the norm was met with resistance, and taking risks in lesson planning or delivery was generally frowned upon.

As a result, my approach to teaching PE became more about conformity than creativity. The initial enthusiasm I had felt started to wane as I realised that my role was becoming one of maintaining the status quo rather than inspiring change. In hindsight, I was becoming more of the same and in my eagerness to please, I allowed it to happen.

Primary Training Troubles

While my experiences during training were less than ideal, for many other teachers, PE training on their trainee teacher courses was almost non-existent, particularly in the primary sector. In my fortunate position of working in a number of primary schools, a common complaint is the lack of PE training received during their initial teacher training. This deficit has led to a significant lack of confidence among teachers when it comes to planning and delivering PE lessons. Many primary educators feel ill-equipped to provide high-quality PE, resulting in a reliance on outsourcing.

The lack of comprehensive training and support for primary teachers in PE highlights a critical need for systemic change. However, this book is focused only on what we as educators can control, and therefore we must consider the importance of on-going professional development. It is crucial that we invest in our teachers, equipping them with the knowledge, skills, and confidence to deliver PE lessons that are not only educational but also enjoyable and inspiring.

Ultimately, it is crucial for educators to continually reflect on their practice, reassess whether they are embodying the teacher they aspire to be, and take proactive steps towards achieving that vision. So, what type of PE teacher do you want to be?

Part 12.2 – Delve
Lee Sullivan

What Type of Teacher Do You Want to Be?
A belief might be defined as having trust, faith, or confidence in (someone or something). It is having a view or an idea that one holds to be true. 'Beliefs are important because they provide a reference point against which to make judgements. They define you as an individual and play a significant part in how you view and interact with the world,' (Everley, Flemons, 2021, Page 54). They might be shaped by prior experiences, social and cultural backgrounds, educational background, research, personal values, etc. For example, if you believe that PE has a responsibility to engage every student, then this will form the foundation of your teaching philosophy and guide your instructional decisions. Conversely, your prior experiences of sport participation might lead you to the belief that PE should be preparing students to perform at a particular level. 'Every human being has a personal life philosophy. It was formed by a complex lifetime mix of genetics, environment, and learning over time,' (Krone, 2014, Page 71).

Harris and Cale (2019) argue that there is a mismatch between two teaching philosophies within PE: fitness for life and fitness for performance. They state that teachers who are inclined towards delivering the fitness for performance philosophy might be influenced by sporting backgrounds, sport science-focused degrees, and 'their limited awareness of and exposure to fitness for life pedagogies' (2019, p.37). As educators, it is important to critically examine our beliefs, recognising their impact on our practice and remaining open to revising them in light of new experiences and knowledge.

Further shaping your teacher identity is the concept of professional or occupational socialisation. Professional socialisation is defined as a person who becomes a legitimate member of a professional society (Shahr et al., 2016) and refers to the process through which individuals learn and internalise the norms, values, attitudes, and behaviours associated with a particular profession. Professional socialisation typically occurs through formal education, training programmes, mentorship, workplace experiences, and exposure to professional networks. It helps individuals adapt to the expectations and demands of their chosen profession and develop a sense of professional identity and belonging. Professional socialisation plays a crucial role in shaping the identities and practices of PE. New teachers undergo a process of professional socialisation that acquaints them with the norms, values, and expectations of the profession. This process involves not only acquiring pedagogical knowledge and teaching skills but also understanding the broader social and cultural significance of physical education. Essentially, your teacher identity encompasses the complex interplay of how you perceive yourself, how you wish others to perceive you, and the qualities and attributes that you use to define yourself as an educator. It is a deeply personal and multifaceted construct that evolves over time through various influences and experiences. There is no one way of teaching PE. Hopefully from this book, and numerous other sources, collaborations and experiences, consider the research and approaches that resonate with you most. By reflecting upon your own PE teacher identity, you gain insights into the factors that have shaped who you are as an educator and deepen your understanding of the values, beliefs, and principles that guide your practice. This self-awareness is essential for continued growth and development as a professional, enabling you to align your actions with your core identity and make intentional choices that support your vision for teaching and learning in PE.

Importance of Reflection

In her article looking at the importance of self-reflection in leaders, Palena Neale (2019) describes self-reflection as 'taking time to think, contemplate, examine and review yourself as part of increasing your self-awareness.' 'Central to your development as a teacher is your capacity and commitment to observe and analyse what is happening in your own lessons and to use your professional judgement both to reflect and act upon these observations and analyses in order to improve pupil learning and your teaching.' (Zwozdiak-Myers, 2021, Page 338).

Reflective practice serves as a compass guiding professional growth and effectiveness. By regularly engaging in reflection, educators can assess their current teaching practices and identify areas for improvement. This introspective process prompts questions about where you stand presently and where you aspire to be. As the world evolves, so too must teaching methodologies and approaches.

Methods of reflection might include, but are not limited to, the following:
- **Observing others and being observed:** PE teachers learn by observing colleagues and being observed themselves, fostering peer learning and self-reflection.
- **Student voice:** Teachers gather input through questionnaires or conversations, incorporating student perspectives into reflective practice for a more holistic understanding of effectiveness.
- **Action research:** Teachers investigate research, collect data, and reflect on outcomes.
- **Professional learning communities:** Teachers collaborate with colleagues, discussing challenges and brainstorming solutions, while also considering student feedback within the group.
- **Mentorship or coaching:** Seeking guidance from a coach provides personalised support, aiding in goal-setting and reflection.
- **Technology integration:** Digital tools facilitate collaboration among teachers and students, encouraging resource sharing and feedback exchange.

Embracing reflective practice empowers PE teachers to adapt to changing landscapes, incorporate new insights, and refine their instructional strategies accordingly. It fosters a mindset of continuous improvement, ensuring that we remain responsive to the evolving needs of our students and the broader educational context.

Pedagogies of the Possible

In his 1988 article: 'Student Teaching and the Pedagogy of Necessity,' Richard Tinning presents the idea of pedagogy of necessity. The article argues that the dominant pedagogy of student teaching in the United States and Australia is characterised as inherently conservative and rooted in technical rationality, embodying an outdated perspective on professional knowledge. This pedagogy often relies on established traditions and external authority rather than fostering innovation or critical inquiry. It is driven by the immediate needs and constraints of the classroom, with little consideration for broader possibilities or alternatives and 'there is little sense of a pedagogy of the possible.' (Page 83).

The challenges surrounding recruitment and the training of PE student teachers are beyond our control as educators, and thus are not addressed in this book. However, some of us have the privilege of serving as mentors to the next generation of PE teachers. While teacher educators effectively share research and innovative practices with student teachers, these ideas often encounter resistance in schools where a rigid 'this is how we do it here' mentality prevails. This mindset, rooted in tradition, can stifle creativity and innovation, representing a pedagogy of necessity that may be outdated.

Our goal is not to mould student teachers into replicas of ourselves, but rather to empower them to explore, experiment, and develop their own teaching identities. They should be afforded the freedom to fail, learn, and test out approaches that resonate with their unique aspirations and beliefs about teaching.

While teacher training lays the groundwork for subject and pedagogical knowledge, embracing the pedagogy of possibility requires ongoing professional development. We must continuously expand our teaching toolkit to remain adaptable and responsive to evolving needs and contexts.

Invest in Yourself

Our teacher training and schools lay a solid foundation, but the responsibility to nurture and refine our professional skills rests on our shoulders. Continuing Professional Development and Learning (CPDL) becomes not just a choice, but a vital commitment for growth and excellence. By embracing CPDL as a personal mission, we empower ourselves to adapt to changing landscapes, deepen our expertise, and ultimately excel in our professional endeavours.

The UK Department for Education shared the following characteristics for successful CPDL in their 'Standard for teachers' professional development,' guidance (2016):
1. Professional development should have a focus on improving and evaluating pupil outcomes.
2. Professional development should be underpinned by robust evidence and expertise.
3. Professional development should include collaboration and expert challenge.
4. Professional development programmes should be sustained over time.

Essentially, strong CPDL offers a collaborative environment where educators engage in discussions concerning both theoretical concepts and practical applications of new ideas. It provides opportunities to implement and experiment with these ideas, observing expertly modelled practices and receiving constructive feedback. Additionally, CPDL should involve the guidance of a coach or mentor to assess the effectiveness of implemented ideas and practices. CPDL should not always be limited to closed professional networks. External challenge and insight can enable teachers to critically evaluate and expand their understanding and practices from outside their immediate context.

Mid-chapter reflection

What new insights have I gained from this chapter so far?

How does this knowledge reinforce or challenge my current beliefs or practices?

Are there areas or concepts I still need to explore further?

Have I identified any gaps in my team's understanding or practice that need addressing?

How can I share or apply this learning to positively influence others in my team or school?

Part 12.3 – Experts

Initial Teacher Education
Ryan Ellis

As a practitioner new to working in ITE, specialising in delivering PE in Primary Years content at the Undergraduate and Postgraduate levels, this section seeks to unpick some of the challenges student teachers face in delivering high-quality PE and the impact therein. These challenges are not specified in order of importance, but I do hope they shine a light on the training landscape and other larger issues at play.

Challenge 1 - What is PE?
"Physical education is the planned, progressive learning that takes place in school curriculum timetabled time and which is delivered to all pupils. This involves both 'learning to move' (i.e. becoming more physically competent) and 'moving to learn' (e.g. learning through movement, a range of skills and understandings beyond physical activity, such as cooperating with others). The context for the learning is physical activity, with children experiencing a broad range of activities, including sport and dance."

Although I tend to share the definition proposed by Association for PE (2019) in my work, as shown above, this question often shines a light on the initial resistance sometimes felt by trainees towards teaching the subject. We all have likes and dislikes, things we enjoy and things we don't and I'm keen to gauge any prospective teachers' views on the subject of PE through discussion and sharing of experiences. Body language is often the first giveaway, but it's not uncommon to hear comments like:

"I hate PE, I'm just not good at sport" or
"I can't teach PE, I don't know how to play cricket"

This doesn't surprise me anymore. I remind myself that my students' attitudes of PE, will, in part, have been shaped by their own experiences of PE as a learner and that their most recent experiences of PE as a learner were from secondary school, and where these experiences are negative, this further compounds students perceived competencies and confidence in teaching the subject (Randall and Keay 2022). From here, the confusion between PE and Sport seems to grow. Often, they are seen as the same entity across society and even Government publications, thus compounding the confusion and narrative that already exists.

The first challenge then, is to address this with students, allowing them to explore distinct differences between PE and Sport, while also acknowledging the ways in which they may crossover in a school curriculum. Sport is not villainised through my work, nor will it ever be. I attribute much of my own teaching characteristics and love of PE to my relationship with sport growing up, but this is not the case for all and it is important to acknowledge the role sport may, or may not have played in the young lives of our students.

Much of a school PE curriculum could be explored through smaller modified games and I place an emphasis on mastery and physical literacy through PE in my work, highlighting the importance of fostering a positive relationship with physical activity and movement (Sport England 2023) for pupils in school, who for some, PE will be the first and only exposure they have to be physically active and develop physical skills that can enhance their lives.

There is often an audible sigh of relief when I tell students they don't 'have' to teach sports in PE. Removing this shackle and viewing PE from a different perspective is only the beginning of the journey. However, it is an important step in challenging the often stereotypical 'sport-based' curriculum that can underserve many children (Casey and Kirk, 2021). Some of these children are now grown up, pursuing their own teaching careers, and will be weaving the threads of a high-quality experience in primary PE for years to come. Answering and clarifying the question 'What is PE?', therefore, is one of the important steps that can start to take students' experience of the subject from dread to delight.

Challenge 2 - Who is teaching the subject?

PE has had its challenges over the years, particularly in Primary Schools where there are an ever-growing number of stakeholders involved in the planning and delivery of the National Curriculum which has led to an abundance of outsourcing of the subject(Blair and Blair 2022). Outsourcing of the subject does have pros and cons and we can't deny the level of knowledge, expertise and enthusiasm at our disposal in the sector, but we do need to question the model of delivery and how it can be best positioned to support students and teachers. Additionally, this outsourcing is often largely, but not exclusively, given to sports coaches and associated organisations, thus perpetuating the narrative raised in challenge 1. Where schools outsource the delivery of the entire PE curriculum to external bodies, the impact on teachers' own professional development and self-efficacy is of concern.

Confidence and competence issues related to the subject are then further exacerbated as 'specialists' take the reins of leading and delivering the subject, creating a cycle in which a teacher's lack of involvement in PE erodes their confidence and 'de-skills' them (Smith 2015), resulting in a retreat from wanting to teach it. In this scenario then, PE starts to become portrayed as a 'specialist' subject to teach (Randall and Griggs 2020).

FROM PE DREAD TO DELIGHT

Ultimately, schools make their own decisions around their PE curriculum and who teaches it, and there are fantastic examples of them working in sync with outside bodies, including team teaching and CPD opportunities through their model of delivery. Where this is the case, as somebody working in ITE, it is preferable for students to be placed in these settings.

It can be disheartening to deliver a PE module to students, watching their motivation, capability, and confidence reach new heights, only to see it extinguished during a school placement where PE delivery is outsourced, leaving them without the chance to apply their learning. Similarly, it's frustrating when a mentor—let's call them a negative influence—is set in their ways, resistant to change, and dismissive of new approaches simply because "it's always been done that way." This lack of opportunity for students to teach physical education while on placement in school was identified by Haydn-Davies in 2008 and continues today. Whilst precautions are taken to ensure students are afforded the best possible placement experiences, there's no denying that the Primary PE landscape is so varied, and some students will undoubtedly only ever experience PE being outsourced or be paired with a 'negative mentor' on placement.

Mentorship plays a vital role for students, particularly in a PE context through how it can help foster innovation and encourage risk-taking in teaching. I see part of my lecturing role in ITE, while students are with me, as that of a mentor, constructing a solid base for my students from which they can dare to push boundaries and continue to innovate. I see this as 'positive mentorship', allowing students to take calculated risks while knowing if things don't work out, that's ok and they will learn and grow from the experience without any judgement from me.

Finding this kind of mentorship when transitioning into the school setting is of paramount importance, forming a common bond with another like-minded teacher or PE advocate. I was fortunate in my first teaching post to have a deputy headteacher who fully bought into the power of PE and physical activity and the positive impact on pupil achievement and wellbeing. This enabled me to continue to pursue my PE passion in a safe and non-judgmental space while having guidance from a perceived 'more knowledgeable other'. This is one of many reasons why I advise my students to get to know a school fully before committing to taking the job. By asking questions, looking at the website and visiting the school, they are more likely to be able to distinguish whether there will be one (or more) positive mentors who can help them thrive.

Finding such a mentor in a physical setting is invaluable, but the power of connecting virtually with others should not be underestimated. I have had individuals I have looked at as mentors online who probably don't even know it themselves, simply through conversations I have had with them on The PE Umbrella podcast, learning from their ways of working and constructing my own understanding of it to implement with my own classes. I would encourage you to curate and connect with others in a similar way to construct your own 'positive mentor' base.

Although research has since questioned the 10,000 hour rule first devised by Anders Ericsson (1993), it is no secret that to master something (as we want our pupils to do in the PE curriculum) we need to have an opportunity to 'do' the thing multiple times, to repeat ideas, to adapt our approaches, to have success and to fail. If we strive for high-quality PE lessons, delivered by teachers, they must be given opportunity and time to do just this, and through this, they will grow and develop as PE practitioners.

A thorough ITE offering with opportunities to build on this in a school environment, supported by positive mentors, is the best way for students to move from dread to delight in teaching PE. I do worry that depriving teachers of the chance to experience this in schools will ultimately, over time lead some of them back to dread once more.

Challenge 3 – Time and CPD

There are time pressures in ITE. It is common knowledge now that many in-service teachers feel/felt inadequately prepared to teach primary PE through their ITE course, and this is largely due to time, or lack of it devoted to the subject (Randall and Keay 2022). I have quipped to those that care to listen, that I could fill five, 8 hour days with PE content and still have more to deliver. Consider that some ITE providers at UG or PG level have less than a quarter of that time across a full academic year, you begin to get a sense of how things need to be squeezed. Then comes the conundrum of priority. In the limited time with these students, what are the most salient messages they need to know to start their journey into teaching PE.

I have often questioned myself as to the 'exact' content that students need to be best prepared to leave ITE and teach primary PE, but I struggle to see knowledge as this 'liquid' that I simply pour into the students' empty cups until they're adequately full. Knowledge acquisition is a never-ending journey, and like a child learning to ride a bike without stabilisers, I give them the starting nudge/push, but more learning continues once they have left me, cycling on different terrain through changing weather. This continued learning happens at a faster rate if they embrace and are given opportunities to teach PE, which circles back to the points raised in challenge 2, and the importance of a positive mentor and a school who embraces the subject. As a minimum here, I look to the professional knowledge model (Randall 2020) and seek to ensure all generalists, as a minimum, understand 'what' to teach and 'why' we are teaching it at the emerging stage, with an emphasis on early movement acquisition and fundamental movement skills.

All of the students come to me with different starting points concerning PE, and as such I do my very best to unpack these experiences with them at the beginning of my modules so I can review the content I will deliver and maximise the impact it will have (Haydn-Davies and Spence 2010). I will start students on their learning journey from wherever their individual starting point happens to be, but with the time constraints in ITE, they will all likely leave with slightly differing endpoints of perceived confidence and competence, despite receiving the same instruction.

Therefore the importance of continued professional development into their early teaching career in a school cannot be understated. In this instance, while some 'pre-packaged' professional development offerings can act as a confidence boost, the best form of development should be personally and contextually relevant to the individual teacher and their needs (Randal and Keay 2022).

Professional development opportunities, then, are essential to continue nurturing learning not just in, but beyond ITE too, as teachers move from dread to delight. However, I have found (not exclusively) challenge 1 and challenge 2 to be barriers in this regard which may keep some teachers feeling a sense of dread for longer than anybody would wish.

Part 12.4 – Apply

The Evolution of 'Training'
Ben Holden

When asked to reflect on this chapter focusing around training, a cold shudder ran down my spine as I was teleported back to my own training year. Undoubtedly the toughest year of my education journey that far exceeded the pressures I experienced during university third year around the dissertation deadline dates. That said, I did exit my PGCE year feeling confident and ready to make that transition from trainee to NQT as it was back then. I attribute this feeling of confidence to the depth and breadth of subject and pedagogical knowledge imparted from my brilliant course lead but also a range of experienced PE teachers that were invited to deliver to our cohort on their own areas of PE specialism.

The workshops we accessed felt more powerful and relevant somehow. I enjoyed the challenge of building up my subject knowledge in areas that I had little or no experience. The workshops during my training year were on Parkour, Street Dance, Cheerleading and Tchoukball. The passion on show from the teachers delivering these workshops was infectious and during my NQT year, I was lucky enough to have a Head of Department that was supportive for me to trial and explore these lesser traditional activities. As a result, some of the aforementioned sports are now main-stays in the school I have just moved on from after 15 years. Whether in my teacher training or through my school, my development would focus mostly on sport-specific coaching. Subject knowledge was topped up with access to National Governing Body qualifications in various popular sports. In fact, the conditions of my offer onto a PGCE were to attend two different NGB Level 1 courses. I felt pretty disconnected and disengaged during both courses as it lacked relevance to teaching. The practices and activities showcased were often tailored to club coaching sessions as opposed to the reality of them being used with a multi-diverse, attitudinally wide-ranging class of 30, year 9s.

As my career progressed, I began to mentor a number of PE teaching trainees and apprentices working within my department. Sadly, it became clear that not all had had the same positive PE training programme that I had been lucky enough to experience. Many idolised their own PE teachers from their school-days. It also became clear that many of these PE teachers receiving this adulation were closer to Mr Glover from Kes than PE teachers that were focused on fostering a love of movement and physical activity in all young people. As such, I felt that a number of my PE mentees had a distorted view on the realities of PE teaching as a profession. They were possibly only seeing PE teachers through their own lens as a 'PE loving' and/or 'sporty child' themselves. I remember providing feedback on many occasions with trainees in the early stages of their training that encouraged them to focus on the wide range of learners in their lessons. Together we considered the range of attitudes and relationships with PE and physical activity from learners within a class, and this helped to remind them that they were not teaching a 12-, 14- or 16-year-old version of themselves.

I reflect back on this activity specific training focus as being indicative of the reality back then. PE was heavily focused on the development of sport specific skills. I am encouraged to see the progression of PE training as moving away from this with a focus on the holistic development of children. Training is more specific to the science of teaching and the focus on nurturing physical literacy in young people.

In my opinion, PE is a progressive subject with the best departments being pupil-focused and outward thinking in their curriculum design. As such, subject knowledge requirements for trainees are broader than ever. That said, a trainee that is proactive in actively addressing subject knowledge gaps and goes above and beyond to further their teaching toolkit will be a trainee that is best prepared for the modern world of PE teaching.

Like the best chefs, who continually experiment and refine practice throughout their careers, the truth is that a PE teacher's training is never finished and is very much a continual process. The best PE teachers are always learning and on the look-out for both innovative and inclusive practice. I encourage all to:
- Actively observe colleagues, in and out of your context/school.
- Surround and submerge yourself into positive PE communities, share best practice and engage in dialogue with the PE community about their successes and challenges.
- Access online and onsite training opportunities throughout your career, stay current, engage in reading around our subject through blogs, literature and more commonly through podcasts and webinars with PE teachers from a range of backgrounds, areas of expertise and context.

PE teacher training at an early stage and throughout a career often provides the tools; the teacher carries this tool kit and through ongoing experiences will begin to utilise the correct tools for each situation to maximise engagement of all pupils in lessons.

Social media and other online platforms have connected us like never before. They enable us to share and find ideas, see how others approach things and challenge the way we think.
This desire to share PE specific ideas was the reason why I launched @WannaTeachPE on X. I share a range of short video clips showcasing coaching and teaching ideas. During my own training, this type of resource was not readily available. This led to a requirement for me to visualise activities and lessons linking them to the context of my classes. I hope many are able to access this account and find some inspiration for their own lessons. However, whenever one accesses any teaching online content or training, they must consider its application in their own context and the students it will be delivered to. Simply copying the videos and hoping for

the best is not going to provide the intended outcome of pupil engagement. Visual content must be studied, planned, adapted, tweaked and delivered with the context of your class at the heart of your consideration process to include that idea into a lesson. This said, a video online of an activity can ignite that spark and encourage you to try something new. Many videos I have seen have led to positive developments in my own teaching. The videos are like an online cooking tuition video, you might need to tweak the portion sizes or adapt the recipe depending on the availability of ingredients and the palette of your class.

Taking Back PE
Sue Pye-Beraet

Physical education plays a vital role in developing fundamental movement skills and fostering a lifelong positive attitude toward physical activity. Yet, for many primary school teachers, the thought of teaching PE often brings a sense of dread. This hesitation is understandable; with the increasing trend of outsourcing PE to external providers and relying on subscription models, many teachers have become de-skilled, and the subject's value and appeal for students has diminished. As Headteacher, I faced considerable anxiety about the potential loss of government funding and the prospect of being left without a PE program. This worry was compounded by the lack of preparedness and confidence among staff. To address these pressing concerns, we needed a comprehensive and strategic approach. We embarked on a transformative journey to reclaim PE as an essential and valued component of our curriculum, ensuring that this effort was a collaborative one, with the active involvement of all staff members.

We decided to conduct a staff voice survey to assess the current impact of our PE program and determine our baseline. The results highlighted a pronounced disconnect between the value teachers placed on PE and their confidence in teaching it. 57% of staff said they did not feel adequately prepared to teach PE, despite 100% of staff strongly agreeing to the subject's importance on the curriculum. 71% of staff said that the current method of delivery was failing to meet the needs of the children and 100% agreed or strongly agreed to wanting further training and support to deliver PE. This feedback was instrumental in shaping our strategy for revitalising PE, providing crucial insights into the areas that required targeted support and development. I work with some incredible staff who are willing to go above and beyond when it benefits the children we teach, so it was great to hear that they understood we needed to do things differently and were open to explore change.

We started by organising our first PE-specific CPD session, focused on debunking myths about PE and boosting teachers' confidence. We dedicated time to listening to teachers' past experiences with PE, many of which included negative memories of certain aspects. By openly discussing these negative experiences, we were able to refocus and clarify what PE should be, and more importantly, what we wanted it to never become. The session culminated in reflecting on our personal "why" for teaching PE. Each teacher had their own unique reason, which we gathered and used to shape the intent of our King's Court First School PE curriculum, ensuring those values were at its core.

Figure 29: Kings Court First School PE Intent

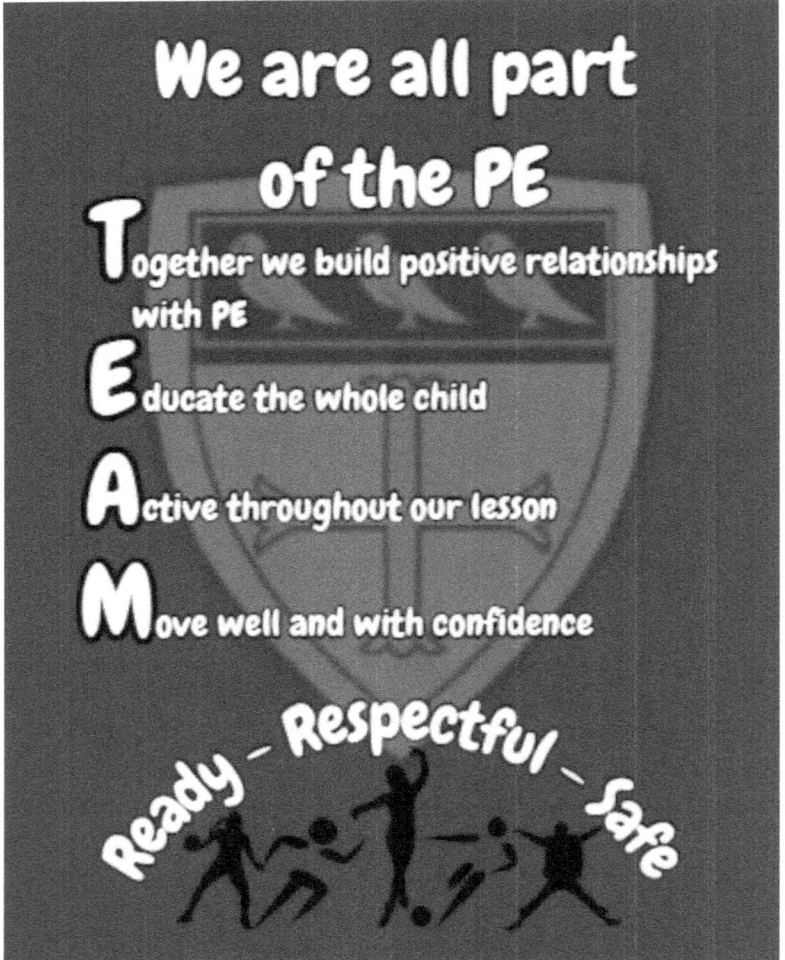

One of our main challenges was overcoming barriers related to time and lesson planning. To tackle this, we introduced the Primary Concept Curriculum, which offered a more holistic approach and flexible lesson plans that could be easily adapted. We also provided targeted training for staff, focusing on what effective PE lessons should look like, facilitated collaborative planning sessions, and implemented a buddy system to support less experienced teachers.

AFTERWORD

These initiatives were aimed at making PE not only a well-structured part of the curriculum but also a subject that teachers felt confident and excited to deliver.

As a result of these efforts, we observed a significant improvement in staff confidence. Teachers began to speak fondly of PE, and students also showed a renewed enthusiasm for physical activity. The changes we implemented were not just about making PE more enjoyable but also about making it relevant to our specific context and needs. We took ownership of the PE program, tailoring it to fit our unique environment and ensuring that it resonated with both staff and students.

Ongoing training, both at the whole-school and individual levels, has been and continues to be a cornerstone of the successful implementation and revitalisation of our PE curriculum. From the outset, it became clear that without consistent, high-quality professional development, we would struggle to bridge the gap between the importance placed on PE by staff and their ability to confidently deliver it.

Whole-school training sessions have played a pivotal role in fostering a unified understanding of the value of PE. These sessions provided a space for staff to openly share their experiences, address misconceptions, and collaboratively shape a shared vision for the subject. Whilst, tailored support through collaborative lesson planning, targeted workshops, and the implementation of a buddy system has allowed for personalised growth and the gradual building of expertise.

However, while we made substantial progress, there is still work to be done. One area that requires attention is assessment. Now that we have a clear understanding of what we stand for in our PE program, we need to develop effective assessment strategies to measure our success and identify areas for improvement. Establishing what we should measure will be guided by our curriculum intent and the holistic approach we have adopted.

In summary, our journey to reclaim and revitalise PE has been both challenging and rewarding. By involving all staff members in the process, addressing their concerns, and integrating PE into a well-structured curriculum, we have transformed our approach to PE. We have made PE our own, aligning it with our context and ensuring that it continues to play a vital role in the development of our students. As we move forward, ongoing training will remain at the heart of our approach, ensuring that staff are continuously supported in their professional journey.

Chapter 12 Summary

Training: from Dread to Delight

DREAD

Rigid Teaching Beliefs:
Some teachers remain stuck in fixed beliefs shaped by their past experiences or training, limiting their adaptability and openness to new ideas.

Stagnant, Tradition-Bound Practices:
Adhering to outdated practices due to a "this is how it's always been done" mentality can prevent innovation and adaptability in teaching.

Outsourced and de-skilled:
PE is outsourced to external providers that devalues and deskills our teachers.

DELIGHT

Reflective and Evolving Teaching Beliefs:
By examining and challenging personal beliefs, teachers can remain flexible, ensuring their teaching evolves to meet diverse student needs.

Embracing a Pedagogy of Possibility:
Teachers explore creative, student-centred approaches, remaining open to experimentation and new methodologies that promote dynamic learning environments.

Investing in Ongoing CPD:
Teachers view CPD as a lifelong commitment, staying informed of the latest pedagogical research and strategies, ensuring they remain effective and adaptable.

Where would you place yourself right now?

DREAD ←——————————————→ DELIGHT

Reflection Questions
- What type of PE teacher do I want to be?
- What are my core beliefs about PE, and how have they been influenced by my own experiences and background?

- Do I lean more towards a "fitness for life" or "fitness for performance" approach in my PE teaching? Why?
- How has professional socialisation influenced my identity as a PE teacher?
- Are there any outdated teaching practices or beliefs I hold onto that may hinder innovation in my classroom?
- In what ways do I actively engage in reflective practice to improve my teaching and student outcomes?
- What actions can I take to ensure my teaching embraces a pedagogy of possibility rather than a pedagogy of necessity?

Call to Action

As we conclude this chapter, it's time to reflect on what you've learned and consider how to apply it. The SHIFT mnemonic can guide you through the next steps: a structured approach to transform your insights into meaningful actions. Take a moment to work through the following questions:

S **Summarise** the key takeaway from this chapter that stands out to you.

H **Highlight** how this takeaway challenges or aligns with your current practices.

I **Initiate** a small change or step right now to put what you've learned into practice.

F **Frame** how this change will contribute to achieving your long-term vision for PE.

T **Take** others on the journey—share your new insights and encourage collaboration.

References

Department for Education. (2016). Standard for teachers' professional development. [Online] Accessed at: https://www.gov.uk/government/publications/standard-for-teachers-professional-development [Accessed on 3 May 2024].

Ericsson, K. A., Krampe, R. T., & Tesch-Römer, C. (1993). The role of deliberate practice in the acquisition of expert performance. Psychological Review, 100(3), 363–406. [Online] Accessed at: https://doi.org/10.1037/0033-295X.100.3.363 [Accessed on 3 May 2024].

Everley, S., & Flemons, M. (2021). Teacher as a reflective practitioner/researcher. In S. Capel, J. Cliffe, & J. Lawrence (Eds.), Learning to teach physical education in the secondary school: A companion to school experience (Chapter 4, pp. 54–69). Routledge.

Milne, A. A., & Shepard, E. H. (2016). The house at Pooh corner. Farshore.

Harris, J., & Cale, L. (2019). Promoting active lifestyles in schools. Human Kinetics.

Krone, B. (2014). A personal philosophy. Journal of Space Philosophy, 3(2), Fall 2014.

Neale, P. (2019). Self-reflection in leadership – Part 1: Ambitions, values, and personality. [Online] Accessed at: https://unabridgedleadership.com/self-reflection-in-leadership/ [Accessed on 2 May 2024].

Shahr, H., Yazdani, S., & Afshar, L. (2019). Professional socialization: An analytical definition. Journal of Medical Ethics and History of Medicine, 12, 17. https://doi.org/10.18502/jmehm.v12i17.2016

Tinning, R. I. (1988). Student teaching and the pedagogy of necessity. Journal of Teaching in Physical Education, 7, 82–89.

Zwozdiak-Myers, P. N. (2021). Teacher as a reflective practitioner/researcher. In S. Capel, J. Cliffe, & J. Lawrence (Eds.), Learning to teach physical education in the secondary school: A companion to school experience (Chapter 20, pp. 338–360). Routledge.

AFTERWORD

The Beginning

I started this book with the end, where I presented two possible futures. To end our book, we will start at the beginning. The beginning of our journey of taking children from dread to delight in PE. Change starts now! If we are to ensure that PE is valued by all, meaningful for all and ensures lifelong engagement in physical activity, major reform is needed, and it starts with us, the teachers. This chapter aims to help teachers consider and take steps to become the teacher they wish to be.

Don't Lose Sight of Delight

As well as my journey as a PE teacher, the most rewarding part of my life is being a father to my children. My role as a dad comes before anything else. One of the reasons I love being a dad, and working with young people, is so that I don't get so wrapped up in being an adult. They remind us that there are other things that are important in life. Children can find joy in the most mundane places, turning a cardboard box into a spaceship or transforming a walk on the pavement into a floor is a lava adventure. It's easy to forget the care-free mindset of a child when we are so bogged down with life.

While reading AA Milne's 'The House at Pooh Corner' to my children one evening before bedtime, I was reminded of the crucial lesson of retaining joy and embracing playfulness in life. The final chapter is titled: 'Chapter Ten, In Which Christopher Robin and Pooh Come to an Enchanted Place and We Leave Them There.' AA Milne had never intended the Winnie the Pooh character to be taken on beyond this book, this story was supposed to be the end. As such, the chapter explains how Christopher Robin must leave his friends behind. Winnie the Pooh is coming to terms with his best friend Christopher Robin leaving the Hundred Acre Woods to join school (though school or indeed where he is going is never mentioned). Christopher Robin tries to articulate that where he is going, the idea of 'doing nothing' and 'joyful play' no longer exist. My children didn't understand the author's intentions with the chapter, but my interpretation had me welling up and holding my kids tighter. Christopher realises that when he leaves his toys, he will no longer be able to play with them ever again. He asks them to remember him and to understand why he has to go. The author is trying to convey that by going to school, Christopher Robin is saying goodbye to childhood. People sacrifice their playfulness, their joyfulness but both are so important in our lives. The book ends with the quote: 'so, they went off together. But wherever they go, and whatever happens to them on the way, in that enchanted place on the top of the Forest, a little boy and his Bear will always be playing,' (Page 179). This quote encapsulates the idea that friendship and the simple pleasures of play transcend time and circumstance, creating a timeless and cherished memory.

So even when teaching is hard, perhaps a lesson doesn't go to plan or a class is giving you a hard time, remember that it really isn't the end of the world. Stop, take a moment to recall the positive impact you have each and every day. Nothing is permanent and those students in front of you won't be there for long. Find the joy in the conversations you have, the moments in a lesson that just seem to click, the one child that you win over or the one who now loves PE but had struggled too previously. Cherish the time we have in our careers, with our loved ones and in this wonderful subject. It will go quickly. We must always find time for playfulness and should look for the joy in all that we do and never lose sight of how and where you find delight.

From Dread to Delight

In this book, we explored themes such as direction, inclusion, learning, holistic development, and the importance of providing a positive experience within PE. By addressing these issues, the book aimed to transform PE from a source of anxiety to a subject of enthusiasm and joy. Each chapter served as a catalyst for critical reflection, urging educators to challenge conventional thinking, integrate current research, and innovate their teaching practices. Ultimately, the book sought to inspire you, the PE teacher, to create an environment where every student could experience the delight of movement and the lifelong benefits of physical education.

We considered what might cause a child to dread our subject. We explored the impact of disregarding students' fundamental needs on their experience and engagement in physical education. How, ignoring belongingness needs can leave students feeling alienated, rejected, and disconnected from their peers and the subject, and consequently diminishing their motivation and enthusiasm for PE. Neglecting esteem needs undermines students' confidence and self-worth, discouraging them from fully participating or pushing themselves in lessons, making PE seem irrelevant to their lives. Additionally, a lack of autonomy and opportunities for self-expression can lead to feelings of oppression, stunting students' holistic development and enjoyment. Addressing these needs is crucial, as students experiencing dread are less likely to engage with physical activity beyond their school years, undermining the goal of fostering a lifelong love for movement.

Most importantly, we reflected on how we might move to ensure more of the children we teach find their way to delight in PE. Cultivating love and belongingness involves nurturing positive social interactions, fostering inclusivity, making the subject matter personally relevant, and infusing lessons with enjoyment. Meeting esteem needs requires recognising and celebrating students' achievements, fostering their sense of competence and confidence through challenging yet achievable tasks, and empowering them to take ownership of their learning journey. Ultimately, striving for delight in PE involves creating opportunities for students to experience growth, autonomy, motivation, self-expression, and a profound sense of satisfaction and pleasure in their physical education experiences. By addressing these needs, we aim to inspire a lifelong love for movement and ensure that PE becomes a source of joy and personal development for every student.

The Beginning: From Dread to Delight

So here it is, the end of this book but the beginning of our new path. A path that takes students from dreading PE to engaging, and seeking further opportunities to engage with PE and movement whatever form they wish. Consider this a call to action! A chance to start afresh, be the change, to try new approaches, to apply the learning shared from this book that aims to change the way all of our students think about PE.

The Future's Foundation

At its foundation, it's imperative that students never feel inadequate, humiliated, or embarrassed within the PE environment. Instead, they should consistently experience a sense of safety, value, and respect. As PE teachers, we play a pivotal role in the ongoing journey of movement that our students embark upon. However, it's essential to remember that PE is not the final destination. Rather, it should serve as a conduit, equipping the young people under our care with the necessary tools, fostering meaningful relationships, and igniting the intrinsic motivation to engage in physical activity for life. At the core of it all, they are human beings first and foremost who deserve to thrive and flourish.

The Future's Journey

Moving from dread to delight is more than a shift in attitude; it is a commitment to fostering an environment where every student feels valued, capable, and excited about participating in physical activity. Every interaction, every lesson, and every encouragement you provide as a PE teacher has the potential to make a profound difference in the lives of your students. Your influence extends far beyond the sports hall, studio or playing field; it permeates their self-perception, their attitudes towards physical activity, and their overall well-being. The journey from dread to delight is ongoing. It is a path filled with challenges and triumphs, but one that holds the promise of profound impact. Let us commit to making every step meaningful and every lesson an opportunity for growth and joy.

The Future's Vision

Imagine a future where each child looks forward to PE, where they find joy in movement and confidence in their abilities. This vision is within our grasp, but it requires dedication, empathy, and innovation. By embracing evidence-informed practices and continually reflecting on our approaches, we can create PE programs that not only enhance physical skills but also nurture the whole child.

Thank you for your dedication to this vital work. Together, we can transform PE from a subject students endure to one they cherish, ensuring that the love for movement and the benefits of

FROM PE DREAD TO DELIGHT

physical activity extend far beyond PE and into every aspect of their lives. We can take our PE students from dread to delight (by baby steps or in giant leaps) and positively change their lives forever.

Afterword

At the start of this book, in the foreword, we listened to real students as they candidly shared their negative experiences of PE, offering a raw and honest perspective on the challenges within the subject.

Now, in the afterword, I am thrilled to highlight a different narrative—voices of young people sharing the positive impact PE has had on their lives. Their stories remind us of the potential PE holds to inspire, empower, and transform.

Thank you for taking the time to read this book and for all that you do to ensure PE becomes a meaningful and positive experience for every young person.

Dareen Janah – Age 15

Since Year 9 onwards, I began to enjoy PE, and I ended up looking forward to the days when I had it. I'd say the reason why my experience changed to a more positive one is that the lessons met our demands—for example, there's barely any fitness lessons because I would say everyone hated and still hates fitness. I even managed to discover a sport that I am relatively good at—badminton. Ultimately, I think the impact on wider life would be continuing to play a sport you like and making it one of your extracurriculars, as well as ensuring you get the basic fitness and physical activity you need from time to time. If there is something that I would want to say to my PE teacher, it would probably be thank you for encouraging physical activity in fun ways that motivated me and my peers, because not only did we benefit from it, we also enjoyed it.

Mayah – Age 15

As the years went on, I gained much more confidence, and I found my voice. I now see PE as one of my favourite lessons that I most look forward to. My experience in PE became much more positive as the teachers started to communicate with all students; they got opinions from everyone and gave everyone a chance to be heard. I see PE as a great way to build someone's confidence. PE makes me feel better about anything that happened that day; it gets my mind off things easily and releases my stress. This impacts me as I now know I can move on to bigger things, such as going to basketball tournaments feeling confident. It also impacts my wider life, knowing I didn't give up on my love for PE, so I know I can do even bigger and better things. If I could say anything to my PE teacher, it would be thank you for motivating me and encouraging me not to give up on what I love. You showed me that I have a voice and that I'm capable of doing a lot. You also showed me my strengths and weaknesses, and what I need help with the most so I could improve.

Elizabeth Sessions – Age 16

Growing up and participating in PE during my teenage years has been a transformative experience that has significantly contributed to my confidence and independence. Through the various sports and activities, I learned the importance of teamwork and perseverance, pushing myself to overcome challenges and setbacks. Each accomplishment, whether it was mastering a new skill or working together with my peers, helped build a strong sense of self-worth. The physical and mental discipline gained from these experiences not only shaped my character but also instilled a belief in my abilities, empowering me to take on new challenges outside of PE and embrace opportunities with a newfound sense of independence. If I could say something to my PE teacher, it would be: thank you. Thank you for the opportunities you've offered me, thank you for creating the perfect environment to grow and develop, and thank you for always wanting the best for me and believing that I can achieve amazing things.

Being a PE ambassador and a sports leader has equipped me with essential skills that will benefit my future in numerous ways. These roles have taught me the importance of teamwork, communication, and leadership, as I've had to motivate and guide my peers in various activities. Additionally, I have developed a strong sense of responsibility and time management, balancing my commitments while ensuring that everyone is engaged and having fun. Teaching and guiding the younger generation has given me a sense of self and purpose, and it has helped me to appreciate the value of teaching and the role of positive role models. By helping to lead the Girls Active Club, I have come to better understand the importance of sport and the detrimental impact of not participating regularly. These experiences not only enhance my CV but also prepare me for future challenges, whether in further education or my career, by instilling confidence and a proactive mindset.

Zara Butt – Age 15

Taking part in PE in secondary school has helped me become the confident, reliable, and strong leader I am today. This is thanks to the support and countless opportunities I have been given to express myself and demonstrate the benefits of PE to younger people. During PE lessons, I discovered a love for rugby and decided to join a club outside of school. Girls' rugby is often overlooked in many schools, but all the PE teachers supported me and worked to show that rugby isn't just for boys.

I also appreciate that we have a voice in PE and get to choose our own pathways. This allows everyone to explore a range of sports and encourages more participation, as students can select activities they enjoy and share with friends. This freedom helps older students make their own decisions and enjoy some autonomy that is often missing in other subjects. The introduction of mixed PE groups for younger years has also been a positive change, allowing everyone to experience all sports, rather than those traditionally associated with their gender. These mixed groups have helped to break down stereotypes and prove that no sport is limited to one gender.

In other subjects, many students may feel like they are just being taught as part of a group, with little personalisation. In contrast, the PE department recognises each student as an individual and makes everyone feel important. The welcoming atmosphere and lack of judgment foster strong relationships between students and teachers. Teachers actively listen to students' preferences, allowing them to voice their opinions about the activities they enjoy or suggest improvements. A strong student voice helps the PE department progress, improving participation and tailoring the range of clubs on offer. Being listened to helps students feel valued and confident to speak up if they face challenges.

The PE department is committed to ensuring every student has the chance to shine. Teachers aim to help students overcome their hurdles, no matter how big or small, by making them feel valued and engaged. This mission to support and empower every individual has had a significant impact, encouraging participation and boosting confidence across the board.

Immy – Age 12

My teacher gave me time to get used to the activities in lessons so I could get involved when I had the confidence to. I now feel understood and listened to. I am comfortable expressing how I feel, whether it is good or bad. I am able to choose an alternative activity that is more comfortable if I want to, which has helped build my confidence. We get to come to school in our PE kits, so I don't feel the negative emotions I had when changing at primary school. It is also good doing PE in our small class, as we are all in the same year group.

I am more relaxed when I do PE now. I don't worry about it because I know if I don't want to take part, I don't have to — but I nearly always do. I feel happy and proud after participating. I feel like I am improving my skills, which makes me more confident to perform in front of others. I feel more comfortable and now do more activities, even those I didn't like before.

PE has definitely had a positive impact on me. I teach my mum what we have done when I get home, making her more active, and we exercise together. It has given me the confidence to do more outside of school, such as Tabata. I now believe I can do things I previously thought I couldn't.

To my PE teacher: you are good at your job! You understand the students, and that helps us feel comfortable doing PE.

FROM PE DREAD TO DELIGHT

Oliver – Year 9

I believe the "Know, Show, Grow" way of teaching PE is beneficial because it helps me understand what I am doing and how it will benefit me, making PE an easier subject to engage with and participate in. This approach has also improved my enjoyment of and attitude towards PE as a whole. Learning and being asked questions about topics beyond just my sports skills has transformed PE from a lesson I once dreaded into one I now look forward to. This fundamental change in the way PE is taught is incredible, and I would highly recommend it to anyone.

Muhammed – Year 9

My experience of PE this year has been really positive so far. Compared to last year, we are actually learning and working towards personal goals. Previously, we were just playing sports without really learning about Physical Education. Last year's lessons felt more like a chance to play and mess around, whereas this year, we have clear learning objectives, the lessons are enjoyable, and I'm actually learning something new in every session. We are also developing important life skills such as respect, etiquette, and fair play, which will benefit us in the future, whether at college, university, or in the workplace.

Alyssa – Year 8

Last year in PE, I never really got involved. We were always told to just join in with the sport but were never given any instructions. We weren't allowed to work at our own pace or build our confidence by practising skills—we just had to play a sport for an hour. Our teacher never taught us about concepts like a growth mindset or comfort zones.

I find that I'm much more comfortable participating because we focus on skill development and are given the choice to either play a full competitive game or practise our skills. We also spend lessons learning about confidence and how we can develop it which is important to me. Our teacher encourages us to take part and takes the time to understand what we dislike about the lesson so he can make it more enjoyable.

I used to make up excuses to avoid participating, but now I genuinely enjoy every lesson. Our teacher adapts the lessons so that I, along with others who may feel uncomfortable, can play at our own pace and in a way that suits us. We spend time working on the skills we lack confidence in, helping us to grow and feel more confident in the sport we're playing. Last year, I was embarrassed to participate, but now I feel much more comfortable with the people around me.

AFTERWORD

Menna – Year 8

My experiences of PE in previous years were not great. If you weren't the fastest or strongest, it often felt like the teachers forgot about you. When I joined Mr Campbell's class, I didn't know what to expect, but after a few lessons, I realised that PE isn't just about sport. I have developed both mentally and physically in ways I never thought possible. Each lesson has clear objectives, and we learn skills that we can carry with us throughout our lives. I enjoy every session, and my confidence continues to grow.

Since learning through the 'Know, Show, Grow' approach, I see not only PE but many other subjects differently. I have started to love PE in a way I never thought I would. In the past, I hated it because I felt different—I was never the best or the most athletic, which made me deeply insecure. I have experienced hurtful comments that have stayed with me for years. But now, my class feels like a family. I am encouraged and supported in everything I do, both by my teacher and my peers.

I honestly cannot express how much PE has done for me. I no longer beg my mum to write me notes to get out of lessons; instead, I look forward to taking part. I leave every PE lesson feeling happy, and I wish my shy, insecure past self could see what I am doing now. I may not be the most athletic, but I always give my best effort. Now, I realise that my best is more than enough, and I'm so lucky to have a teacher who believes in me—because for many years, I didn't believe in myself.

www.ingramcontent.com/pod-product-compliance
Lightning Source LLC
Chambersburg PA
CBHW082107230426
43671CB00015B/2624